GATEWAY STATE

POLITICS AND SOCIETY IN MODERN AMERICA

*William H. Chafe, Gary Gerstle, Linda Gordon,
and Julian E. Zelizer, series editors*

For a full list of books in this series see: http://press.princeton.edu/catalogs
    /series/pstcaa.htm

Gateway State

HAWAI'I AND THE CULTURAL TRANSFORMATION OF AMERICAN EMPIRE

SARAH MILLER-DAVENPORT

PRINCETON UNIVERSITY PRESS

PRINCETON & OXFORD

Published by Princeton University Press
41 William Street, Princeton, New Jersey 08540
6 Oxford Street, Woodstock, Oxfordshire OX20 1TR

press.princeton.edu

Portions of chapter 4 originally appeared in Sarah Miller-Davenport,
"A 'Montage of Minorities': Hawai'i Tourism and the Commodification
of Racial Tolerance, 1959–1978," *The Historical Journal* 60, no. 3
(September 2017): 817–842.

LCCN 2018955220
ISBN 9780691181233

British Library Cataloging-in-Publication Data is available

Editorial: Eric Crahan, Pamela Weidman
Production Editorial: Terri O'Prey
Jacket/Cover Art and Design: Layla Mac Rory
Production: Jacqueline Poirier
Publicity: Tayler Lord, Julia Hall

This book has been composed in Arno Pro

Printed on acid-free paper. ∞

Printed in the United States of America

10 9 8 7 6 5 4 3 2 1

For my parents

CONTENTS

vii

ACKNOWLEDGMENTS

I HAVE ACCRUED innumerable personal and professional debts over the course of writing this book. One of the fun parts about finishing it is the chance to get sentimental and thank all the people who have, in one way or another, shaped the final product. I am reminded as I write this how lucky I am that I get to spend most of my time surrounded by really smart people. Many of them have offered constructive criticism and asked pointed questions that forced me to clarify, deepen, or otherwise rethink my central claims. This project is undoubtedly richer and more informed as a result. All flaws are my own.

First, I could not have asked for a better dissertation committee at the University of Chicago. Mark Bradley has been a model advisor and mentor. He is exceptionally accessible, kind, and wise. It was my good fortune that he came to Chicago during my second year of graduate school. In the many years since he has shepherded me through the process of becoming a professional historian and teacher, all the while allowing me space to develop my own ideas. Jim Sparrow has likewise been essential to the development of this project, from the very first phone conversation we had when I was applying to graduate school. He always managed to unearth the larger significance of my research, even when I could not see it myself, and his good humor is matched by the depth of his knowledge. Jane Dailey provided crucial interventions when this project was in need of direction, and she has always been a warm and generous host at the many dinners she has held at her home. Matt Briones helped me to see how my project fits into the larger history of the Asian American experience. Amy Stanley, though not a member of my dissertation committee, influenced my work in significant ways, particularly in my attention to the economic aspects of Hawai'i statehood. Her teaching—along with that of Adam Green, Bruce Cumings, Julie Saville, and Christine Stansell—was a large part of why my first few years of graduate school were so exciting.

The University of Chicago has a reputation for being a cold and competitive place, but in my eight years there I found the opposite to be true. The members of my off-the-books dissertation workshop—Chris Dingwall, Susannah Engstrom, Emily Remus, and Katy Schumaker—remain close friends and collaborators. Emily and I have continued the traditions started there after we moved into full-time jobs, and her emotional support, quick mind, and forthright comments on countless draft chapters have sustained me through the ups and downs of academic life. I am also grateful for the friendship and feedback of other members of my Chicago cohort: Celeste Moore, Emily Marker, Peter Simons, Katie Turk, Jake Betz, Sam Lebovic, and Jake Smith. Members of the Social History and International History workshops—including John Mc-Callum, C. J. Álvarez, Patrick Kelly, Korey Garibaldi, Kai Parker, Dan Webb, and Lael Weinberger—have also left their mark on my work.

This project is a product of multiple institutions. A number of professors at Oberlin College inspired me to pursue history as a major and, later, encouraged me to become a historian myself. I am particularly thankful to Moon-Ho Jung, Wendy Kozol, and Leonard Smith. The seminar on decolonization at the National History Center was a formative experience. It was essential to the existence of at least one chapter of this book and for helping me to think more broadly about the place of Hawai'i in the larger history of decolonization. Jen Foray, Dane Kennedy, William Roger Louis, Philippa Levine, and Jason Parker were all excellent seminar leaders who steered my research in newly global directions. Marilyn Young skipped my seminar year, but I was lucky enough to spend just enough time with her before her death to know why she was so beloved. *Gateway State* has also benefited from the contributions of Seth Archer, Henrice Altink, Eric Avila, Beth Bailey, Elizabeth Borgwardt, David Clayton, Mona Domosh, Nick Guyatt, Kristin Hoganson, Julia Irwin, Monica Kim, Henry Knight Lozano, Piers Ludlow, Katherine Marino, Daniel Matlin, Kevin Murphy, Lien-Hang Nguyen, Meredith Oda, Matthew Pratt-Guterl, Andrew Preston, Federico Romero, Ellen Schrecker, Giles Scott-Smith, Jay Sexton, Brian Ward, and Ellen Wu. Daniel Immerwahr, a frequent co-panelist, has been a generous and incisive reader of multiple papers and chapters that form this book.

A work of history is only as good as its sources, and for that I am thankful for the assistance of the staff at multiple archives, particularly Melissa Shimonishi, Ricki Aikau, Victoria Nihi, and Gina Vergara-Bautista at the Hawai'i State Archives; Dore Minatodani, Jodie Mattos, and Sherman Sasaki at the University of Hawai'i; and Chris Abraham at the Eisenhower Library.

I got a job offer at the University of Sheffield mere days before receiving my PhD and at the time I had no idea what to expect of this rather surprising career development. But I lucked into a truly welcoming and collaborative department at Sheffield, where I have accumulated many wonderful friends and colleagues. In addition to their comradeship, Andrew Heath, Simon Middleton, James Shaw, and Simon Toner all provided important advice on my manuscript at various stages of the process. Dina Gusejnova, Tehyun Ma, Máirín MacCarron, Caoimhe Nic Dháibhéid, and Colin Reid have helped make

Sheffield a home. I was privileged to start as a first-year lecturer at Sheffield at the same time as Eirini Karamouzi, who has guided me through the idiosyncrasies of the British higher education system with patience and humor; I also appreciate her pretending that my Greek pronunciation is acceptable. Beyond the city of Sheffield, there is a growing community of American-trained academics in Yorkshire that has made living away from home a little less disorienting. Shaul Mitelpunkt and I started together at Chicago and then by stroke of fortune found ourselves a short train ride apart on the opposite side of the Atlantic. Amanda Behm and Elisabeth Leake keep me sane, reminisce with me about superior U.S. plumbing—and make my work better.

Princeton University Press has been an ideal press to work with. I am particularly indebted to Gary Gerstle for inviting me to submit to the Politics and Society in Modern America series, and to the other series editors—William Chafe, Linda Gordon, and Julian Zelizer—for including me in it. Gary's insights on my research and continued faith in me throughout my revisions have been invaluable. The detailed and penetrating feedback of Penny von Eschen and other peer reviewers helped make this book both broader and more focused. Eric Crahan has been an exemplary and engaged editor who has tolerated my endless questions and nitpicks with good cheer and intelligence. Terri O'Prey, Pamela Weidman, and Theresa Liu made this book's publication process a seamless and rewarding experience. Thanks also to Jack Rummel for his excellent copyediting.

This project would not have been possible without the generous support of a number of funders, including the Doris Quinn Foundation, the Eisenhower Institute, the Society for Historians of American Foreign Relations, the George C. Marshall Foundation, the Eisenhower Foundation, the Textbook and Academic Authors Association, and the Center for the Study of Race, Politics, and Culture at the University of Chicago. The University of Sheffield provided funding for a number of key research trips. The Center for the United States and the Cold War at New York University offered me a visiting fellowship that provided me the crucial time and space to complete my manuscript. I am grateful to Timothy Johnson and Mike Koncewicz for making it happen.

Many people outside of academia have given me much-needed encouragement and, as importantly, reminded me that there is a world beyond it. Kate Silverman Wilson, Sarah Kogel-Smucker, Laura Paley, Erin Finnerty, Dan Sershen, Laura Silber, Laura Wickens, and Sarah Olsen have all been steadfast friends. My many Chicago cousins, but particularly Linda Camras and Jerry Seidenfeld, fed me regularly and offered parental guidance when my own parents were hundreds of miles away. Multiple stays in Washington, DC, were made warmer, and cheaper, because of the hospitality of my cousins in and around that city. Ana Greene and V. J. Hyde and Debbie Fertig and

Jonathan Levy were generous enough to put me up while I did research at the National Archives.

Finally, my parents, Batya Miller and John Davenport, have been my unstinting champions. Not once did they question my decision to pursue a PhD in history, despite the many financial reasons to do something—anything—else. They instilled in me from a very young age the notion that there is more to life than making money, and that learning about the world is a worthwhile goal in itself. They are also, not incidentally, terrific copyeditors, and my dad has endured the rare feat of reading my entire manuscript twice at different stages of its development. In properly placed semicolons and in many other ways, this book has their indelible stamp on it.

GATEWAY STATE

Introduction

IN A MOVE that signaled a break with Democratic Party tradition since the New Deal, John F. Kennedy declared in the summer of 1960 that, rather than opening his campaign in Detroit on Labor Day, his bid for office would officially launch in Honolulu, followed by a stop in Alaska. To Kennedy, Hawai'i was a powerful example of the "New Frontier," the vague but evocative theme of his campaign and, eventually, his presidency. Suggesting to Americans that global developments demanded a new kind of labor, Kennedy extolled the "spirit of adventure" that had led their nineteenth-century forebears to seek novel experiences in Hawai'i. He insisted that this spirit "must be awakened again in the American people if we are to maintain our position as a leader in the free world." Hawai'i, Kennedy claimed, was not only a product of past expansionist sentiment, but must also be a site for its rechristening—and for the work of securing America's political and ideological influence abroad. As the nation's first state with a majority Asian population, Hawai'i held great symbolic value to America's expansionist global mission. "It represents the outstanding example in the world today of peoples of many races and national origins living and working together in peace and harmony," Kennedy said. "It represents as well a bridge to Asia."[1] But while Kennedy was concerned about international perceptions of American race relations and praised Hawai'i as an example of a racially tolerant society, he was notably reluctant to pursue an active civil rights agenda during either his campaign or his presidency. Perhaps Hawai'i, with its glint of newness, appealed to Kennedy because the island state seemed to be removed from the troubles of the mainland, and from the burdens of its history.

Kennedy did not, in fact, launch his campaign in Hawai'i, choosing instead to open in Alaska and send to Honolulu in his place vice presidential candidate Lyndon Johnson, who had gone to great lengths to secure Hawai'i statehood in the Senate. As with civil rights, Kennedy, in contrast to Johnson, was better at rhetoric than action. Kennedy's original intent proved prophetic, however, when his whisker-thin victory over Richard Nixon was secured with the help of a recount in Hawai'i that showed Kennedy just 115 votes ahead of his opponent—a reversal of the original count that managed to put Hawai'i's three electoral votes in the Democratic column and triggered a dramatic last-minute notification to Congress shortly before it was due to certify the election.[2] In its first full year as a state, Hawai'i played an outsized role on the American political stage.

But in September 1960, Kennedy could not have known that Hawai'i would be a flashpoint in his election. To him, Hawai'i was as much an idea as a place. He did not have to experience its magic to invoke it. Of course, Hawai'i *was* a place, one whose culturally mixed society and geographic proximity to Asia had given form to the visions that surrounded it. Those characteristics would be deployed in the service of various policy- and money-making projects that brought unprecedented numbers of people to the islands in the decades following Hawai'i's admission as a state in 1959. Only a small fraction of mainland Americans would come to know the islands firsthand, however. Like Kennedy's use of Hawai'i to suggest broader themes about America's role in the world, Hawai'i's resonance in American politics and culture far exceeded its size.

For a few crucial decades in the second half of the twentieth century, America looked to its newest and outermost state for ideas on how to live in an increasingly interdependent world. Hawai'i—a lonely north Pacific archipelago, its jagged curve of islands pointed like a finger toward Asia—was perhaps never more relevant to the United States than it was in the years after statehood. For in Hawai'i, an array of powerful people saw the future, one in which the United States was no longer shackled by old ideas of race, culture, or territoriality. They sought to construct Hawai'i as a site for both understanding and transcending human difference and for projecting U.S. global power—twinned projects that came together in Hawai'i and rippled outward.

This book explores how and why Hawai'i was invested with such significance at the height of American Cold War hegemony. It marks the passage of Hawai'i from territory to state, a process that also transformed Hawai'i from a suspect alien land into an imagined racial and consumer paradise and conduit for American-Pacific relations. The core producers of this new vision of Hawai'i were centered in both Honolulu and the mainland United States, drawn mainly from the often-interlocking ranks of Hawai'i's Democratic leadership, Pacific-oriented members of Congress, modernization advocates in higher education and in the federal government, popular liberal writers, and Hawai'i's business community, notably those in the tourism industry. These elites helped institutionalize Hawai'i as a space where the United States met Asia—and where Americans could encounter Asians—in fruitful, and lucrative, exchange.

While developments in Hawaiʻi may at first glance appear to be peripheral to broader changes in postwar America, I argue that Hawaiʻi statehood represented a key transitional moment in how Americans defined their nation's role in the world, and how they negotiated the problem of social difference at home. Hawaiʻi may have been thousands of miles away from the rest of the United States, but it was this very remove that made it so influential in this period.

Unlike all forty-nine states that came before it, Hawaiʻi's full inclusion in the nation was based on claims that emphasized *not* Hawaiʻi's sameness to the rest of the United States, but rather its fundamental difference. Hawaiʻi had met the constitutional criteria for statehood well before World War II, and its political and educational institutions followed mainland practice. But its mixed and majority ethnically Asian population was a perpetual obstacle to statehood, even up until the late 1950s. By 1959, however, Hawaiʻi was valuable to the United States precisely because it was home to so many people of Asian descent.

Other states, such as Oklahoma or New Mexico, experienced protracted statehood campaigns because of their sizable nonwhite populations. But Hawaiʻi was the only one with a majority of people whose race, for most of its territorial history, made them ineligible for naturalized citizenship—thus making its eventual admission as a state a powerful marker of historical change. But just what was the nature of that change? Why did postwar Americans, from tourists to Peace Corps officials, decide to embrace Hawaiʻi, both the place and the idea, so enthusiastically after rejecting its people for so long?

The answer lies in the intersection of global decolonization and the delegitimation of legalized racism in U.S. politics and culture. These were related developments, as other scholars have shown.[3] *Gateway State*, however, brings postwar racial formation in the United States and global decolonization into the same frame—not just analytically, but materially, as Hawaiʻi's change in legal status was based on a reimagining of race, culture, and foreignness. Hawaiʻi statehood, in marked contrast to the parallel issue of Alaska statehood, transcended its more prosaic implications to become part of a larger national reckoning over the meaning of American democracy in the era of civil rights and decolonization.

Once a racially problematic overseas territory whose population was deemed unassimilable, Hawaiʻi by the 1960s was being touted as a global exemplar of racial harmony and an emblem of the New Frontier. This was a concept that signaled a more expansive understanding of American national identity—both in terms of who could be counted as American at home and what areas of the world were considered to be within the U.S. sphere of influence.

Continental U.S. territories were expected to become states and were incorporated as part of the United States on the basis of their adherence to norms of whiteness and European culture; this was of a piece with the larger movement toward national consolidation in the Americas and Europe in the nineteenth century.[4] Hawai'i statehood was likewise a result of a broader global development—decolonization—that also promoted national consolidation. But Hawai'i statehood, in this context, had very new implications for the links between nation and race.

Global decolonization and Hawai'i statehood complemented U.S. efforts to promote the nation-state as the primary building block of the postwar global order. As the leading power of the noncommunist world, the United States "startlingly naturalized the free nation," drawing on the tradition of Open Door diplomacy to advance its own political and economic interests as European colonialism collapsed.[5] Against this background, Hawai'i, as an overseas colony legally distinct from the rest of the United States, appeared to many as an aberration needing resolution.

But American support for the nation-state, and Hawai'i statehood along with it, were also a response to the demands of the peoples of the decolonizing world. Grassroots, revolutionary forces abroad had transformative effects on the U.S. state and society in the postwar period. The United States may have sought to control the process of decolonization, but it did not originate it. And while many Americans may have welcomed the end of European empire, they nonetheless found themselves in a reactive position when the calls for self-government across Asia and Africa roared onto the global stage after World War II. American postwar policy, though it certainly altered the course of colonialism's demise, collided with a global movement that had already been set in motion, one that in turn shaped the Cold War itself.[6] Ordinary people in the colonial world demanding their right to self-determination changed the course of global history, often upending the domestic societies of their former rulers.[7] Britain and France may have experienced the most visible reverberations, but the impact of decolonization on the United States was likewise transformative, if less immediately obvious. Hawai'i statehood was one such transformation.

As a non-self-governing territory with a mostly Asian population—many of whose members became eligible for citizenship only in 1952, when Congress overturned anti-Asian naturalization laws—Hawai'i was a problem for the United States, belying its anticolonialist, antiracist rhetoric. The only perceived solution, however, was not to grant independence, as was done in the Philippines, but to bind Hawai'i ever more tightly to the continental United States. In the process, Hawai'i was brought closer to the United States at the same time that it was being instituted as a portal to the foreign.

Statehood, according to its supporters, would be a boon to U.S. foreign relations, and a practically cost-free one at that. It would, with one piece of legislation, demonstrate to the decolonizing world that America practiced what it preached on the issue of self-government. And by making Hawai'i a fully equal part of the nation, as opposed to casting it off, the United States could counter Soviet claims of American racism and show the Third World that it valued non-Western culture. Hawai'i—as a site of American settler colonialism and as "bridge to Asia" during a period in which the Pacific was of increasing strategic importance to the United States—required self-government without severance.

Gateway State exposes the links among postwar racial formation, decolonization, and U.S. global expansion. It demonstrates that the United States was not only engaged in influencing the outcomes of various struggles for decolonization abroad, but was also the author of its own project of decolonization, one that shaped popular conceptions of race and national identity. In the context of global decolonization, it was no longer enough for the U.S government to promote straightforward Americanization, either at home or abroad. With Third World nationalists calling for an end to foreign domination, the United States needed to convince them that it respected others' cultural traditions.

Hawai'i, as the most recent state to join the union and the most seemingly different, was portrayed as the perfect staging ground for America's newly ambitious foreign policy and as an antidote to accusations of American racism and cultural chauvinism. Moreover, unlike many parts of the mainland that called into question America's commitment to racial equality, Hawai'i appeared to present a ready-made model of interracial amity; it needed only to be exploited, not fostered through legislation or painful social change. Although Hawai'i had long been known among social scientists as the "melting pot of the Pacific" for its mix of Polynesian, Asian, and European cultures, with statehood that cosmopolitan reputation acquired new stakes, and new valence.

The positive emphasis on Hawai'i's mixed racial and ethnic makeup stood in contrast to earlier national debates over the corrosive impact of racialized immigrants on America's white-dominated culture. Much of the popular discourse around immigration during the late nineteenth and early twentieth centuries had focused alternately on exclusion and assimilation, with the two positions sharing a common fear of the foreign. Instead, in postwar discourse Hawai'i was lauded not only as a model of successful Americanization but as something more complex—as an example of useful foreignness.

Besides bringing the United States closer to Asia, Hawai'i could impart lessons of racial tolerance to Americans in the continental United States. Meanwhile, the immigrant population in Hawai'i and its desire for statehood reaffirmed American faith in its national superiority.[8] The acceptance of Asians in Hawai'i as full U.S. citizens thus depended, ironically, on their Asianness.

Even before statehood was secured, powerful advocates in Hawai'i and on the mainland had begun working to harness the islands' newfound prominence toward concrete foreign policy ends. In particular, they sought to turn

Hawai'i into a center for "mutual understanding," where Americans and Asians could encounter each other under ideal conditions. By 1962, Hawai'i was home to the East-West Center, a federally funded graduate program at the University of Hawai'i aimed at cultural and technical "interchange" between Americans and Asians, as well as the Peace Corps' largest training site for American volunteers during the 1960s. Peace Corps officials hoped that interaction with Hawai'i's multiracial society would catalyze the psychological refashioning they believed was necessary for "inter-cultural communication."

Meanwhile, Hawai'i's people were enlisted in the effort to solidify the new state's role as bridge to Asia. American elites were not only engaged in an effort to demonstrate to the decolonizing world Americans' respect for racial and ethnic minorities, as other scholars have shown. They were also keenly interested in tapping the cultural knowledge of those minority populations, particularly people of Asian descent, and using it to win friends in Asia. According to Jack Burns, Hawai'i's most influential governor (1962–74), the people of Hawai'i possessed valuable knowledge about "the problems the Asiatic peoples have in adjusting to the new modes of life" and so constituted "our best mediator with those peoples."[9] Asian Americans in Hawai'i thus never lost their perceived connection to Asia or became "white," as had other immigrant groups; instead, their racial and cultural difference was transformed into a marketable resource, one that could be deployed to help other Americans navigate an increasingly globalized world dominated by an expansionist United States.[10]

In short, Hawai'i's difference was turned into an instrument of American foreign policy. The conversations about Hawai'i in the postwar era also reverberated beyond the foreign policy establishment. Hawai'i statehood thus helped usher out a strictly assimilationist paradigm for addressing racial and ethnic difference in American politics and culture. Instead, as administrators of the University of Hawai'i's new East-West Center claimed, the fiftieth state was supposed to exemplify "the useful employment of diversities for mutual good"—a concept that, I argue, represented an early iteration of what would later be called multiculturalism.[11]

"Mutual good" in this instance referred to the spread of American modernization practices to the decolonizing world. Most accounts of multiculturalism in the United States have attributed its formation to a domestic, grassroots effort by minority communities to assert their rights to cultural recognition in the wake of formal legal equality. But as the ideas circulating in and around Hawai'i during the statehood era attest, the emergence of multiculturalist ideology among liberal elites and at the highest levels of policy was, in part, a product of American global expansion, and appeared in inchoate form as early as the 1950s. *Gateway State* shows how postwar liberal multiculturalism was developed in Hawaiʻi as a tool of global power, and then embraced, reformulated, and contested by ordinary Americans.

The ideas on multiculturalism developed in Hawaiʻi were not mere rhetoric: poststatehood Hawaiʻi became a physical center for facilitating the new cultural encounters of the Cold War, with varying degrees of success. For those Americans seeking to sway the loyalties of people in Asia and the Pacific, Hawaiʻi was not only seen as a symbolic representation of America's commitment to democracy and diversity; it was also a place where people from both Asia and the U.S. mainland were physically transported in order to prove the veracity of that message. But those cultural encounters did not always go as planned. Moreover, they often revealed the cultural chauvinism of the Americans who orchestrated them, despite their claims that such encounters were intended to prove otherwise.

Meanwhile, popular media and other forms of cultural production amplified the image of Hawaiʻi as land of social amity and cultural mixing. As liberal writers and activists looked to Hawaiʻi as a model for domestic race relations, food writers and garment manufacturers promoted Hawaiʻi cuisine and fashion as vehicles for expressing one's cosmopolitanism and racial liberalism. The Hawaiʻi tourism industry, above all, helped to solidify the vision of the islands as a racial paradise. Aided by the backing of the new state government, the Hawaiʻi tourism industry suggested to ordinary Americans that they could take part in the same kinds of cultural exchange experienced by Peace Corps volunteers and East-West Center students.

As the varying narratives of statehood-era Hawaiʻi suggest, much of Hawaiʻi's allure lay in its novelty, and in its mutability. As such, those looking to Hawaiʻi for solutions saw what was useful to see, for whatever political or economic purpose. Hawaiʻi, a place with its own complex past, much of it disconnected from that of the West, reflected back to them an idealized version of the United States, as if it had always been so. But the production of Hawaiʻi as a model of racial amity distorted the reality of life in Hawaiʻi as well as the sources of racial inequality on the mainland. A decade after statehood the movement for ethnic studies at the University of Hawaiʻi challenged the liberal multiculturalism of state institutions and helped to fuel the nascent Hawaiian sovereignty movement. Both called into question the myths around Hawaiʻi as a symbol of American democracy, anticolonialism, and racial egalitarianism.

What these debates would eventually reveal was the contested nature of Hawaiʻi statehood itself. Statehood was a paradoxical form of "decolonization" that had broadened U.S. democracy but did not overturn colonialism. Rather, decolonization and colonialism overlapped in Hawaiʻi. For Hawaiʻi's people of Asian descent—whose presence in Hawaiʻi was itself a result of American empire—statehood was a form of decolonization: they gained equal national representation as part of a state that was now fully integrated, legally, with the continental United States. This coincided with, and reinforced, their transformation in status in American immigration law and in U.S. popular culture. For Native Hawaiians, however, statehood was an extension, and a definitive normalization, of U.S. settler colonialism and the illegal overthrow of the Hawaiian state. It was at once an admission and a denial of American colonialism that placed the prospect of Hawaiian independence even further out of reach. So while statehood represented the expansion of American society and law to include a wider swathe of peoples and cultural norms, this expansion was accompanied by a process of national consolidation that limited the political options for those who might not want to participate in the U.S. project.[12]

These paradoxes and contradictions provide insight into the ways in which decolonization reshaped both U.S. foreign policy and domestic society in postwar America. Hawai'i, I argue, embodied many of the tensions inherent in America's national self-image as an anticolonial global power. A product of American conquest, the state of Hawai'i was now being extolled as the embodiment of American democracy. These same disjunctures shaped American actions in the decolonizing world, where the United States repeatedly announced its benevolent, anti-imperial intent while simultaneously using military violence to police intolerable behavior—namely, anything resembling an embrace of communism—by Third World nations.

Just as Hawai'i statehood represented both widening social participation and national consolidation, American Cold War policy at the global level promoted both broader multicultural inclusion and new limitations on acceptable forms of political economy. Hawai'i, as a site for promoting mutual understanding and as the base for various military interventions aimed at containing communism in Asia, was located at the nexus of these two projects. Indeed, Hawai'i's designation as a staging ground for projecting American cultural power grew out of its history as the center of U.S. military operations in the Pacific, and America's seemingly conflicting missions of mutual understanding and military coercion often coincided in Hawai'i. The notion of Hawai'i as "gateway to Asia" emerged in the nineteenth century among military strategists who were seeking a coaling station for navy steamships. As a result, the military quickly became a major force in the islands, and it has profoundly shaped their relationship to the United States and affected Hawai'i's own economic, social, and spatial landscape. It was the U.S. military presence in Hawai'i that made it a target for the Japanese attack that triggered America's entry into World War II. Later, Hawai'i's transition out of a plantation economy went hand in hand with massive military spending in the islands.[13]

This is not to say that the uses of Hawai'i as a center for global exchange hid an ulterior motive or served as cover for more nefarious activities. Rather, I take seriously the utopian discourses around Hawai'i while maintaining a critical eye toward their practical implications, evasions, and inconsistencies. Rhetoric rarely served as simply a deceptive veil in U.S. foreign policy, but usually originated from deeply held ideological assumptions.[14] Moreover, the very disconnect between rhetoric and action itself shaped American foreign relations during the Cold War. U.S. empire, as Amy Kaplan argues, has been fundamentally incoherent—simultaneously pursuing conflicting goals, such as national boundedness and colonial expansion.[15] One distinguishing feature of U.S. empire has been the presence, going back to the early republic, of powerful anti-imperial forces within the United States.[16] This long-standing strain of anti-imperialism, however myopic or hypocritical, animated the ways in which the United States behaved as a global superpower.

Nevertheless, while the founders of Hawai'i's Pacific-directed institutions in the years after statehood did not always work deliberately to further U.S. domination in the Pacific, they did operate within a set of assumptions that narrowed the scope of action and debate. Many seemed genuinely to believe that Americans had much to learn from other peoples. Yet this view existed in tension with a system of beliefs, written into the very structure of those institutions, that took for granted the superiority of America's economy, political organization, and social relations.

Historical scholarship on modern Hawai'i has been limited in scope, and for the most part has not delved deeply, if at all, into questions about the relationship between social change in the United States and American postwar expansionism. Much of it has focused on the impact of American intervention on the islands—with annexation serving as the pivotal moment in defining Hawai'i's relationship to the United States—or the particularities of Hawai'i's local social structure and politics. The stories of American missionary settlements in Hawai'i, the subsequent growth of Hawai'i's plantation economy and immigrant labor force, and American annexation of the islands have been relatively well covered. Few accounts, however, have explored the impact of Hawai'i on the United States, or how changing American attitudes toward Hawai'i represented broader social and cultural developments. The literature on statehood often treats it as solely a political issue.[17] Some scholars have begun to explore the international dimensions of Hawai'i statehood, placing statehood in the context of the Cold War and American foreign policy. But the focus of these analyses is limited to policymakers and major news coverage of congressional debates and takes a limited view of statehood's larger meaning and impact.[18]

Gateway State seeks to delocalize and open up the study of Hawai'i statehood by locating it within the context of both U.S. foreign relations and domestic politics and culture. As Asia came to occupy a central place in U.S. Cold War strategy, so too did Hawaiʻi. Those strategic concerns in turn had a far-reaching impact on policy, politics, and culture in both Hawaiʻi and the rest of the United States.

This study expands on a burgeoning historiography that situates twentieth-century American history within a wider global frame that draws on many of the themes and methodologies of traditional diplomatic history while also expanding its analytical scope and bringing attention to a broader set of agents of American foreign relations.[19] Many newer scholars of U.S. foreign relations have also sought to "deprovincialize American history" by demonstrating the impact of foreign developments on American society.[20] Most of these works have challenged assumptions of American exceptionalism, either explicitly or implicitly, by exploring the ways in which American institutions and politics have evolved in relation to global developments.[21] They show that the domestic looks different if we take the foreign into account. *Gateway State* likewise illuminates the permeability of the "domestic" by focusing on Hawaiʻi as an ambiguously foreign place within the nation—one whose connection to Asia was strategically deployed in the postwar era to suit the demands of American expansion in the decolonizing world.

To elucidate the longer history of how Hawaiʻi came to be an object of decolonization, *Gateway State* draws on the growing body of historical literature on American empire. As Paul Kramer argues, the category of the imperial helps open up the United States to global history and focuses our attention on questions of power and its asymmetries in American relations with other peoples.[22] Rather than treating America's acquisition of overseas colonies in 1898 as an accident or aberration, this imperial historiography emphasizes the centrality of empire in U.S. history from at least the era of Manifest Destiny onward.[23] While America's formal empire never reached the size or scope of its European counterparts, it was nonetheless embedded in that global colonial system.

Most relevant for my purposes here, the imperial lens helps situate the history of American racial formation in a global context. The era of high imperialism led to the intensification of cross-cultural contact around the world, and with it, new racial categories used to justify colonial subjugation. But whereas in Europe the concept of racial difference has always been directly linked to colonialism and its aftermath, those connecting threads have often been less visible in U.S. history. For centuries, national racial discourse in America was mainly focused on differences of white and black in the context of domestic slavery. It was a system whose roots lay in New World colonialism and the expansion of global trade, yet one that was usually talked about as an institution "peculiar" to the American South.[24]

Slavery, however, was not the only historical development shaping racial formation in the United States. As the United States expanded to reach Pacific shores and enter Asian markets, which together fueled a massive influx of Asian laborers, Asians came to occupy an increasingly prominent place in American racial imaginings.[25] Meanwhile, America's acquisition of overseas territories in 1898 further complicated the relationships among American expansion, immigration, and race. As newly colonized peoples were thrust into the chaotic mix of American racial forms, they both challenged and reified concepts of difference and exclusion through their designation as American subjects without citizenship rights.[26] Adding to the confusion over empire, race, and national belonging was the ambiguous legal status of the new colonies. Unlike Hawai'i—which was made an incorporated territory eligible for statehood because of its large white settler population—the Philippines, along with Puerto Rico and Guam, were designated as "unincorporated" American territories that were ineligible for statehood. This was a new juridical invention for the age of American formal empire.[27]

While the Philippines may have been the most populous and most contentious of the new possessions, the annexation of Hawai'i perhaps best represented the increasingly Pacific-oriented nature of American empire. Hawai'i's colonial relationship to the United States is often told separately from other histories of American empire, perhaps because Hawai'i's annexation was not part of the spoils of the Spanish-American War.[28] But Hawai'i is central to understanding American imperial relations in the Pacific, as well as anti-Asian racism in the United States. If America's growing relationship with Asia and the Pacific was defined as much by external as by internal change, it was in Hawai'i—which was both a long-standing object of American expansionist ambitions and a central site for Asian immigration—where these interlocking developments converged most starkly. Not coincidentally, Hawai'i was a major conduit for Asian migration to the mainland, where nativists sought to sever the human ties between the United States and Asia by passing exclusionary immigration laws.

America's presence in Hawai'i went back to 1820, when a group of American missionaries arrived in the islands. It was their descendants who orchestrated the overthrow of the Hawaiian monarchy in 1893 and, five years later, Hawai'i's annexation to the United States.[29] Unlike Puerto Rico or the Philippines, Hawai'i was unburdened by vestiges of European colonialism. It had no official colonial bureaucracy to speak of and was largely free from interference from Washington. And yet, mainland norms had thoroughly penetrated island culture, simultaneously masking the colonial nature of the American project in Hawai'i and demonstrating its effectiveness. Moreover, Hawai'i served as the inaugural site of U.S. military operations in the Pacific, with a navy coaling station first set up in Honolulu in 1860 and exclusive American rights to Pearl Harbor established in 1887.

White minority political dominance, coupled with a monocrop economy and preferential terms of trade with the United States, made Hawai'i a classic island colony to rival any of Europe's. The islands' wealth was concentrated among a handful of families who were direct descendants of the missionaries who came to Hawai'i in the 1820s and 1830s. Meanwhile, of all the new overseas possessions, racial structures in Hawai'i most closely resembled those of the mainland, albeit in jumbled and idiosyncratic fashion. The white elite in Hawai'i, who oversaw a regime of imported Asian labor, evoked the omnipotence of the planter class in Southern slave states. Despite Hawai'i being admitted as an incorporated territory, and thus eligible for statehood, whites in Hawai'i deliberately forestalled any changes to its territorial status out of concern that doing so would threaten their political and economic control.

The politics of race in Hawai'i cannot be uncoupled from a system of labor that insistently linked race and class. Planter rule was founded on a racially stratified system designed to limit labor organizing by assigning jobs based on ethnic descent and correlated with perceived skill and intelligence, with northern Europeans at the top, Chinese and Japanese laborers in the middle, and Filipinos at the bottom. This labor regime was also influenced by discourses of race and nation that existed apart from the plantation economy. Hawai'i politics exposed the tensions between empire and nationalism, republicanism and industry, heterogeneity and racial hierarchy. Before annexation, whites were deeply divided on what Hawai'i's economy and society should look like. Throughout the nineteenth century, fearing the dilution of Hawai'i's imported American culture, an increasingly powerful class of nonplanter white elites—merchants, newspapermen, and other professionals—worked to prevent nonwhites from becoming too numerous. Believing they had carved out a pristine replica of New England society in the north Pacific, these men led the movement for annexation.[30]

Colonialism thus existed in uneasy alliance with American nativism in Hawai'i. Although the two impulses were not mutually exclusive in practice, their ideological inconsistencies gave rise to a Hawai'i society that was both highly culturally diverse and aggressively American. Annexation helped bring whites in Hawai'i together and consolidate their rule, but it could not reconcile the inherent conflict between categories of racial difference and democratic practice. In Hawai'i, as it did throughout the conquered world, that conflict played out in a colonial register, with the problems of race, local political power, and Hawai'i's subordinate relationship to the mainland all intertwined.

Global decolonization fundamentally undermined the concept of racial hierarchy that was at the core of colonial ideology. Around the world, colonized peoples challenged the racialized structures of control erected by colonizers, often drawing on Enlightenment rhetoric and veneration of human equality espoused by colonizers themselves.[31] The struggles against colonialism in Asia and Africa also enlisted the support of oppressed racial minorities in the United States, who worked to expose the parallels between colonial rule and discriminatory policy at home.[32]

While decolonization and the global movement for racial equality challenged systems of racial difference, it did not erase them. Decolonization helped spur massive worldwide migration as workers and refugees from Asia and Africa sought opportunity in former colonial metropoles, forcing Europeans to confront racialized minorities on a larger scale than ever before. Hawaiʻi statehood shows that decolonization had a parallel impact on the United States. In particular, it demonstrates that postwar rearticulations of difference in both the domestic and foreign spheres were intimately connected. The legitimation of antiracist discourse in domestic politics and the overhaul of racist legislation in American law were not only influenced by policymakers' concerns over how the United States projected itself to the decolonizing world. New theories on race and culture that emerged in the postwar period in relation to Hawaiʻi also shaped American foreign relations. Global-minded institutions such as the East-West Center and the Peace Corps both contributed to national discourses around changing notions of difference and sought to inject those new ideas into foreign policy making.

The discourses around difference in Hawaiʻi, I argue, augured the rise of multiculturalism in U.S. culture more broadly during the later decades of the twentieth century. Well before college admissions offices advocated for the importance of cultural diversity in enriching the undergraduate experience and corporations instituted "cultural sensitivity" training programs for their employees, the Peace Corps was teaching cultural sensitivity in Hawaiʻi and the islands' business and political class was selling the new state as "a montage of minorities."[33]

There is a vast scholarship, much of it written in the 1990s by sociologists, philosophers, and literary critics, that theorizes multiculturalism and examines its manifestations in academia, politics, and everyday life.[34] I treat the ideology of multiculturalism, as malleable and imprecise as it may be, as a historical phenomenon that emerged out of a specific temporal moment in U.S. politics and culture. Multiculturalism, unlike its ideological antecedents, pluralism and cosmopolitanism, is not only an idea, but also an institutional practice linked to increasing globalization in the latter half of the twentieth century. Scholars have mostly focused on multiculturalism's association with education, chronicling the efforts of those seeking to diversify humanities curricula in response to demands to end white cultural hegemony. This story is often told as a declension narrative, in which the original, radical multiculturalist ideal was diluted, and contained, often at the expense of promoting diversity at a structural level.[35]

In contrast to the prevailing analysis, I argue that multiculturalism was not only a way for racial and ethnic minorities to assert their right to cultural recognition.[36] Nor was it simply a means for people in power to pander to those restive minority communities. Multiculturalism, from its origins, was a discursive and institutional tool for liberal policymakers and business leaders, who saw the celebration of social difference as a means to both facilitate American expansionism abroad and make money at home. This was not a straightforward story of co-optation. Indeed, liberal corporate multiculturalism emerged before critical leftist multiculturalism.

Broadly defined, multiculturalism refers to the ideology and practice of celebrating social difference in a heterogeneous society. In contrast to assimilationism or traditional racial liberalism, multiculturalism stresses particularity over universality. It represented a response to the challenges of negotiating group difference in the post–civil rights, postcolonial era. Once legal rights and protections were granted to racial minorities and immigration law was stripped of its racial restrictions, once formalized inequality was replaced with more nebulous forms of repression and racialization, multiculturalism offered a way to talk about social difference as an ongoing, and ultimately unresolvable, part of modern life.

The term *multiculturalism* can be traced back to the mid-1970s and its rise in popular media tracks a similar upward trajectory as "globalization."[37] "Multicultural" was already in limited use in the 1960s—significantly, one of its first mentions in the *New York Times* came in an article about the University of Hawaiʻi.[38] Its conceptual genealogy goes back further, particularly toward the discourse of cultural pluralism, first articulated by Horace Kallen in his radical rejection of the melting pot and later picked up by social scientists and in progressive circles during the interwar period.[39] These "oppositional networks" persevered throughout World War II, despite the external pressures of wartime consensus culture, widespread indifference to civil rights claims, and Japanese internment.[40] But they were never mainstream. Moreover, when state institutions involved themselves in navigating the problem of racial and ethnic diversity in this period it was generally to promote coercive Americanization.[41]

By the late 1950s, as the debates on Hawaiʻi statehood demonstrate, national policymakers and the producers of popular culture had begun adopting much of the rhetoric of cultural pluralism, and using it toward new ends. They also began interweaving it with a cosmopolitan ethos, which—as exemplified by the emphasis on racial mixing in Hawaiʻi—upheld the benefits of cross-cultural borrowing over the preservation of autonomous cultural traditions.[42]

This also involved a remarkable transformation in the legal status and popular images of Asians in the United States, who went from being agents of a "Yellow Peril" to a "model minority." During the Cold War, as Christina Klein and Melani McAlister have shown, Orientalist ideas of a binary opposition between East and West gave way to more flexible and heterogeneous representations that often emphasized the affinities between Americans and the people of "the East"—even as many policymakers continued to view the people of Asia through an Orientalist lens.[43]

That multiculturalism came out of a period marked by aggressive American expansionism is no coincidence. The negotiation of difference was increasingly played out on the global stage in the postwar era. Just as more Americans than ever were leaving the United States as tourists, government workers, and business travelers, a new wave of migrants from the so-called Third World was changing the American social landscape. These two trends were tightly entangled. Like Hawaiʻi statehood, immigration reform was a central plank in U.S. government efforts to prove American good intentions to people of color around the world, and particularly in Asia.[44] Meanwhile, the architects of such expansionism, both in government and outside it, asked Americans to demonstrate their racial tolerance to ease the process of exerting U.S. influence abroad.[45] Thus the new inclusionary ethos that marked elite discourse in the postwar era was not simply the product of moral or intellectual enlightenment; it also fulfilled the strategic demands of American empire.

The scale and scope of U.S. global engagement, which Hawaiʻi represented in microcosm, necessitated a new paradigm for managing social difference in both national and foreign affairs. One of the ways of doing so was to fold "race" into "culture" or "ethnicity." After the passage of civil rights reform, liberal elites increasingly subscribed to the idea that race was an illegitimate category of analysis—a biological fiction that should be discredited as an explanation for group differences. Multiculturalism helped to replace archaic theories of race and instead drew on anthropological notions of culture as linked to ethnic descent, wherein everyone, from American WASPs to Filipino villagers, was reared in specific norms and practices that shaped their individual identities.

However, as poststatehood Hawaiʻi demonstrates, the foregrounding of difference left open a number of questions. To what extent should respect for difference give way to various homogenizing forces, such as political democracy, modernization, capitalism, or nationalism? How should the groups that comprise a multicultural society be defined and delineated? Where did indigenous people fit into the multicultural paradigm? And how could multiculturalism address the thorny problem of racial inequality, at once a biological fiction and a structural reality?

Hawaiʻi boosters left many of these questions unanswered, choosing instead to project an image of Hawaiʻi as a place that was at once American and foreign, internally diverse and racially transcendent, melting pot and salad bowl. Such inconsistencies, rather than reflecting a nuanced understanding of the complexity of Hawaiʻi life, were more often driven by the logic of profit and strategic national interest than by social justice.

Gateway State reconstructs and critiques the postwar utopian vision of Hawaiʻi through an analysis of the people and institutions that crafted it and contested it. As a hybrid work of political and cultural history, it assumes that political and cultural change are mutually constitutive. I thus give equal weight in my analysis to food writers, members of Congress, State Department staff, university students, state officials, and others seeking to shape Hawaiʻi's image and its future. To that end, *Gateway State* tracks Hawaiʻi statehood and its effects in roughly chronological order, with each chapter focusing on the perspective of a different set of historical actors who emerged as prominent voices in the discourses around Hawaiʻi at particular moments in time.

The first chapter explores the post–World War II congressional debates on Hawaiʻi statehood. It was not until the statehood debates that Hawaiʻi began to acquire a popular reputation as a vibrant interracial community where "East meets West." This image emerged only through contentious political struggle, as statehood advocates battled opponents who believed Hawaiʻi's people were a threat to white supremacy. Mainland opponents, most of them Southern Democrats, assailed statehood as a colonialist maneuver that would dilute U.S. national identity. Many of these opponents feared that Hawaiʻi would provide the crucial votes necessary for civil rights legislation if the territory were made a state. Statehood advocates at first claimed Hawaiʻi should be granted statehood because of its similarity to the mainland. By the end of the statehood debates, however—as Asia grew in importance in U.S. Cold War policy—Hawaiʻi was promoted by its supporters as a place whose cultural connections to Asia could be used to advance American global interests.

Chapter 2 examines how activists, journalists, and writers constructed Hawaiʻi as a paradigm of racial equality in the context of the national civil rights movement. While the vision of Hawaiʻi as a racial paradise went back to social science discourses of the interwar period, the statehood debates of the postwar era politicized the Hawaiʻi fantasy. Best-selling author James Michener was the most prominent media figure to champion the idea that Hawaiʻi could serve as a model for mainland race relations. The black press and many civil rights activists likewise turned to Hawaiʻi as proof that "integration works." This was an aspirational picture that overlooked Hawaiʻi's own racial tensions, which would eventually rise to the surface as the glow of statehood dimmed. Moreover, these accounts ultimately helped promote the new state as a place where mainlanders could escape the hostile race relations of mainland—one of the implicit messages of Hawai'i's tourism industry—rather than a viable social model that could be emulated.

The third chapter investigates how the idealistic imaginings of America's newest state were institutionalized through an effort to establish Hawai'i as a center for global educational exchange. Hawai'i statehood arrived at a moment when the United States was increasingly going beyond its borders to draw foreign peoples into its orbit. The East-West Center and the Peace Corps both enlisted Hawai'i in this effort by designating it as an ideal site for fostering mutual understanding, as a place where foreigners could be trained in American economic and cultural practices and where foreign ways could be demystified for Americans. These efforts would in turn win over people from the decolonizing world, whose racial and cultural differences were seen as obstacles to be conquered in the service of modernization. The ideas on inter-cultural communications developed at the East-West Center and the Peace Corps would eventually be taken up more broadly, notably by the military in its campaign to secure the allegiance of South Vietnamese peasants.

While the East-West Center and the Peace Corps training program repre-sented Hawai'i's attempt to promote itself as a center for cultural exchange, it was the tourism industry's efforts to sell race and racial tolerance that truly revolutionized Hawai'i's political economy.[46] Chapter 4 studies the Hawai'i tourism industry's efforts to market Hawai'i as a multicultural paradise where positive racial experiences could be bought and sold. Although Hawai'i had long been a draw for wealthy tourists, jet travel, which arrived the same year as statehood, allowed a larger and broader cohort of mainland Amer-icans to vacation in the islands, which the tourism industry portrayed as a quasi-foreign space where mainlanders could experience social amity and forge multicultural self-identities in the comfort of a safe, American milieu. In the process, I argue, tourism helped turn race and racial tolerance into saleable—if intangible—commodities. Meanwhile, a massive military rest and recreation (R&R) program in Hawai'i for combat soldiers during the Vietnam War exposed the limits of global mutual understanding and racial tolerance. Instead of encouraging its consumers to learn from Hawai'i's mixed multicultural society, R&R in Hawai'i upheld the nuclear family and sought to insulate servicemen from the wider world, where American–foreign encoun-ters often did not go the way the U.S. government envisioned. The tourism industry epitomized the ways in which much of the liberal racial discourse in the post–civil rights era conflated race, culture, and ethnicity, and in the process, depoliticized all three.

A fifth chapter asks why white, middle-class American women were so fascinated with all things Hawai'i in the two decades after statehood, and why Hawai'i's export market linked racial and ethnic boundary-crossing with women's self-fulfillment. The mainland marketing of Hawai'i offered a virtual version of the kinds of cross-cultural exchange taking place in Hawai'i itself, urging ordinary mainland women to envision themselves as liberated, globe-trotting cosmopolitans. Cookbooks and apparel manufacturers suggested that the acts of eating Hawaiian food and wearing clothes produced in Hawai'i could catalyze a new, more relaxed, racially enlightened worldview. Yet the mainland consumption of Hawai'i was also made possible by the expansion of racially segregated suburban developments, where racial liberalism could be performed without disrupting racial inequality.

The final chapter challenges the progressive narrative of Hawai'i's boosters by analyzing the rise of opposition movements in Hawai'i, particularly groups advocating for ethnic studies programs at the University of Hawai'i and related, nascent movements for native rights. While the liberal multiculturalism of state boosters went largely uncontested in Hawai'i in the years before and after statehood, by the late 1960s Hawai'i's colonial history and its consequences would be reawakened as excitement over statehood gave way to widespread discontent among those excluded from statehood's rewards. Like the architects of Hawai'i's cultural exchange institutions, radicals in Hawai'i were also responding to Third World movements for cultural nationalism—as movements not to counteract, but to emulate.

As ethnic studies activists were quick to point out, Hawai'i never did live up to the idealistic rhetoric surrounding it. But to many liberals at mid-century and the decades after, the idea of Hawai'i as a multicultural utopia was a plausible one, even as it appeared to be increasingly at odds with a country wracked by racial inequality and mired in an imperialist war in Southeast Asia. Why did this seemingly peripheral state come to play an outsized role in liberal visions of the nation's racial future, and of the U.S. place in the world? Hawai'i's unexpected and enduring relevance in American life is what this study seeks to explain.

1

"The Picture Window of the Pacific"

AMERICAN FOREIGN POLICY AND THE
REMAKING OF RACIAL DIFFERENCE IN
THE CAMPAIGN FOR HAWAI'I STATEHOOD

ON A TYPICALLY balmy November afternoon in Honolulu, a city some 2,500 miles from the continental United States, Hawai'i governor William F. Quinn took to a podium with a speech that spoke to the lofty expectations attached to Hawai'i statehood. A few months earlier, in March 1959, Congress had passed a bill to admit Hawai'i as the fiftieth American state, which took effect in August, and Quinn and much of the rest of Hawai'i were still in a celebratory mood. Standing in front of I'olani Palace, the seat of the state government and former royal headquarters of the once-sovereign Hawaiian nation, Quinn offered a portrait of a poststatehood Hawai'i that was at once romantic and utilitarian. "We have long proclaimed how important it was to our country that Hawaii be a state—that we, Hawaiians of all racial ancestries, be given full and equal rights of citizenship," he said. "Now we must bring the strength of our various races to the service of our nation in the Pacific world." By making Hawai'i a state, Quinn argued, the United States had "struck a great blow for freedom in the world of the Pacific." He went on to describe how Hawai'i lay at the center of a changing vision of the United States:

> No more will we be challenged as a colonial nation. No more will it be charged that we maintain a colony in the Pacific because its inhabitants are largely non-Caucasian. . . . Instead [other peoples] see us broadening our horizons not by conquest—not as master and slave—but by concord—by solemn vows of everlasting equality. We have great hopes for this new state. . . . We see ourselves, with the beautiful harmonic blend in our society, as an instrument for the advancement of the true brotherhood of man. We want to share this harmony—we want to exemplify the beauty of it

to the people of the world. We want it to be known for what we think it is—the purest embodiment of the philosophy of American government yet known to man.[1]

In his brief address, Quinn hit all the key themes of the protracted congressional debate that surrounded Hawai'i statehood throughout the 1950s. During the thirteen years that statehood remained on the legislative docket, the problem of Hawai'i's political status had become a way to talk about a wide array of challenges facing postwar America. From worldwide decolonization to domestic racial inequality, from the expanding role of the United States in the world to the changing role of the state at home, Hawai'i was a discursive battleground for contesting all of these pressing concerns. Such issues, as exhibited by Quinn's speech, were not always so neatly separated. Rather, more often than not, they were discussed in tandem with each other, as if they were interlocking pieces in the same puzzle.

Indeed, Hawai'i did represent something of a puzzle. Hawai'i's postwar prominence raised new questions about how to define the territory's place in both the United States and in the world—and how to define American national identity more broadly. With its location in Polynesia and large ethnically Asian population, could Hawai'i still be considered American—and, if so, would that change the meaning of the very concept of Americanness? Should difference be repressed or celebrated? Hawai'i statehood served at once as an answer to and an evasion of these vexing questions. Quinn seemed to want to have it all ways at once, with Hawai'i representing a microcosm of the world and of the United States, an exceptional community and an all-American one.

Whether Hawai'i represented the embodiment of or notable exception to American culture, it was clear by the time Hawai'i finally became a state that it had acquired great symbolic stature for all sides of the issue. As the postwar period progressed, Hawai'i quickly went from being an administrative and legal problem to being an ideological one, revealing major divisions over what the role of the United States in the world should be and what American society itself should look like.

The statehood debates demonstrate that the delegitimation of racism in national discourse was bound up with the changing global role of the United States. The policymakers who promoted statehood explicitly linked the cause of American postwar expansion with the need for a more inclusive racial policy in the domestic sphere. As the United States proclaimed its support for decolonizing nations while simultaneously expanding its global influence, Americans began articulating a new national story—one codified in both culture and law—in which racial and ethnic difference were no longer obstacles to full citizenship but instead were characteristics of American society that should be celebrated. America's internal diversity came to be a signal of national strength as it demonstrated the power of American ideals to encompass people from different ethnic origins. The emphasis on Hawai'i's diversity also helped cover over uncomfortable questions about the islands' colonial history and indigenous opposition to statehood, as the success of Asian Americans in Hawai'i supposedly proved the consensual, democratizing nature of American expansion.

The ambiguousness of Hawai'i—as both a territory and a potential state— shaped the discourses around statehood legislation throughout the 1940s and 1950s. Within this protean discourse, the same reasons given in support of statehood might also be used to oppose it. Hawai'i's location, racial composition, and its taint of colonialism appeared as arguments on both sides of the congressional debate. But while statehood was an issue of global significance to its supporters, its opponents were concerned mainly with Hawai'i statehood's domestic relevance. They objected to admitting Hawai'i not only because of its large Asian population but also because of a more abstract fear of the potential ripple effect of Hawai'i's integrationist example. Opposition to Hawai'i statehood was therefore about race in the broadest possible sense.

By the time Hawai'i was admitted in 1959, it was not simply another U.S. state. It was, as Senator Henry Jackson put it, "our diplomatic state . . . next door to over half the population of the world."[2] Midway between the United States and Asia, and home to a majority population of people of Asian descent, Hawai'i's value lay in its racial difference and in its ambiguity—as a part of America that was also a "bridge" to the decolonizing world. Rather than being a direct extension of the mainland, Hawai'i became a place whose uniqueness defined its relationship to the rest of the United States. After more than a century of Americanization efforts in Hawai'i, the success of the statehood campaign ultimately hinged on foregrounding Hawai'i's connection to Asia.

———

Considering the stakes, it is perhaps not surprising that Hawai'i statehood took as long as it did. The debates around Hawai'i statehood were among the most contentious of any statehood debates in American history. The issue was subject to more than thirty congressional hearings and reports, totaling several thousand pages, and made Hawai'i "the most thoroughly studied, the most exhaustively investigated, and the most rejected by Congress" of all U.S. territories that went on to become states.[3] Beginning soon after Hawai'i's annexation in 1898, the territory would regularly seek admission from Congress, but these requests were more perfunctory than sincere. For much of the first half of Hawai'i's territorial history, the islands' white elite had no reason to seek increased democratic participation. Indeed, until the eve of World War II, white Americans in Hawaiʻi—known as haoles, the Hawaiian word for foreigners—had much to lose if their territory became a state. Since the arrival of American missionaries in Hawaiʻi in 1820, haoles had gradually created for themselves a comfortable enclave of wealth and power, from which they ruled over a racialized working class. They lived in high style, attending lavish parties and going home to palatial island estates. One reporter in 1893 claimed that he had seen more people in evening dress in Hawaiʻi than anywhere in the United States.[4] Many Native Hawaiians and Asian laborers, by contrast, lived in extreme poverty underwritten by political disenfranchisement. Any increased power that statehood might confer on them would necessarily undermine the haole way of life. Up to and beyond the first organized push for statehood in the 1930s, haoles in Hawaiʻi were among the key proponents of the idea that the islands' heavily Asian population was unassimilable. Even as most haoles came to advocate statehood, they remained deeply influenced by the tradition of white supremacy in which they were raised.

That tradition was established through a combination of persuasion and force. White settlers in Hawaiʻi were also lucky. The first American missionaries came at a moment of dramatic transition. For centuries Hawaiʻi had developed without any foreign contact outside of the Polynesian Pacific. When English explorer James Cook landed on Kauai in 1778, he helped set in motion seismic changes in Hawaiian society and the islands' relationship to the rest of the world. By 1810, the introduction of guns had allowed chief Kamehameha to unite the Hawaiian islands, which had previously been ruled through a system of decentralized chiefdoms. But at the same time that Kamehameha was working to establish the new kingdom's sovereignty and ensure internal cohesion, the islands were confronted with challenges from the outside. Traditional Hawaiian ways were under threat from sandalwood merchants, whalers, and other western traders who brought with them germs, a rowdy port town culture, and new notions of commodity exchange.

By the time the American missionaries arrived, Native Hawaiian society was in deep distress. Chiefs had begun levying heavy taxes on commoners to pay off debts to foreign traders, thereby upsetting older systems of communalism and feudal patronage. Western diseases, such as smallpox, were wiping out whole communities throughout the islands.[5] As Hawaiians were roiled by change, American missionaries saw an opportunity for thoroughgoing reform. They immediately set about evangelizing Native Hawaiians and imposing American cultural, social, and legal norms. Their relatively small numbers belied their outsized influence. The names of those early American settlers—Thurston, Judd, Baldwin—would echo in the halls of power in Hawaiʻi for more than a century.

By converting many members of the monarchy to Protestantism, the Americans quickly gained a foothold in Hawai'i's royal governance structure. Through the overhaul of Hawai'i's legal and political regimes, they sought to transform everyday custom and practice in the islands. In 1840 they helped usher in a constitutional monarchy. Over the course of the next several years, the establishment of an independent judiciary, a civil service, and universal male suffrage further eroded the authority of the king and local chiefs, while privatization laws allowed foreigners to purchase land, leading to the near-total displacement of Hawaiian commoners.[6] Haoles used the opportunity provided by Hawaiian land reform to buy up large plots and turn them into sugar plantations manned by imported Asian labor.[7] Land ownership firmly cemented haole power in Hawai'i. In 1875, at the urging of the haole elite, Hawai'i and the United States signed a reciprocity treaty in which the United States agreed to lift all tariffs on Hawaiian sugar in exchange for rights to the land that would become Pearl Harbor. Though the treaty did little to help Native Hawaiians, it was mutually beneficial for both haoles and the U.S. government, which had been eyeing Hawai'i as a site for a naval coaling station. Meanwhile, sugar plantation profits soared.

Haole ascendancy culminated in the overthrow of the monarchy and Hawai'i's annexation to the United States. In 1887, under threat of violence, King Kalākaua acceded to yet another American-written constitution, this one allowing haoles even greater influence in the Hawaiian legislature. Six years later, a group of haole conspirators, supported by the American foreign minister to Hawai'i and a company of U.S. Marines, ousted Queen Lili'oukalani, who had attempted to restore the monarchy's power. For five years the new Republic of Hawaii called for annexation to the United States, though President Grover Cleveland effectively put off the unprecedented move of acquiring an overseas American territory. By the middle of the Spanish-American War, however, the expansionist mood in the United States was at a high pitch, and Hawai'i was increasingly recognized as a strategic base for American imperial ambitions. In the summer of 1898, at the urging of President William McKinley, Congress officially annexed the islands.[8]

Haoles were left to administer Hawai'i as they saw fit. Indeed, congressional support in 1900 for Hawai'i's Organic Act, which laid out the new territory's governing structure, was contingent on assurances that the white oligarchy would continue its reign. According to an official at the Department of Interior, "It was accepted without question that Hawaii was to be governed by a 'ruling class' of approximately 4,000 Americans and other Anglo-Saxon peoples" who would dominate the territory's other 145,000 residents. Because American law prevented Asians from becoming naturalized citizens, some 60 percent of the islands' population at the time of annexation was unable to vote.[9] Although

Native Hawaiians comprised an absolute majority of registered voters until 1925, they had been effectively chastened by earlier demonstrations of haole force. With a few notable exceptions, they largely declined to challenge the haole political elite, which held a firm grip on the Hawai'i legislature via the Republican Party.[10] The white oligarchy was also traditionally consulted by the president when he appointed the territorial governor. Meanwhile the islands' economy, now based almost entirely on sugar and pineapple production, was dominated by a cartel of haole-owned firms known as the Big Five, which presided over nearly all aspects of sugar production in Hawai'i, from the plantations to processing and shipping.

The dominance of white settlers in Hawai'i was also the reason the islands were designated by the Organic Act as an incorporated territory—like all previous U.S. territories—and thus eligible for statehood. The other possessions acquired during and after the Spanish-American War, with smaller white populations, were given the newly invented status of "unincorporated" territory, which had no provisions for statehood. Haole support for the territorial status quo in Hawai'i nonetheless remained strong for decades. It took a turn in fortune to drive home the limitations of territorial status. The Sugar Act of 1934, which imposed a quota on Hawaiian sugar imported to the mainland, posed a direct challenge to haoles' base of economic power and lead to a near-reversal of opinion on statehood among much of Hawai'i's white community. By 1935, the territory had thrown its full weight behind statehood by establishing an official statehood lobbying organization known as the Equal Rights Commission (later the Hawaii Statehood Commission). That same year a House subcommittee delegation held extensive hearings in Hawai'i. The subcommittee's report postponed any endorsement of statehood without "considerable further study." In 1937 another congressional delegation visited the islands only to recommend that Hawai'i's statehood bid be tabled once again, citing concerns about the loyalty of Hawai'i's Japanese population.[11]

The greatest push for statehood came after World War II, however, and coincided with the rise of Hawai'i's Nisei population, the children of Japanese plantation laborers. Statehood bills were introduced in every session of Congress, passing in the House three times (in 1947, 1950, and 1953) and in the Senate once (in 1954) until a bill finally passed in both houses in 1959. Despite majority support for statehood in both the House and the Senate, opponents were able to use procedural tactics to stall statehood for more than a decade.

In the end, Congress could no longer plausibly reject Hawai'i statehood after Alaska's admission in 1958. But this chronology of events obscures as much as it reveals. Alaska, which was significantly less populated and less developed than Hawai'i, began its postwar statehood campaign by hitching its fate to Hawai'i's. The fact that Alaska became a state first was partly due to partisan politics: Hawai'i's history as a GOP stronghold helped it garner support among mainland Republicans, while Alaska had traditionally gone Democratic. But the Hawai'i elections of 1954, which resulted in the capture of the territorial legislature by a multiracial Democratic Party, complicates any such reductionist argument about why Alaska went before Hawai'i. The issue of Alaska statehood, although it had opponents, including Dwight Eisenhower for much of his presidency, never reached the level of controversy that Hawai'i elicited.[12] The base of opposition to Hawai'i statehood was not the Democratic Party as a whole, but a small group of powerful Southerners who looked at Hawai'i—with its racially mixed society—and saw ominous portents of national integration.[13] Congressional traditions and procedures—such as preventing subcommittees from reporting out bills for floor debates or threatening to filibuster—allowed them to wield tremendous influence over the terms of debate.[14]

Those Southern Democrats were going against the tide of public opinion. After World War II, the number of Americans favoring statehood ranged between 60 and 80 percent in Gallup polls.[15] Popular views on Hawai'i speak to a decline in the blatant public racism that had shaped American policies on immigration and offshore possessions before the war as well as growing support for civil rights. And yet to paint statehood opponents as a retrograde minority is to overlook the significance of the transformation in American politics and culture that Hawai'i statehood represented.

For one, some segregationists supported statehood and opponents existed outside the South, with many of them in Hawai'i itself, where they were against statehood for diverse reasons. On the mainland, opposition beyond the South often reflected the deep-rootedness and geographical reach of anti-Asian racism. After the Japanese bombing of Pearl Harbor, people of Japanese descent were singled out for mass internment in the U.S. West and relentless stereotyping in popular media, helping to fuel a brutal race war in the Pacific.[16] Given the unprecedented nature of incorporating an overseas territory as a U.S. state, combined with the vehemence of wartime anti-Japanese sentiment and the prominence of Hawai'i's Japanese population, statehood's success is more surprising than not.

Facing the many challenges in making the case for statehood, advocates struggled to put forth a coherent argument. Initially, many supporters, particularly those in Hawai'i, focused on the territory's legal right to statehood. The Hawaii Statehood Commission, established by the territorial legislature in 1947 to succeed the Equal Rights Commission, initially took a cautious approach to promoting its cause. With board members appointed by the territorial governor and comprised mostly of haoles—many of whom were connected to the islands' business community—it represented Hawai'i's centrist-conservative guard. To counteract the opposition's portrayal of Hawai'i as a hotbed of labor radicalism and wary of feeding into the hands of mainland nativists, they sought to present Hawai'i as an anodyne, average American community. Its earliest arguments for statehood framed the issue in terms of Hawai'i's worthiness. Hawai'i was just like any other American territory looking to become a state: its entitlement was located in constitutional law, not ideology.[17]

Yet the Statehood Commission was also reluctant to speak explicitly on the injustice of Hawai'i's unequal relationship to the rest of the United States. Drawing too much attention to Hawai'i's inequality with the mainland risked highlighting its subordination to the rest of American society. Walking the line between highlighting Hawai'i's interdependence with mainland society and lauding its self-sufficiency, statehood advocates in Hawai'i in the 1940s suggested that it was in fact a culture of *independence* that linked the islands to the rest of the United States. According to Victor S.K. Houston, a former congressional delegate for Hawai'i, Congress had "taken care" of American Indians on the mainland, Eskimos in Alaska, and Filipinos in the Philippines, but in Hawai'i, "the Territorial government was left to take care of its own needs, without help from the parent government."[18] Although the Philippines had achieved independence after a period of American "tutelage," Houston was offering the opposite argument for why Hawai'i should be granted a change in status: it was a *lack* of tutelage that made Hawai'i an appealing candidate for statehood.

Hawai'i's Americanization was another common trope in the early years of the postwar statehood campaign. "The visitor to Hawaii today finds in Honolulu all the characteristics of a mainland metropolis," the Statehood Commission asserted. "Large department stores and smart shops line Fort Street, modern multi-story office buildings and banks front on Bishop Street." Parks in the capital were filled with Honoluluans who had embraced "the familiar frenzy of our national sport" of baseball, along with tennis and golf.[19] It is notable that in this description of Honolulu the Statehood Commission chose not to mention that most of the city's baseball diamonds were in parks with Hawaiian names, that surfing was arguably a more popular local pastime than golf or tennis, or that Bishop and Fort streets wove through heart of the city's sizeable Chinatown district. Instead, it chose to project a more generic image of Hawai'i—and of America. Designed to be inoffensive, it intentionally rejected the particularities of place.

Hawai'i statehood advocates had reason to be defensive on the question of Hawai'i's Americanness. And it was not only those actively opposing Hawai'i's admission as a state who worried statehood advocates. Even after the bombing of Pearl Harbor, Hawai'i often had a hard time shaking the notion that it was a foreign country. The Statehood Commission believed that correcting this impression, wherever it might come up, was part of its mission. In one case, it protested a University of Minnesota decision in 1947 not to admit students from Hawai'i on the basis of their supposedly "foreign" status. The university's admissions office came back with a strikingly obtuse response. Ignoring the Statehood Commission's pleas to recognize Hawai'i as part of the United States, the Minnesota letter writer cheerfully pointed out that "there is a certain advantage in being classified as 'foreign,'" at least when it came to membership in the university's Cosmopolitan Club.[20] For the Statehood Commission in the late 1940s and early 1950s, no slight was too insignificant and no organization too small to be schooled on Hawai'i's American credentials. In a letter to Henderson Publishing in Peoria, Illinois, the Statehood Commission complained on behalf of a Hawai'i resident who had attempted to subscribe to *National Livestock Producer* and *National Rabbit Raiser* but was told the magazines could not accept foreign subscriptions. This was a "particularly sensitive" issue, the Statehood Commission explained. As the islands were "now on the threshold of attaining the status of a state. . . . we do not relish having the term 'foreign' applied to the Territory of Hawaii."[21]

As these interactions demonstrate, people in Hawai'i were accustomed to managing mainlanders' confusion over terms such as foreign, country, and territory. But mainlander ignorance was not just a nuisance. It cut to the heart of Hawai'i's dilemma: in the eyes of many Americans, Hawai'i simply was not American enough to be considered "an integral part" of the United States. This was not to say that most Americans actively objected to Hawai'i's role as an incorporated territory or a potential state. Rather, many mainlanders simply did not give much thought to Hawai'i's official status. Part of the reason for their ignorance on Hawai'i's relationship to the United States was because an overwhelming array of institutional structures, ranging from textbooks to maps to federal departments, had for decades downplayed, ignored, or hidden America's colonies from view.[22]

But the biggest factor marking Hawai'i as foreign was the racial difference of its people. It was also race that stubbornly linked Hawai'i to Puerto Rico and other nonwhite lands beyond the contiguous United States. As one opponent of statehood suggested in an appeal to Congress in 1949, Hawai'i was part of conspiracy of foreign invaders seeking to break down the barricades erected around white America. "To make a State of Hawaii would mean to give free access to the hordes of Yellows, Blacks, Filipinos, Koreans, Japanese, Puerto Ricans, etc.," Maryland resident David Aitchison wrote to his state representatives in a letter obtained by the Statehood Commission. The "huge inter-racial center" of Hawai'i would be an entry point for nonwhites seeking "to annihilate the White Anglo-Saxon stock."[23]

Even milder notions of the islands' racial difference were seen as threatening to the statehood cause in late 1940s and early 1950s. For instance, the

Statehood Commission worried that the tourism industry, which had done so much to promote Hawaiʻi as a tropical idyll populated by locals of exotic racial extraction, was undermining the message of Americanization. A friendly, if strained, exchange between the Statehood Commission and the Hawaii Visitors Bureau in 1947 revealed the tensions over how Hawaiʻi should be portrayed to the mainland. According to the Visitors Bureau, "The glamour of Hawaii from our point of view and from the point of view of the visitor is not in seeing another white man, but seeing the brown and oriental races of the Pacific." The Statehood Commission, distressed that a magazine advertisement for Hawaiʻi tourism had underrepresented the number of whites living in the territory, saw its mission as separate from that of the "glamour boys" at the Visitors' Bureau, who "are selling a different Hawaii than we are." To placate the Statehood Commission's anxiety over Hawaiʻi's image as a land of brown and oriental peoples, the Visitors Bureau, perhaps disingenuously, promised to "plug for the caucasian" from then on.[24]

As such an exchange illustrates, the Statehood Commission in the late 1940s hewed closely to traditional ideas about white supremacy. While often arguing on the one hand that Hawaiʻi's race issues were unique to the islands, the Statehood Commission, in a contradictory effort, also sought to represent the territory as racially analogous to the mainland—often by deliberately minimizing the fact that whites were a minority in the territory. Such a move required a delicate mix of evasion and selective reporting. Anticipating the question of whether the people of Hawaiʻi were "capable of maintaining a State government" at an upcoming subcommittee hearing in 1948, Joseph Farrington, Hawaiʻi's congressional delegate and a fixture of white Honolulu society, encouraged commission-sponsored witnesses to highlight the similarity of public officials in Hawaiʻi to those on the mainland. According to Farrington, "A simple statement of racial heritage does not convey to a mainlander the true picture of racial conditions in Hawaii." Speakers should "use a very broad racial analysis footnoted to indicate that, although the person in question may be an 'Hawaiian-Caucasian' . . . to all appearances the person is distinctly a Caucasian."[25] Understanding that mainland questions on Hawaiʻi's readiness for statehood were in fact coded racial critiques of the "maturity" of the islands' majority nonwhite population, Farrington sought to make Hawaiʻi appear more white. While he knew that Hawaiʻi residents of Asian descent would never be considered white by the standards of the Eightieth Congress, he was willing to wager that "Hawaiian-Caucasians" might get a pass.

Other Statehood Commission tactics in these years involved statistical or historical distortion. In a typical letter to the editor in a mainland newspaper, printed in March 1947, it sought to deny Hawaiʻi's Asianness. "Many people are under the impression that the Hawaiian legislature is in danger of control by persons of oriental ancestry," the letter lamented. But they "do not realize that Hawaii's 519,000 population is composed of well over 85% bonified [sic] United States citizens, and citizens of Caucasian background outnumber citizens of Japanese background."[26] Such statistics appear deliberately dishonest as they were likely based on inclusion of military personnel in Hawaiʻi, which during and immediately after World War II gave a significant yet temporary bump to the islands' white population, enough to disrupt the usual balance between whites and Japanese. By 1950, after demobilization, people of Japanese descent again achieved a demographic plurality akin to prewar figures—37 percent of the population to whites' 23 percent.[27] The Statehood Commission also erased the Asian influences on Hawaiʻi society by repeated reference to the legacy the New England missionaries who arrived in Honolulu harbor in 1820. In a letter to Thomas J. Lane, a Democratic representative from Lawrence, Massachusetts, the Statehood Commission claimed that, just as in Lane's home state, "the heritage of New England is likewise dominant" in Hawaiʻi, and that Hawaiʻi owed a debt to missionaries from Lawrence who had "firmly entrenched" American culture in the islands.[28]

Statehood supporters beyond Hawaiʻi likewise often sought to consciously downplay non-Western influences in the territory. Seth Richardson, a Washington, DC, lawyer who had spent time in Hawaiʻi before the war, insisted before a Senate committee in 1948 that "there is not a corner of Hawaii where it is not American." However, he was distressed by residents' "constant invitation" to eat raw fish. Richardson suggested that people in Hawaiʻi should not be so open about this practice, which is common in both Japanese and Hawaiian cuisine. The consumption of raw fish was doing Hawaiʻi "a disservice," he said, as it "convinces the person from the mainland that they are not quite civilized."[29]

But the strategy of belaboring assimilation in Hawaiʻi was that it could, paradoxically, undermine the case for statehood. If Americanization was the only yardstick by which Hawaiʻi's readiness for statehood was measured, opponents could simply stress that Americanization had not gone far enough. Given the circumstances on the ground, the efforts to make Hawaiʻi seem less diverse were largely futile: Hawaiʻi's polyglot reality could not be ignored.

And indeed, in the early years of the statehood campaign, when members of Congress looked beyond the Statehood Commission for local perspective, a more complicated racial picture emerged.[30] When congressional delegations visited Hawaiʻi in 1946 and 1948 to seek residents' opinion on the statehood issue, much of the testimony revolved around race. Witnesses often began their testimony by explaining their ethnic background (though this did not seem to be the case for those who identified as white) and many highlighted the racial diversity of the islands.

For instance, in testimony before Senate Committee on Public Lands in January 1948, Donald Fujimoto, a student at Farrington High School in downtown Honolulu, was insistent on emphasizing Hawaiʻi's heterogeneity. "I would like to state that Hawaii is polyglot," he told the committee. "We feel sure that this is no obstacle and should not stop us from having statehood."[31] Another statehood supporter, C. T. Wong, a representative of the Chinese Chamber of Commerce, proudly declared that "our population here in the islands is composed of the biggest race mixture." This was one of Hawaiʻi's strengths, said Wong. "Being cosmopolitan, our lives are molded together in almost every respect. We all grow up together, play together, mingle together socially, join together in business partnerships and I would like to say that I believe there is no other place in the world that has such a sociological background."[32] Similarly, Mrs. Chester Robinson—a housewife from Honolulu who did not discuss her ethnicity and who was, presumably, white—also argued that Hawaiʻi had exemplary race relations. Both her dentist and her doctor were Japanese, she pointed out, and "we deal all the time with the Chinese, Filipinos, and Japanese and they treat us fair and square and we get along beautifully with them." Moreover, according to Robinson, given the racism in the U.S. South, Hawaiʻi was "a bright spot in the country and I think the United States should be proud to have us as a State."[33]

The Statehood Commission, however, was right to worry about how mainlanders might react to the prospect of a racially mixed state. It knew that Hawaiʻi's Asian majority and its reputation as a land of loose racial barriers would raise hackles in the context of desegregation, as many in the South were concerned that statehood might hasten the end of Jim Crow. At the same time, statehood threatened to unearth well-worn tropes of the Yellow Peril, particularly in the West.

While the histories of racism against African Americans and Asian Americans are usually told separately, they often overlapped in significant ways. Both groups found themselves legally segregated from wider American society: the former by means of Jim Crow laws in the South and discrimination everywhere and the latter by both state and national legislation. Of all immigrant groups entering the United States, Asians were singled out as hopelessly unassimilable and thus barred from naturalization (as people of African descent had been prior to Reconstruction). While most other immigrant groups were increasingly accepted as "white" after the introduction of quota-based immigration law in 1924, immigrants of Asian descent, like blacks, continued to be seen as racially distinct and inherently inferior by many white Americans. It is notable that the racial bars to immigration and naturalization for Asians were not eliminated until the McCarran-Walter Act of 1952, at the same time that Jim Crow being overturned.

Despite the fact that discriminatory legislation against Asians was on the wane in the postwar period, anti-Asian sentiment continued to be a galvanizing force in nativist circles and this antipathy was often made explicit in arguments against Hawai'i statehood. Groups such as the Native Sons of the Golden West and the California Joint Immigration Committee drew on the tradition of Western nativism to actively oppose statehood, claiming that the islands' large Japanese-American population was "in effect unassimilated" and therefore threatening.[34] Yet the West Coast did not have a monopoly on racism against people of Asian descent. Perhaps the most prominent foe of Hawai'i statehood outside of Congress was Nicholas Murray Butler, the former president of Columbia University who, though blind and dying, marshaled the energy—along with a typist—to launch a public appeal against the admittance of any new states. According to Butler, "To add any outlying territory hundreds or thousands of miles away, with what certainly must be much different interests than ours and very different background," could lead to "the beginning of the end of the United States as we have known it."[35]

Such xenophobia, it should be said, was common even within the territory itself. Local opponents often based their objections on the prominence of people of Asian descent in Hawai'i, particularly the Japanese community. While it appears that a large majority of Hawai'i residents supported statehood, antistatehood forces were a vocal presence at the congressional hearings in the islands in 1946 and 1948. Many came to complain about bloc voting, wherein ethnic Japanese citizens supposedly only voted for each other. If allowed to continue, according to witness John Stokes in 1946, "this will have been accomplished what the Government of Japan attempted toward the end of the nineteenth century, namely, the control of Hawaii by Japanese." Stokes—an Australian immigrant and former curator at Honolulu's Bishop Museum—described Japanese immigrants as "enemy aliens" whose crime was seeking to instill Japanese culture in their children.[36]

Perhaps the most prominent, and most persistent, statehood opponent within Hawai'i was Alice Kamokila Campbell. A territorial senator representing Maui and heiress to a wealthy Hawaiian-haole family, Kamokila Campbell came out strongly against statehood in the 1946 congressional hearings in Hawai'i. Like many statehood opponents who testified before visiting members of Congress, Campbell expressed concerns over the demographic dominance of Hawai'i's Japanese population. The children of Japanese immigrants, she claimed, were not assimilated—Shintoism was "still deeply impregnated into their very blood stream"—and their cultural and numerical dominance must be curtailed "for the good of the entire community."[37] Kamokila Campbell framed the problem as one of patriotism and national security, suggesting that the United States would make itself vulnerable to another Pearl Harbor if Hawai'i were to become a state, and frequently expressed her own pride in being an American citizen. But she also spoke in more a subtle register as a Native Hawaiian. Kamokila Campbell was worried that statehood would mean that "we should forfeit the traditional rights and privileges of the natives of our islands for a mere thimbleful of votes in Congress, that we, the lovers of Hawaii from long association with it, should sacrifice our birthright for the greed of alien desires to remain on our shores." Ultimately, she said, Hawai'i wanted "nothing else but to be left alone."[38]

Kamokila Campbell refused to accede to statehood's inevitability. She sued the territory in 1948 over the use of taxpayer funds to support the Statehood Commission's efforts to galvanize public opinion in favor of admission, and she continued to petition Congress to reject statehood bills well into the 1950s.[39] Kamokila Campbell is today seen by many as a key figure in native resistance to U.S. colonialism, though her targeting of Hawai'i's Japanese population and declarations of American pride complicate this image. It is impossible to know, however, the extent to which she represented Hawaiian objections to statehood before 1959. While there were murmurs of native discontent at the time—the Statehood Commission, for instance, reported with alarm in 1951 that Hawaiian taxi drivers were arguing against statehood to tourists—other Hawaiians were enthusiastic participants in the statehood movement.[40] With the exception of Kamokila Campbell, private apprehensions did not translate into the kind of vocal opposition that would come more than a decade after statehood. And yet, as John Whitehead suggests, Kamokila Campbell's lament over the "continuing loss of influence and position for the Hawaiian community she cherished" likely did reflect deeper anxieties among Hawaiians, even those who "were willing to give statehood a try" in 1959.[41]

The most powerful opponents of statehood were Southern Democrats, as their opinion determined whether statehood bills would come to a vote. Rarely in public did Southern opponents provide explicitly racial reasons for their objection to statehood, though occasionally, and tellingly, their racism would slip out. Rather, they would usually offer a host of other explanations for why Hawai'i should not become a state, such as its geographical location or alleged infiltration by communists. Still, the Statehood Commission courted Southerners anyway, hoping that their opposition was rooted in a straightforward fear that two senators from Hawai'i might tip the balance in favor of civil rights legislation. As explained in 1951 by George Lehleitner—a New Orleans businessman and statehood supporter who served as the Statehood Commission's unofficial representative in the South—Southern congressmen used arguments over noncontiguity or communism as cover for a "deeprooted (but unuttered) fear" that two senators from Hawai'i would support the "repugnant measures contained in the President's 'Civil Rights Program.'"[42]

FIGURE 1. Alice Kamokila Campbell testifying at a congressional hearing in Honolulu, 1946. *Honolulu Star-Advertiser.*

To make clear that Hawai'i would not be inclined to support such "repugnant measures," the Statehood Commission worked to convince Southerners that people in Hawai'i were uninterested in mainland race relations, as they had already overcome their own racial challenges. "Attempts to legislate racial 'tolerance' have not met with general acceptance in Hawaii, but rather with opposition or indifference," the Statehood Commission insisted.[43] Hawai'i governor Oren Long echoed the point in a letter in 1953 to Georgia senator Walter George, claiming that Hawai'i need not "be feared by any other American community." Hawai'i, he said, was "an unusual society" whose atmosphere of racial harmony had emerged on its own, without the kind of state intervention civil rights advocates were proposing for the South. "No influence outside, no individual outside of Hawaii, no executive branch or legislative branch of government outside of Hawaii gave this manner of living to us." Moreover, he wrote, since the people of Hawai'i themselves would resent any external interference in their society, they would never "compel the people of other communities to do something in the realm of human relations and human attitude."[44]

By framing the issue in terms of states' rights, Long hoped to underline the parallels between Hawai'i and the South. But in making the case for Hawai'i's indifference to Jim Crow, he and other statehood boosters in Hawai'i also underscored the notion of Hawai'i's cultural distance from the mainland, contradicting any claim that Hawai'i was a little New England. In its appeals to Southern policymakers to vote for statehood, haoles like Long were willing to pursue a range of tactics. But most of these continued to treat Hawai'i's racial makeup as a problem, and all were designed to make Hawai'i appear racially innocuous.

Long's logic worked on a few Southern politicians, notably Senator Russell Long (unrelated) and Representative Henry Larcade, both prosegregation Democrats from Louisiana who supported Hawai'i statehood. Larcade justified this seeming contradiction by saying that what people did in Hawai'i "was their business, and they are entitled to their way of life. In the South we do not approve of this way of life, and this should be our business."[45] For the most part, however, Southerners in Congress refused to acknowledge any parallels between their argument for states' rights and Hawai'i's right to statehood. What the appeal to states' rights failed to address was that the problem posed by Hawai'i's racially mixed population was not simply that it might be seen as sympathetic to civil rights: it was that it was mixed to begin with. For baldly racist politicians like Texas senator Tom Connally—who in 1952 declared on the floor of the Senate that he was "a better American than a great many people who live in Hawaii" because "the majority of the people there are not of American ancestry or descent"—the assurance that the people of Hawai'i would not interfere with the South's apartheid society held little sway.[46]

Overt racism was relatively rare in congressional debates, especially when compared to prewar debates over Hawai'i statehood or American immigration policy. But racism was often lurking beneath the surface of statehood opponents' rhetoric. The antistatehood camp in Congress, led initially by Nebraska senator Hugh Butler, eventually fixed on the supposed threat of communism in the islands, which provided a useful Cold War hook for their opposition. Butler led an investigation into communism in Hawai'i in 1948, which was followed by a visit by the House Un-American Activities Committee in 1950. Although there was no evidence of communist infiltration in the islands, the suggestion that there was helped to delay a floor vote on statehood in the Senate. Those claiming that Hawai'i was contaminated by communists often argued that the territory was particularly prone to foreign pressures because of its ties to Asia. Butler claimed that the "oriental traditions" that "set the tone of the entire culture" in Hawai'i made people resistant to "any sound concept of American ideals."[47] Retired admiral Ellis Zacharias went even further, asserting that if Hawai'i were granted statehood, the children of Chinese immigrants in Hawai'i (or "Chinese 'Nisei,'" as he inaccurately referred to them) would fall under the spell of Communist China and pose "a direct menace" to national security. Politicians from Hawai'i would also face "enormous pressures from Asia" to promote "gambling and narcotics rings" in the United States.[48] The reference to drug smuggling and other illicit activities often associated with the Yellow Peril stereotype further racialized Hawai'i residents, linking all people of "oriental extraction"—not only ethnic Chinese who might have family connections to China—under the rubric of subversion.

Anticommunist opponents to statehood pointed to a series of strikes in Hawai'i in the 1940s as proof of the territory's susceptibility to communism. One reason for such alarm was that the strikes were unexpected and unprecedented. Until the 1930s, Hawai'i's labor force had been largely unorganized and disempowered, partly due to the racial and language differences among workers, which managers exploited. Bolstered by the new labor protections of the New Deal and increased cross-racial collaboration among workers, union membership exploded after the war. In 1946, for the first time in Hawai'i's history, a mixed-race coalition of workers led a successful territory-wide strike against sugar plantation owners; three years later, an even more disruptive strike of Hawai'i's dockworkers also led to a settlement in favor of workers.[49]

Business leaders' incredulity over the strikes meant that communist charges also found traction among the haole elite, which had initiated the statehood campaign and which for the most part publicly supported statehood. But a newly powerful, multiracial labor movement represented a threat to their class interests, and a number of scions of haole society came out against statehood on anticommunist grounds.[50]

Haole opponents of statehood wanted to maintain both their power over Hawai'i's nonwhite workforce and the islands' close ties to the United States. Mainland opponents, by contrast, often talked about Hawai'i's relationship to the United States in antagonistic terms. To them, Hawai'i was an external threat seeking to harm or in some way corrupt the continental nation with "alien traditions." This way of thinking "invert[ed] the role of colonizer and colonized," to borrow a concept from Amy Kaplan.[51] The problem of Hawai'i's racial difference that so preoccupied Butler and other mainland statehood opponents thus betrayed American colonialism in the islands: it was the colonial project that had produced the racially mixed society that they found so troubling. Moreover, it was Hawai'i's racial difference that helped define it as a colony. Since its annexation as an incorporated territory eligible for statehood, Hawai'i's relationship to the mainland had more closely resembled those of the new unincorporated possessions. Like the territories acquired from Spain, Hawai'i, because of its "unassimilable" population, was a colonial outpost rather than a state-in-waiting.

Most statehood advocates, both in Hawai'i and on the mainland, also glossed over questions of conquest. Instead, they presented a celebratory account of Hawai'i's annexation and its aftermath. Hawaiians, in this version of the story, "asked for" annexation after a long period of mutually beneficial relations between the United States and the sovereign Hawaiian nation.[52] "The Hawaiian people have been drawn to America almost since the dawn of their modern history," Massachusetts representative John McCormack declared. The 1893 revolution and 1898 annexation were distilled to a one-line story in which "Hawaii became a republic, and negotiations for annexation were immediately undertaken."[53]

To present a more historically accurate recounting of Hawai'i's relationship to the United States in the 1890s—one that would have been easily available to members of Congress in the form of an 1893 congressional investigation into the overthrow of the Hawaiian monarchy known as the Blount Report, among other accounts—would have shattered the notion that the United States was and always had been an anticolonial power. When Joseph Farrington insisted that "Hawaii constitutes one the few groups of islands in the Pacific that have not at one time or another been under the control of some European power," and that Hawai'i had always been "completely self-governing," he was speaking to a broader American national mythology. It was one in which the United States, unlike European nations, sought not control of other peoples, but to bequeath them self-rule.[54]

Still, the problem of Hawai'i's colonial relationship to the mainland dogged the debates over statehood. One of the most compelling arguments for statehood to emerge in the early 1950s—that ending Hawai'i's unequal status would demonstrate America's anticolonial credentials to the world— was also an implicit confession of America's role as an imperial power. And yet this acknowledgement came wrapped in denial. Supporters of statehood engaged in rhetorical acrobatics to reconcile the notion that overturning Hawai'i's unequal status could be a symbol of American anticolonialism without admitting that Hawai'i was an American colony. The United States, Wyoming senator Joseph O'Mahoney announced in a floor debate, "has no colonial aspirations, and the people of the United States are interested only in spreading freedom among the peoples of the world." But in postponing state-hood "we shall be giving fuel to the propaganda flames of the Soviet [sic] in their efforts to capture the minds of the people of the world." O'Mahoney then compared Hawai'i statehood to Philippine independence, all without pausing to concede the subordinate roles that linked them (let alone the differences between statehood and independence). The best rebuttal to the Soviet claim that the United States was a colonial power, O'Mahoney said, "is to prove once again, as we have already done, when we set the Philippines free, when we set Cuba free, that we want freedom and self-government for peoples all over the world."[55] O'Mahoney and other statehood supporters, while avoiding the word decolonization to describe Hawai'i statehood, nonetheless hung their arguments on the demands of a decolonizing world.

The Hawai'i statehood issue often begged discussion of the larger cohort of U.S. territories, not all of them "set free" like the Philippines or Cuba. Such comparisons inevitably highlighted their continued lack of full self-government, despite the insistence of O'Mahoney and others on America's history of anticolonialism. Puerto Rico, an offshore territory also angling for an overhaul of its legal status in the postwar years, was the most obvious parallel to Hawai'i. Among American dependent territories, Puerto Rico was the most similar to Hawai'i, owing to the size of its population and social and economic ties to the mainland. At the same time, however, due to Puerto Rico's unincorporated status and the relative lack of popular local support for joining the United States, statehood was only a remote possibility in the postwar era. The Caribbean island's eventual reorganization in 1952 as an American commonwealth with limited self-rule had tabled the statehood question for the near future.

Still, Puerto Rico raised uncomfortable questions about Hawai'i's own statehood ambitions: why *should* Hawai'i be a candidate for statehood when Puerto Rico was not? Legal technicalities aside, how was Puerto Rico's relationship to the mainland different from Hawai'i's? Statehood opponents insisted it was not. Moreover, they argued, to admit Hawai'i as a state would not only open the door to Puerto Rico statehood, it would invite any area under U.S. influence to assert that right. "Where is the line to be drawn? Have we learned nothing from the lessons of the old Roman Empire?" Democratic representative Woodrow Jones of North Carolina asked in 1953.[56]

Hawai'i statehood advocates often navigated the Puerto Rico question by insisting that Hawai'i was more American and thus more deserving than Puerto Rico, with the Caribbean island serving as a model of inadequacy. In response to the suggestion by a group of Southern senators that Hawai'i also pursue commonwealth status—a move also supported by Kamokila Campbell and by the staunchly anticommunist Ingram Stainback, the Tennessee-born former Hawai'i governor—Hawai'i congressional delegate Elizabeth Farrington responded sharply. "The people of Hawaii," she said, "do not want to be like Puerto Rico, which has been the poorest section of our Nation."

Farrington, who succeeded her husband after his death in 1954, went on to denigrate Puerto Rico by reference to its exemption from federal taxes. People in Hawai'i, she said, "believe that the Republic of the United States is the greatest government conceived by man, and therefore we want to share all the responsibilities as well as the privileges of government. We do not want to get out of paying our taxes."[57] In short, commonwealth status was a poor substitute for the full political participation to which Hawai'i was entitled.

Southern opponents of statehood were aware of the contradictions inherent in promoting Hawai'i statehood as an act of decolonization and used them to their rhetorical advantage. "The propagandists of Russia say we are reaching far out into the Pacific, far out into Europe, that we are controlling Greece and Turkey, that we are controlling this, that, and the other country in an effort to gain world power," said Georgia representative Prince Preston. "They will capitalize on the fact that we are trying to give Hawaii statehood. They will say it is just another example of our policy of reaching out and gaining world power."[58] Arkansas senator William Fulbright argued that granting Hawai'i commonwealth status would result in more self-rule for Hawai'i than would statehood, underscoring his argument by pointing out that "the only country that is moving to acquire and dominate other areas is Russia."[59]

Texas representative W. R. Poage went so far as to suggest that the proposal for Hawai'i statehood was part of a larger movement to take away self-rule from all Americans, particularly those in the South, who were under threat by "a great many people wanting to run the affairs of everybody else and wanting to run the affairs in States where they do not live." Proclaiming Southern segregationists to be part of "an awakening all over the world" of people fighting for self-rule, Poage worried that Hawai'i statehood might result in "two more votes in the Senate to deny local self-government in the United States."[60] Poage's astonishing effort to link white rights claims in the Jim Crow South to the global movement of decolonization may have been novel, but the relationship between racism and anti-imperialism was not. As Paul Kramer shows, anti-imperialist movements in the United States were historically tied to nativist groups who feared the demographic power of nonwhite colonists, much like Southerners who dreaded the destabilizing effects of two senators from Hawai'i.[61]

While they might have been able to sidestep the question of whether Hawai'i was a colony in congressional debates, statehood advocates had less control over the discourse around Hawai'i and decolonization in the international sphere. Undercutting the claim that Hawai'i was already self-governing, the United States was required to transmit information on Hawai'i to the United Nations under Article 73 of the UN Charter, which called for annual progress reports on the "administration of territories whose peoples have not yet attained a full measure of self-government." The fact that the United States complied with this requirement for both Hawaiʻi and Alaska riled California senator William Knowland, who in 1956 told the State Department that he was "greatly shocked" over the matter because the two territories "are destined to become States of the American Union." Secretary of State John Foster Dulles responded by insisting that the original logic behind reporting on the two territories was that it "would greatly enhance United States prestige" in a decolonizing world. But Dulles also indicated that the reporting was a mostly nominal, perhaps even disingenuous, exercise, pointing out that there was an "absence of any agreed United Nations definition of the term 'non-self-governing.'"[62] Knowland failed to stop Article 73 reporting on the territories of Hawaiʻi and Alaska—international politics trumped domestic unease over admitting to America's less-than-democratic relationship with its overseas possessions.

Indeed, by the mid-1950s, questions of U.S. foreign policy were coming to dominate the debates over Hawaiʻi statehood. Hawaiʻi, as America's western frontier and host to the U.S. Pacific Command, was gaining new strategic and symbolic importance as the Cold War pivoted toward Asia. This was a development that also helped push domestic political power westward. Whereas American Cold War policy had focused primarily on Europe in the 1940s, by the next decade it was Asia that most worried the foreign policy establishment. The communist victory in China, North Korea's breach of the Thirty-Eighth parallel, and the push for decolonization in Southeast Asia combined to draw American attention to the Pacific, leading to profound changes in the U.S. role in the world. Now that China could no longer be America's main ally in East Asia, the United States turned to Japan, pursuing a policy of "reverse course" that pulled back on democratic reforms and drew the two former adversaries closer together in pursuit of Cold War aims. This project, as Naoko Shibusawa shows, also necessitated a "reimagining" of the Japanese people in American public discourse—one that was often driven by the U.S. government, which worked to overturn wartime stereotypes. With Japan now America's most important friend in Asia, Japanese people went from being "subhuman, buck-toothed apes with Coke-bottle glasses" to being held up as subservient foreign allies abroad and upstanding citizens at home.[63] Meanwhile, U.S. efforts to build up Japan's industrial economy entailed a reliance on raw materials from Southeast Asia, making that region's political developments of great interest to the United States. And in return for economic aid, Japan cooperated in American military ventures Asia, the first of which was the Korean War. That conflict, lasting from 1950 to 1953, propelled the massive and sustained growth of the U.S. military. Its global expansion was focused on the Pacific and its domestic growth in the South and the West, spurring migration to the defense industry jobs in California and Washington and amplifying the national profile of the western states.

The U.S. West was changing in other ways as well, as a combination of grassroots civil rights activism and top-down pressure worked to overturn the region's anti-Asian traditions. In the context of the Cold War, white Americans in the West increasingly believed that anti-Asian racism was unpatriotic, leading to what Charlotte Brooks has called a "startlingly rapid racial transformation" in her study of housing practices in California.[64] Long-serving Washington senator Henry Jackson—a hardline cold warrior and tireless campaigner for local defense contracts—perhaps best exemplified the fusion of West Coast boosterism and the emerging Pacific emphasis in foreign relations. Significantly, he was also one of the most vocal advocates of Hawai'i statehood.

This new Pacificist orientation in U.S. foreign policy was, as Bruce Cumings argues, unilateral and coercive.[65] But it also demanded nonmilitary means of legitimating the U.S. presence in Asia as the region became an ideological battleground of the Cold War, where both the Soviet Union and the United States sought to undermine the other's claims to benevolence. As the two superpowers traded accusations of imperialist intent in Asia, Soviet propagandists took advantage of the U.S. record of legalized racial discrimination, which was difficult to defend. Through its own propaganda programs—and through concrete civil rights and immigration reform, which scholars have linked to Cold War concerns—the United States sought to project an image to the world of a racially egalitarian nation.

The increasing salience of race and decolonization in the Cold War, together with the Cold War's expansion into Asia, helped shift the conversation around Hawai'i statehood. The Statehood Commission's tactic of emphasizing Hawai'i's sameness to the mainland had largely failed. Given the opposition camp's antipathy to Hawai'i's multiracial population, the Statehood Commission gained little legislative traction by trying to convince Congress that race had no bearing on statehood. Its flimsy claim that Hawai'i represented New England society transplanted to Polynesian shores was not enough to galvanize the indifferent, and the argument that representatives from Hawai'i would refuse to vote for civil rights could not sway the obstinate Southern bloc.

In fact, it was mainland politicians who helped reframe the debate by advancing the idea that Hawai'i's Asian-inflected culture and mixed racial composition might be assets, rather than problems. Hawai'i statehood, they argued, could be a weapon in the ideological conflict in Asia, where people interpreted Hawai'i's continued territorial status as a sign that the United States was not fully committed to either decolonization or racial equality. "Hawaii should not be required to apologize for or minimize the significance of its heterogeneous racial complexion," said Harry Truman's interior secretary Oscar Chapman.

"What we do in Hawaii is watched and weighed throughout Asia, in Japan, the Philippines, India, Indonesia, and China. The granting of statehood to Hawaii can be a very real contribution to our fight against communism, a fight in which the people of Hawaii join." In the "Era of the Pacific," Chapman said, the United States must not "fail to take any action which will bind Hawaii even closer to the United States."[66] By transforming Hawai'i's status, Chapman and others argued, the United States would send a powerful message to Asia that it was committed to self-government and racial equality. It was the twinned critiques of racism and colonialism that made *statehood*—as opposed to independence, with its connotation of segregation—appear as the natural solution.

The idea that Hawai'i's mixed race population had something to offer the United States had been a perennial argument for statehood since the beginning of the postwar period, but it had often competed with the more conservative prostatehood arguments espoused by the Statehood Commission. For instance, in the early years of the statehood debate, statehood advocates frequently pointed to the wartime service of Hawai'i's 100th Infantry Battalion, composed nearly entirely of Nisei soldiers, as an example of the contributions Hawai'i's Japanese-American population had made to the nation. But discussions of the 100th Battalion were also usually offered as proof of Nisei loyalty to the United States—as a way to allay any lingering doubts around the Americanness of Hawai'i's people. In the early years of the statehood debate even those who claimed admiration for Hawai'i's "melting pot" culture were often uncertain about the value of using Hawai'i's diversity as an argument for statehood. (The melting pot metaphor, with its assimilationist connotations, also revealed ambivalence over the extent to which Hawai'i's connection to Asia should be highlighted.) After lauding Hawai'i's "remarkable record" of racial mixing, Oregon senator Guy Cordon expressed sympathy for those less open-minded than himself. Despite his own support for statehood, Cordon told a Senate subcommittee in 1948, Hawai'i's "intermingling of racial differences, the basic differences in antecedent ideologies and religions, are such that it would be readily understandable to me if many of the wisest among you should suggest a little more time."[67]

With the intensification of the Cold War, however, statehood advocates became less equivocal in emphasizing Hawai'i's non-Western cultural connections. As the conflict increasingly moved into Asia, Hawai'i's role as a strategic U.S. outpost in the Pacific was amplified, giving new weight to claims that the United States might benefit by having a state oriented toward the "Far East." Mike Masaoka, Washington representative of the Japanese American Citizens League and a frequent witness in statehood hearings, argued that Hawai'i's racial composition was "one of the most potent arguments for—and contrary to those who insinuate otherwise, not against—statehood." This was because "to the millions of dark-skinned people who are the most numerous of the earth's peoples" America's denial of statehood to Hawai'i was proof of the claims of "Communist hatemongers" that the United States was racist and anti-democratic.[68] Another prostatehood witness testified that Mohammed Roem, the former vice prime minister of Indonesia, had proved Masaoka's thesis when Roem told the Hawai'i legislature that Indonesians "were watching to see if the United States will grant statehood to 'racially tolerant Hawaii.'"[69]

In the context of the Cold War battle for the Third World, statehood would be not only a show of good will toward Asians, but also a show of power. According to a 1950 congressional report, statehood "would solidify America's stature in the Pacific by sending notice to the people of the Pacific and to the world that this country intends in no sense to retreat from its position of leadership in the Pacific . . . and on the contrary proposes that every legitimate step be taken to preserve and strengthen the objectives achieved in that struggle."[70] Statehood, by this logic, would convey a greater sense of American power than territorial status because it carried an ideological message of racial amity at home and respect for divergent cultures in the international sphere. American influence was thus believed to be dependent on a sense of democratic legitimacy and moral righteousness.

Statehood bridged domestic and foreign policy in new ways during the postwar era as foreign developments appeared to demand domestic change. This shift can be discerned in internal discussions within the Eisenhower administration over how to frame the statehood issue in the president's 1956 State of the Union address. Initially, Eisenhower's aides resisted mentioning statehood in the context of U.S. foreign policy. Secretary of State John Foster Dulles warned that statehood was "a pretty tricky thing from the standpoint of foreign policy," because while it was easy to point to the Philippines as a "shining example" of America's commitment to national self-determination, the people of Hawai'i "don't want to be independent—they want to be part of us."[71] Significantly, however, the final speech emphasized the foreign policy aspects of the proposed legislation. "In the Hawaiian Islands, East meets West," Eisenhower told the nation. He continued in this vein:

> To the Islands, Asia and Europe and the Western Hemisphere, all the continents, have contributed their peoples and their cultures to display a unique example of a community that is a successful laboratory in human brotherhood. Statehood, supported by the repeatedly expressed desire of the Islands' people and by our traditions, would be a shining example of the American way to the entire earth.[72]

In this version of the speech, it was not the Philippines that was the world's "shining example" of American anticolonialism, but Hawai'i. Eisenhower thus elided Dulles's problem of whether Hawai'i was a domestic or a foreign policy issue. For Eisenhower, it would seem, the fact that the people of Hawai'i "want to be part of us" was the very thing that made statehood a matter of foreign policy.

Just as Eisenhower and other mainland policymakers were promoting the foreign policy uses of Hawai'i statehood, events on the ground in Hawai'i were challenging the conservative approach of the Hawaii Statehood Commission and the old territorial politics it represented. In 1954, a coalition of labor organizers and Nisei veterans propelled the Democratic Party to power in the territorial legislature, upending the Republican Party's five-decade rule. After passing a comprehensive platform of progressive legislation only to have it vetoed by the territory's federally appointed Republican governor, Hawai'i's Democrats intensified their efforts to secure statehood. In 1956 Democratic Party chair John Burns was elected as Hawai'i's congressional delegate. He actively courted moderate Southern Democrats in Congress, most importantly Senate majority leader Lyndon Johnson. Although Johnson was initially opposed to Hawai'i statehood because it might upset the partisan balance in the Senate, he ended up being instrumental in securing its passage.

The mid-1950s marked a turning point for other reasons as well. Johnson's reversal reflected the weakening of the obstructionist Southern bloc. In the wake of the Supreme Court's landmark decision in *Brown v. Board of Education* in 1954, which enjoyed widespread support among the American public, many moderate Southerners, especially those seeking to attract investment in a "New South" built around high-tech industry, were coming around to the inevitability of desegregation.[73] Since becoming majority leader in 1955, Johnson had been nudging his Southern colleagues toward that position, believing that compromise on civil rights was the only way to avoid Democratic marginalization at the polls. In 1959, two years after Congress passed the first civil rights legislation since Reconstruction, Hawai'i was again on the table in the Senate. By 1959, however, with Johnson one of statehood's staunchest supporters, the time was ripe to end the deadlock. It helped that it was increasingly clear that Hawai'i would send a largely Democratic delegation to Congress. But it also seems that Johnson's commitment to Hawai'i ran deeper. According to a biography, he saw in Hawai'i an "example [that] could help the South with its own racial problems," and in statehood a demonstration to the world "that the United States truly believed in multiracial equality."[74] Claiming that "the undeniable evidence of history, as well as the irresistible persuasiveness of Jack Burns, removed the scales from my eyes," Johnson put his full weight behind Hawai'i statehood.[75]

In a few years as a delegate representing a changing Hawai'i, Burns, with the help of Johnson and other Democratic allies, managed to accomplish what his more timid Republican predecessors had failed to do over more than a decade. Believing that it was ambivalence within the territory, rather than mainland opposition, that had delayed statehood, Burns helped to solidify a more forceful prostatehood argument that did not whitewash Hawai'i's demographic profile.[76] No longer would the emphasis be so heavily on the islands' Americanness, as the Farringtons had done. Instead, in the emerging narrative that Burns and other statehood advocates promoted, Hawai'i's claim to full representation lay less in its similarity to the mainland than in its difference. "The citizen of Hawaii, that new man of the Pacific," declared Burns, "will be our most effective bridge to the Asian world."[77] According to Burns, besides sending a strategic message to the peoples of Asia, Hawai'i statehood would enhance American power by drawing the new state's people, with their ethnic knowledge of Asia, closer to the United States.

As Burns knew, the usefulness of Hawai'i's people to U.S. policy and American society was a growing theme among statehood supporters in Congress. "The racial background of Hawaiian people gives the Nation a unique medium of communication and understanding with Asiatic people," Montana senator James Murray argued, perhaps betraying a form of Orientalist thinking about the limits of discourse between white Americans and Asians. If granted statehood, according to Murray, Hawai'i's representatives in Congress would "have intimate knowledge of trans-Pacific affairs and could well become the center of administration of our interests in the Pacific and in Asia."[78] Meanwhile, Senator William Knowland, one of Hawai'i statehood's strongest advocates, insisted that Americans would benefit not only from Hawai'i residents' expertise on Asia, but from their capacity to "interpret the spirit of America to the Far East."[79]

For some statehood supporters, Hawai'i's didactic potential went beyond the realm of foreign policy. Just as they might serve as experts on Asia, the people of Hawai'i could also tutor mainland Americans on racial tolerance. Massachusetts representative John McCormack claimed that Hawai'i's racial harmony could rub off on mainland Americans, saying, "With the closer association between the islands and the mainland which would accrue from statehood, continental Americans would become more acutely aware of the degree to which democracy is practiced in Hawaii." This, he argued, "surely would have a salutary effect on race relations in the United States."[80]

Such a proclamation was short on details—just how would "this salutary effect" come about?—but it helped bolster the expanding image of Hawai'i as a bastion of racial harmony that could, by process of osmosis, produce wide-ranging benefits to the United States. In McCormack's framing, Hawai'i made American racial problems seem less intractable, requiring lessons in tolerance rather than dramatic social upheaval. At the same time, the portrayal of Hawai'i as a land free of racial animosity masked the islands' own troubled racial past, in which white American settlers had simultaneously displaced Native Hawaiians from power and worked to ensure that the Asian laborers they imported were politically disenfranchised.

The children of Asian laborers themselves helped erase this history by emphasizing both their service in the highly decorated 100th Infantry Battalion and their postwar economic success. In the process, the ideal they conveyed of a racially tolerant United States helped to further obscure colonialism in Hawai'i and delegitimize any Native Hawaiian opposition to statehood, however inchoate that opposition was.[81] Nisei statehood advocates, in holding up their rights to full U.S. citizenship, ignored the long-standing, competing rights claims of Native Hawaiians who sought not membership in the American union, but independence from it.[82]

That Nisei became the face of the Hawai'i statehood movement must not be simply dismissed as simply another example of Americanization, however. While other scholars have argued that statehood's success was based on claims that Hawai'i had assimilated to American norms, it is clear that any such tactic was ineffective on its own. For much of the Hawai'i statehood campaign, the effort to prove Hawai'i's Americanness had existed in tension with concomitant claims that Hawai'i was a bridge to Asia and the decolonizing world. As the statehood debates dragged on, however, supporters grew less concerned with delineating the boundary between the foreign and the domestic in Hawai'i and instead began to speak of Hawai'i as a place that transcended such rigid characterizations.

In a Senate subcommittee hearing in 1959, Eisenhower's secretary of the interior, Fred Seaton, captured the burgeoning idea of Hawai'i as a place that was at ease with its duality. Much of Hawai'i was "modeled after the way of life in vogue in the continental United States," he said, echoing many of the early Statehood Commission arguments that sought to prove Hawai'i's Americanness. But then he turned this vision outward. Hawai'i was not like the mainland in at least one important sense. Rather than existing solely as a mainland duplicate, "Hawaii is the picture window of the Pacific through which the peoples of the East look into our American front room. This is and will be particularly important in our future dealings with the peoples of Asia, because a large percentage of the population of Hawaii is of oriental or Polynesian racial extraction." The racial link between Hawai'i and the broader Pacific was key, Seaton said, because when "the peoples of those eastern lands washed by the waters of the Pacific" looked at the multiethnic state of Hawai'i, they would see that "we do, indeed, practice what we preach."[83]

Seaton's speech may have heralded a growing level of comfort with Hawai'i's cultural and geographic difference from the mainland. But it also betrayed the shallowness of the narrative around Hawai'i. In Seaton's framing, Hawai'i was valuable for its propaganda purposes. Once statehood was achieved, the islands could be a site for global spectacle—a tableau constructed for global consumption as one might display a purposefully decorated living room in view of passing neighbors. But this carefully crafted portrait of Hawaiʻi, like a home whose well-appointed appearance belies a chaotic family life, papered over a number of discrepancies that might derail the effort to normalize statehood as the predestined outcome of national progress.

By early 1959, Hawaiʻi statehood indeed seemed inevitable to enough members of Congress to override the objections of its opponents. After making the tactical move of delivering statehood to Alaska first, in 1958, as a way to placate pro-Alaska Democrats, Johnson pushed the Hawaiʻi bill through the relevant Senate subcommittees, intimidating those who questioned his strategy and standing down segregationists who threatened to filibuster. Not even arch-segregationist Strom Thurmond—who asked in the final floor debates, "Can two diametrically opposed mental approaches be fused with a harmonious result? The answer is an emphatic 'No.'"—could stand in the way.[84]

After Congress passed the admission bill in March 1959 the message that statehood was inevitable, and had always been, was promoted in other ways as well. In a territorial plebiscite mandated by Congress and held in June, Hawaiʻi residents were asked to vote on whether to join the United States as a state. Voters came out overwhelmingly in favor, with 132,773 to 7,971—or 17 to 1—voting for statehood.[85] With records indicating that 90 percent of registered voters participated, statehood advocates could point to the plebiscite as a definitive reflection of statehood's popularity. But the design of the plebiscite itself also helped to produce this affirmative outcome. Notably, it only offered voters the choice between statehood or territorial status—independence was not on the list. Hawaiian sovereignty activists have since argued that this limited choice was a means of denying Hawaiʻi's colonial history and of repressing any potential native opposition to statehood.[86] Indeed, as activists have pointed out, the United States, as a member of the United Nations, was expected to offer the option of independence when non-self-governing territories voted to change their status.[87] While there is no compelling evidence to suggest that a sizeable number of Hawaiʻi residents would have opted for independence, surely some would have. And although it is unlikely that those devising the plebiscite worried that a choice of independence would derail statehood, their decision guaranteed that statehood would appear to be the only viable future for Hawaiʻi.

Statehood, of course, was not the fulfillment of Hawaiʻi's—or America's—destiny. It was instead the product of more than a decade of debates that were informed both by Hawaiʻi's complex territorial history and by the particular demands of America's expanding role in the postwar world. Hawaiʻi emerged as something indisputably unprecedented when it became a state in 1959. With statehood, Hawaiʻi was transformed into a liminal space where the

FIGURE 2. A girl in Hawai'i celebrates statehood. Hawai'i State Archives.

concepts of the national and the global were often consciously—sometimes strategically—blurred. Hawai'i's liminality was not only shaped by geography. The mixed population of the islands had long confounded any attempt to slot people into categories of racial, ethnic, or national identity. But in the process of becoming a state, Hawai'i's people came to be portrayed by its champions less as a burden than a national asset, as they could now be deployed as agents in the effort to intensify the U.S. presence in the Pacific.

The progressive Hawai'i ideal also helped bolster a larger liberal project to forge national consensus around a hopeful and inclusive image of the United States. American national identity in the postwar period was becoming increasingly disassociated from race in favor of a concept of citizenship that stressed individual claims on the state. Race never stopped being a key marker of difference and a foundation of personal and group identity, however. It was this combination of the persistence of race as a category of difference along with the gradual abolition of race as a factor in access to formal citizenship rights that made Hawai'i statehood possible and gave it larger meaning in American public discourse.

Despite the progressive aura around Hawai'i statehood, its success sent a mixed message on American attitudes toward racial equality. Many statehood advocates—especially those who were prosegregationist Southern

Democrats—held up Hawai'i as proof that racial tolerance need not be legislated. Leaving aside the irony that Jim Crow represented legislated racism, for those looking for evidence that civil rights laws were unnecessary, Hawai'i society presented a case study. Because Hawai'i had no antidiscrimination laws on its books at the time of statehood (it had no antimiscegenation laws either), this allowed even some of those who were against civil rights legislation to celebrate racial integration in Hawai'i. The example of Hawai'i as promoted in popular culture would give comfort to those, both inside and outside the South, who believed racial inequality was the outcome solely of individual prejudice.

Statehood signaled a reformulation of the meaning, and value, of racial difference. During and after the statehood debates, Hawai'i was portrayed as a model racial community that had solved the problem of difference without political strife and had produced upward mobility for its Asian population. But this was a narrative that implicitly critiqued others—particularly African Americans—who failed to achieve political and social equality without confrontation. Congressional supporters of statehood were notably quiet on the 1954 territorial elections in Hawai'i, in which a multiracial coalition led by prolabor forces overturned the haole status quo. The reality of a once-disenfranchised community that had won political power through activist means did not dovetail with the racial romanticism promoted by many mainland statehood advocates.

Hawai'i statehood also illuminates the ways in which the Cold War shaped postwar racial liberalism, with uneven consequences for different racialized groups depending on their importance to U.S. foreign policy. While Hawai'i's Asian population was celebrated because of how they might aid U.S.-Asia relations, Native Hawaiians, with no obvious racial role to play in the Cold War, were largely absent in the statehood debates. Meanwhile, in the continental United States, Native Americans during the postwar period were subject to renewed assimilation efforts by the federal government, which marked a regression from New Deal programs that had supported increased tribal autonomy.[88] And in stark contrast to the discourses around Asians in Hawai'i, Puerto Ricans were portrayed by statehood supporters as backward and undeserving of full equality with other Americans.[89] The difference in treatment between Hawai'i and Puerto Rico—and between Asian Americans and Latinos in postwar America more broadly—might be explained by the relative importance of Asia compared to Latin America in the Cold War.

The terms of postwar immigration reform likewise suggest that specific national priorities determined who should be allowed to enjoy full citizenship rights. The McCarran-Walter Act of 1952, though it overturned racial bars to naturalized citizenship, nonetheless maintained strict country quotas based on Americans' national origins and barred entry to anyone ever associated with the Communist Party—going so far as to mandate the deportation of naturalized citizens involved in "subversive" activities. That act, together with the Hart-Celler Immigration Act of 1965, also solidified the notion of "good immigrants" by favoring those with special job skills that might contribute to particular industries. And significantly, while Hart-Celler eliminated national origins quotas and raised total immigration numbers, it imposed restrictions for the first time on immigrants from the Americas.[90]

In the debates over Hart-Celler, the new congressional delegation from Hawai'i furthered the idea that Asian immigration was useful to American foreign policy objectives in Asia—and that the people of Hawai'i were uniquely placed to speak to those objectives. "We in Hawai'i, perhaps to a greater degree than the people of any other State, are particularly aware of the objectionable features of our present immigration law," said Representative Spark Matsunaga, who was of Japanese descent. "And insofar as the provisions of our immigration law relate to Asians, we are able, because of our geographical location, to speak from the vantage ground of actual observation and experience."[91] Senator Hiram Fong, meanwhile, used his own life experience to tell an exemplary story of Asian American upward mobility. Standing on the floor of the Senate, the Chinese-American Fong—who had been a successful businessman before turning to politics—declared it "remarkable that the descendent of one of Hawaii's plantation laborers, coming from the Far East," should be able to participate in a legislative debate over immigration policy.[92] Together, such statements linked statehood to a broader progressive narrative on race and immigration, one with Asian Americans at the center.

The national imperatives that demanded an end to anti-Asian discrimination in the postwar period structured the debates around Hawai'i statehood, with wider implications for how race continued to shape social relations in the United States as well as in Hawai'i itself. With statehood, Hawai'i was lauded as an example of American multiculturalism and an emblem of America's democratic credentials to the decolonizing world. In the process, however, one national history was erased and replaced with a new one. Hawai'i's colonial past and the inequalities it had produced were overlooked in favor of a utopian image that served U.S. interests in Asia. Hawai'i's transformation from territory to state did not resolve many of the questions that had animated the often-contentious statehood debates, though it might have given the appearance of resolution. Eventually, excitement over statehood would fade, as would the national narrative of racial tolerance that Hawai'i had helped to tell. In both Hawai'i and on the mainland the problem of race would reemerge in new forms—and with new outcomes.

2

Through the Looking Glass

HAWAI'I AND THE PROBLEM OF RACE
IN POSTWAR AMERICAN CULTURE

AMONG THE MANY striking images from the 1965 civil rights march from
Selma to Montgomery, Alabama, one in particular stands out as incongruous,
even strange: Martin Luther King, Jr., flanked by Ralph Bunche, Abraham
Joshua Heschel, and other civil rights leaders, their arms linked to form a
human chain and their necks draped in plumeria leis. Unlike in most pictures
from the time showing public figures wearing leis—many of them photographed disembarking a jet at Honolulu International Airport, with faces
radiating broad smiles—the expressions of King and the other marchers were
solemn. Long associated with tropical fun for most mainland Americans, the
Hawaiian leis were now being deployed in a wholly different context, their
symbolism both dislocated and elaborated.

But for anyone who had been paying attention in recent years to the debates
over Hawai'i statehood and popular media accounts of the new state as a land
free of racial conflict, the leis might not have seemed so out of place. They had
been a gift from a delegation of marchers from Hawai'i, who also brought with
them a banner reading "Hawaii Knows Integration Works" that was thrust
in the air as they made their way past violent hecklers and chanted over the
whirring of army helicopters.[1]

Another unusual photograph taken the same year as the Selma march would
seem to suggest that integration did "work" in Hawai'i—or at least work differ-
ently there than elsewhere in the United States. This one shows a four-year-old
Barack Obama at the beach, smiling joyfully atop his grandfather's shoulders
as the Pacific swirls lazily around them. The picture is not only striking for the
resemblance it reveals between the black child and his white grandparent, but
also for its historical novelty. It is difficult to imagine such an image of carefree racial mixing at that time produced anywhere other than Hawai'i, where

FIGURE 3. Martin Luther King and other civil rights leaders on
the march from Selma to Montgomery, 1965. Getty Images.

Obama's white mother met his Kenyan father, and where Obama spent his
childhood. Despite the civil rights reforms of the mid-1960s, segregation on the
mainland was only beginning its uneven dismantling when young Obama gam-
boled in the sand with Stanley Dunham. Indeed, it was not until the Supreme
Court banned antimiscegenation laws in *Loving v. Virginia* in 1967 that the
union of Obama's parents would be legal throughout the American South—
with the exception, of course, of the most southern, and newest, U.S. state.

Six years before the Selma march, King had spoken before the Hawai'i state
legislature, mere weeks after President Eisenhower signed the bill to make
Hawai'i a state. The significance of Hawai'i's reputation as a successful multiracial society was not lost on King. He flattered his audience, telling them:

> As I think of the struggle that we are engaged in in the South land, we look to
> you for inspiration and as a noble example, where you have already accom-
> plished in the area of racial harmony and racial justice that which we are
> struggling to accomplish in other sections of the country, and you can never
> know what it means to those of us caught for the moment in the tragic and
> often dark midnight of man's inhumanity to man, to come to a place where
> we see the glowing daybreak of freedom and dignity and racial justice.[2]

FIGURE 4. Barack Obama with his grandfather in Hawai'i, 1965.
Obama Presidential Campaign.

King quickly moved to a larger critique of segregation and racial inequality
in the United States. In doing so, he at once abstracted Hawai'i and situated
it against the wider backdrop of the problem of race in mid-century America. In King's formulation, Hawai'i was less a real place than a rhetorical foil,
an instrumental example of integration that served to highlight the evils of
its opposite. King, like so many others during the years surrounding Hawai'i
statehood, saw in Hawai'i what he wanted to see.

Ironically, at least for those who subscribed to a utopian vision of Hawai'i
society, King's speech sparked a clamorous debate on the floor of the legislature over the merits of federal civil rights legislation. A few weeks earlier,
Hiram L. Fong, the newly elected Republican senator from Hawai'i and the

first Chinese American in Congress, had suggested that he would join Southern senators in their opposition to civil rights. Arguing that "it is difficult to
legislate a mode of life," and that segregation was "an emotional problem that
will be cured by time," Fong surprised many on the mainland who believed
that his ethnicity would translate into a vote to end Jim Crow.[3]

Despite such indications that Hawai'i was not quite the epitome of racial
liberalism that many mainlanders had imagined, that was the dominant image
of the new state that emerged over the course of the postwar period. Hawai'i's
protracted statehood campaign helped to establish the islands' national reputation as a place free of racial tension. Meanwhile, popular media expanded
on and refracted this policy discourse, melding older images of Hawai'i as
an untroubled dreamland with claims that the islands offered a vision of the
future for American race relations, one of the most pressing issues in postwar
American society by the 1960s.

As various mainland policymakers, writers, and activists turned to Hawai'i
as a racial model, they found that the islands did not bend so easily to a
utopian narrative. The "melting pot of the Pacific" had its own racial tensions and entrenched hierarchies. In key ways, Hawai'i *was* different from the
mainland—the colonial system created by white elites coexisted with widespread interracial marriage and a population dominated by people of Asian
descent. But in others, such as the prevalence of residential segregation,
Hawai'i was very much in line with mainland racial norms. The utopian image
of the islands as a racial paradise was based in the reality of Hawai'i's unusually
mixed society. But it was a fantasy nonetheless, one that overlooked persistent
inequality rooted in decades of colonialism.

The stories mainlanders produced about race in Hawai'i reveal something
about the islands themselves. More so, however, they speak to a search for an
alternative to the mainland's racial problems, with Hawai'i serving as an object
of projection. That Hawai'i was both like the mainland and unlike it, both
American and foreign, only amplified its allure. Mainlanders writing about
race in Hawai'i saw the islands through the prism of their own experience.
At the same time, they saw in Hawai'i a pathway out of the American racial
dilemma, its foreignness providing a crucial pivot for reimagining the domestic racial order. Hawai'i could thus serve as both fantasy and legitimate racial
model, sometimes simultaneously. It helped Americans to tell themselves a
narrative of national racial progress even as Hawai'i's cultural and geographical
distance often served to lessen its impact on mainland race relations.

Martin Luther King, a savvy student of the media who was attuned to the
power of evocative language and visual messages, saw something useful in
Hawai'i and its iconography. This is not to exaggerate Hawai'i's importance to
the African American struggle for civil rights. Indeed, Hawai'i's connection

to the mainland civil rights movement was always rather vague, both in rhetoric and in practice. But neither is it to say that King's interest in Hawai'i was arbitrary or purely opportunist. Why did Hawai'i evoke for King and others a dream of social harmony? How did Hawai'i go from an uncomplicated land of hula dancers and surfers to a symbol of American racial liberalism in U.S. popular culture? In short: why, during the crucible of the civil rights movement, was Martin Luther King wearing a lei?

———

Hawai'i statehood was not a clear-cut issue of racial justice in the postwar years. President Harry Truman had listed statehood for both Hawai'i and Alaska as part of his civil rights message to Congress in 1948, but other than claiming that the territories deserved "a greater measure of self-government," he did little to elaborate on the links between statehood and civil rights reform.[4] His secretary of the interior, Oscar Chapman, went a bit further in his testimony during Senate committee hearings on Hawai'i statehood, arguing that "Hawaii should not be required to apologize for or minimize the significance of its heterogeneous racial complexion" and that "Hawaii offers an example to many of the States."[5] Still, despite Chapman's efforts to portray Hawai'i as a model for the mainland, it remained open to question just how Hawai'i might help mainlanders overcome the problem of racial inequality. If Hawai'i was indeed so effortlessly amicable, how could its example translate into a course of action for those struggling daily with entrenched racism?

For Truman's successor, the connection between Hawai'i statehood and civil rights was even more tenuous. Eisenhower entered office without a strong civil rights agenda, and his support for civil rights reform later in his presidency was unenthusiastic at best.[6] Whereas the Truman administration had submitted to the Supreme Court numerous amicus briefs supporting school desegregation, Eisenhower refused to publicly back the Court's endorsement of integration in *Brown v. Board of Education* in 1954. But even though Eisenhower took a hands-off approach to civil rights at home, he was acutely sensitive to the image problem Jim Crow was causing overseas, where the Soviet Union was pointing to America's poor record of ensuring social equality for its own citizens. Indeed, one of Eisenhower's most celebrated moments—his decision in 1957 to send federal troops to enforce school desegregation in Little Rock—was likely made out of concern for America's image abroad.[7] After three weeks of inaction, Eisenhower finally ordered federal troops to Arkansas with the declaration that "thus will be restored the image of America."[8]

For the Eisenhower administration, Hawai'i could likewise serve an ambassadorial function. As such, Hawai'i was less an example to other U.S. states than evidence of America's benevolent intentions to the rest of the world. Eisenhower's support for Hawai'i statehood was more strategic than ideological. Tellingly, Eisenhower did not want Alaska to become a state; he believed that the military's control over large swaths of unpopulated land in the territory might prove unsustainable if Alaska were granted increased self-rule. Whereas Truman had called for statehood for both Hawai'i and Alaska under the rubric of promoting self-determination, Eisenhower was more calculating when it came to such matters. Hawai'i statehood, Eisenhower believed, would only bolster American dominance in the Pacific, whereas Alaska may as well remain a territory. Although Alaska had significant numbers of nonwhite, native peoples, it was Hawai'i—with its large population of people of Asian descent—that would capture the imaginations of people in Asia.

For the Eisenhower administration, however, Hawai'i's racial difference should *only* matter in the realm of foreign relations. Unlike his predecessor Oscar Chapman, Fred Seaton, Eisenhower's secretary of the interior, made no direct mention of Hawai'i's significance to mainland race relations in his appearances before Congress. Rather, he consistently stressed the notion that statehood's greatest symbolic value lay in the fact that it would "prove to the world—and particularly Asia—that we practice what we preach."[9] According to Seaton, the benefits of Hawai'i's racially egalitarian society would be realized primarily in the global arena.

This emphasis on the importance of Hawai'i's Asian population to U.S. foreign relations show that postwar discussions on race were not always subject to a simple black/white binary. The "Negro question" tended to dominate both domestic and global scrutiny of America's race relations in the postwar period. But shifting American attitudes toward people of Asian descent existed in parallel to, and sometimes in tension with, the renegotiation of African Americans' role in U.S. society. Throughout the postwar era, new legal norms around race and citizenship sought to make the United States more equal—at least at the level of formal rights. This new rights regime was geared at changing not only the status of African Americans, but other racial minorities as well. Immigration reform eliminating racial restrictions to naturalization came only a few months before the Supreme Court began hearing arguments in *Brown v. Board of Education* in 1952. Two years later *Brown* overturned *Lum v. Rice*, a 1924 Supreme Court decision upholding the exclusion of Asian students from white schools. The trend continued into the 1960s. The 1965 Immigration Act, which abolished the national origins quota that had been in place since 1924, came on the heels of the Voting Rights Act, the definitive and most muscular piece of legislation of the civil rights era.

Yet even as these changes were happening simultaneously, and even though both stemmed from the ascendency of "civic nationalism" over "racial nationalism" in the postwar period, many white commentators at the time glossed over the historical relationship between anti-Asian and anti-black racism.[10] Like the Eisenhower administration, the mainstream press often elided the question of Hawai'i's relationship to African American civil rights. The message they promoted was not so much that Hawai'i could prove that "integration works," but that integration was already working. Echoing Secretary Seaton, most press reports with a prostatehood bent emphasized the global implications of turning the multiracial territory into a state. According to a 1950 editorial in the *New York Times,* statehood would be "a most convincing demonstration to our friends in Asia, at a time when we badly need friends in Asia, that this nation as a democratic state has no place for any theory of racial supremacy or superiority." The editorial had been in response to a statement by Joseph Farrington, Hawaii's congressional delegate, arguing that segregationists were seeking to derail statehood. However, rather than addressing the ample evidence supporting this claim, the *Times* simply declared, "We hope Mr. Farrington is wrong," and "Ours in not a racist state."[11]

The *Washington Post,* in a prostatehood editorial from 1953, similarly avoided discussing the very problem of American racial inequality that statehood was supposed to counteract. "Nothing would do more to prove to the world that the United States really practices its belief in the political equality of all citizens than for the Congress to admit Hawaii as the forty-ninth state," the editorial asserted.[12] In so doing, it suggested that statehood, by serving as "proof" of American democracy, was more urgent than any other legislative reform geared at advancing concrete political equality. Moreover, the image of Hawai'i as inherently harmonious erased any hint of social struggle in the islands, whether past or present.

The civil rights struggle on the mainland was also conspicuous for its absence in "The Case for Hawaii," a 1954 *Saturday Evening Post* story by Hodding Carter. The piece portrayed Hawai'i as a land of affable interracialism and cultural novelty. Carter's account included a tour through the islands' various ethnic enclaves and his accompanying gustatory adventures: soy curds with a Japanese coffee farmer on the Kona coast, sushi with a group of Nisei veterans in Honolulu, lomi-lomi salmon with a mixed crowd of Kauai businessmen and labor leaders. These experiences convinced Carter that Hawai'i "has less religious or political animosity than does any other area in the world." They also led him to believe that statehood for Hawai'i, with its happy and successful Asian communities, would deliver a "counterpunch" to Asia. "The success of these Asiatic immigrants has a far happier importance to all of us," Carter wrote, "for not only is it the American essence but it also demonstrates to all of Asia what the United States offers to Americans of all racial origins it also offers to all."[13]

Of course, the United States in 1954 did *not* offer success to Americans of all racial origins, a fact of the nation's racial apartheid that Carter would have known all too well. Carter, the Louisiana-born editor of the *Delta-Democrat Times* in Greenville, Mississippi, was guilty of a sleight of hand when he conflated Hawai'i's race relations with those of the mainland. This distortion was of a piece with his record as a moderate Southern newspaperman, one who sought to rehabilitate the South's status by advocating for gradual racial desegregation. Though he supported black voting rights and integration at the university level, Carter was notably against public school desegregation—the most visible civil rights issue of 1954 because of *Brown v. Board of Education*—believing it could reignite the Civil War.[14] Carter's attitude was similar to that of Henry Larcade, the Louisiana congressman and Hawai'i statehood supporter who thought Southerners and people from Hawai'i alike should be free to determine their own "way of life." Carter did not want the South to be "tweaked by outsiders. That was for him to do from the inside." He and a small group of gradualist Southern editors sought to walk the line between stemming the tide of racist extremism in the South and convincing the rest of the nation that the region was on the path to enlightenment.[15] Against this background, there was both an irony and a wistfulness to Carter's description of Hawai'i as a place that "can teach all of us, and the world, more about democracy."[16]

But even if the cognitive dissonance Carter displayed in "The Case for Hawaii" reflected his Southern upbringing, it was a blind spot shared by many of his northern counterparts. By focusing on successful Asian Americans in Hawai'i as a demonstration of America's racial egalitarianism, the mainstream press could ignore the central cause of global criticism of U.S. race relations: Jim Crow. By 1954, Asian exclusion laws had been overturned by Congress. Meanwhile, the situation in the South was a gathering storm, as both black protest and massive resistance to integration were intensifying. Despite this, much of the mainstream press had yet to realize the significance of the civil rights movement. Carter and his moderate friends often served as the main informants on Southern race relations for northern publications, even as African American journalists were risking their lives to report on the plight of Southern blacks. It would not be until things turned bloody in the aftermath of *Brown*, revealing the ferocity of Southern white racism, that most major newspapers began assigning dedicated reporters to the "race beat."[17]

Mainstream journalists' superficial understanding of the movement for racial equality helps explain their evasive treatment of Hawai'i's connection to civil rights. But for many of those to whom the future of American race relations was a pressing everyday concern—rather than an abstract matter of policy—the campaign for Hawaiʻi statehood stood plainly within a larger matrix of racial justice issues. The black press, which served as a key vehicle for galvanizing civil rights activism across the country, followed closely Hawaiʻi's bid for statehood throughout the 1940s and 1950s. As it was portrayed in the black press, Hawaiʻi statehood had everything to do with the problem of race on the mainland. This was in part because statehood opponents had made it so. "Southern senators, led by the states of Mississippi and Virginia, have come to regard their fight against admitting Hawaii to statehood as a fight [against] establishing a civil rights law abolishing segregation in America," the Associated Negro Press reported in 1953. "Official sources here say that if Hawaii loses its fight to become the 49th state, civil rights legislation is doomed for another set-back." Hawaiʻi statehood was thus not only a civil rights issue unto itself, but a bellwether for the civil rights crusade as a whole.[18]

Dixiecrats did not invent the linkage between Hawaiʻi statehood and mainland civil rights. In fact, according to many in the black press, Southern politicians *should* worry that statehood would lead to comprehensive civil rights reform. A 1946 opinion piece by Honolulu NAACP head Fleming R. Waller in the *Baltimore Afro-American* predicted that "because the population [in Hawaii] is made up of minorities, it is very probable that in the interest of self-preservation their vote will be liberal. It is impossible to see otherwise, since any Congressional measure aimed against colored people would act like a boomerang and hit them too." Waller, who served briefly on the Hawaii Statehood Commission, went on to call for solidarity among mainland African Americans and Hawaiʻi residents of Japanese descent, arguing, "If the colored here could win over the Japanese, consolidate his forces with theirs, point out to the Japanese the far-reaching implications of the color problem with all its ramifications, a real gain shall have been made. Their power would be felt in Congress."[19]

The black press was undergoing a period of transformation during this time, with national papers, such as the *Pittsburgh Courier* and the *Chicago Defender*, doubling their circulation between 1940 and 1946.[20] Much of this was due to the wartime revival of the civil rights movement, which black publications played a crucial role in shaping. For instance, it was the *Pittsburgh Courier*— the largest-circulating African American newspaper—that spearheaded the "Double V" campaign calling for victory in the fights against fascism abroad and Jim Crow at home. The expansion of the black press was also part of what Adam Green calls "an evolving premise of national black feeling," one that was geared both toward consolidating black culture and identity and also toward integrating African Americans into the larger national community.[21] The Associated Negro Press (ANP)—a wire service with stringers and correspondents throughout the United States and abroad and boasting a subscription roll that included nearly all black newspapers—was indicative of this trend. Although founded by Claude Barnett, a disciple of Booker T. Washington, the ANP was decidedly diverse in the range of black thought it represented. Still, it was part of the widespread embrace by African Americans of "classic liberalism as the dominant structure of black life."[22] African Americans, Green emphasizes, were not mere recipients of postwar white liberalism or victims of the crackdown on dissent during the Cold War; rather, they actively helped shape the very terms of liberalism itself. Throughout the debates on Hawai'i statehood, for instance, black reporters repeatedly stressed Hawai'i's salience to domestic race relations. In doing so, they were at the vanguard of popular efforts to find social substance in the question of Hawai'i statehood.

In the postwar black press Hawai'i society was often framed as a rebuke to mainland race relations. A consistent trope was the notion that Hawai'i could serve as a racial refuge—a haven for African Americans who were tired of the daily struggle on the mainland. Hawai'i's African American population in the postwar period was small—including members of the armed forces, it was estimated at only a few thousand in 1948, according to the ANP.[23] Its allure for African Americans thus lay as much in its novelty as its reputation for racial liberalism. Much like the accounts of the north as a land of opportunity that helped propel the Great Migration, many stories on postwar Hawai'i in the black press portrayed Hawai'i as the antithesis of the Jim Crow south. According to the ANP, "the territory offers an opportunity for the colored American to lose his racial identity in a melting pot which is almost totally free from discrimination and segregation."[24]

Similarly, an article in the *Baltimore Afro-American* in 1947 opened with this breathless lede: "If you're seeking a place this side of Heaven where liberty abounds and opportunity is not limited by color, then Hawaii is the place." The piece attributed that sentiment to Fleming Waller on the occasion of his stepping down as head of the Honolulu branch of the NAACP and returning to his home in Virginia. Describing Waller's experiences in Hawai'i, the article continued, "You may go anywhere you please, he said, patronize the finest hotels, restaurants, theatres and other places of amusement 'and no one stares at you as though you did not belong there.'" The only real incidents of racial violence, according to Waller, were perpetrated by members of the armed forces.[25]

Hawai'i's "heavenly" race relations were often attributed to the commonness of interracial marriage—that most entrenched of racial taboos on the mainland, where the "tragic mulatto" born of mixed raced parentage was still a figure of pity and contempt. A piece in the *Chicago Defender* insisted that interracial marriage had led Hawai'i's people to discover "the key to the race problem": parents and statisticians were choosing not to classify newborn babies by race. "Interracial marriages have so confused the situation that no one can determine how to classify anyone. So what do you do? You do as they are now doing in Hawaii—just forget it and make a note that the population has been increased by one."[26] While the mainstream press also regularly mentioned Hawai'i's high rates of interracial marriage, the significance of intermarriage was likely far greater to African American readers. Hawai'i's lack of antimiscegenation laws and its seemingly lax attitudes toward racial classification would have resonated powerfully with black audiences. Indeed, it was the prohibition against interracial sex from which all other segregationist laws derived their ideological legitimacy. Jim Crow was based, foremost, upon the fiction of "racial integrity" and the accompanying "one-drop rule" mandating that anyone with a trace of African ancestry be designated as black. In purporting to ensure white racial purity, antimiscegenation laws thus served as "the ultimate sanction of the American system of white supremacy."[27] The notion that one's race could simply be "forgotten" in Hawai'i stood as a direct challenge to the very foundations of Jim Crow.

Hawai'i had long been held up by racial liberals as a society that disproved the logic of racial classification. There was a bit of both truth and illusion in portrayals of Hawai'i as a place where people cared less about race. Indeed, Hawai'i did have very high rates of interracial marriage relative to the rest of the United States. In 1967, the year of *Loving v. Virginia*, mixed unions were estimated at 33 percent in Hawai'i, more than ten times the national average of 3 percent.[28]

These statistics had long been a point of fascination for people studying race relations. During the interwar period, as progressive social scientists such as Franz Boas and Ruth Benedict were beginning to unravel biological notions of race—arguing that culture, not genetics, determined social difference—Hawai'i became a key site for studies on the malleability of both race and racial identity. One of the founders of Hawai'i sociology was Romanzo Adams, a graduate of the University of Chicago, who arrived at the University of Hawai'i in 1920 and pioneered the study of what he called Hawai'i's "unorthodox race doctrine."[29] His Social Research Laboratory, which ran until the 1960s, helped raise the national profile of the university and turned the territory into a breeding ground for liberal ideas on race. (Not incidentally, the Adams lab also became a frequent consultant to the Statehood Commission on matters of demography and social relations.)

A decade after Adams's arrival, University of Chicago sociologist Robert Park, who was shaping the study of racism and race mixing as an academic field, came to Hawai'i for a stint as a visiting scholar. He was soon followed by a number of his students, who flocked to Hawai'i for research "as if it was a pilgrimage site."[30] Park's breakthrough theory of the "race relations cycle" had focused on white immigrants moving through the stages of assimilation. What made Hawai'i so appealing to Adams, Park, and others was that it offered the opportunity to study how Asians, who were targeted as uniquely *un*assimilable in American law and popular culture, moved through this same cycle. Researchers frequently referred to Hawai'i itself as a "laboratory"—a term that was picked up by nonacademic writers—which referred to the islands as both an object of examination and an incubator of positive race relations.

These social scientists, like many writers for the postwar black press, pointed to Hawai'i's high rates of intermarriage as both cause and effect of the islands' racial amity. Intermarriage, which Adams traced back to the openness of Native Hawaiian culture, was perhaps the most common theme of interwar social science research on Hawai'i. It was the subject of a number of books published during this period, including Adams's *The Peoples of Hawaii* (1925)—in which he claimed that Hawai'i's different ethnic groups "are in the process of becoming one people"—as well as Adams's later *Interracial Marriage in Hawaii* (1937), and Sidney Gulick's *Mixing the Races in Hawaii: A Study of the Neo-Hawaiian American Race* (1937). Similarly, in a nonacademic text, journalist Clifford Gessler called the people of Hawai'i "the golden race, the new people" in 1937.[31] Such works went against the grain of the eugenicist science of the early twentieth century, whose widespread acceptance in American academia and wider society cannot be overstated. Popular texts like Madison Grant's *The Passing of the Great Race* (1916) had declared that the purity of the genetic lines of Nordic peoples was being contaminated by inferior racial "stock." By contrast, Adams and others argued that race mixing in Hawai'i was in fact producing favorable results, with people in Hawai'i simultaneously forging a new "race" and assimilating to American norms.[32] While many of these authors did not necessarily reject biological ideas of race—the people of Hawai'i, after all, were simply melding their races—they both allowed for the possibility of racial transformation and heralded racial mixing as a positive phenomenon, rather than a mark of decline.

Such studies gave academic legitimacy to the idea that Hawai'i was a racial paradise. Yet, in its insistence that Hawai'i society was "uniquely unburdened by prejudice and fundamentally defined by the crossing of racial lines," the work of Adams and others tended to ignore evidence all around them that undermined this utopian vision. For instance, as Adams was lauding race mixing in the islands, the eugenicist Stanley Porteus, a colleague in the psychology department at the University of Hawai'i, was arguing that Asians and other nonwhites were undermining white racial integrity. Moreover, as Shelley Sang-Hee Lee and Rick Baldoz show, in their descriptions of mixed marriages the studies of the Adams laboratory tended uphold the white culture as the end goal of assimilation and leave underexplored their own findings of

Hawai'i's persistent racial tensions.[33] And many of these works, influenced by what Gary Gerstle calls the "deep naturalism" of the Chicago School, rejected the idea that social or political structures should be reformed to promote racial equality—to do so would be to intrude upon a supposed "natural tendency toward harmony, equilibrium, and progress."[34]

Reports in the black press did acknowledge the existence of racial prejudice in Hawai'i, but like the NAACP's Waller, they often attributed it to mainland whites transplanted to Hawai'i by the war, rather than to the islands' longer colonial history. "Natives of this 'melting pot of the Pacific' saw first signs of the American Dixie influence shortly after Pearl Harbor, with the influx of Southern Race-baiting whites, intent on barring Negroes from all public places, where before they had been welcomed," the *Chicago Defender* reported.[35] Indeed, as Beth Bailey and David Farber have demonstrated, in addition to bringing an unprecedented number of African Americans to Hawai'i, World War II also transported thousands of Southern whites, accustomed to strict racial segregation, to a place where interracial marriage was normalized. The resulting encounters—among black and white soldiers, and between the soldiers and Hawai'i residents—were both transformative and tumultuous. African American soldiers were emboldened by the relative openness of Hawai'i society, while many white soldiers furiously resented blacks' newfound self-confidence.[36] In one simultaneously disturbing and humorous example, blacks reported that they were often asked by people in Hawai'i if they had tails—an insulting rumor spread by white troops. As a result, black soldiers "dropped drawers all over Hawaii" in an effort to disprove that racist myth.[37] Black/white tensions continued to shape the social landscape in postwar Hawai'i, as many mainland soldiers and war workers stayed on after the conflict. "Migrants are bringing their native racial prejudice to the Hawaiian Islands," an ANP headline from 1946 read. "Just how far Hawaii will lean towards racial patterns of the mainland remains to be seen."[38] Unlike many reports in mainstream publications, the black press saw potential for corruption in mainland influence.

In this way the black press often portrayed postwar Hawai'i as a site where contesting racial ideologies jockeyed for dominance, but where progressive racial attitudes would ultimately win out. While many reports pointed to the military as a conduit for exporting racial prejudice to Hawai'i, others suggested that Hawai'i in fact had a moderating affect when it came to race relations in the military. Reporting from Schofield Barracks in central Oahu, the *Chicago Defender* claimed: "Many race theorists would get quite a start if one day they could look in on this army post, where soldiers of all racial extractions and religions live, contrary to their buddies in America, in peaceful accord and good will."[39] The article, which was published in 1946—two years before Truman

FIGURE 5. An African American soldier with his family, Honolulu, 1947.
Schomburg Center for Research in Black Culture, Photographs
and Prints Division, The New York Public Library.

issued an executive order abolishing segregation in the armed forces—did not
make explicit reference to Hawai'i's multiracial society, but its implication that
Hawai'i was not "in America" pointed to the idea of Hawai'i's exceptionalism.
A 1948 ANP story, which deemed Hawai'i a "Mecca for Sailors," was more
explicit. According to the author, "I found Filipinos, Japanese, colored and
white persons carrying out orders of their superiors with a sense of pride and
joy." The piece concluded by praising the efforts of those on the base "to have
harmonious relations between all personnel."[40]

Reinforcing the notion of Hawai'i as a "mecca" for African Americans were
advertisements in the black press for Hawai'i package vacations. The deals
never explicitly mentioned racial tolerance in Hawai'i, but such a message was
implicit: African American tourists avoided traveling to places where they
would be unwelcome or treated disrespectfully. At the same time, the lack of
attention to race in these Hawai'i tour ads reflected the efforts of postwar black
media—epitomized by *Ebony* and Johnson Publishing—to present a fuller
picture of black society, one that emphasized "the happier side of Negro life."[41]
To many in the black press—and, presumably, the readers who answered the

ads for a Hawai'i tour package—Hawai'i appeared to offer a chance at that happier life.

Not all reports from black newspapers were so laudatory of Hawai'i society, however, especially as the statehood fight wore on and black correspondents in Hawai'i became more familiar with the islands. Many noted the continued influence of Hawai'i's white business elite, who in 1947 shut down an attempt to create a territorial Fair Employment Practices Commission despite the fact that "citizens have come forward with the necessary proof" of employment discrimination.[42]

In another story challenging the notion that Hawai'i was a racial heaven on earth, an ANP article from 1950 reported that whites in Honolulu were using restrictive lease terms to maintain residential segregation in tony city neighborhoods. In a nod to Hawai'i's colonial history, the report explained: "When the missionaries came here to save souls, they also grabbed land, either by marrying Hawaiian nobility or simply by robbing the natives. These holdings have been handed down to descendants with the stipulation that they were never to be sold." New residents usually had to agree to decades-long leases rather than purchasing the land outright, thus perpetuating haole control of the area. While acknowledging that a few wealthy Chinese people and other nonwhites were able to buy into white neighborhoods by offering hefty sums for fee simple home ownership, the article noted that such rare examples hardly augured the end of residential segregation. It ended by deflating the claim that Hawai'i was truly exceptional from the mainland: "Anyway you figure it, it's still white supremacy. But what else can you expect? Hawaii is yet a part of America, isn't it?"[43]

Some of the most nuanced reporting on postwar Hawai'i came from Frank Marshall Davis, an African American writer and activist—and a close friend to Stanley Dunham and occasional counselor to the young Barack Obama on racial politics.[44] Davis, a native of Kansas via Chicago, came to the islands for vacation in 1948 as an editor for the ANP and stayed there until his death in 1987. He and his wife, who was white, had supposedly gone to Hawai'i at the suggestion of Paul Robeson shortly after Davis, "a closet Communist," had come under scrutiny from both the Federal Bureau of Investigation and the House Un-American Activities Committee. For Davis, Hawai'i offered relief from the political pressures he faced on the mainland as well as an opportunity to experience a more racially liberal society. Upon arriving in the territory, Davis felt an immediate affinity with the islands' increasingly vocal interracial labor movement and he soon became a columnist for the *Honolulu Record*, a radical weekly newspaper founded in 1948 by Nisei labor activist Koji Ariyoshi.[45]

Yet Davis was far from quixotic in his portrayal of race relations in Hawai'i. In a series of articles for the ANP in 1949 under the theme "Democracy:

Hawaiian Style," Davis provided black readers on the mainland with a subtle analysis of Hawai'i's mixed society that acknowledged the ways in which the territory's colonial history continued to shape its complex social relations. While celebrating Hawai'i's ethnic diversity and the relative fluidity of racial ideology in Hawai'i compared to the mainland, Davis also highlighted the racialized inequalities and simmering resentments that characterized territorial life. After calling Hawai'i a "rainbow land of beautiful color mixtures," Davis quickly pointed out that the islands were no utopia. "Despite this amazing and wonderful ethnic hash found here in the 'crossroads of the Pacific,' there are prejudices," he wrote. "Out here many dark Puerto Ricans are insulted if they are mistaken for Japanese; the Portuguese bitterly resent being called being called 'haole' or mainland white. . . . There is sizable prejudice against both Japanese and mainland whites."[46] He ascribed bias against the haole population to economic inequality, claiming that the majority of people in Hawai'i resented haole power. Moreover, although haoles may have held the highest economic rank in Hawai'i society, their minority status meant that other groups tended "to join together to present something of a united front" against their attempts at racial subjugation.[47]

Meanwhile, according to Davis, there existed in Hawai'i an undercurrent of deep distrust of any newcomer, not least mainland African Americans. "Hawaii's colored people have a shifting place in this complex mosaic of prejudice. As the last to arrive, they have yet to 'prove' themselves as have other peoples." Ironically, because many African Americans had come to Hawai'i during the war, they were "classed together" with white soldiers and war workers by many locals. Still, Davis insisted, "anti-colored prejudice is not static by mainland standards. It is flexible and, for that reason, can be eliminated or allowed to crystallize largely by the efforts of colored Americans themselves."[48]

Obama would later express similarly complex sentiments about growing up black in Hawai'i. His grandparents, Obama writes, had moved there out of a sense of adventure and, upon encountering its mixed race society, "threw themselves into the cause of mutual understanding." He describes watching his affable white grandfather befriend people of all races and take up many of their cultural customs. By the time the adolescent Obama met Davis in the 1970s, African Americans—most of them connected to the military—had carved out a tiny but consistent presence in the islands. Hawai'i was, according to Obama, a place where black people "said what we pleased, ate where we pleased; we sat at the front of the proverbial bus." And yet, even in Hawai'i Obama found that because of his race he had "a limited number of options at my disposal" compared to the other teenage boys around him. In Obama's recollections of his conversations with Davis—who comes across as a kind of cynical truthteller—his grandfather's friend insists that Obama's white family will never be able to relate to the experience of being black, no matter how progressive they are or how much they love Hawai'i's multiracial culture. Meanwhile, Obama writes, his growing awareness of his blackness meant that he had to look east across the Pacific for cues on how to be African American, an identity, Obama suggests, that he could not fully own until he moved away from Hawai'i.[49]

Like Obama, Davis in his postwar writings painted a portrait of postwar Hawai'i as a multidimensional, fluctuating, and often-contradictory society. His account of a place that had produced at once an "ethnic hash" and a "complex mosaic of prejudice" reflected an understanding of both Hawai'i's colonial history and of its turbulent present. In the late 1940s, when Davis arrived in Hawai'i, the islands were on the cusp of a social revolution, one all the more extraordinary given the odds against it. Prewar Hawai'i was a place of sharp economic disparity and racial divisions, much of it due to the efforts of the territory's haole elite to consolidate and maintain its hold over the islands' politics and economy—at the expense of both Native Hawaiians and Asian laborers. Haole rule was amplified through the domination of the Republican Party, which loyally served the interests of the Big Five in the territorial legislature.

But near the end of World War II, workers in Hawai'i organized a powerful interracial labor movement that would eventually curtail the monopoly power of the Big Five and bring the Democratic Party to power in 1954, ushering in a period of Democratic political control that continues in Hawai'i to this day. As a result, "seemingly overnight . . . the protracted period of entrenched racial divisions [was] displaced by a protracted period of durable interracialism."[50] In the process, argues Moon-Kie Jung, Hawai'i's working people came to see their race and class interests in alignment, though not necessarily identical. Contrary to accounts of Hawai'i as a "deracializing" melting pot, Jung writes, "It was through race, not its erasure, that Hawaii's interracial working class was made."[51]

But while locals in Hawai'i were fighting for economic and political rights, mainlanders were rarely exposed to the complex racial logics that characterized Hawai'i society. Instead, prostatehood policymakers and mainstream media accounts tended to portray the islands as a timeless paradise free of racial or class strife. As such, they often overlooked the ways in which any cross-racial solidarity that did exist in Hawai'i was less a product of natural social mixing than of class struggle. Rarely did the mainstream press, for example, address the intense fight for worker control that helped overturn the racial divisions created under the Big Five regime. When the contentious labor relations of the late 1940s were mentioned, it was usually in the context of statehood opponents' claims that Hawai'i was a communist stronghold.

For example, the *New York Times,* in a 1950 editorial supporting a congressional investigation into communism in Hawai'i, claimed that the territory's bid for statehood—"surely a question of extraordinary gravity"—combined with "the facts of geography," meant that labor unrest in the islands should be scrutinized. The "paralysis of waterfront activity and impeding of shipping through direct strikes" in Hawai'i had demonstrated that the territory's economy was especially "vulnerable."[52] Thus, in the early years of the statehood campaign, just as Hawai'i's was becoming arguably more democratic, Hawai'i's labor movement was often portrayed as an impediment to statehood in mainland discourse, while the issue of race in Hawai'i was divorced from any discussion of either rights or class.

By 1959, however, the mainstream press had long buried any concerns that Hawai'i was a hotbed of class strife. With the announcement of its admission as a state, Hawai'i was now firmly a symbol of progressive democracy and racial egalitarianism. Mainland readers were flooded with newspaper and magazine stories extolling the islands for their "astounding mixture" of ethnicities and the "easy and admirable geniality" that prevailed among them.[53] Hawai'i statehood proved to the world that Americans "do not stand for any theory of racial superiority," wrote the *New York Times*. The *Boston Globe* claimed that "in fulfilling Hawaii's dream of statehood, we also fulfill the belief of our founding fathers in the declaration that all men are created equal."[54]

But Hawai'i was not merely proof of long-standing American ideals. It also represented the American future. News stories emphasized Hawai'i's novelty. The people of Hawai'i, according to the *Times,* were "a new version of the American people."[55] An article in the *Washington Post,* echoing the language of interwar sociology, declared Hawai'i "one of the world's most conspicuous centers of integration" and the breeding ground for "a new race or strain: a sort of Pacific man, olive-skinned, lithe, handsome."[56] Similarly, an editorial in *Life,* anticipating the "New Frontier" trope of John F. Kennedy's 1960 presidential campaign, hailed Hawai'i as a place of innovation, a "laboratory" that both embodied the old American frontier spirit and reinvented it. While Alaska, with its vast natural resources, was a traditional "physical frontier" that could act as a "safety valve for the footloose," Hawai'i was something altogether different—its frontier was not physical, but conceptual. "When democracy has the courage of its convictions, it becomes a frontier of its own," wrote *Life.* The new Pacific state was "an advertisement to all the world, especially the Orient, that all races can get along in equality when the political auspices are right." The editorial then went on to compare Hawai'i's favorable economy to that of segregated Mississippi, long ago a western frontier itself whose standard of living was now lowest in the nation.[57]

Yet in their message that Hawai'i represented something "new" such portrayals left open the possibility that Hawai'i was less a model for the U.S. than an anomaly within it. In highlighting the islands' uniqueness, they suggested that Hawaiʻi might only have a limited impact on mainland race relations. Indeed, this paradox—of Hawaiʻi as racial utopia and "bridge to Asia," as both part of and apart from the rest of the United States—was at the heart of Hawaiʻi's image in postwar American culture.

Still, Hawaiʻi's new prominence in mainstream discourse signaled shifting racial attitudes. Hawaiʻi, for instance, figured prominently in popular efforts to rehabilitate Japanese Americans after the war, when tens of thousands of Issei and Nisei were illegally interned in federal relocation camps under the auspices of preventing treason. *Go for Broke!*—a popular and critically acclaimed film released in 1951 and based on a Pulitzer Prize-winning piece by Hodding Carter—told the story of Nisei troops in the 442nd Regimental Combat Team and the 100th Infantry Battalion, the latter of which was comprised mostly of Hawaiʻi residents. (The 442nd's motto, "go for broke" was supposedly Hawaiʻi pidgin for betting everything in a gambling game.) The units, which combined together in Italy, saw heavy fighting across Europe, and its soldiers were among the most decorated in U.S. army history. The film was remarkable at the time for giving significant screen time to positive images of Asian characters. It portrayed the Nisei soldiers in heroic light, ending with their climactic rescue of the "Lost Battalion" from Texas that got itself trapped by German forces in the Vosges Mountains. But white characters remained at the center of the narrative, as it chronicled the evolution of Lieutenant Michael Grayson from bigot to defender of Nisei honor. Grayson spends much of the film trying to reunite with his original unit from Texas—the very one that the 442nd ends up rescuing. By the end of the film, Grayson has clocked a fellow Texan for using the epithet "Japs." Critics were warmed by the picture of racial amity and Nisei patriotism in *Go for Broke!*, with some suggesting that viewing the film could lead white audiences to the kind of redemptive arc experienced by Lieutenant Grayson. Bosley Crowther, writing for the *New York Times*, called it "a forceful lesson in racial tolerance and friendliness" that "aptly revealed and demonstrated the loyalty and courage of a racial minority group."[58] The *Washington Post* editorial page suggested that senators deciding on Hawaiʻi statehood might see the film and be more inclined to reward the Nisei for their heroism in the face of "stupid discrimination" during the war.[59]

As its political star rose, Hawaiʻi was also becoming the object of increased attention in lighter popular fare. Throughout the 1950s and early 1960s, Hawaiʻi, which had long occupied a niche market in mainland cultural production, was fast emerging as a touchstone of American mass culture. From the hula hoop craze of 1958 to the popularization of surfing through films such as the *Gidget, Endless Summer,* and the Elvis Presley vehicle *Blue Hawaii* and its sequels, Hawaiʻi references were everywhere. *Hawaii Calls*, a Honolulu-based weekly radio show of Hawaiian music that began in 1935 and spawned dozens of albums, reached its peak popularity during this period—broadcast on some 750 stations worldwide in 1952.[60] Television, outpacing films as Americans' entertainment medium of choice, was likewise enamored with Hawaiʻi. *Hawaiian Eye,* a detective series that took place largely at the Hawaiian Village Hotel in Waikiki, ran for four seasons, from 1959 to 1962. Several popular television shows, including *I Love Lucy* and *Father Knows Best,* featured a Hawaiʻi vacation story, an episode theme that remains a sitcom mainstay to this day. These early postwar representations of Hawaiʻi rarely gave more than a nod to the islands' multiracial character. Still, they elevated Hawaiʻi's cultural status at a time when the narrative around statehood was emphasizing the islands' mixed race society.

This embrace of Hawaiʻi was part of a broader normative shift away from the racist and antiforeign sentiment that had dominated debates on race, ethnicity, and immigration before World War II. Against the background of postwar immigration and civil rights reforms that were overturning legalized racism, many Americans were now glorifying the United States as an inclusive society. As John F. Kennedy put it in an essay commissioned by the Anti-Defamation League in 1958, the United States was "A Nation of Immigrants." Kennedy himself appeared to represent the consummate immigrant success story—he was a Catholic and descendant of Irish immigrants, a decorated veteran of World War II, and now the charismatic junior senator from Massachusetts. His essay presented an appropriately romantic version of U.S. immigration history that dwelled little on racist immigration law and highlighted immigrants' plight only to demonstrate their eventual triumph over adversity.[61] While Kennedy and other liberals would continue to advocate restrictive caps on immigration, the celebratory tone of his 1958 essay nonetheless marked a turn away from earlier popular immigration discourse calling for racial exclusion. And though "A Nation of Immigrants" focused almost entirely on European immigration, Kennedy would expand the text's pluralistic ethos to nonwhites when, during his presidential campaign in 1960, he called Hawaiʻi's racially mixed population an "outstanding example in the world today of peoples of many races and national origins living and working together."[62]

Such ideas were also fostered by cultural producers who worked in parallel with liberal policymakers to promote racial tolerance among white Americans—particularly in regard to people of Asian descent, as their allegiance was seen as crucial to winning the ideological battle with the Soviet Union. During the postwar period, an interconnected group of "middlebrow intellectuals," among them James Michener, Norman Cousins, Thomas Dooley, Oscar Hammerstein, and Pearl S. Buck, helped mediate the relationship between the United States and Asia for American audiences through their films, musicals, books, and other cultural texts. As Christina Klein argues, together they sought to deprovincialize Americans and rid them of their racial prejudices—"to replace the old nationalist map that Americans carried in their minds, in which the United States filled the frame, with a new internationalist one, in which the United States and 'free' Asia alike were embedded within a larger world system."[63] This was decidedly a Cold War project, one aligned with the work of the U.S. government to demonstrate American benevolence and racial tolerance to the decolonizing peoples of Asia.

Overt expressions of xenophobia and racism were no longer socially acceptable in polite society in many parts of the United States—due in part to both shifts in policy and to the efforts of middlebrow intellectuals to shame American audiences for their biases against "people whose eyes are oddly made / And people whose skin is a diff'rent shade."[64] This change in norms, as well as its limitations, were reflected in attitudes toward black civil rights. White public opinion, at least in the North, was overwhelmingly in favor of civil rights reform, albeit to varying degrees of urgency. A Gallup poll from 1956, for example, found that more than 70 percent of whites outside the South agreed with the Supreme Court's desegregation ruling in *Brown v. Board of Education*, though less than 6 percent considered civil rights to be the nation's most pressing concern.[65] So while many white Americans may not have been personally committed to overturning Jim Crow—and while many continued to perpetuate less brazen forms of segregation in the north—it is clear that it was becoming popular to declare one's allegiance to antiracist ideology.

Such declarations had increasingly global resonance. After World War II the antiracist theories of Franz Boas, Robert Park, Romanzo Adams, and other liberal social scientists gained traction on the world stage—albeit with ambiguous results that revealed the persistence of race and racism. Among the more notable transnational projects of the postwar period was a series of statements on race issued by UNESCO aimed at "disseminating scientific facts designed to remove . . . racial prejudice."[66] The American-dominated cultural agency of the United Nations, UNESCO stood at the center of international postwar discourse on the problem of race. This was a discussion prompted in part by revelations of the Nazis' use of racial classification toward genocidal ends. It was also a response to the demands for both self-determination and racial equality waged by people of color around the world. To address this, UNESCO organized a transnational group of social science scholars to revisit scientific definitions of race. The resulting statements issued in 1950 and 1951, however, demonstrate profound ambivalence toward the delegitimation of race among postwar scholars. In line with progressive social scientific theory, the first statement bluntly claimed that race was a "social myth" rather than "biological fact." But that declaration garnered more backlash than assent within the international academic community. Under pressure from race scientists, UNESCO organized another panel, which issued a new statement the following year. This one was far more equivocal. While the panel claimed to repudiate the scientific racism of an earlier era, it nonetheless supported a biological definition of race—and even allowed for the possibility of racial differences in intelligence.[67]

Given the lack of scholarly consensus on race it should not be surprising that postwar Americans also espoused confused and contradictory opinions when it came to the problem of social difference. Moreover, the reality of race in America clashed with the postwar discourse of antiracism, which left little room for a wider critique that addressed issues of economic inequality or de facto racial segregation. Yet many liberal policymakers and writers invested antiracism with great hope, believing the primary long-term solution to the problem of racial inequality in America was to cure individual Americans of their racism.

For sociologist Gunnar Myrdal, arguably the most influential writer on "the Negro problem" in the postwar era, Americans needed to be made aware of the dangers of racial prejudice. White Americans, wrote Myrdal, were "all good people" who "want to be rational and just," but they allowed their irrational prejudices to corrupt otherwise virtuous American institutions.[68] The United States as a nation thus needed to reconcile the "American creed of liberty, equality, justice, and fair opportunity for everybody" with the treatment of black citizens.[69] This Myrdal identified as the "American Dilemma": the disparity between American national greatness and blacks' exclusion from it. Moreover, the solution to the American dilemma was of global significance. Not only would America's "well-being" increase at home, but equally important, argued Myrdal, "America's prestige and power abroad would rise immensely" if it were to overcome the challenge of racial inequality. "In this sense," wrote Myrdal, "the Negro problem is not only America's greatest failure but also America's incomparably great opportunity for the future."[70]

James Michener, like many others in the postwar period, turned to Hawai'i for answers to the "American dilemma." The bestselling author of tomes of historical fiction, Michener was one of the most prominent postwar figures to popularize the image of Hawai'i as a racial model for the mainland. In a book manuscript from the late 1950s on the problem of racial prejudice in American society, Michener held up Hawai'i as the embodiment of American democracy and a panacea for the racial strife of the mainland. In his introduction to the book, which Michener intended to be a collaborative project with Pearl S. Buck and Oscar Hammerstein, Michener wrote that his goal was to alert readers to "the peril that faces us all unless we stop our nonsensical behavior regarding race prejudice."[71] He was certain, however, that this peril could be surmounted. Prejudices, according to Michener, were "unfounded, automatic and irrational," and thus "the intelligent man fights against them."[72] Moreover, Michener saw in world history a tendency "to greater communion between races, not less; toward greater equality, not less; and toward greater acceptance of the essential brotherhood of the world, not a retreat from that principle."[73] Hawai'i, for Michener, was the superlative example of this progressive narrative, and he devoted his final chapter to analyzing its social relations and deploring its stalled bid for statehood. "Whenever I despair of American democracy, whenever I am irritated by the stupidities we Americans are capable of, I think of what a democratic system of government has accomplished," Michener wrote of Hawai'i. "And if I sometimes seem over hopeful of what democracy will one day accomplish with the American Negro, it is because I know the miracles of which this form of government is capable."[74]

Michener did not overlook the racial divisions in Hawai'i society, but he sought to situate them within his larger story of racial progress and American democracy. Beginning with the American missionaries who arrived in Hawai'i in the 1820s, Michener worked to show how each successive migrant group to the islands appropriated American norms to their own ends. Chinese laborers, though treated badly by American plantation owners, "quickly found that the Hawaiian pattern of life, fashioned in large part after New England principles, favored men who saved money, who worked with good will, and who got their children educated."[75] Even more so than the Chinese, the trajectory of Hawai'i's Japanese was a "tribute to the transforming capacities of American democracy" since they arrived further along in the process of Hawai'i's Americanization. "I can think of no other nation in the world in which a laboring group, brought into a country at a disadvantage, so promptly became full fledged citizens," Michener wrote of the Japanese experience in Hawai'i.[76] Native Hawaiians, who Michener portrayed as eager to "cede" their kingdom to the United States, likewise benefitted from American beneficence. The willingness of American men to marry women of Hawaiian nobility in order to gain access to land meant that Hawaiians were brought fully into the American fold.

The contradictions in Michener's portrayal of the United States as a benevolent expansionist power were especially notable in his discussions of Native Hawaiian history. America's colonization of Hawai'i often appeared to be an inconvenience to Michener's story of American racial progress. In his unpublished manuscript and elsewhere he repeatedly emphasized that Hawaiians both welcomed American interference in their homeland and were better off for it. And while he tended to depict Hawaiians as noble, he also represented them as primitive and susceptible to corrupt leadership—and in need of Americans' guiding hand. Their very arrival in Hawai'i was because they were a "defeated people" escaping Tahiti, and this was a weakness that was carried across generations. For Michener, Hawaiians' own hospitality, in combination with their need for external direction, made their colonization practically inevitable.[77]

Even if the Americans who came to Hawai'i were themselves greedy and racist, the ideals they carried over from New England planted high-yield seeds. In Michener's convoluted telling, the efforts of Hawai'i's white elites to secure their power through racialized labor policy were ultimately trumped by the very American system of government they brought with them. While individual plantation owners or others promoting racial discrimination may have distorted America's core values, the American way of life itself remained sound. Michener thus sought to subsume Hawai'i's history of colonialism and white supremacy into a narrative of American righteousness. At the same time, he portrayed the movement among mainland segregationists to thwart Hawaii's bid for statehood as an aberration, albeit a potentially dangerous one. The actions of "a few stubborn senators," Michener wrote, threatened to bring racial hatred to "a hitherto uncontaminated Hawaii."[78]

In suggesting that racist individuals represented a stain on America's—and Hawai'i's—otherwise exemplary record, Michener echoed the larger efforts of U.S. policymakers to transform global condemnation of Jim Crow into a vehicle for promoting American democracy. Just as Myrdal had framed prejudice against blacks as a departure from the "American creed," the U.S. government sought to counter Soviet criticism of American race relations by portraying segregation as an anomaly within a larger triumphant nationalist story. "The lesson of this story," Mary Dudziak writes, "was always that American democracy was a form of government that made the achievement of social justice possible, and that democratic change, however slow and gradual, was superior to dictatorial imposition."[79] In short, American laws and norms contained the germ of racial progress, even if that progress was not yet fully realized.

But even in postwar Hawai'i progress could be elusive. At the end of his book manuscript, Michener provided an ironic account of his own confrontation with racial prejudice in Hawai'i, one that undermined his earlier assertion that the islands were "hitherto uncontaminated." When looking to buy a house in the islands with his Japanese American wife, Mari, Michener discovered that she was barred from certain neighborhoods because of her ethnicity. Michener sought to rationalize such overtly segregationist practices, however, saying that "I have no fight with people who want to live with their own groups." He went on to argue that "in the aspects of my life which really do matter—where a man can really be hurt—there are no discriminations" in Hawai'i, where anyone could be a lawyer, teacher, or politician regardless of race. Racially restrictive housing covenants were thereby relegated to the realm of the private for Michener. Still, the incident seems to have shaken him. Despite his opening claim that this was a book whose goal was to help eliminate personal prejudice, after Michener had finished grappling with his own experience of discrimination in Hawaiʻi he ended the manuscript with a much less ambitious aspiration: "The reason I want to live in Hawaiʻi, is that here you have people who have discovered a way of allowing diverse human beings to follow in their private and personal animosities, while at the same time forbidding them by law to practice these discriminations in public," Michener explained. "And that is all I want for the rest of America."[80]

As it would turn out, "private and personal animosities" did matter. Michener would eventually leave Hawaiʻi for the mainland in the early 1960s, saying that he and his wife "met with more racial discrimination in Hawaii than we did in eastern Pennsylvania, where we had previously lived."[81] Meanwhile, his book on racial prejudice never got published. In a cover note to the manuscript he grumbled that while he had done his part for the project, his "foolishly" enlisted coauthors Buck and Hammerstein "never did theirs. . . . and all this effort went to nothing." Michener admitted, however, that he was able to use much of the research he had done for the failed manuscript "as the basis for the central theme of the Hawaii book."[82] That "Hawaii book" was *Hawaii*, Michener's fictionalized saga of Hawaiʻi history and, respectively, the third and second bestselling title of 1959 and 1960. *Hawaii* was a triumphal story of disparate groups, brought together by geographic circumstance, forging social bonds through their shared perseverance and common humanity. In Michener's novel, as in his unpublished book manuscript, Hawaiʻi was meant to stand in as surrogate for the whole of the United States.

Hawaii marked a turning point in Michener's career. It cemented his status as a go-to author for book clubs and helped make him a regular on the *New York Times* bestseller list. In addition to prodigious book sales, the novel earned Michener a record-breaking $600,000 film deal and a reputation for bankability that would ensure him a lifetime of lucrative publishing contracts.[83] With *Hawaii* he landed on a profitable formula—a narrative of epic sweep that followed the descendants of multiple families as they lived through dramatic historical change—that resonated deeply with American audiences. It was a formula he would return to again and again.[84]

Topping out at nearly a thousand pages and often tedious, *Hawaii* must have felt like a slog to many of its readers. It was frequently didactic, weaving Michener's liberal antiracist agenda into the fictional narrative. Its grand chronological structure, which favored a bird's-eye perspective over character or plot, made the novel seem more historical than literary, and thus more "accurate." Despite these potential handicaps, its popularity—its "must-read" status in the late 1950s and early 1960s, boosted by the support of the book club juggernaut—attests to the power of middlebrow producers to set cultural norms. The hallmark middlebrow institution, the Book-of-the-Month Club was invented during the 1920s to target busy college graduates plagued by status anxiety and their "inability to project to others the image of being au courant." Book-of-the-Month Club ads stoked these fears and vowed to relieve them. "What a deprivation it is to miss reading an important new book at a time when everyone else is reading and discussing it," went a standard pitch, which then proposed a solution to this "deprivation" in the form of a club subscription. Another ad invited potential customers to "join the intellectual élite of the country."[85] The business model worked: during the postwar period, the Book-of-the-Month Club was a powerhouse on the publishing scene, boasting nearly a million subscribers and shaping the tastes of a wide swath of the American reading public.[86]

Hawaii, typical of book club selections, offered its readers both edification and cocktail party conversation fodder. Hawai'i was more visible than ever, and *Hawaii* fed the public's fascination with the islands while promising a deeper understanding of the new state. Reviewers tended to praise it as an accurate and educational portrait of Hawai'i. Horace Sutton, for instance, lauded it as a definitive text. Hawai'i "is so well covered," he wrote in the *Saturday Review,* "that it may be a long time before anyone essays another major work on the islands."[87] Though it was presented as fictional, *Hawaii* declared that it was "true to the spirit and history of Hawaii," and it told its characters' stories within the context of a series of larger events that appeared to be straightforwardly nonfiction. Critics at the time and since have pointed to the book's many misrepresentations, particularly around Hawaiian cultural practices, yet the book nonetheless managed to convey a sense of scholarly gravity through its "historical" framework.[88]

Beginning with an extended description of the geological formation of the Hawaiian archipelago, the novel ended with a section titled "The Golden Men." In between, Michener chronicled the interwoven family histories of the Kanakoas, the Hales, the Kees, and the Sakagawas up through World War II—an account that often relied heavily on familiar tropes of licentious natives, gorgeous scenery, and sun-kissed beach boys. The final part of the novel, however, pointed toward a future iteration of the Hawai'i paradise, with Michener's yet-unidentified narrator speaking hopefully of "a new type of man being developed" there. This was a Golden Man: "A man influenced by both the west and the east, a man at home in either the business councils of New York or the philosophical retreats of Kyoto, a man wholly modern and American yet in tune with the ancient and the Oriental." It was not intermarriage that had produced the Golden Man, but a new "way of thought." Thus, wrote Michener, "his awareness of the future and his rare ability to stand at the conflux of the world he owed to his understanding of the movements around him."[89]

Michener's Golden Man trope bore the imprint of Romanzo Adams, Robert Park, and other interwar scholars of race in Hawai'i.[90] This was Adams's "unorthodox race doctrine" translated for a mass audience. Michener's Golden Man, however, was a subtly updated version of the Chicago School iteration. For one, he was both American *and* "in tune with the Oriental," thereby suggesting that assimilation should have limits. His ability to make friends around the world, from New York to Kyoto, was one of his key assets. Whereas Park was keenly interested in the Asian "marginal man" who was in the process of abandoning his traditional culture, Michener's Golden Man was a cultural omnivore. Moreover, Michener's narrator claimed, a person's racial or ethnic background was in fact irrelevant to the development of the Golden Man mindset. Rather, one needed to have life experiences that would cultivate the inner Golden Man.

Hawai'i, according to Michener, was the ideal setting for developing this cosmopolitan sensibility, one that could even be a site of moral redemption for the most hardened bigot. Clyde V. Carter, a character who appears toward the end of *Hawaii*, is introduced as a clichéd Dixiecrat—a congressman from Texas and stalwart opponent of Hawai'i statehood who "hated to the point of nausea anyone who wasn't a white man."[91] But after spending some time in Hawai'i under the auspices of investigating the territory's fitness for statehood, Carter has a near-epiphany on the corner of Fort and Hotel streets:

> And as he stood there in the late afternoon, in the heart of Honolulu, watching the varied people of the island go past, he had a faint glimmer of the ultimate brotherhood in which the world must one day live: Koreans went by in amity with Japanese whom in their homeland they hated, while Japanese accepted Chinese, and Filipinos accepted both, a thing unheard of in the Philippines. A Negro passed by and many handsome Hawaiians whose blood was mixed with that of China or Portugal or Puerto Rico. It was a strange, new breed of men Congressman Carter saw, and grudgingly an idea came to him: "Maybe they've got something. . . . Maybe this is the pattern of the future."[92]

Carter's hosts, among them the haole-Hawaiian Hoxworth Hale—the leader of the Fort, Michener's fictionalization of the Big Five—quickly hijack his reverie and convince him to stand firm in his opposition to Hawai'i statehood. Nonetheless, Michener suggested that Carter may have completed his transformation from bigot to Golden Man had he stayed in Hawai'i.

Ultimately, however, it is the patriarch Hale who is redeemed at the end of Michener's novel. After the Fort loses control over the territorial legislature and his daughter marries Shigeo Sakagawa, a Democratic Nisei politician, Hale identifies himself as the novel's narrator. With this surprise reveal, Michener seems to have been asking his mostly white readers to embrace the onrushing social transformation that Hawai'i portended. After decades at the helm of Hawai'i's economy and politics, Hale, "a proud, lonely man, descendant of missionaries and owner of the islands," loosens his grip on the reins of power without relinquishing them completely: "So at the age of fifty-six I, Hoxworth Hale, have discovered that I, too, am one of those Golden Men who see both the West and the East, who cherish the glowing past and who apprehend the obscure future."[93] In ending the novel with this line, Michener suggested to his audience a path toward sublime surrender to the new social order. Hale was not so much abandoning his past identity, but evolving. If a man who had every reason to resist change could look ahead to the "obscure future," so too could white Americans on the mainland.

Michener's anodyne concluding vision of Hawai'i in *Hawaii* did not portend the kinds of racist encounters that drove the author and his wife to leave the islands two years after the novel's publication. Nor did it offer anything in the way of concrete solutions to the problem of racial prejudice Michener set out to ameliorate in his unpublished manuscript. Moreover, although the ending was clearly meant to be hopeful, it was also ambiguous. Read one way, it inadvertently conveyed the scale of the difficulty in tackling racial prejudice in America. In focusing on Hawai'i's unique ability to challenge bigotry, Michener implied that it was only in the islands, or through contact with Hawai'i's people, that whites could overcome their racism—that distance from the mainland and its racial norms was necessary for national racial progress.

But the portrait of social amity and white racial tolerance that *Hawaii*'s ending painted would continue to be reproduced and expanded on in American culture throughout the ensuing decades—including during the Selma march in 1965, when King's lei signified both the superficial and substantive meanings attached to Hawai'i in postwar American culture. In 1967, a few months after the Supreme Court banned antimiscegenation laws, Hawai'i made a brief but pivotal appearance in the landmark film *Guess Who's Coming to Dinner,* which, much like the ending of *Hawaii,* chronicles the evolution of a white man from prejudice to racial tolerance as he comes to accept that his daughter is marrying a black man. It was in Hawai'i where the young interracial couple met. Although their courtship in the islands takes place off-screen, the new state nonetheless serves as the initial catalyst for a decline, however small, of mainland racism.

Such themes would permeate the poststatehood discourses around Hawai'i, in both the policymaking and cultural realms. Most notably, they would be embraced by people in Hawai'i who were looking to transform the islands' political economy. Michener and likeminded cultural producers, in using well-worn representations of Hawai'i combined with newer claims for its deeper social relevance to the United States, offered a script for others seeking to promote the new state. Whatever the reality of Hawai'i, for those charged with constructing the islands' poststatehood identity, the image of the islands as a racial paradise would prove to be both popular and profitable.

3

The Power of Mutual Understanding

AS OPERATION ROLLING THUNDER battered Vietnam during the spring of 1965, President Lyndon Johnson told an audience in Honolulu that he wanted to promote peace. "We hear of wars and rumors of wars, but too often the . . . steady work of achieving peace goes unnoticed in this world in which we live," Johnson declared to the board members of Hawai'i's East-West Center (EWC). Yet "there is nothing that really matters more than working toward peace, trying as best we can to replace strife and suspicion with respect and with understanding between men." That was where the East-West Center came in, Johnson said, by helping to ensure that "all of us can live in a world ultimately of peace, of friendship, and of a reasonable standard of living for all humankind."[1]

The East-West Center, an international educational exchange and graduate program at the University of Hawai'i, along with the university's Peace Corps training program for volunteers to Asia, were part of a broader reimagining of U.S. global authority, one that was decidedly Pacific in orientation. Their location in Hawai'i, on the periphery of the American nation-state, was seen as vital to that expansionist mission. Hawai'i, though far from the center of power in Washington, was a wellspring of ideas for the newly ambitious foreign policy making of the 1960s. As America's "bridge to Asia," Hawai'i helped formulate new strategies for securing U.S. cultural and economic influence in the decolonizing world.

The East-West Center and Peace Corps training program represented an effort to turn the islands from metaphorical bridge into a formal site for promoting U.S. foreign policy interests under the rubric of cultural exchange. Over the course of the statehood debates, proponents had transformed Hawai'i's cultural ambiguity into an asset to U.S. foreign relations. Hawai'i—part Asian, part American—became a space between and apart that could take on various cultural forms as necessary. Advocates of exchange believed Hawai'i offered an ideal setting for what they called "mutual understanding": a place where foreigners could be trained in American economic and cultural practices and where foreign ways could be demystified for Americans. By the end of 1960, on Johnson's initiative, Congress had established the East-West Center and two years later the islands would become host to the largest domestic training center for the Peace Corps, Kennedy's experimental program "to promote world peace and friendship" by sending young American volunteers abroad.[2]

These developments seized on, and crystallized, an assumption already circulating in both liberal policy circles and American popular culture: America's global identity must be remade to meet the demands of a decolonizing world. Earlier development and cultural diplomacy efforts had focused disproportionately on Europe, but by the end of the 1950s policymakers were shifting their gaze to the "Third World," where the Cold War was to have its most dramatic impact.

Resistance to American power in the decolonizing world, however, forced the U.S. government to seek new ways of communicating its intentions. Cultural exchange in Hawai'i was one way. Hawai'i, with its multiracial population and apparent social harmony, was celebrated by various policymakers and social scientists as a symbol of America's commitment to racial diversity and cultural pluralism, and—paradoxically—of the universalism of American ideals. The islands were "living proof that peoples of all races, cultures and creeds can live together in harmony and well-being," where "democracy as advocated by the United States has in fact afforded a solution to some of the problems constantly plaguing the world."[3] At the same time, however, Hawai'i was also viewed as a place whose difference from the rest of the United States—its Asian-inflected culture and seeming lack of racism—made it the ideal meeting ground between Americans and Asians.

People in Hawai'i itself helped to produce this image of their home state. A rising political and business class in the islands, led by Governor John Burns, saw much to be gained by hitching Hawai'i to the kinds of ambitious foreign relations efforts promoted by the Kennedy administration. But these local leaders were not simply followers or recipients of Washington policy initiatives. Rather, they helped shape the terms by which Hawai'i was constructed as a bridge to Asia and which, in turn, influenced how other Americans understood racial and cultural difference in a global context.

Advocates of cultural exchange in Hawai'i emphasized the islands' uniqueness as much as their Americanness. In doing so, they instrumentalized difference in the service of U.S. foreign policy. The EWC, for instance, rejected the "bland assimilation of differences" in favor of "the useful employment of diversities for mutual good."[4] In stressing difference over assimilation they helped to develop multiculturalism as both discourse and institutional practice. But they also set restrictions on the level of difference to be tolerated while suggesting that the celebration of difference must be channeled toward particular ends. Not all differences were equally valid in practice. "Mutual good," meanwhile, meant American-style modernization. The foreigners at the East-West Center and those targeted by the Peace Corps were expected to reject communism and shed many of their "traditional" cultural attributes. The "modern" capitalist values to replace them happened to be American, but they were also assumed to be global. In effect, the United States was willing to accommodate some of Third World societies' alien cultural traditions so long as they accepted American economic ideas.

Hawai'i, as a "decolonized" U.S. state, was now to serve as a conduit for American expansionism. Hawai'i statehood was in many ways an expression of the tensions and contradictions inherent in America's national self-image as an anticolonial global power. Although the state of Hawai'i was a product of the global campaign for decolonization, the dominant narrative of statehood ignored Hawai'i's colonial history while simultaneously promoting the new state as a symbol of American credibility in the decolonizing world. And so—while the state of Hawai'i was refashioning itself as center for global cultural exchange and for "mutual understanding" over "bland assimilation"—it was also informed by a larger foreign policy framework that emphasized the importance of promoting U.S. interests abroad. Indeed, as Hawai'i shows, the development of an emerging multiculturalist discourse in the postwar era cannot be divorced from American global expansionism.

The fixation on mutual understanding reflected an assumption that the peoples of the decolonizing world must be exposed not only to American products and development models, but to American ways of thinking—and, above all, to Americans themselves. At the same time, mutual understanding was a skill that *Americans* must to learn in order to exert influence in the decolonizing world. Mutual understanding needed to be regulated, however, if it was to be effective in promoting American foreign policy. Advocates of "free interchange" in Hawai'i prized the islands' liminality and mutability, but they also sought control over social relations in Hawai'i's exchange programs.

At the same time, the discourses of mutual understanding and interchange obscured the disparities in power between Americans and the peoples of Asia and the Pacific. Those who sought to promote Hawai'i as a site for both cultural exchange and the projection of American power ignored the inherent conflicts between these two aims—though, to them, there was no conflict between those goals, or between American and Asian interests. America's presence in Asia, however, was often based less on friendship or even friendly coercion than on brute force. In May 1961, two days after Johnson plunged a shovel into the earth at the East-West Center groundbreaking ceremony, President Kennedy, believing the Vietnamese people were mishandling their independence from France, ordered an increase in U.S. advisors and covert operations in South and North Vietnam.[5] By the time Johnson made his appeal for peace to the East-West Center board in 1965, America had launched a full-blown war, with Hawai'i as command center, against the people it insisted it wanted to help. Ultimately, the disconnect between interchange and modernization resulted in a limited multiculturalism in Hawai'i, one that celebrated difference only if it advanced "mutual good" as defined by those in power.

—————

The East-West Center and the Peace Corps were heirs to earlier Cold War endeavors to bolster U.S. global power with nonmilitary initiatives. They also drew on a longer history of nonstate projects aimed at improving relations between different ethnic groups. Beginning in the interwar period, progressive anthropologists, internationalists, and other activists argued that both global and domestic stability depended on better human understanding across cultural divides. While some focused their efforts on teaching Americans to be less provincial—through such programs as junior year abroad for college students and intercultural education for school-age children—others were more interested in promoting understanding of American culture as a way to secure U.S. influence overseas.[6]

Many of the ideas developed by these internationalists were then taken up by the U.S. government during the Cold War as part of its effort to project a friendly image of the United States to the rest of the world. Cultural diplomacy, as its proponents called it, was meant to convince people abroad to reject communism in favor of the "American way of life," which was defined by a high standard of living that was the product of democracy and free market capitalism. Within a few years after World War II, the basic architecture of cultural diplomacy was in place. The first of these postwar cultural initiatives, the Fulbright Act of 1946 promoting educational exchange, was soon followed by the Smith-Mundt Act in 1948, which funded various propaganda efforts, such as the Voice of America's radio broadcasts and public exhibitions on American culture in Western Europe. By 1953, when the Eisenhower administration established the United States Information Agency (USIA), the United States was sending abroad thousands of people and propaganda materials in an attempt to "win hearts and minds" in the battle against communism.[7]

American cultural diplomacy hit a stumbling block, however, when it came to the question of U.S. race relations. The United States attempted to represent itself as a bastion of democracy to the world, but back on American soil the civil rights movement was ramping up its efforts to secure equality for African Americans—prompting segregationists to launch a violent campaign of massive resistance. Stories of racial violence and discrimination damaged America's ideological standing in the decolonizing world, where the Soviet Union, whose propagandists excoriated the United States for its treatment of African Americans, threatened to gain the advantage. Meanwhile, civil rights activists, adjusting their tactics to suit the circumstances of the Cold War, also sought to exploit the disparity between America's rhetoric of equality abroad and the reality of Jim Crow at home. In response, U.S. government propagandists worked to simultaneously deflect international attention away from the American South and to paint a picture of the United States as an egalitarian society, one that represented a departure from European colonialism.[8]

Many historians, in focusing almost entirely on America's international image problem during the Cold War as it pertained to black-white race relations, have largely overlooked the fact that the U.S. government was also deeply concerned about perceptions of American racial attitudes more broadly. As Asia and the Pacific became an increasingly important region to the twinned goals of American military and economic expansion, U.S. policymakers sought to encourage deeper cultural and social ties between Asians and Americans through initiatives such as the USIA's People-to-People program, which funded the movement of nongovernmental "ambassadors" to Asia and elsewhere. This was bolstered by the campaign of "middlebrow intellectuals" to rid American popular culture of Yellow Peril tropes and portray the United States as a racially tolerant society, one in which Asian immigrants could flourish and that viewed with empathy those living on the other side the Pacific.[9]

But although James Michener and others may have been seeking to bring together the United States and Asia in what Christina Klein calls a "global imaginary of integration," their pleas for cross-cultural friendship were nonetheless informed by a structure of knowledge that viewed global relations in much more stark terms.[10] The dominant theoretical framework for understanding the relationship of the United States to the people of Asia was based on the concept of three worlds, not one. The three worlds rubric divided the globe into the capitalist First World, the Communist Second World, and the Third World of everyone else, tenuously bound together by their lack of easy categorization.[11]

The Third World, unaligned, most of it emerging from the yoke of colonialism, had become the battleground for competing communist and capitalist visions of postcolonial modernity.[12] To formulate such a vision, and to make it appealing to peoples of the decolonizing world, the U.S. government enlisted the help of various nongovernmental actors in higher education and the foundation sector. The scale of the effort was unprecedented, contributing to the greatest expansion of higher education in American history.[13]

Initially the focus was on developing foreign language skills and scholarly knowledge of the specific peoples and regions with new strategic importance to the United States—an interdisciplinary project known as area studies that emerged during World War II and was quickly drafted into the Cold War.[14] While area studies tended toward the particular, there was also a movement to develop broad, universal laws of human behavior that could explain, somewhat paradoxically, differences in culture and political economy. By the late 1950s, American social scientists had woven into the three worlds concept a theory that claimed to understand why the Third World remained poor and "underdeveloped." Rather than looking to the exploitive practices of colonialism or global capitalism, modernization theory explained the relative social and economic positions of the first and third worlds by placing each on a spectrum that ranged from "traditional" to "modern." Modernity, in tautological fashion, was in turn defined by how deeply a nation's economy was integrated with global markets and by how closely its society resembled those of the democratic capitalist nations of the West.[15]

According to its adherents, modernization theory, unlike colonialist discourses of civilization and savagery, promoted mobility and transformation. All nations, save perhaps the United States, had been "traditional" at some point in their histories, enslaved to superstition, provincialism, and feudal social relations. Nations and peoples could slide up the modernity spectrum, if given the right tools, information, and some capital to hasten industrialization. In this way, modernization theory injected a certain flexibility into the rigid three worlds rubric at the same time that it reified the Third World's subordinate status and demanded U.S. intervention in its economies.[16]

Modernization theory drew on the assumptions of French and British colonial reformers who believed their job was to teach colonized peoples how to be modern subjects. But while European colonial administrators often viewed modernization as a means of slaking natives' desire for independence—and thereby extending colonial rule—Americans viewed modernization as a homogenizing project that would enmesh formerly colonized peoples in the new world system of independent nation-states.[17] And though America's actions in the decolonizing world often defied its rhetorical commitment to self-determination, such rhetoric nonetheless shaped American development policy, often toward contradictory ends. During the era of decolonization, "it was no longer politically possible to divide the world between advanced and primitive beings," as Frederick Cooper argues. "Distinctions in level of development persisted, to be sure, but they could be overcome."[18] Such possibilities often went unfulfilled, certainly, but the onrush of decolonization meant that the United States had to base its modernization policies on theories that explicitly eschewed racialized notions of human development. At the same time, American concerns that people in the Third World might be swayed by communist ideology reflected an acknowledgment of Third World agency. Decolonizing nations had a choice, however limited, and it was up to the U.S. government to ensure that they made the right one.

It was against this background that statehood advocates began circulating proposals for using Hawai'i as a center for cultural exchange, linking the cause of statehood to larger U.S. foreign policy aims. But while the construction of Hawai'i as a mediating space was part of American efforts to secure its influence in the Third World, it was also born out of the specific circumstances of the Hawai'i statehood debates, which themselves contributed to the burgeoning sense that the United States must reshape its national life in light of global developments. In both Hawai'i and on the mainland, the labeling of Hawai'i as a "bridge to Asia" helped give meaning to, and to an extent normalize, what might otherwise have been a rather strange turn of events: the incorporation of an archipelago 2,200 miles from the American continent as a fully equal part of the nation.

Statehood advocates believed Hawai'i's people could provide a model for how to accommodate difference within the framework of the nation and, at the same time, use such difference as leverage for advancing American interests abroad. "Hawaii's citizens of Japanese, Chinese, Korean, and other oriental ancestries are American to the core," John Burns, Hawai'i's congressional representative and later the state's most influential governor, proclaimed in a Senate hearing in 1957. "They also understand and appreciate the problems the Asiatic peoples have in adjusting to the new modes of life. They can be our best mediator with those peoples." To Burns, who predicted that in the future Asia would be an increasingly significant trading partner for the United States, it was only natural that "Hawaii will be our center for these relations."[19]

As Burns predicted, the people of Hawai'i would soon come to serve as ambassadors for mediating relations between the United States and Asia. Within months of statehood, Hawai'i sent to Asia its most prominent "American to-the-core" citizens of Asian descent, Hiram Fong and Daniel Inouye. The two men had just been elected as members of Hawai'i's first voting delegation in Congress—Fong as a Republican senator and Inouye as a Democratic House member. Each was first in other ways as well, with Fong the first Asian American senator and Inouye the first Japanese-American member of Congress. At the end of 1959, the two men traveled separately to Asia, meeting with government officials and journalists, and touring military and cultural sites, with the State Department celebrating the visits as a way to foster friendship between the United States and the "Far East."[20]

But people in Hawaiʻi had more ambitious plans for the islands beyond being home base for the world's most notable Asian American politicians. During the statehood era, Hawaiʻi's business and political leaders were casting around for new industries to attract capital to the islands. For a century Hawaiʻi's sugar and pineapple cartels had been the backbone of the Hawaiʻi economy; now world-wide production of the two commodities was increasingly moving to Southeast Asia. Meanwhile, the labor movement in Hawaiʻi, once notably weak, had gained a foothold in local politics. Hawaiʻi's plantation system, with its accompanying sharp social divisions and colonialist practices, was on the decline.

Along with tourism, educational exchange appeared to many in the islands as a way for Hawaiʻi to recast its global identity, reaping hefty financial rewards in the process. The specific contours of that identity—how different or un-different Hawaiʻi should be, and toward what ends—would remain in flux, even after statehood was secured. Nonetheless, as Burns's 1957 testimony suggests, by the end of the 1950s many Hawaiʻi boosters had come to embrace the ambiguity of Hawaiʻi, viewing the islands' liminality as a source of prestige and profit. Ignoring earlier debates about whether Hawaiʻi was foreign or American, different from or representative of mainland society, Burns and others claimed Hawaiʻi was all things at once: an exceptional place that was also an exemplar of America. Hawaiʻi was envisioned as a protean cultural space, one that could serve as staging ground both for Americans acquiring new cosmopolitan personalities and for people from the decolonizing world adjusting to "new modes of life." In the midst of a drawn-out debate over statehood that had largely hinged on how to define Hawaiʻi's cultural identity, Hawaiʻi was now seeking to foreground its "bridge" capabilities.

There was already a strong tradition of global engagement in Hawaiʻi. Despite Hawaiʻi's geographical isolation, Native Hawaiians retained historical memory of their ancestors' Pacific voyages and understood their archipelago to reside at the nexus of a larger island universe; after European contact, traveling Hawaiians saw their homeland as part of a wider indigenous world.[21] In the twentieth century, settlers in Hawaiʻi saw the islands as an ideal site for the rising internationalist movement. The Pan-Pacific Union, founded in 1917, and, later, the Institute of Pacific Relations (IPR), established in 1925 with funding from the Rockefeller Foundation, sought to turn Hawaiʻi into "our new Geneva" through conferences and research programs aimed at increasing cultural links between the United States and Asia.[22] Like advocates of postwar cultural exchange in Hawaiʻi, they believed Hawaiʻi's multiracial character and geographic and cultural liminality positioned it to assume a leadership role in Pacific affairs. However, by the early 1930s, as the IPR expanded and gained more adherents on the mainland, its headquarters was transferred to New York; IPR leadership believed Hawaiʻi was too provincial.[23]

After the war, with the promise of statehood on the horizon, Hawai'i boosters were eager to eradicate any hint of Hawai'i's provincial reputation. Indeed, they argued, it was Hawai'i's distance from New York and other traditional centers of American power and intellectual ferment that made Hawai'i *un*-provincial. In 1945, there was a short-lived campaign to make Hawai'i—a place where it was "easy for people of all countries to feel at home"—the home of the United Nations headquarters.[24] Later, a plan jumpstarted by Hawai'i governor Sam King and the U.S. Department of the Interior created the basic conceptual framework for many of the Hawai'i training and exchange initiatives that would follow, before and after statehood. In 1954, King succeeded in convincing the State Department to establish the International Cooperation Center (ICC) in Honolulu as a site for "conditioning" Asian trainees en route to various educational exchange programs in the continental United States.

Straddling a delicate line between emphasizing Hawai'i's resemblance to mainland society and highlighting its cultural ties to Asia, the outline for the ICC claimed that Hawai'i could serve multiple purposes at once. Hawai'i, much like Samarkand, Uzbekistan—a "transitional area" where the Soviets sent Asians before bringing them to Russia—provided the "perfect environment" for acculturation. Since much of the islands' population was of Asian descent, this meant that in Hawai'i "many Asian cultural values are preserved and there is an unusual degree of knowledge and understanding of Asia." But Hawai'i was also "a thoroughly American community" whose people were "living happily and prosperously in a modern world." In an attempt to reconcile this potential contradiction, the ICC proposal defined Hawai'i as " 'mid-passage' into the American way of life."[25]

"Conditioning" in Hawai'i would take several forms, from the material to the emotional and intellectual. At the most rudimentary level, Hawai'i would help Asians to become acquainted with the basic elements of daily life in the United States, including American money, transportation, and table manners.[26] At the same time, Hawai'i's cultural environment would be legible to Asian visitors, who would encounter "foods and habits more closely allied to their native patterns than are available elsewhere in the United States," thus presumably lessening their susceptibility to culture shock.[27]

As important, Hawai'i provided a key forum in which to educate Asians on the state of American race relations. And yet the authors of the ICC plan equivocated when it came to how to define the problem of race in the United States—as one of reality, of international perception, or of some combination of the two—and how Hawai'i might solve it. On the one hand, the plan claimed that Hawai'i's "high degree of inter-racial harmony and equality of opportunity" made the islands "a living refutation of the picture of the inferior status of non-whites in the U.S. which is a major point of nationalist and communist anti–U.S. propaganda in Asia." However, although in Hawai'i itself "there are no problems of race to embarrass" Asian visitors, it was also true that they would most likely encounter racial prejudice once they got to the mainland. Here, the plan's authors suggested that Hawai'i was less a refutation of America's national image than it was an exception to it—the islands, as a liminal area between East and West, were "the *only* part of the United States where these conditions may be found." Nonetheless, Hawai'i still had an important role to play by providing the visitor "a free climate [in which] he can discuss the barriers he will face elsewhere" and learn about "progress toward which has been made in alleviating these conditions."[28]

Hawai'i might also serve as a conditioning site for Americans, according to the ICC proposal. Just as it did for Asian trainees, an orientation program in Hawai'i for Americans would also provide them the opportunity to observe a racially integrated society, offering "the hope of reducing any race prejudices which a technician might have." In addition, Hawai'i could teach Americans about the customs and achievements of the societies they would be traveling to, "thus reducing the possibility of giving offense" upon arrival, and inculcating "a degree of modesty necessary to the success of their missions." However, lest it be assumed that only Asians needed instruction in American cultural practices, the plan for the ICC made clear that Hawai'i-based training for Americans should also include activities that would "indoctrinate them . . . in the essentials of the American way of life."[29]

The problem of cultural difference, ICC supporters optimistically believed, could be solved simply by bringing people together within the controlled setting of Hawai'i society. In pursuit of that stated goal the ICC had by 1959 conducted training in subjects ranging from animal husbandry to perfume manufacturing for some three thousand Asian participants from thirty countries. Meanwhile, plans were in the works in Hawai'i and in Congress to use the ICC as a model for the much more ambitious East-West Center.[30] And while the ICC never became a conditioning center for Americans going to Asia, it did articulate many of the basic assumptions that a few years later would undergird training programs in Hawai'i for Peace Corps volunteers and Agency for International Development (USAID) workers traveling to Vietnam.

Not everyone believed the ICC should serve as a blueprint for future endeavors, however. Critics argued that, when it came to cultural exchange, Hawai'i's difference from the mainland was a deficiency rather than an asset. In enshrining Hawai'i's exceptionality the ICC threatened to undermine its own universalistic mission. If Hawai'i was even a little bit Asian, and thus different from the mainland, how could it the best representative of *American* culture to Asians, or to anyone else?

Moreover, Hawai'i could not logically serve at once as refutation of *and* antidote to mainland racism. Whether or not Hawai'i was a truly racially harmonious society, its status as a place apart from the rest of the United States left it open to both praise and skepticism within foreign policy circles. In reporting on his visit to the ICC in 1957, the American diplomat in charge of educational exchange in Indonesia warned that while Hawai'i might be a cultural bridge to Asia, it was not the best stopping place for Asians coming to the United States for technical training. With residents insisting "that they really are different from the Americans on the mainland," an Indonesian spending time in Hawai'i might return home believing that "his exaggerated conception of U.S. race problems has been verified" and that Hawai'i was truly an exception to American racism. Moreover, trainees in Hawai'i would then face "additional adjustment . . . in going on from Hawaii to Washington."[31] While Hawai'i might be more similar to Indonesia than the continental United States, it was not American enough to serve as an effective introduction to mainland racial norms.

Even after Hawai'i statehood was secured, American diplomats in Asia were wary of plans to scale up the ICC model into the much more ambitious East-West Center that Lyndon Johnson and John Burns were hatching in Congress. Indeed, the State Department in general was resistant to the EWC. In the spring of 1959, as Congress was hammering out plans for the establishment of the EWC—to be housed at the University of Hawai'i and overseen by the State Department—officials at State were urging lawmakers not to place the EWC under their jurisdiction. Assistant Secretary Robert Thayer suggested that any entity of the University of Hawai'i, because of its status as a U.S. land grant institution, should be sponsored by the Department of Health, Education, and Welfare. But EWC backers in Congress countered that "the objectives of the center lay in the field of international education and cultural relations," and thus ought to fall to the State Department to administer.[32] Significantly, the State Department lost the argument.

Once the EWC had been established by Congress and plans for its construction were underway, Thayer continued to express doubts about the new institution. He feared "that our friends from the Far East will feel that they are being discriminated against by not coming to the mainland of the USA," he wrote. He likened Hawai'i to Puerto Rico, "where Latin Americans felt this discrimination when they were assigned to the University of Puerto Rico for study rather than to the mainland."[33] Thayer's comparison of Hawai'i to Puerto Rico is notable, as the two offshore territories had had a similarly ambiguous relationship to the U.S. mainland since their annexation in 1898. More recently, the two had been linked in discussions in Congress on the issue of their status as non-self-governing territories in the age of decolonization.

Although advocates for Hawai'i statehood had worked to distance Hawai'i from Puerto Rico by claiming that the Pacific territory was the more American of the two—and therefore deserving of something better than Puerto Rico's awkward new designation as a semi-independent commonwealth—Thayer suggested that neither one could claim full U.S. pedigree yet.

State Department staff in the field supported Thayer's claim that there was a perceived stigma attached to foreign training programs in Hawai'i. It was unclear, however, just where the stigma originated. A diplomat in Korea, after admitting that many Koreans he had spoken with were in favor of the EWC, stated that U.S. embassy officials did not want most Korean grantees to "receive their chief—or even major—impressions of American life in Hawaii." This was because "neither Honolulu nor the University of Hawaii have reputations as major American intellectual, scientific or cultural centers. Above all, Hawaii is, by its very size and distance, isolated from the centers of American culture."[34] Another State Department official echoed this sentiment, saying that Hawai'i was "too atypical, sociologically . . . for the vast use envisaged in the 'East-West Center' idea."[35]

Defying its critics in the State Department, the framers of the EWC made the case that Hawai'i was coming into its role as a global powerhouse unto itself, one that did not need to rely on mainland intellectual centers to authorize its legitimacy. Moreover, they argued, Hawai'i represented a relocation of the point of contact between the United States and the world—arguing for a Pacific orientation to supplement, even supplant, America's traditional Atlantic fixation. Hawai'i was "a *new* State, permeated to the core with a zest for the future and its role in shaping that future, particularly in Pacific and Asian affairs."[36] With statehood, the islands no longer had to tread carefully to appease those uncomfortable with their duality. The University of Hawai'i, for its part, could now fulfill its role "as an intellectual, cultural mediary [sic] between the peoples of Asia and the peoples of the Americas." Statehood had come at a time of "growing realization of the need for better mutual understanding between peoples," and Hawai'i was poised to take advantage of this new global consciousness.[37]

But, as State Department correspondence makes clear, even many U.S. officials posted in Asia seemed to believe that "the centers of American culture" lay somewhere other than Asian-inflected Hawai'i. Despite the claims that Hawai'i could be at once culturally Asian and "American to the core," the State Department, charged with dealings between discrete states, struggled to assimilate this nebulous characterization into their framework of understanding. The resistance to the EWC among State Department officials, who were drawn from the East Coast WASP elite, shows that the emerging multiculturalist discourse germinating in Hawai'i was still very much contested.

The State Department of the early 1960s was still wedded to Eisenhower-era notions of spreading "Americanism"—in all its seemingly unambiguous solidity—to the people of Asia. It did not see any benefit in emphasizing internal differentiation within the United States, as represented by polyglot Hawai'i. For someone like Robert Thayer, a former lawyer for a white-shoe New York firm, the notion that the United States might itself be a little bit Asian would have been suspect—not something to advertise to the world.[38] This reluctance of the State Department to support the EWC demonstrates that Hawai'i, far from being merely a tool for policymakers in Washington, was actively shaping foreign policy in the 1960s by generating new ideas about the benefits of celebrating America's cultural and ethnic diversity.

State Department concerns aside, by the end of 1961 the EWC had already enrolled its first class of students in its graduate degree program and had received a group of senior scholars working on short-term research projects. Students, most of them men, came from India, Indonesia, Japan, the Philippines, and numerous other countries throughout Asia and the Pacific. About 30 came from the United States. The foreign students—198 of them—nearly doubled the typical number of new students from Asia and the Pacific enrolled annually in U.S. universities.[39] They could choose from a wide array of courses, with subjects ranging from agronomy to social work to overseas operations, and were also offered field trips and training sessions at several of Hawai'i's government agencies and major private companies.[40]

The EWC claimed to represent a new kind of educational exchange policy. "It is a place. It is a people. It is an ideal," went a typical brochure.[41] That ideal, and the EWC's "primary objective," was "the increase and development of mutual understanding between the peoples of the countries of Asia, the Pacific area and the United States."[42] This emphasis on "mutual understanding" reflected a belief that the battle for the alliance of the Third World depended in large part on the performance of cultural respect. The lack of understanding that the EWC sought to combat was, foremost, that of nationalists in the decolonizing world. Between 1945 and 1960, the United Nations nearly doubled as it included forty-four new members—a number that would only rise with the ongoing disintegration of European colonialism in Africa and Asia.[43] Formerly colonized people, however, did not blithely accept America's message of benevolence, especially in the face of U.S. armed intervention in societies that rejected American development models. The people of the Third World were thus suspicious of American intent, even if many of them embraced modernization. To many, U.S.-led development bore a resemblance to the "civilizing" missions of European colonists who had sought to overturn the basic way of life of colonized peoples. Decolonizing nations were not only fighting for political and economic sovereignty, but for cultural autonomy as well. They longed both to improve basic quality of life and forge new societies that broke with the colonial past. Rather than engage in "obscene emulation," wrote Frantz Fanon, the revolutionary theorist of decolonization, peoples fighting for independence must reject the "outmoded games" not only of Europe but also of the United States—which Fanon called "a monster where the flaws, sickness, and inhumanity of Europe have reached frightening proportions."[44]

The goal of cultural regeneration was on full display at the Bandung Conference in 1955. At this historic conference, which brought to Indonesia representatives of newly independent nations from across Asia and Africa, participants repeatedly stressed their desire to reclaim indigenous culture. Defying colonial discourses of Western cultural superiority, Bandung's Final Communiqué insisted that Asia and Africa were in fact "the cradle of great religions and civilisations which have enriched other cultures and civilisations." Cultural suppression, the Communiqué argued, had been central to the larger colonial project, which had denigrated native practices and belief systems and severed ties between non-Western peoples. Bandung participants thus sought to establish both cultural sovereignty and cultural cooperation among themselves— "to renew their old cultural contacts and develop new ones"—as part of their larger effort to prevent neocolonialism.[45]

The Communiqué proposed that Asia and Africa take part in their own cultural exchanges, separate from the West. Such ideas, together with the larger goals of the Non-Aligned Movement that came out of Bandung—which called for the Third World to reject formal allegiance to both the United States and the Soviet Union—were alarming to many in Washington, where nonalignment was equated with communism. Even if they misread the ideological implications of nonalignment, the American foreign policy establishment was rightly worried that efforts to resist external influence could derail U.S. efforts to shape Third World development.

Meanwhile, there was rising concern in diplomatic circles that representatives of the United States in the Third World were behaving badly—and undermining the message that Americans represented a break with the elitism and cultural chauvinism of Europeans. That was the central claim of the bestselling novel *The Ugly American,* published in 1958, which painted a portrait of American diplomats in Southeast Asia who lived in luxurious compounds and knew and cared little about the history, language, or culture of their host countries. (The eponymous "ugly" American, and the book's hero, was Homer Atkins, a homely engineer who lived among the local people.) The book— which was based on the real-life experiences in Asia of coauthors William Lederer, a Navy captain, and Eugene Burdick, a political scientist—caused a stir among foreign policy officials. Its most direct impact was serving as one of the inspirations for the Peace Corps.

FIGURE 6. Thai Pavilion at the East-West Center, ca. 1970s. Courtesy of the East-West Center.

Against this background, the EWC defined its mission as one of breaking old patterns of negotiating difference—it sought "not to erase differences
between people, but to make possible respect for the ways in which we are
unlike" by emphasizing "the free interchange of information and ideas."[46]
Such ideals were embedded in the physical construction of the EWC, whose
campus plan was supposed to promote cross-cultural encounters. EWC residential services, for instance, aimed to encourage "idea-trading" by placing
several lounges on each floor of its dormitories and urging American students
to room with students from Asia.[47] Other buildings were designed to invoke
Hawaiʻi's links to Asia. Teak from Thailand paneled the walls of the administration building, with a pavilion donated by the Thai monarchy erected just
next to it in 1967.[48] The administration building also overlooked a gift from a
group of businessmen from Japan—a garden with a stream running through it
in the shape of the Japanese character for "heart" and said to illustrate, according to John Burns, "the concept of the peoples of the world working together
and appreciating each other's virtues."[49] The East-West Center theater, this
one paneled with Burmese teak, proudly proclaimed its capacity to stage both
Asian and Western dramas.[50]

But the notions of interchange and mutual understanding glossed over the ways in which questions of global power undergirded EWC programming, which was charged with deepening American ties to Asia under the amended Mutual Security Act. Since its original passage in 1951, this legislation had promoted American interventionist actions abroad through massive military, economic, and technical assistance to foreign allies. The EWC's lofty mission was thus at once quixotic and strategic. Its constant use of "mutual" was not so much an attempt to veil ulterior American motives in Asia; rather, it suggested the extent to which the EWC—and the policymakers who created it— assumed the mutuality of American and Asian interests.

In the context of nationalist calls for sovereignty, convincing people in the decolonizing world of that mutuality of interests proved a challenge. But what proponents of mutual understanding took away from Fanon and other critics of Western imperialism was not the need to overturn generations of European intervention or upend class hierarchies in decolonizing nations. Instead, they sought to sell Third World audiences, from elites to peasants, on the legitimacy of American modernization programs (which would, theoretically, lead eventually to social equality). *How* to convey the message of American benevolence, one that would override competing messages of Third World nationalism, became a major topic of concern among modernization theorists in the overlapping networks of government and academia. For them, it was not racism, colonialism, or U.S. policy that was fueling anti-Western sentiment in the Third World, it was a problem at once more elusive and more solvable: a failure to communicate.

The techniques the U.S. government used to communicate with the Third World became more sophisticated and extensive under the Kennedy administration. As Jason Parker shows, public diplomacy efforts in the 1960s relied increasingly on market research, communications theory, and a recognition of the agency of Third World audiences—leading to a general shift in tone "from bombast and propaganda to persuasion." This was accompanied by a new faith in the importance of communication to U.S. foreign policy.[51] Mutual understanding and cross-cultural communication were not simply addendums to a larger development strategy. Rather, effective cross-cultural communication was seen as key to reconstructing decolonizing societies along American lines. Modernization theory rose in parallel with communications studies as an academic discipline, which was likewise drafted into the Cold War.[52]

The uses of communication in modernization was the subject of a month-long conference hosted by the EWC in the summer of 1964. Led by Daniel Lerner and Wilbur Schramm—"the founder of communication study" and later director of the East-West Communication Institute at the EWC—the theme of the conference was "Communication and Change in the Developing

Countries."[53] The two men were some of the most vocal proponents of using mass media to dismantle outmoded ways of thinking in decolonizing societies. Lerner's 1958 book *The Passing of Traditional Society,* for instance, claimed modernity and mass media went hand in hand—and was one of the first major works in modernization theory.

In the edited volume that came out of the conference, which had a foreword written by President Johnson and an author's list that included Lucian Pye and Max Millikan, Lerner argued that at the heart of modern consciousness was a sense of global interconnectedness cultivated by effective communication across cultures. Echoing the EWC's emphasis on interchange, he advocated for the rejection of the old colonialist binary of a "spiritual East" and "material West" in order to forge cross-cultural ties. "Is there really such a sacred cleavage between 'us' and 'them'?" Lerner asked. But U.S. communication with Third World peoples needed to pierce their "ethnocentrism," which often took the form of a "historical, and sometimes hysterical, jag of anti-West sentiment." Westerners, Lerner claimed, had risen above such provincialism in part by embracing mass media, which fostered empathy for people outside one's immediate environment. "Traditional society," by contrast, "deploys people by kinship into communities isolated from each other and from a center" and traditional people were thus "lacking bonds of interdependence." For Lerner, modernity was universal while traditional societies were particular and insular. Yet despite his proclaimed anti-ethnocentrism, Lerner also insisted on the East's subordination to the West. "Candor enjoins us to recognize that what the West is . . . the East seeks to become." Here Lerner suggested that the East-West binary was not imagined, but rather something to break down. "Do they really want only to be 'like them'? If so, why do they turn to us for aid and why do we give them aid?"[54]

With his explicit Western chauvinism, Lerner seemed to contradict the basic principles of interchange. But he also exposed the inherent imbalances of interchange as practiced at the EWC, where the mutual interests of the United States and Asia were ultimately determined by the United States. For one, the EWC was more engaged in straightforward technical training than cross-cultural communication. Technical training, in turn, reflected unspoken assumptions of American superiority. The EWC, whose official name was the Center for Cultural and Technical Interchange between East and West, may have promoted cultural mixing between Asians and Americans, but on the technical side, interchange was only meant to travel in one direction. While it offered some classes in areas such as Asian Art or Asian Studies, the vast majority of EWC courses focused on training students in American-developed science and social science. In 1961, for example, more EWC students were enrolled in tropical agriculture courses—including soil science, plant pathology, botany, poultry science, and agricultural economics—than in any other field.[55] The next most popular courses, namely English as a second language, government, and education, demonstrated a commitment to modernizing the central institutions of Third World societies.[56]

The recruitment of EWC grantees similarly reflected a bias toward Western knowledge production over mutual interchange. While EWC students were overwhelmingly from Asia and the Pacific, the country of origin of senior specialists carrying out research projects at EWC was weighted heavily toward the United States. For instance, in 1965, of 72 senior specialists, 33 were American—nearly one half—with only six Pakistanis representing the next largest national group.[57] Meanwhile, by the end of that same year, of the 1,413 students who had been enrolled in the EWC since its founding, only 435—less than one-third—were American.[58]

In the case of students from the U.S. Trust Territory, interchange could be used to directly uphold U.S. colonialism in the Pacific. According to the EWC's 1959 report to the State Department, there was "a growing awareness among the metropolitan powers that the future prestige of such powers will largely depend on what they do to help in the training of leadership" in their non-self-governing territories.[59] The use of the term metropolitan here, with all its associations with European colonialism, is revealing. The Trust Territory—thousands of small islands in Micronesia taken over from Japanese control during World War II—existed in a political limbo. While there were no plans to transform the status of these islands, they were asked to look toward the new state of Hawai'i as a modernizing example. The EWC's focus on cultivating "leadership" in the Trust Territory was an implicit nod to international pressure to promote self-government, yet it also sought to boost metropolitan "prestige" by a show of U.S. mastery in its overseas possessions.

The belief in American technical supremacy was embedded even in the EWC's more culture-oriented initiatives. The EWC's theater, for example, was officially described in a brochure as a place "where the theatrical traditions of Asia can blend with those of western civilization." And yet, the theatrical training program at the EWC in practice sought to educate only Asian theater workers, whose "slavish imitation" of western theater had resulted in "neither good Western nor good traditional Oriental staging." Fortunately, the trainees at the EWC understood that modern Asian theater "will not advance beyond its present hole-in-the-corner insignificance until those who work in it are trained in modern methods of production."[60] As this account of EWC training suggests, modernization theory, and its attendant belief in decolonizing nations' need for American tutelage in technical methods, informed the EWC approach to even those cultural realms that might appear peripheral to the cause of industrial development.

The EWC's focus on skills training reflects the hegemony of modernization discourse among many liberal policymakers in the 1960s. But the mission
of the EWC more broadly also spoke to a seemingly contradictory fixation,
within some quarters of the foreign policy establishment, on alternative visions
of development that eschewed high-modernist infrastructure investment in
favor of bottom-up, community-level initiatives. As Daniel Immerwahr shows,
at the height of modernization's popularity, the United States was also sponsoring small-scale "community development" that relied on local leaders to design
their own projects.[61] It is worth pointing out that the stated goal of the EWC,
at least in its early years, was not to modernize Third World societies. It was
to bridge national divides, one culturally respectful conversation at a time, in
order to contribute to the "betterment of American relations with [Asian and
Pacific] countries."[62] As with community development, the notion of interchange implied that the people of the Third World could actively determine
the shape of U.S. intervention in their societies. And yet, within the EWC,
attempts to foster interchange existed alongside with more orthodox modernization efforts that reflected the logic of larger U.S. projects aimed at top-down
transformation. Modernization and small-scale interchange were not opposing
concepts at the EWC, but complementary ones, with interchange serving as
vehicle for convincing Third World representatives of modernization's benefits.

The EWC emphasis on modernization and technical training was also
a reaction to political contest over the nature of U.S. foreign aid programs.
Despite EWC attempts to link cultural and technical interchange as complementary causes, it was under pressure from Congress to ramp up the technical side of its mandate. After the introduction of a House proposal in 1963 to
severely cut federal appropriations to the EWC, Hawai'i representative Tom
Gill said that part of the problem for some members of Congress was "that
the emphasis at the Center is unduly heavy on the cultural side." The foreign
policy value of some of the EWC's more culture-oriented initiatives evoked
"unfavorable visions of 'ivory towers' and 'long hairs,'" Gill told EWC supporters. "If you can imagine the difficulty a Midwestern Congressman might
have explaining the Senior Scholar Program to an Iowa corn farmer, you may
have an inkling of what I mean." While Gill admitted that the whole of the
State Department budget was "the happy hunting grounds" for conservative
members of Congress seeking to discredit the Kennedy administration's foreign policy, the singling out of the EWC indicates the unstable foundations on
which "cultural interchange" stood. According to Gill, for the EWC to prove its
usefulness to provincial Midwesterners, it had to link its mission more forcefully to concrete development goals.[63]

While attempts to defund the EWC were unsuccessful, the controversy
over EWC appropriations revealed the broader challenges of implementing

the utopian rhetoric surrounding Hawai'i. Even the most high-minded idealists at the EWC and elsewhere had to contend with policymakers in Washington who insisted on a more hard-nosed approach to foreign policy. One EWC administrator admitted skewing programming "toward technology" in order to ensure congressional support, insisting that, "whether the people in the humanities like it, their day is past."[64] Skeptics in Congress who believed the EWC should focus on technical programming dismissed the goals of advancing racial harmony and cross-cultural exchange as worthy in their own right. To them, mutual understanding had to directly advance American interests in order to warrant congressional appropriations, especially as the escalation of the war in Vietnam led to cuts in the foreign aid budget. This in turn shaped the kind of cross-cultural programs that were implemented in Hawai'i and limited their scope.

Due in part to pressure from Congress, by 1968 the EWC had significantly altered its official mission, with research and technical training taking a more dominant role under the rubric of "problem-oriented, research-directed programs."[65] Critics of this transition within the EWC decried the move away from the founding ethos of mutual understanding and insisted that the EWC would now be treading ground already covered by other aid organizations. A petition circulated at the University of Hawai'i called for a reinvigoration of the EWC's original goals of interchange, stating, "Asia has something more to offer the West than its problems."[66]

But the petition overestimated the effectiveness of the EWC's original mission of promoting mutual understanding, which had often proved elusive in practice. One EWC instructor reported in 1963 that there were "serious problems involving the morale of East-West Center students," among them the fact that white Australian students were racist, Indian students had "a superiority complex," and, in general, there was "very little intermingling" among students of different ethnic groups.[67] An evaluation of student satisfaction at the EWC published a year later revealed a similar dissonance between the EWC's idealistic public image and the challenges of achieving mutual understanding. While American students believed they harbored no stereotypes about people from Asia and the Pacific, students from Asia and the Pacific disagreed: half of those in their first year of school said that Americans were prejudiced. Significantly, that number went up to two-thirds for Asia/Pacific students in the second year, indicating that greater exposure to American students led to *less* mutual understanding. As a result, compared to American students, students from Asia and the Pacific "are more skeptical about interchange really having occurred among grantees."[68] It is telling that American students had more faith in the progress of mutual understanding than their foreign peers. In their refusal to acknowledge their own chauvinistic behavior while at the same time extolling the goals of abolishing prejudice, the American students suggested that their task was not to actively eradicate racism, but to demonstrate to the world that they were already racially enlightened.

Ultimately it was the Peace Corps, not the EWC, that sought to address more directly the kind of ignorance exhibited by American EWC students and the diplomats in *The Ugly American*. The Peace Corps, the hippie stepsister of the U.S. foreign policy establishment, took an alternative tack from more traditional foreign aid and mutual understanding programs. The Peace Corps' training program in Hawai'i was, in many ways, the counterpart to the East-West Center, and its mirror opposite. While the stated goal of both institutions was to increase mutual understanding between Asia and the United States, the Peace Corps, unlike the EWC—and unlike most other American foreign aid programs—was explicitly intended to serve as a training initiative aimed at preparing both Third World peoples *and* Americans for "new modes of life." While inheriting many of the elements and ideologies of its more traditional development counterparts, the Peace Corps differed in its focus on Americans themselves as objects of social and psychological reform. And, again, Hawai'i was identified as a central site for facilitating that transformation.

The Peace Corps' Hawai'i training program was the largest of all Peace Corps training programs in the 1960s and by the end of the decade one in ten volunteers had passed through Hawai'i. Based in Hilo, a working-class city on the Big Island, the largest and southern-most island in the Hawaiian archipelago, Hawai'i became the primary training conduit for volunteers traveling to East Asia and the Pacific.[69] It was no fluke that during the Peace Corps' formative years Hawai'i was home to the biggest and, arguably, most influential of its training programs. As they had with the East-West Center, state and university officials lobbied hard for the Peace Corps contract. To its promoters, the Hawai'i training program was a statewide project, encompassing everyone from the governor to "housewives and Hilo sampan drivers," all of whom served as "a human link between eastern and western worlds."[70] The whole of Hawai'i, as "link" between the United States and Asia, was ready to rally to the Peace Corps cause.

The Peace Corps, meanwhile, emerged out of the same debates as those around the EWC over how to use the nation's human resources to advance its aspirations to global leadership. For many in both Washington and Hawai'i, the multiracial state seemed a perfect fit with the Peace Corps' dual mission of promoting "a better understanding of the American people" in host countries and "a better understanding of other peoples on the part of the American people."[71] The islands, home to numerous immigrant groups and ethnic descendants of the nations in Asia to which Peace Corps volunteers would be assigned, offered what many believed was a unique opportunity for productive cultural friction. Just as the architects of the ICC envisioned that institution as a potential "conditioning" center for Americans traveling to Asia, the Peace Corps likewise viewed the Hawaiʻi training program as a cultural stepping-stone for its Asia-bound volunteers.

The Peace Corps imbued Hawaiʻi with the power to transform volunteers from parochial middle-class Americans into worldly "intercultural workers"—globe-traveling chameleons fitted with the skills needed to navigate an increasingly integrated world. The thinking behind using Hawaiʻi as a training site was based on the belief that Hawaiʻi provided volunteers with exposure to a society that embodied both a range of foreign cultures and successful cultural mixing. But it was also grounded in the assumption that the islands, in what was becoming a dominant trope in discussions of Hawaiʻi's role in U.S. foreign policy, were an amorphous cultural space in which multiple objectives could be realized.

Hawaiʻi was thus not only envisioned as a place that could help facilitate changes in the mindsets of the people of the decolonizing world. It was also seen as a site where Americans could refashion themselves. Indeed they *must*, according to the Peace Corps. Historiography on American foreign relations during the Cold War often overlooks the ways in which the U.S. government sought to shape the behavior and practices not only of foreign peoples, but of Americans as well. The Peace Corps stood at the forefront of this effort. It pioneered the practice of "cultural sensitivity" training, calling on Americans to engage in personality reinvention by developing both an understanding of cultural difference and the capacity to overcome it in the service of American foreign policy.

The Peace Corps, its founders insisted, was an organization of the future, one born to help shake a sclerotic foreign policy establishment of its bad habits—the kind immortalized in *The Ugly American*. Kennedy proposed the creation of Peace Corps during his presidential campaign. Underscoring his call for a broader reform of diplomatic practices, he envisioned the new organization as one directed at American youth who would ultimately go on to long-term employment in the State Department and replace the old guard.[72]

One of the key goals of the Peace Corps was to repair America's global reputation, as well as its own self-image, particularly around the issue of race. According to Sargent Shriver, the organization's first director, the United States was a society characterized by love, not social discord, with the Peace Corps "part of the real 'other America' that exists somewhere beneath the tinsel, the neon signs, the racial hatred, and the poverty."[73] As another Peace Corps official described it, the Peace Corps should not simply reveal this other America, but play an active role in serving as an agent of change at home by "altering the behavior and attitudes of average Americans—building new people."[74] Kennedy himself stressed the connection between building better Americans and good relations with newly decolonized peoples abroad. He lamented the fact that, in contrast to the Soviet Union, the United States had no diplomatic representatives in any of the six of the newly independent African states— "nations that can affect our security." And when mission chiefs were sent to new nations, he argued, "the indications are that he will have no briefing papers on African customs and problems—no staff member that speaks Swahili or Urdu or other local language—and no staff member who is not also a member of the white race." Unlike the current State Department, Peace Corps volunteers would be better trained in non-Western culture and recruited "from every race and walk of life," thus helping to usher in a new era in both domestic race relations and global understanding.[75]

But despite its flower-child image, the Peace Corps was not immune to the pressures of technocratic thinking or insulated from the more aggressive foreign policy ideology of the Kennedy and Johnson administrations. As Michael Latham shows, the Peace Corps, despite its emphasis on interchange, was one among a number of Kennedy-era development initiatives whose ultimate intention was to disseminate American ideology and practices.[76] Similarly, Molly Geidel argues that the Peace Corps was fundamentally neocolonial in its promotion of the idea that poverty in poor Third World societies was the result of a failure to fully embrace market values.[77] At the same time, however, the Peace Corps was rhetorically more committed to the cause of cultural exchange than any other government foreign aid program of its time, and its volunteers did not necessarily hew the government line. And unlike USAID, whose personnel generally directed large infrastructure projects, Peace Corps volunteers were often assigned to create local, small-scale community development programs with little guidance from officials in Washington.[78]

Joining the Peace Corps, meanwhile, allowed volunteers to defer military service, and the organization, particularly during the Vietnam War, was framed as both a supplement to America's military efforts and as a way to present a less bellicose image of the United States. As a result, the Peace Corps sat uncomfortably within the foreign policy establishment. Indeed, the Peace Corps reflected many of the tensions and contradictions of U.S. government policy under the Kennedy and Johnson administrations. Peace Corps officials, who were notorious for resisting clear policy directives in the organization's formative years, were often torn between conforming to the administration's technocratic interventionist foreign policy and working to subtly counteract it.

Peace Corps training reflected the organization's belief in its difference from other development programs. Rather than emphasizing the accumulation of information, Peace Corps training focused on "chang[ing] people, emotionally and fundamentally rather than intellectually."[79] The first step in this was to cultivate volunteers' "cultural sensitivity." Trainees must be made to "see

American culture as only one of the many valid expressions of man's cultural potential" and "demonstrate respect for the foreign culture and the individuals within it."[80] This was to be done not by simply informing trainees about the society they would be encountering as volunteers; instead, a trainee would learn how to handle cross-cultural interaction through immersive experience. This was a new, more modern approach to cultural education, according to the Peace Corps. While it may have relied in part on the historical and cultural knowledge amassed by area studies, "cross-cultural studies, as the title implies, are more personal than area studies." The Peace Corps' disdain for area studies also reflected one of the basic assumptions of modernization theory—that all of human behavior could be explained by a set of universal laws. In cross-cultural studies, students would come to see themselves as participants, not just disinterested observers, of the mechanics of culture, broadly construed. The trainee would learn how to be an "inter-cultural worker," a job that entailed "confront[ing], physically or intellectually, a world that is different from his, a world in which he is the curiosity."[81]

Peace Corps ideas on interculturalism borrowed heavily from the work of anthropologist Edward T. Hall, who had pioneered the move within postwar anthropology to study not only the cultural practices of foreign people, but also Americans' relations *with* those people. Most crucially for the Peace Corps was Hall's insistence that Americans, too, were products of culture, one that "controls behavior in deep and persisting ways."[82] In his book *The Silent Language*, published in 1959, Hall argued that Americans' ethnocentrism and ignorance of the ways in which they were shaped by culture were getting in the way of American foreign policy. While Hall's demand for better interethnic relations drew on anthropological ideas first developed in the interwar period, what was new about Hall was his desire to convert those ideas into teachable skills that could be used to advance foreign policy. Hall had cut his teeth as a consultant for the Foreign Service Institute, the training arm of the Department of State, where he advised future diplomats on how various nonverbal cues and behavior signaled broader cultural norms and beliefs. Like Kennedy, Hall found many foreign service officers lacking in intercultural skills. He called on Americans to "stop alienating the people with whom we are trying to work."[83]

Peace Corps materials asserted that attention to one's own culture would allow volunteers to discern the seams holding all societies together. Adopting the theories of sociologist Erving Goffman, training literature likened the experience of the volunteer to that of an actor joining a cast whose social relations constituted staged performances, wherein the volunteer was "always on stage even though sometimes playing a minor role."[84] Goffman's influential 1959 work, *The Presentation of Self in Everyday Life,* used the metaphor of dramaturgy to deconstruct the mechanics of everyday interaction. The Peace

Corps used Goffman's dramaturgical analogies to emphasize the necessity for volunteers to behave as self-aware actors.

For the Peace Corps, cultural sensitivity was a craft, much like acting. Honing it was just as important as acquiring knowledge about a specific place or society, if not more so. It urged trainees to employ Goffman's theory of "impression management" to crack the code of social performance and achieve "communication control."[85] A successful volunteer "continuously monitors his social environment and tries to read the communication from it and at the same time to evaluate the effectiveness and relevance of the message he is sending to it."[86] It was this heightened awareness that Peace Corps training was supposed to cultivate by exposing volunteers to foreign cultures in a controlled setting. Once immersed in an alien environment, unmoored from the familiar, they would become more aware of the ways in which they had been socialized to react, often without much thought, to everyday situations.

This was where "third culture" training came in, with the third culture representing a group whose traditions differed from the trainees' own and, often, those of the eventual host country. Following on Goffman, third culture training was framed as a dress rehearsal for the live performance in front of the host country audience. The third culture could be any disenfranchised, marginal, or otherwise non-mainstream group living near the training site. By this definition, immigrant Thai communities in Hilo, Native Americans living on a reservation, and poor African Americans in urban "ghettos" all constituted "third cultures."[87] Systematic interaction with such groups would supposedly generate a sense of fruitful unfamiliarity that could help trainees to "feel the reality of cultural differences and the existence of coherent other ways of life."[88] They could also help rattle volunteers' preconceived notions about their own place in American society, making them realize that "we are strangers in our own land."[89] All this would prepare them for the inevitable strangeness they would be confronting in their field assignments.

Hawai'i was seen by many in the Peace Corps as an ideal site for exposing trainees to a third culture. This was because "nowhere else in the U.S. can you duplicate the combination of flexible facilities, climate, a local population of Asian background, and natural setting (big plantations, small farms, mountains, jungle, ocean, etc.)."[90] The physical plant of the training center, a converted hospital, was described as a kind of "Peace Corps College," complete with a dining facility where trainees were served "a mixed Asian-American diet that may be the best Peace Corps training food anywhere." The center's facilities were designed to help condition trainees for overseas life without causing unduly harsh cultural dislocation. For example, once trainees were "weaned" off milk, which would not be easily available in Asia, they were said to quickly develop a taste for the foreign food offered in the Peace Corps cafeteria.[91]

Cultural education was also supposed to take place outside the training center in Hilo and the surrounding area. Hilo, which had long been a major production center for Hawai'i's sugar industry, still possessed a largely plantation-based economy during the 1960s, one that relied heavily on labor from Asian immigrants and their descendants. The Peace Corps sought to take advantage of Hilo's demographic makeup, emphasizing its foreignness, and at the same time suggested that the Big Island community offered a level of cultural accessibility that might not be found in the host country. Hilo residents, from housewives to Sampan drivers, were expected to play the part of interlocutors for Peace Corps trainees.

Because Hilo was at once foreign *and* American, some argued, it provided Peace Corps trainees with a smoother transition to overseas life than would in-country training in the host nation. Immersion without preparation, according to Phillip Olsen, director of the Hawai'i Peace Corps program in 1970, would lead to "culture-shock instead of cultural understanding." In Hawai'i, by contrast, a trainee would be allowed to acquire confidence and skills in a relatively comfortable environment—"to *test* his abilities and experience some of the problems of inter-cultural relationships in local communities" and then "relate these to his forthcoming experience in a specific Host Country." Without the pressure to adjust to an overwhelmingly foreign culture, trainees in Hawai'i would be better able to hone their "sensitivity to cultural difference."[92] For all its talk about experiential education, the Peace Corps seemed to prize a certain level of critical distance when it came to cross-cultural encounters.

According to the Peace Corps, trainees needed only to leave the center for routine everyday activities to develop their cultural sensitivity. A report on the Thailand training program in Hilo suggested that trainees could acclimate to Thai culture by virtue of their daily activities in the city and surrounding area. It extolled the opportunities they would have to visit Asian shops and restaurants, where they would "encounter an Asian atmosphere and deal with people of Oriental ancestry."[93] Volunteers spent much of their time at the center learning the Thai language, but it was these kinds of off-site cultural experiences that the Peace Corps stressed as most useful. As one trainee reported, "Perhaps more important than fluency in Thai is the far more subtle knowledge of how to live with and by liked by the Thais."[94]

A more intensive experience involved a weeks-long stint in the Waipi'o Valley, a remote enclave on the Big Island, for what the Peace Corps called "Transition Training." The Waipi'o Valley, the seat of power for many early Hawaiian kings, had been flooded by a tsunami in 1946 that wiped out the small Chinese community that had settled there. By the time the Peace Corps arrived in the early 1960s, the valley—accessible only by a jeep ride along a tortuous and dangerously steep dirt road—was home to handful of Native

FIGURE 7. Peace Corps volunteers train with water buffalo in the Waipiʻo
Valley, 1960s. Photograph by Francis Haar, courtesy of Tom Haar.

Hawaiians growing taro. The Peace Corps treated the valley as a staging
ground for introducing trainees to an "exact replica" of the rural environs of
Thailand, the Philippines, Malaysia, and other countries in the region.[95] Here
Hawaiʻi, in contrast to its portrayal by the EWC as a paragon of modernity,
offered a throwback to a premodern way of life. An evaluation report of the
training interlude at Waipiʻo painted an idyllic scene of acculturation to simple
living: trainees would sleep in tents while building the camp, which involved
activities like "cutting grass in hip-deep swamps" to make huts, working with
water buffalo, watching cockfights, digging latrines, and taking care of a passel
of pigs. On Saturday afternoons, they would kill one of the pigs for a nighttime
luau on the beach.

The valley experience was supposed to inspire trainees to embrace physical
adventure and demonstrate flexibility in the face of unfamiliar material hardship, but it was interpersonal flexibility that the Peace Corps prized above all
else. In the middle of the evaluation report's description of trainees roughing it
together in the Waipiʻo Valley, there appeared a brief but revealing reference to
a scheduled weekly foray into cultural improvisation. On Sundays, the report

FIGURE 8. Peace Corps volunteers watch a cockfight during training in the Waipiʻo Valley, 1960s. Photograph by Ray Kramer, courtesy of the University of Hawaiʻi Library.

said, the trainees—presumably still digesting Saturday night's luau pig—"are taken out in pairs and dropped, usually unannounced, at various small Filipino and Japanese plantation worker camps nearby to learn what they can and make friends." This ad hoc approach to cultural training, in which it was thought that casually delivering a group of college-educated mainlanders to a community of unsuspecting Hilo farm laborers would produce interethnic friendship, evoked the parallel experience of volunteers being "dropped" at their overseas field assignments.[96]

An evaluation of Peace Corps training for volunteers to the Philippines similarly stressed the possibilities of interaction with Filipino immigrant populations in Hilo, yet it also implied that trainees should not yet seek to fully immerse themselves in Filipino culture. Adopting the tone of the anthropological discourse of the day, it claimed the Filipino villages around the site of Hilo's sugar industry provided volunteers with a chance to peek in on a representative tableau of Filipino culture, allowing them "to observe the behavior of the Filipino community, and to gain some familiarity with the homely but important aspects of Filipino personal life." Such exposure to Filipinos in Hawaiʻi would likely make volunteers "better equipped to deal with Filipino life in the Philippines—the differences between the two cultures notwithstanding."[97]

The possibility that Filipino immigrant life in Hawaiʻi might indeed be significantly different than Filipino life in the Philippines was of little concern to Peace Corps officials in the 1960s. Instead, Peace Corps training literature emphasized the need for volunteers to become cultural generalists. Third culture experience was supposed to help gird trainees for all manner of cross-cultural interaction. In the third culture approach, trainees would not be inundated by information on the particularities of a given host country. Instead, it would "prepare a trainee to work in any cross-cultural situation, rather than in a specific country."[98] Training was meant to provide volunteers with the emotional and intellectual tools for understanding social relations and effectively communicating with people in a variety of contexts. The discourses around Peace Corps training suggested the notion that once a person attained a high level of cultural fluency, he or she could simply be "dropped" in a foreign society and be able to flourish, even with scant prior knowledge of its history or local customs.

This approach to culture downplayed the social conditions and particularities that culture reflected. Instead, all too often the Peace Corps favored facile generalizations over an acknowledgment of the ways in which history, economic interests, and global relations of power had shaped—and continued to shape—Americans' relationship with the people the Peace Corps sought to understand.

Meanwhile, in Peace Corps training, the people of Hilo themselves, with their "designation as a human link between eastern and western worlds," were turned into cultural abstractions.[99] Like the people of the Third World for whom they were meant to stand in, they became objects onto which the Peace Corps projected its theories. In these discussions, as in many others around the fiftieth state, Hawaiʻi and its residents were open to seemingly endless interpretation. Hawaiʻi was chosen as a training site both for its Americanness and for its Asianness, as a place that was simultaneously modern, modernizing, and home to premodern enclaves such as the Waipiʻo Valley. It was Hawaiʻi's liminality that made it a model that could be replicated and applied to infinite "cross-cultural" situations.

And yet Peace Corps officials continued to return to a reductionist notion of Hawaiʻi's Asianness in justifying the training center's location. It is notable that, as in the Hawaiʻi statehood debates, Native Hawaiians were almost entirely absent from discussions of Hawaiʻi's usefulness as a Peace Corps training site, despite the fact that they might also have constituted a "third culture." Ultimately, it was Hawaiʻi's geographical and cultural proximity to Asia—the main site of American intervention during the Cold War—that made it an appealing place for Peace Corps training, and which reveals the ways in which intercultural training was used as a tool of power, even if its adherents did not see it that way themselves. Peace Corps volunteers were supposed to be "change agents" in their field assignments, and the main purpose of the Peace Corps was to transform host society culture, not simply to promote some vague notion of cross-cultural understanding. The latter was intended to facilitate the former.

For all its emphasis on fostering cultural understanding, the Peace Corps was invested in promoting *American* culture above all. And American culture, in classic exceptionalist fashion, was framed as both unique and universal. It was thus necessary that volunteers continue to see themselves as Americans. The goal was not for them to become so enamored of another culture that they adopted it as their own. It would be counterproductive, wrote one training manual, to send a volunteer who was susceptible to "'going native' [as] a means of reducing tension." Rather, volunteers must be capable of "adapt[ing] their own values, needs, etc., to those of the culture within which they wish to work, without losing their identity as Americans."[100] After all, the Peace Corps suggested, it was volunteers' very Americanness—their technical expertise, work ethic, and open-mindedness—that made them valuable to a host country. Why else would they be there?

The Peace Corps, as a complex, ambiguous expression of American power, may have represented an alternative to military action in the Third World. And indeed, there was not much overlap between those who enlisted in the Peace Corps and the Marine Corps. But the Peace Corps's use of military nomenclature also suggested the complementarity between the missions of civilian and military intervention during the Cold War. Hawai'i, again, illuminates these connections. In addition to its designation as cultural bridge to Asia, Hawai'i was also the staging ground for America's largest post–World War II intervention in Asia: the Vietnam War. As the site of the U.S. military's Pacific Command—"the earthly foundation for a truly awesome power projection across some 100 million square miles of land and sea"—Hawai'i was Washington's base for conducting the war and was usually the final U.S. way station for troops bound for Vietnam.[101] Although Hawai'i was far removed from Vietnam's battlefields, the war had a deep, if sometimes invisible, impact on the state. For instance, during the war's height, one in seven Hawai'i residents was either a member of the military or a dependent, and its population suffered a significantly higher proportion of combat deaths than any other state.[102]

Hawai'i's role as a conduit for American power in the Pacific, both before and after the Vietnam War, was rooted in its deep historical ties to the military. For decades, beginning with the U.S. acquisition of exclusive leasing rights to Pearl Harbor in 1887, the rhetoric around Hawai'i as "gateway to the Pacific" had a decidedly martial inflection. Hawai'i, according to U.S. naval strategist

Alfred Thayer Mahan in 1893, was "unrivaled" in its "geographical and military importance" to America's effort to establish naval dominance over China.[103] Later, it was the Japanese attack on the U.S. naval fleet at Pearl Harbor in 1941 that alerted many mainland Americans to Hawai'i's relationship to the United States, and of Hawai'i's importance to American expansionist ambitions in the Pacific. In 1947, Truman established the United States Pacific Command in Hawai'i—the first of its kind—unifying all branches of the armed forces serving in the Pacific under one authority and solidifying Hawai'i's position as America's largest and most important military hub. That role was amplified a few years later with the outbreak of the Korean War and the massive military expansion it entailed.

Hawai'i's military significance was consistently obscured, however, in statehood-era public discourse on the islands' role as "bridge to Asia." Politicians such as Daniel Inouye—one of America's longest serving senators and a World War II veteran who consistently championed the defense industry—labored in closed committee rooms to maintain a constant flow of military dollars into the state. But the image state officials and other Hawai'i boosters broadcast to America, and to the world, was of a place that advanced international cooperation through nonviolent vehicles such as the EWC and Peace Corps training. Thus, even as the Pentagon was quietly moving personnel from Hawai'i to Okinawa in anticipation of a major troop buildup in Vietnam in May 1965, President Johnson praised the East-West Center for fostering "a world ultimately of peace, of friendship."[104] And yet the effort to promote Hawai'i as a center for mutual understanding was not simply a means of masking its parallel role as a military hub. Rather, the two projects often drew inspiration from and amplified each other.

The principle of mutual understanding as a tool of modernization was deployed even in the violent context of the American invasion of Vietnam, where it was understood as both antidote and adjunct to military action. While the U.S. government devalued the individual lives of the Vietnamese people, it emphasized the need to capture the "hearts and minds" of the Vietnamese masses through propaganda and development programs. Working with the South Vietnamese state, the United States promoted development as form of counterinsurgency. This was exemplified by the Strategic Hamlet Program, which relocated peasants into fortified areas that were subject to "social engineering" geared toward transforming rural life. Often referred to as "the other war," pacification's stated goal was to "win loyalties rather than kill insurgents."[105] By offering peasants the benefits of modernity—infrastructure, schools, agricultural technology, healthcare—the pacification campaign aimed to strengthen the legitimacy of the South Vietnamese state and combat the lure of communism.[106]

Hawai'i again found itself at the center of the efforts to secure American military power in the Pacific through its relationship with USAID. The agency targeted Hawai'i to help push forward the "second front" in Vietnam for familiar reasons: "because the island state's tropical environment, multi-racial population and rural community patterns are unique in the United States" and thus offered a "total environment most conducive to achieving the training objectives of cross-cultural communication" in Vietnam.[107] In support of a special USAID recruitment effort aimed at the people of Hawai'i, Governor Burns in 1965 appealed to state residents to join USAID's ranks in Vietnam by praising them as "uniquely equipped" with "native ability" to "maintain effective and harmonious relationships" and to "adapt to alien cultures and rapidly changing conditions."[108]

Vietnam, in this framing, was little different from the Philippines, Thailand, or other U.S. allies in Asia linked to the EWC and the Peace Corps. It should be similarly receptive to Hawai'i's singular brand of social harmony and its modernizing example. And civilian involvement in wartime Vietnam would raise Hawai'i's profile, according to Burns, as it would further the ongoing effort to "gain even greater recognition for Hawaii's capabilities as the hub of influence in the Asian-Pacific world."[109] As the state's most tireless cheerleader, Burns saw in Vietnam another opportunity to demonstrate Hawai'i's cultural exceptionality, and thereby its enduring usefulness to the United States, beyond the islands' strategic location. But while he glossed over Hawai'i's warmaking ties to Vietnam by emphasizing its role as a cultural bridge, Burns also exposed the conceptual and material links between Hawai'i's cultural exchange programs and U.S. military intervention.

By the spring of 1966, USAID had established the Asia Training Center (ATC) at the University of Hawai'i for its staff en route to Vietnam. The center marked the intensification and centralization of USAID's pacification efforts in Vietnam, which would come under direct military control the next year as part of the new Civil Operations and Revolutionary Development Support program (CORDS). It also demonstrated the impact on the wider foreign policy establishment of the cultural training practices being developed in Hawai'i. The curriculum of the ATC, which was initially headed by Peace Corps program director John Stalker, was based on Peace Corps training in Hilo. Indeed, the university was chosen for USAID training because of its "demonstrated competence in training Peace Corps Volunteers for service in South and East Asian countries."[110]

Like the Peace Corps, the ATC stressed cultural sensitivity as a tool of modernization. Training emphasized the necessity of psychological transformation—for both USAID workers and the Vietnamese—as the first step toward advancing pacification. The people of Vietnam needed to be made to feel invested in "the business of development," which in turn required "understanding, experience, sensitivity and a new order" on the part of USAID workers.[111] To inculcate this new understanding among USAID trainees, the ATC employed what was essentially "third culture" theory: "intensive" residential training would facilitate regular contact between USAID workers and Asian members of the training staff, and trainees would also take part in "imaginatively planned field experiences" in Hawai'i's ethnic enclaves "to simulate the conditions" AID officers might find in Vietnam.[112] In contrast to State Department resistance to using Hawai'i as a "conditioning center" a decade earlier, it was now embracing Hawai'i's foreignness.

Unlike Peace Corps volunteers, USAID staff trained in Hawai'i had an explicitly military mission. Reflecting this orientation, the USAID program was located near Pearl Harbor, rather than embedded in a civilian community like the Peace Corps' Hilo campus. But the parallels in approach demonstrate the ways in which mutual understanding was meant to bolster American power, both military and cultural, in the Pacific. Fittingly, military training in Hawai'i relied on the same tactics adopted by the ATC and developed by the Peace Corps. As Simeon Man shows, to prepare soldiers for guerrilla combat, training exercises used Asian and Hawaiian personnel to act as Vietnamese "natives" in elaborately constructed mock villages in O'ahu's jungles— practices that "collapsed the distinction between Hawai'i and Vietnam."[113] Similarly, USAID training in Hawai'i collapsed the boundaries between military and cultural strategies for advancing American expansion. For USAID, the cultural sensitivity learned in Hawai'i was supposed to secure American military victory in Vietnam. While mutual understanding became an adjunct to development, development became a tool of military strategy. This was especially true after the formation of CORDS, which made clear to USAID staff that development was "a means [rather] than an end," with winning the war the ultimate goal.[114]

The contradictions between development and military intervention in Vietnam were brought into relief in a more visible forum when President Johnson called for a high profile summit of South Vietnamese and American leaders in Honolulu in February 1966. Hawai'i's capital was frequently the site of such meetings, but this one stood out for its content and for the unprecedented level of publicity it garnered. Johnson, who attended the summit himself, hastily arranged the event to focus on pacification and development. Just as Governor Burns had downplayed Hawai'i's involvement in the war by emphasizing the state's identity as peaceful "bridge to Asia," Johnson, by highlighting the "nonmilitary" aspects of the war, hoped to deflect attention from the resumption of Operation Rolling Thunder and stave off growing public criticism of escalation.[115] To that end, the closing statement of the summit focused not

FIGURE 9. President Lyndon Johnson arriving in Hawai'i for the Honolulu
Conference on the Vietnam War, February 5, 1966. Photographed by
Yoichi Okamoto, courtesy of the LBJ Presidential Library.

on military aims, but on a positive message of promoting democracy and
development. The governments of the United States and South Vietnam, it
promised, were dedicated to "a true social revolution" and to constructing "a
modern society in which every man can know that he has a future."[116]

The Declaration of Honolulu, as the statement was labeled, encapsulated
the ironies of Hawai'i's role as a center for both "mutual understanding" and
warmaking—and of the broader tensions between America's dual commit-
ments to ideological and military expansion in the Third World. Indeed, both
ideological and military intervention failed in Vietnam: the war would go on
for another six years, resulting in millions of deaths and the unification of
the country under a communist government. Nor did the Declaration appear
to have any short-term effect. Within weeks of the conference, a coalition of
Buddhists, dissident members of the South Vietnamese military, and students
demonstrated the bankruptcy of pacification by organizing a massive months-
long uprising in South Vietnam to oppose the American-supported military
junta. The movement was eventually extinguished not through mutual understanding, but by South Vietnamese forces, further undermining American
and South Vietnamese claims to political legitimacy.[117] Meanwhile, escalating
costs for the war in Vietnam meant cuts in federal funding for the EWC and
other cultural diplomacy programs.[118]

The gap between the discourse of mutual understanding and the violence perpetrated in Vietnam did not go unnoticed in Hawai'i. The University of Hawai'i, like other campuses across the United States, was a site of antiwar activism. But it was a small number of antiwar students at the nationally funded EWC who raised the most concern among federal and state officials.[119] Indeed, EWC students who opposed the war threatened to reveal the limitations of cultural interchange—and of the hypocrisy of the government's stated commitment to mutual understanding between the United States and Southeast Asia while waging a war against Southeast Asians. One EWC student, John Witeck, a native of Virginia who was working toward a graduate degree in Asian Studies, courted the attention of the State Department when he burned his draft card on campus in April 1968. Witeck, presumably, came to the EWC because of its claims to foster mutual understanding, but now he denounced the EWC as an agent of a corrupt U.S. government. "Moral imagination," Witeck wrote in an editorial in the EWC's student newsletter, was being "suppressed at this American-financed Center, which chooses instead to conduct business as usual, despite the slaughter of thousands of Vietnamese a week by this Center's patron." He criticized EWC grantees for enjoying the benefits of living in a "'disneyland' of unreal, intercultural inertia," while being "unwilling or unable to demonstrate their convictions." Interculturalism, Witeck implied, could serve to blind its adherents to global injustice and inequalities of power—students were performing interculturalism in the rarefied setting of the EWC without understanding how cultural encounters played out, often violently, in reality.[120]

EWC chancellor Howard Jones worried that radicals like Witeck might jeopardize the center's funding. In a letter in April 1968 to Governor Burns about the visit to the EWC by a congressional investigative team, Jones warned that they might recommend substantial budget cuts if students like Witeck, "who disagreed publicly with U.S. policy on Vietnam," were allowed to remain enrolled.[121] Although the cuts never came, the Witeck case exacerbated tensions between the University of Hawai'i and the State Department, which insisted the "national interest" mission of the center set it apart from the rest of the university. While Jones was reluctant to expel Witeck for fear of fueling further student protest and provoking criticism abroad, Assistant Secretary of State Edward Re viewed the matter in starker terms. Re urged Jones to expel Witeck on the basis of "conduct considered by the Center to be prejudicial to its program."[122] Though Re halfheartedly deferred to the authority of the university administration to decide Witeck's fate, he clearly chafed at the State Department's lack of control over university disciplinary matters. Whereas Re's predecessors had wanted to eschew responsibility for the EWC when it was conceived, the State Department now recognized it as an instrument of foreign policy.

Concerns over the University of Hawai'i's execution of the EWC's national mission prompted Washington to wrest ever more control, eventually leading to the EWC's incorporation in 1975 as an autonomous organization funded by the federal government.[123] Like the increased emphasis on technical training years earlier, this severance from the university underscored the declining belief in interchange for its own sake, with the government now making clear that the EWC serve as a more direct agent of national interests. Interchange, though always framed in terms of its benefits to foreign policy, now needed adequate direction, and containment, if it were to realize those benefits. The instrumentalism of cultural exchange was now made explicit.

The ideas of interchange and cross-cultural communication developed in Hawai'i had not been discredited. Far from it. But they had been transformed over the course of the 1960s. Mutual understanding and cultural sensitivity were no longer end goals, offering vague promises of international goodwill; they were now tools to be mastered and applied with precision. This was exemplified by the military's efforts to weaponize cross-cultural training for use in Vietnam, where mutual understanding was expected to serve particular strategic objectives.

Meanwhile, these ideas were also being codified as the basis for a new industry. As the Peace Corps was transitioning to host country training programs in the early 1970s, administrators of the Hawai'i program noted that the knowledge trainees had acquired could serve them well in future careers. "From the Peace Corps experience have come thousands of Americans with skills in intercultural relations, many of whom are now applying these skills in assignments such as ghetto teaching," asserted a report. It went on to predict that Hawai'i would be at the center of the development of "a new profession" under the rubric of "Applied Human Science." Building on its experience in providing intercultural training to Peace Corps volunteers, the university might incorporate such programming into its general curriculum, to produce "qualified cross-cultural practitioners who could become involved in the rapidly proliferating training industry."[124] Going beyond vague ideas of mutual understanding, the proposal envisioned the professionalization of cross-cultural skills.

Hawai'i was indeed at the forefront of intercultural training, which took off with rapid globalization in the 1970s and 1980s and is now a mainstay of institutional life in the United States and Europe. In 1970 UH-Hilo inaugurated the Center for Cross-Cultural Training and Research—by all evidence the first of its kind. Headed by Phillip Olsen, fresh off his stint as director of the Hawai'i Peace Corps program, the center, among other activities, produced a quarterly journal, *Trends,* dedicated to research on intercultural communication.[125] Although the center at Hilo was short-lived, UH continued to be at the forefront of this emerging field, with several of its key figures based in Hawaiʻi—including Wilbur Schramm, who stayed on as emeritus professor after his directorship of the EWC's Communication Institute, and K. S. Sitaram, an early leader in establishing intercultural communication as a legitimate academic discipline, who began his career as an assistant professor at UH in the early 1970s.[126]

Meanwhile, cultural sensitivity would become a foundational term of multiculturalist ideology. The way these related developments evolved in Hawaiʻi illuminates the links between the nature of American empire in the 1960s and changing racial paradigms in domestic American society. The ease with which advocates of cultural sensitivity could transition from discussing the experiences of Peace Corps volunteers overseas to the applicability of such skills in American "ghetto" schools is remarkable. It demonstrates how U.S. policymakers, educators, and others understood the problem of social difference in the context of global expansion. The discourses around 1960s Hawaiʻi—a state residing at the nexus of the domestic and the global—also help track the shift toward multiculturalism as a replacement for the rigid racial frameworks of the past. At the same time, the emergence of multiculturalism in Hawaiʻi points to an increasingly popular assumption among policymakers and social scientists that all social difference could be explained by culture, rather than race or structural inequality. That idea would be reinscribed and elaborated in Hawaiʻi's culture industries themselves, which sought not to master difference or even understand it, but to profit from it.

4

Selling the "Golden People"

HAWAI'I TOURISM AND THE
COMMODIFICATION OF RACIAL TOLERANCE

FOR AMERICANS AT the height of the jet age, a Hawai'i vacation started at thirty thousand feet. To conjure an aura of glamour and excitement around travel to Hawai'i, the major air carriers with routes to Honolulu sought to ensure that a plane trip to the islands would be unlike any other domestic flight. Claiming that "for most people a visit to Hawaii is not just a routine journey but a fulfillment of long-held expectations," United Airlines promised its passengers would "step into Hawai'i" when boarding its Royal Hawaiian Jet, where stewardesses in tropical print uniforms would serve a "full-course gourmet adventure" consisting of Filet Mignon Teriyaki or "Hawaiian style" lobster.[1] In a similar vein, Hawaiian Airlines entreated its inter-island customers to picture themselves flying in comfort while sipping a Mai Tai served by stewardesses representing "the many ethnic heritages of Hawai'i" and emanating the "gentle spirit of fellowship and goodwill" said to be the core characteristic of Hawai'i society.[2]

For all its claims that Hawai'i was a dream vacationland of effortless calm and sociability, the tourism industry's work to maintain such appearances was anything but effortless. Behind the relaxed façade of the Hawai'i holiday was an army of marketers, managers, and service workers laboring to provide tourists with a seamless experience of paradise. Though the tourism industry sought to impart a timeless quality to Hawai'i's paradise image, the ways in which the islands were marketed in the poststatehood era were shaped by larger economic, political, and cultural forces of the era. It was with statehood in 1959 that mass Hawai'i tourism industry was born—and with it, new ways of selling, traveling, and imagining multicultural selfhood.

With jet service in Hawai'i also arriving in 1959, the tourism industry, aided by the state government, worked to exploit the state's newfound prominence, luring planeloads of mainlanders who thronged its beaches, hotels, and cultural spectacles. As Hawai'i sought to distinguish itself from other vacationlands, it spun a dual narrative of racial difference and racial mixing to help sell the islands as a unique destination where mainlanders could purchase a transformative leisure experience. This was part of a larger discourse around Hawai'i's special role as a multiethnic offshore state of the United States. But it also took on a life and logic of its own as race was deployed in the service of large-scale financial gain.

For a geographically isolated archipelago in the middle of the Pacific without much in the way of an industrial or financial sector to draw large numbers of business travelers, such numbers are remarkable. The most visible impact of the rise of Hawai'i tourism after statehood would be on Hawai'i itself, but Hawai'i tourism also left its mark on American culture and society more broadly, if less conspicuously. As tourism grew to be an increasingly important driver of economic growth in other U.S. states and in nations around the world, Hawai'i positioned itself at the forefront of this global trend and heralded a shift to a service-oriented economy in the wake of deindustrialization. In this new political economy, occupational skill was increasingly measured in terms of personal presentation and performance, and less by one's productive capabilities. In the case of Hawai'i, such performance was often centered around the representation of positive race relations.

Hawai'i tourism helped turn racial tolerance into a saleable, if abstract, commodity. To be sure, the tourism industry sought to entice mainlanders with the allure of warm weather and scenic beauty. But it also coaxed them with an invitation to partake in the islands' celebrated "Aloha Spirit": an elusive vision of social harmony that was supposedly the defining feature of the Hawai'i vacation. By attending ethnic festivals, eating exotic food, and interacting with locals—dubbed "the Golden People" in tourism literature—visitors might even bring some Aloha Spirit home with them. Hawai'i's multiethnic society thus became not only a site of consumption, but also an object of consumption itself.

The consumption of racialized commodities or cosmopolitan experiences was nothing new.[3] But the consumption of Hawai'i during the mid- to late twentieth century represented something different. After a statehood campaign that succeeded by framing Hawai'i's admission as a boon to American foreign policy, the tourism industry's portrayal of Hawai'i as a racial utopia must be seen as part of the ascendency of American liberalism in the era of decolonization. Situated in this context, the modern Hawai'i tourism industry was not simply an extension of its colonial antecedent, although the legacies of Hawai'i's colonial past would continue to haunt touristic imagery. Tourism producers in the poststatehood era were selling a packaged experience of both ethnic difference and racial tolerance. Rather than traveling to Hawaiʻi to psychologically affirm their commitment to white supremacy as their colonialist predecessors had done, mainland tourists to Hawaiʻi in the poststatehood era were participating in the commodification of an emerging multiculturalist ideal, one that validated American liberal beliefs in racial progress.

Americans' embrace of multiculturalist ideology was made possible, and necessary, by the same structural processes of globalization and decolonization that turned Hawaiʻi into both an American state and a site for mass tourism. As the colonial system came to be replaced with less formal structures of economic and political power, America—and Americans, equipped with passports and plane tickets in their back pockets—acquired a larger global presence than ever before. The impact of American expansionism was not only felt by foreign peoples, however. America's rising global status also required Americans to acquire new outlooks and new practices. To prove their nation's benevolent intentions, Americans were asked to perform their racial tolerance—at home and abroad—for a global audience.

The records of the Hawaii Visitors Bureau, an institution heavily subsidized by the new state government, offer a lens onto how state and business interests together created a corporate multicultural vision for Hawaiʻi. Marketers seized on the discourses around Hawaiʻi statehood, which portrayed multiracial Hawaiʻi as a "bridge to Asia" that would help the United States win the allegiance of the decolonizing world by demonstrating its commitment to cultural diversity, anticolonialism, and racial egalitarianism. In the wake of statehood and Hawaiʻi's designation as a site for "mutual understanding," the tourism industry suggested to ordinary Americans that they too could take part in international cultural exchange. And they did not have to go to "the Orient" to see it: Hawaiʻi could provide them with an entertaining crash course in cosmopolitanism.

At the same time, tourism literature implied that Americans could overcome the domestic racial divisions of the post–civil rights era through the buying and selling of racial tolerance. But the marketing of Hawaiʻi revealed the contradictory nature of racial discourse during the latter half of the twentieth century. Tourists were invited to be entertained by Hawaiʻi's Golden People, who were portrayed as both a blended race and a collage of disparate ethnicities. Such rhetoric evoked the tension at the heart of the emerging global discourse of multiculturalism—over whether the goal of liberal society was to protect difference or to incorporate difference in service of unity—and scrubbed it of any political salience.

Not all tourists, however, were sold on a vision of Hawaiʻi as a multicultural paradise. Servicemen on leave from Vietnam, who accounted for one-fifth of tourism revenue in the late 1960s and early 1970s, came to Hawaiʻi to visit the

United States, not to experience Asia—where the United States was waging a war that relied on an assumption of American superiority over Asian society and culture. Against this background, the Hawai'i R&R program relied in part on older Orientalist tropes about the dangers of East–West encounters.

These inconsistencies reflected both the limits of racial liberalism as well as a prioritizing of revenue at the expense of ideological coherence. The tourism industry only asked as much of its consumers as it believed would be profitable. Ultimately, the racial enlightenment that the Hawai'i tourism industry was selling was intended to serve commercial ends, not political ones. The iconic Hawai'i tourist in the marketing materials of the poststatehood years was a member of Francesco Adinolfi's jet-setting "cocktail generation": worldly but not radical.[4]

Just as many tourists were invited to buy into racial tolerance, the people of Hawai'i were asked to provide that racial tolerance for tourists to consume. As tourism became an ever more significant sector of Hawai'i's economy, the tourism industry increasingly sought to rationalize the Aloha Spirit, its expression now an economic imperative of poststatehood society rather than its foundational ethos. The progressive veneer of Hawai'i tourism literature thus often obscured the more conservative goals of many tourism boosters, who were less committed to advancing social justice than to promoting capitalist development in Hawai'i—though they often claimed, and many seemed to believe, that the latter reinforced the former. In turning race and racial tolerance into commodities, sold by laborers in an expanding service sector, the Hawai'i tourism industry of the 1960s and 1970s is a prime example of the postmodernist turn in American culture. Postmodern culture has been shaped by a system of late capitalism that celebrates the performance of difference while denying the structures of power undergirding it. In Hawai'i, the politics of difference were glossed over in favor of a simulacrum of racial harmony. While the Aloha Spirit may not have been entirely imagined, its representation in the service of capitalism changed its valence, neutering it of history and complexity.

———

Before the bombing of Pearl Harbor, Hawai'i occupied a position of near-reverence in American popular imagination—a dreamland physically unreachable for all but the most fortunate. The touristic image of "Hawaii," as Beth Bailey and David Farber write, "had been purposefully constructed by businesses that lived on tourism, and then elaborated in thousands of public and private fantasies in the new consumer culture of America."[5] While such representations of Hawai'i tourism in mass culture were largely an early twentieth century phenomenon, the Hawai'i tourism industry itself had been a large part of Hawai'i's economy since the nineteenth century. Beginning well before the United States annexed the islands, boosters in Hawai'i sought to profit from America's emerging tourist class. At the same time, as Christine Skwiot argues, touristic literature and travel writing fundamentally shaped Hawai'i's relationship to the United States, helping to create the ideological justifications for American white settlement in Hawai'i as well as the islands' eventual annexation.[6] Celebrated travel writers such as Robert Louis Stevenson and Mark Twain—who famously deemed Hawai'i the "loveliest fleet of islands that lies anchored in any ocean"—helped create Hawai'i's reputation as an exotic, almost transcendent tropical paradise ripe for both tourists and white settlers.

This was also an image underwritten by the state, first under the monarchy, which funded steamship lines and the construction of the first Royal Hawaiian Hotel, and later the revolutionary and territorial regimes. After the overthrow of the Hawaiian monarchy, the territory's highly organized business interests worked to consolidate the tourism industry, founding the Hawaii Promotion Committee in 1902, a public-private venture that would morph into the Hawaii Visitors Bureau (HVB) in 1945.

Meanwhile, local business elites, previously focused almost entirely on agriculture, began expanding into tourism. The Matson Navigation Company, the territory's dominant shipping line, started carrying a new kind of cargo— wealthy tourists—on a series of ever more opulent liners. Matson reigned over pre–World War II tourism in Hawai'i, transporting visitors as well as housing them in grand hotels, including the new Royal Hawaiian Hotel, the grand "Pink Palace" that opened in 1927 and continues to anchor the Waikiki strip. Amplifying the tourism industry's promotional efforts was a series of films set in in the islands, many of them romantic dramas such as *Bird of Paradise* (1932) and *Waikiki Wedding* (1937), that cemented the image of Hawai'i as paradise. A popular radio show, *Hawaii Calls,* which began broadcasting to the mainland in 1935 from the Moana Hotel, featured languorous, steel guitar–heavy music that quickly became synonymous with tropical holidaymaking.

Tourism bolstered haole power by attracting affluent mainlanders to the Royal Hawaiian and other luxurious Waikiki resorts "designed to keep social and racial inferiors at bay."[7] This social inequality that haoles celebrated was inscribed onto Hawai'i's landscape, as tourism transformed marshy Waikiki from a neighborhood of local farmers and fishermen into an enclave for elites.[8] Meanwhile, white supremacy in Hawai'i was reinforced by the primitivist discourse—distilled in the image of a "lovely languid lady strumming the ukulele on the beach"—that dominated tourism materials in the prestatehood years.[9] Hawai'i's early tourism industry relied on a set of visual tropes that portrayed the islands as havens of "soft primitivism," embodied by the friendly and sexually available hula girl.[10] This spectacle of the hula girl—in performances both in Hawai'i and on the mainland—was also part of an anti-Asian discourse that "erased Asians from the territory" during much of the first half of the twentieth century.[11]

But while luaus and hula girls would certainly remain stock components of Hawai'i tourism imagery, during the statehood era such tropes came to coexist with the equally powerful theme of Hawai'i as an egalitarian multi-racial paradise for a new age—one in which Native Hawaiians often consti-tuted one among several ethnic groups in the islands' "montage of minorities." Statehood, which made Hawai'i legally equal to the rest of the United States, along with the concurrent development of jet service to Hawai'i, changed the tourism game, both in terms of tourism's revenue-generating potential and the ideological stakes of the visitor industry's portrayal of the new state. The transformation of the Hawai'i tourism industry from an important sector of Hawai'i's economy to *the* driver of economic growth was fundamentally shaped by statehood.

As the image of Hawai'i as a multiracial paradise emerged from the state-hood debates, the tourism industry worked to alter its own vision of Hawai'i-as-paradise to suit this new narrative. It suggested that to visit Hawai'i was to partake in a nationalist project that advanced both American foreign policy and the negotiation of racial difference at home.[12] American tourism boosters had long linked nationalism and vacationing.[13] During the Cold War, however, tourism was invested with new meaning as the tourism industry and the U.S. government worked together to spread American ideology and development models abroad.[14] Tourism to Asia, as Christina Klein argues, became a "form of geopolitical engagement" for ordinary Americans. To that end, the State Department during the height of the Cold War instructed American tourists abroad not to behave arrogantly or violate "common bonds of decency."[15] As the U.S. government sought to win friends in the so-called Third World, it asked Americans—passports in hand—to perform their embrace of diversity for a global audience. Poststatehood Hawai'i offered the perfect stage for this per-formance. As a former colony with a majority Asian population that was now America's newest state, and as a symbol of American egalitarianism that was also a gateway for Americans into the realm of the foreign, Hawai'i met multiple ideological demands at once. In Hawai'i, a space between the domestic and the global, the national and international objectives of tourism cohered.

After 1959, the state became ever more engaged in promoting Hawai'i tour-ism, helping the quasi-public HVB to become a highly organized marketing machine that would play a determinative role in the trajectory of the poststate-hood economy. At the same time, tourism was instrumental in bringing about the rise of the modern promotional state, which viewed attracting investor dollars through the branding and selling of "Hawaii" as equally important as governance. Indeed, many conservatives in Hawai'i believed promoting tourism was a better use of state funds than social service expenditures.[16] The HVB in the poststatehood years went from being a basic travel promotion agency focused mostly on short-term goals to a state-mandated "marketing arm of tourism for the entire State of Hawaii," with the task of "making tourism the keystone of the Hawaiian economy" and serving as catalyst for other economic growth sectors.[17] To that end, its budget tripled between 1958 and 1968 and the proportion of government investment in it rose from a little over half to nearly three-quarters.[18]

Those efforts paid off. After witnessing steady but modest gains in visitor arrivals in the decade and a half after World War II, the number of continental American tourists to Hawai'i nearly doubled between 1958 and 1960, leading the Hawai'i state planning office to brag that "more Americans dream about taking a vacation in Hawaii than any place else in the United States."[19] Tourism quickly outpaced Hawai'i's other leading industries, notably defense, along with sugar and pineapple production. By 1968 tourism's share of GDP had eclipsed that of military expenditures, and by 1977 it was producing more revenues than all federal spending in Hawai'i combined.[20] By 1970, Hawai'i would be host to 1.7 million annual visitors—ten times as many as the year before statehood.[21] That meant that Hawai'i, with a population of less than 800,000 in 1970, had more than twice as many annual visitors as residents. This was a trend that would only intensify; by the end of the twentieth century annual visitors would outnumber residents by nearly six to one.

Such changes took place as Hawai'i was experiencing unprecedented national attention, with books, films, and print media feeding eager mainland audiences with stories and images of America's newest state that emphasized the islands' mixing of cultures. James Michener's wildly popular *Hawaii*, an epic fictional account published in 1959 of "how disparate peoples . . . ultimately joined together to build America's strong and vital fiftieth state," was the third bestselling novel of the year.[22] As the debates around statehood increasingly focused on Hawai'i's polyglot society, it became difficult for the tourism industry to ignore the emerging narrative possibilities. This was a point driven home by prominent travel writer Horace Sutton, who urged Hawai'i's tourism industry in 1960 to make better use of the islands' multiethnic culture. Why, he asked, were people in Hawai'i "so proud of your Asian ties socially and politically, and so shy about them touristically?" He went on to question traditional marketing strategies that left mainlanders in the dark about "the magnificent lore brought here and still cultivated by the Chinese, the Japanese, the Filipinos and the Koreans" and uninitiated in the exotic foodstuffs—such as fresh ginger, water chestnuts, and watercress—that were prominent in Honolulu grocery stores yet absent from hotel restaurant menus.[23]

Within a few years, Hawai'i's tourism industry had begun to put Sutton's advice into practice. This was partly driven by perceived market demands. Hawai'i, according to the HVB, had much to offer the visitor in terms of "eating, drinking, loafing, relaxing, recreational sporting, and enjoyment of beautiful scenery and equable climate."[24] But this was not enough. While the islands had made great advances in securing a reliable base of visitors from the West Coast, the Hawai'i tourism industry had its eye on all mainland consumers, and in particular the lucrative East Coast market. As a result, it was in competition with other scenic warm-weather destinations, such as Florida or the Bahamas, that had geographical proximity on their side. Part of the solution, according to the HVB, could be found in increased capital for tourism promotion. To that end, it consistently called on the state to ramp up funding for its work, claiming in 1960, for instance, that "tremendous sums are being spent elsewhere by other tourism promotion agencies—expenditures which are proving to be highly profitable investments." While Hawai'i's tourism promotion budget was only $1.6 million for 1960–61, it pointed out, Bermuda was close behind at $1.5 million and Nassau substantially ahead at $2.3 million.[25]

Lack of adequate funding for tourism promotion was only part of the problem, however. The HVB believed that the content of tourism marketing and of touristic experience itself were just as important, if not more so. Noting that the Hawai'i tourism industry oversaw the production of "a single intangible product—'visitor satisfactions,'" the HVB warned that Hawai'i must find a way to distinguish the "intangible" qualities of a Hawai'i vacation if it wanted to draw tourists away from other destination areas. "Unless Hawaii continues to provide visitors with more high quality satisfactions per visitor dollar than do competing arenas," it said in 1961, "Hawaii cannot continue its rapid growth as a world travel center." Increasingly in the poststatehood years, such visitor satisfaction was believed to hinge on providing visitors with positive racial experiences. Against the background of an expanding foreign market for American tourists, the Hawai'i tourism industry saw itself as up against not only other tropical vacationlands, but also the whole of Western Europe, which in the postwar years had become the most popular overseas leisure destination for Americans. According to a 1961 HVB survey of mainland tourists who had chosen to visit places other than Hawai'i, around half of those interviewed had gone to Europe instead. This, the HVB surmised, was because Europe had "intellectual-cultural" appeal—unlike Hawai'i, whose reputation as a "sensuous paradise" had obscured its more substantive attributes. "The need for self-improvement, for cultural development, for widening of intellectual horizons, is a strong one, and appears to be the powerful magnet drawing visitors to Europe," the marketing survey concluded. It ended by declaring that "a clear implication of this study is the desirability of developing the intellectual-cultural appeals to supplement (not replace) the physical-sensuous." In order for Hawai'i to realize the "rich potential in this neglected area," it must do a better job of selling the "unique diversity and intermingling of races and cultures" to potential tourists.[26]

To that end, the tourism industry set out to entice visitors with the promise that a Hawai'i vacation consisted not only of sun, sand, and fruity cocktails but also included a life-changing encounter with Hawai'i's racial difference and the islands' culture of ethnic harmony. Tourists were urged to come to Hawai'i and immerse themselves in the glow of the Aloha Spirit, a concept that, in the tourism industry's phrasing of it, called up a vision of social amity, ethnic spectacle, and general well-being all at once. It was a term that had been used by the tourism industry before statehood, but usually as a vague reference to Polynesian hospitality and the friendliness of Hawai'i's "local color" rather than a more layered invocation of the ideal of liberal pluralism.[27] In the period after statehood, the Aloha Spirit acquired new meaning. While the language and imagery around the Aloha Spirit alluded to earlier touristic portrayals of Hawai'i as a welcoming Polynesian paradise—indeed, the Aloha Spirit was said to have originated among Native Hawaiians—they also drew on broader social and political discourses that emphasized Hawai'i's unique status as a multiethnic American state in the heart of the Pacific.

The Reverend Abraham Akaka, arguably the most famous Hawai'i clergyman of his time and pastor of the historic Kawaiaha'o Church in Honolulu (once the chapel of the Hawaiian royal family), offered an extended description of the concept of the Aloha Spirit in 1966 that reflected common usage of the term in the poststatehood era. To mainlanders who wondered, "How it is that here people of such divergent cultures can thrive without hostility or prejudice," he first reviewed the most popular sociological theories: Hawai'i's small size, its mild climate, its history of intermarriage. But, he went on, "there is something more." He explained:

> This we call the "Aloha Spirit"—the heritage each man finds if he adopts these Islands as his own. Those of us who hold this theory believe God designed these Islands for immigrants. Everyone here, from the members of the oldest Hawaiian families to the visitors disembarking from planes today, are immigrants. . . . Despite the great numbers of immigrants, the Hawaiians—the first settlers of the Islands—have survived the influence of the newcomer. While each immigrant group brought something of its native culture to Hawaii, it also adopted a way of life from the Hawaiians. It absorbed what we call the "Aloha Spirit"—the friendliness, humbleness of

the Hawaiians. To the malihini—the newcomer—the word "aloha" at first means simply "hello" or "goodbye." But it does not take the newcomer long to learn that there is a deeper meaning to "aloha"—kindness and gracious-ness, love and understanding. . . . Yet the "Aloha Spirit" is not something we of the Islands wish to retain only for ourselves. We offer it to the world.[28]

Akaka's account of the Aloha Spirit could have comprised a church sermon. Indeed, it likely started out as one. And so it is telling that this particular pas-sage appeared not in a sermon, but inside the pages of United Airlines' maga-zine. The use of lofty messages in the service of selling Hawai'i was a consistent theme in tourism literature. The HVB often sought to portray Hawai'i as "more than a pretty place" in its effort to reach those sophisticated tourists who might be considering other destinations with more "intellectual-cultural" cachet.

In doing so, the tourism industry worked to ensure that American tourists to Hawai'i could feel virtuous in their choice of vacation destination—without any exposure to Hawai'i's troubled racial history or American conquest over Native Hawaiians. Touristic references to the Aloha Spirit helped to nor-malize Hawai'i's relationship to the United States by reviving colonialist tropes, in which Native Hawaiians welcomed white American settlers, and coupling them with the postwar narrative of the United States as a nation of immigrants.[29] Such evocations of the Aloha Spirit suggested both a sense of Hawai'i's exceptionalism and its representativeness of American plural-ism. While tourism literature tended to trace much of Hawai'i's culture to native origins, it simultaneously, and contradictorily, conceived of Hawaiians as one slice in a colorful multiethnic pie that also included Japanese, Chi-nese, Filipino, and other Asians in Hawai'i. Even Akaka, though singling out Native Hawaiians as inventors of the Aloha Spirit and the original settlers of the islands, nonetheless situated them as one immigrant group among many. At a time when white Americans were "discovering" their own family ancestries—a movement endorsed by Congress through the Ethnic Heritage Studies Act of 1972—Hawai'i offered an exotic mirror version of this mainland ethnic revival.[30]

In another melding of sales and seriousness, Hawai'i's governor Jack Burns used an advertorial in the New York Times in 1966 to urge mainland investors to look on Hawai'i, with its booming tourism-based economy, as the vanguard of a new Pacific era. Flanked by color photographs of pristine white-sand beaches, the Waikiki skyline, and lei-wearing children representing a "happy mixture of races and cultures," Burns's message suggested that Hawai'i offered a palliative to the seemingly insurmountable problems that arose from both modern mainland life and misunderstandings among nations. While Amer-icans "are faced with the disruption of Viet Nam, the enigma of Communist

China, the uncertainties of Indonesia," and are "not quite prepared to cope with these new problems," Burns said, "the people of Hawaii, proud of their role in the American experience and of their cosmopolitan heritage, are oriented in their thinking to meet [these] challenges."[31] Burns's opening message thereby framed the rest of the thirty-six-page supplement, much of which was devoted to advertisements for Hawai'i tourism. In doing so, it demonstrated the efforts of the state to yoke the pressing task of global racial progress with tourism development.

Most materials produced by the Hawai'i tourism industry were less heavy handed, portraying Hawai'i's multiethnic culture as a site of leisure and amusement as well as personal enrichment. The tone of a 1971 HVB advertisement to promote Hawai'i as "more than a pretty place"—which appeared in more upmarket magazines such as *The New Yorker*—straddled the line between high-minded and frivolous. Based on consumer research showing that visitors craved "a sense of involvement," the ad promised tourists that they could acquire both new cultural knowledge and a pleasure-filled holiday if they came to the islands. Visiting Hawai'i was a chance to "see the Orient. And Micronesia. And Europe." It was "almost like taking an international tour on six islands."

But lest potential tourists be scared off by the linguistic and cultural hurdles associated with a foreign vacation, the ad reminded them that "most of the people you'll meet speak your language." In a place where foreign ways were filtered through an American idiom, one could enjoy adventure without exertion: "You can order a Portuguese breakfast or an Indonesian banquet without consulting a dictionary.... Our mixed-up Hawaiian heritage presents some odd little surprises. Go to a ball game and you can order a hot dog—or a steaming bowl of fish soup." As more Americans were traveling to foreign countries—not just in Europe but in Asia, Latin America, and other regions of the Third World—the HVB claimed that Hawai'i might serve as a microcosm of all things foreign. "In Hawai'i," the ad said, "you'll find out what it's like to speak in a different language, worship in a different church, even live in a different colored skin"—all, presumably, without actually requiring any foreign language proficiency or ponderous soul searching.[32] Not incidentally, Hawai'i also had the added benefit of offering a "foreign" vacation within the U.S. at a time when the government was urging Americans to "See America First" to help correct a growing balance-of-payments problem.[33]

As the "More than a Pretty Place" ad suggests, the tourism industry often sought to depict Hawai'i as both a place of distinct ethnicities—Asian, Micronesian, European—and of "mixed-up," Americanized culture. At the same time that the HVB was sponsoring ethnic pageants, such as the Cherry Blossom Festival and Fiesta Filipina, that delineated cultural identity, it also worked to craft a portrait of Hawai'i as a society that had transcended old ideas of race

Hawaii's State Capitol, Honolulu, symbolizes the volcanic origin of the Islands.

American spoken here.
Also Japanese, Portuguese, Chinese,
Hawaiian, Tagalog, Korean,
Samoan and Pidgin.

While you're in Hawaii, see the Orient. And Micronesia. And Europe. They're all here. And all-American.

It's almost like taking an international tour on six islands. Except that most of the people you'll meet speak your language. Or something close to it.

That can come in handy. You can order a Portuguese breakfast or an Indonesian banquet without consulting a dictionary. And pay your check without a computer.

Our mixed-up Hawaiian heritage presents some odd little surprises. Go to a ball game and you can order a hot dog — or a steaming bowl of fish soup. There are big surprises too. Things you might not expect to find in an island paradise.

You can first-night a performance of La Tosca in one of the world's most acoustically perfect theaters. Or groove to a rock concert in the sweet air. There's a great cultural center where you can explore Polynesia's multi-colored past. And a magnificent aquatic museum where her future is on display.

There's a city of refuge where ancient warriors once sought sanctuary from the wrath of their gods and their fellow men. (And where you can do the same today, if that's the kind of year it's been.)

In Hawaii you'll find out what it's like to speak in a different language, worship in a different church, even live in a different colored skin.

The airlines and steamship companies have done everything but bring Hawaii to your doorstep. There are hotels in all price ranges and tours for every taste.

So before you go anywhere in this world, talk to your travel agent. He'll tell you it's all happening in Hawaii.

Hawaii
IT'S MORE THAN A PRETTY PLACE.

On behalf of the Islands of Hawaii, Kauai, Lanai, Maui, Molokai and Oahu.

FIGURE 10. "More Than a Pretty Place," Hawaii Visitors Bureau ad, 1971.
Hawaii Visitors and Convention Bureau.

and ethnicity. While this contradictory representation of Hawai'i on one level spoke to the complex reality of negotiating identity in the post-World War II period, on another level it reflected an attempt to hedge on the question of race and its significance. Was the Hawai'i tourism industry in the business of selling racial difference or racial transcendence? Without any seeming thought given to the difference between the two, it unabashedly worked to sell both.

This strategy was exemplified by a campaign launched by the HVB in the late 1960s titled "The Golden People of Paradise" and at the time deemed to be "the most ambitious marketing campaign ever devised to promote travel to the 50th State."[34] Driven by market concerns, it was intended to "even out the seasonal peaks and valleys of visitor flow into the State.[35] Along with a sixteen-page print media insert expected to reach 5.7 million mainland homes, the campaign included other promotional tie-ins, among them partnerships with the West Coast magazine *Sunset* to sell Hawai'i foods in major West Coast supermarkets, and with *Vogue,* which would coordinate merchandising of Hawai'i fashions at department stores in twenty-three metropolitan areas.

The content of the print advertisement made reference to James Michener's figure of the "Golden Man," who appeared at the end of *Hawaii.* Indeed, it was the audience for *Hawaii*—educated, liberal, middle-class whites—who the HVB was targeting when it sought to sell Hawai'i on the basis of its "intellectual-cultural" appeal. Michener, not coincidentally, was also one of the most prominent boosters of Hawai'i tourism. In a speech before the Civil Aeronautics Board shortly after statehood in 1959, Michener spoke on behalf of Hawaiian Airlines and called for the expansion of trans-Pacific aviation routes, which were then dominated by Pan Am. Hawai'i, Michener insisted, "can function as the western frontier of the United States, the gateway between the Orient and the mainland." But tourism had to be amplified for this promise to be realized. Speaking as a resident of the islands, Michener insisted that Hawai'i's "vital role in the Pacific" was possible "only if aviation increases even faster than our population, faster than our investments, and I would say faster than our development of hotel rooms."[36]

Michener suggested that Hawai'i, with a burgeoning visitor industry, could produce a nation of cosmopolitans ready to serve U.S. interests. This cosmopolitan ideal was personified by *Hawaii*'s Golden Man—"a man at home in either the business councils of New York or the philosophical retreats of Kyoto."[37] Michener had insisted that the Golden Man notion was not based on Hawai'i residents' physical coloring due to "racial intermixtures" but was instead "a product of the mind."[38] The HVB Golden People campaign, however, appeared to reject the notion that race could somehow be transcended. Instead, it played up the racial and ethnic differences of—and among—people in Hawai'i. The text of the Golden People campaign was accompanied by

It is a marvel now, the qualities we have created
a montage of minorities, a bounty of cultures . . .

FIGURE 11. "Golden People" ad campaign, Hawaii Visitors Bureau, 1969.
Hawaii Visitors and Convention Bureau.

photographs of Chinese temples, marching luau dancers, Japanese women parading in traditional dress, and described Hawai'i as "a festive land" where one would be immersed in a parade of "masks, firecrackers and multi-lingual chantings." Even as the term Golden People signaled racial blending, the substance of the ad—with lines such as "we have created a montage of minorities, a bounty of cultures" and "we move daily in an extraordinary spectrum of colors and feelings"—implied that Hawai'i's dynamism lay not only in the elaboration of cultural differences, but in their dramatic juxtaposition.[39]

Notably, the Golden People campaign did not include whites in this montage, suggesting that haole culture was not part of the entertainment Hawai'i had to offer. By turning Hawai'i's ethnic groups into a spectacle for a white audience, the Golden People campaign recalled earlier examples of white consumption of racial difference at places such as world's fairs, black nightclubs, or hula shows, where performers were expected to display their primitivism. But the broader social and cultural context of this consumption of difference had changed in the decades after the Second World War. While Michener, Myrdal, and the U.S. government were urging Americans to abandon racial prejudice, the Hawai'i visitor industry of the jet age was inviting white tourists to publicly affirm their admiration of other cultural traditions in the context of Hawai'i's poststatehood society, where multiracial cooperation was equated with modernity.

But the Golden People campaign, launched a decade after the publication of *Hawaii*, was also appealing to white racial liberalism at a moment when it was under intense strain. By the late 1960s, as de jure civil rights reform proved insufficient for overturning centuries of oppression, many northern whites had begun to recoil from black activists' attacks on economic inequality and segregation in northern cities.[40] Speaking to this unrest, Governor Burns noted that "Hawaii has not been racked with the civil disturbances that many of the less fortunate states have been undergoing," attributing this to "the manner in which the multi-racial people of Hawaii live and work together."[41] In this context, the safe multiculturalism presented in the Golden People campaign suggested that Hawai'i might serve as a respite from the racial discord on the mainland—and as a way for white tourists to prove their lack of prejudice in the face of increasingly radical critiques of inequality. At the same time, however, the language of multiculturalism obscured the racial and class privilege that enabled so many mainland tourists to travel to Hawai'i, where nonwhite service workers would help to affirm their racial liberalism.

But Hawai'i was not merely a stage for performing racial tolerance. The tourism industry also held out the possibility that visitors might be transformed by their experience of racial otherness in Hawai'i. From its very beginning, as William Leach argues, modern capitalism has sought to manufacture and harness consumers' impulse for personal expression through novel experiences.[42] But, if modern capitalism calls for acquisitive boundary crossing, certain boundaries are nonetheless more navigable than others at specific temporal moments and in distinct places. In Hawai'i in the two decades following statehood, the boundaries consumers were entreated to cross were racial. Drawing on 1960s advertising discourses that Thomas Frank identifies as "hip consumerism," tourism literature suggested that visitors to multiracial Hawai'i could become more free-spirited, cool, and likeable in their everyday lives.[43]

Not surprisingly, given Hawai'i's reputation as a site of interracial sex, tourism boosters often hinted at the possibilities for sexual experimentation. A 1972 article in the Hawaiian Airlines in-flight magazine by local Hawai'i novelist Scott Stone claimed that the islands represented the vanguard of the sexual revolution. Younger tourists, he wrote, "have brought their own sense of freedom to the Islands only to encounter a situation wherein morality is a personal thing and Hawaiians do not sit in judgment. . . . there just aren't many uptight Hawaiians." Male visitors open to new experiences—and men were clearly Stone's intended audience—would find a "marvelous lack of bigotry" in Hawai'i and might even wind up marrying an islander. Mainland women, too, exhibited "a new-found freedom" while on a Hawai'i holiday. "They will be using as much Hawaiian slang as they can muster and talking knowledgeably about The Point After and the Kamaaina Bar and the Top of the Ilikai. They will be trying, for the first time, malasadas and saimin and char siu, and they will be digging every moment of it." Stone even suggested mainland women could become less white as they exposed themselves to the dazzling Hawaiian sun: "They turn up on the beaches, mostly, their pale skins soaked in various kinds of oils and lotions; in a matter of days they will be suffused with the glow that comes from both a tan and a newfound confidence."[44]

Stone's glorification of the transformative effect of bronzed skin referenced the popular association between leisured class status and suntanning.[45] But it also suggested a kind of racial metamorphosis. Just as the "More Than a Pretty Place" campaign promised visitors they might "even live in a different colored skin," much of the discourse around Hawai'i tourism implied that one could take on a new racial identity, if only temporarily, by participating in Hawai'i's commercialized ethnic spectacles—by, for example, learning the hula or donning a kimono and attending a Japanese tea ceremony. The tourism industry's coaxing of white visitors to free themselves by embracing Hawai'i's laxity and racial otherness echoed Norman Mailer's invitation to white society in "The White Negro" to throw off "the inefficient and often antiquated nervous circuits of the past" by adopting black culture.[46] But while Mailer located the power of such racial appropriation in its transgressiveness and the appeal of black life in its precarious, "psychopathic," valence, the Hawai'i tourism industry aimed to point consumers to a middle road of safe experimentation. The racial and ethnic differences mainlanders would experience in Hawai'i were meant to be exciting rather than threatening. Moreover, unlike many people living in Hawai'i, experimental white tourists could revert to their white identity at will.

This form of racial mobility, however ephemeral, was made possible in part by the broader mobilities of the jet age. Ordinary Americans could harness the technological and geopolitical power of the United States to cross all sorts of new boundaries during the postwar period. Aviation, in particular, "propagated the comforting fiction that the air could somehow dissolve political sovereignties, along with differences and inequalities they signified."[47] But the fictions produced by air travel were grounded in the reality of its transformative power. Aviation collapsed time and distance, creating what Wendell Willkie called "a navigable ocean of air blanket[ing] the whole surface of the globe. There are no distant places any longer; the world is small and the world is one."[48] While aviation had long been associated with glamour and heroism in American popular culture, the introduction in the late 1950s of commercial jet aircraft—which flew nearly twice as fast as propeller planes and were more efficient and cheaper to operate—made aviation available to middle-class Americans.

The rise of American commercial aviation after World War II was fundamentally shaped by the postwar ideology of nationalist internationalism. As a symbol of high modernism and American technological prowess, aviation, writes Jennifer Van Vleck, "was a powerful conduit of ideas about the world." Aviation promised its passengers the world. And with flying came a sense of entitlement to even the most remote corners of the planet. Jet age travel was both liberal in its inclusionary rhetoric and imperialistic in its scope. The iconography of aviation in the postwar era elaborated and legitimized American postwar expansionism by presenting flying as a means of facilitating cross-cultural knowledge and understanding. Perhaps the most famous icon of the jet age was the logo of Pan American World Airways, which was comprised of a blue globe crisscrossed by white latitude and longitude lines—a world wiped of geography.[49]

Just as aviation was a powerful conduit for ideas about the world, it was also a conduit for ideas about the self. The anonymity associated with airports and airplanes, the speed with which passengers traveled from one destination to another, and the newly accessible destinations themselves all contributed to the notion of jet travel as a means of self-reinvention.[50] This was a phenomenon experienced by passengers and airline staff alike and one strongly linked to a new iteration of jet-fueled cosmopolitanism. As Christine Yano demonstrates in her study of Nisei Pan Am stewardesses who were based, not coincidentally, out of Honolulu, the airline industry produced an ethos of metaphysical boundary crossing. By creating "a contact zone of mobility and interaction," airlines such as Pan Am generated a "sense of pioneering previously uncharted waters of race, language, and culture."[51] One could board a plane in Los Angeles and arrive only hours later in Tokyo or Hong Kong or some other foreign city—or in Hawai'i, which offered a taste of multiple foreign cultures.

And yet, the rootlessness of the jet age could also be disconcerting. For Roland Barthes, flying represented the incoherence of modern life, in which freedom and confinement could emerge from the same source. "The jet-man," Barthes wrote in 1957, embodied a paradox in which "an excess of speed turns into repose."[52] Adventure was always just on the other side. The ease and passivity with which jet travelers careened through space recalled the hollowness felt by Jackson Lears's bourgeois antimodernists in the early twentieth century, when it seemed "a weightless culture of material comfort and spiritual blandness was breeding weightless persons who longed for intense experience."[53]

But while the unprecedented mobility of the jet age allowed for "intense experience" once passengers disembarked, it also facilitated their mass production. In Hawai'i, the selling of intense experience became increasingly rationalized. As airlines became more reliant on their Hawai'i routes—spurring the construction of ever-larger hotels in the islands—the tourism industry could no longer rely on the euphoria surrounding statehood to draw enough visitors to meet the exponential growth in visitor facilities.[54] But with the boom in tourism came local resistance to it. To both perpetuate and justify the pervasiveness of tourism, the state and the visitor industry worked to ease its integration into everyday life and to school Hawai'i's people on its benefits. According to the HVB, one of its key jobs was to spread the "gospel of aloha" not only among tourists, but, more importantly, among Hawai'i residents who had "direct contact" with tourists.[55] As a result, activities and practices that had once resided in a cultural sphere mostly independent of tourism were brought under the umbrella of the promotional state.

A state resolution in 1965 dramatized this cultural restructuring. In directing the HVB "to preserve and maintain the 'Hawaiian Spirit of Aloha,'" the legislature sought to commodify Hawai'i's culture and streamline its production.[56] Increasingly, instead of the visitor industry tapping local culture to promote tourism, it took on the role of shaping local culture for touristic ends. For instance, whereas Hawai'i's ethnic festivals previously had been funded by local communities, by 1967 they were subsidized in whole or in part by the HVB.[57] Likewise, the HVB began working with the Department of Education to develop "appropriate educational programs" whose goal was to inculcate the Aloha Spirit through the teaching of "customs, arts, crafts and cultures of our various ethnic groups which are an inseparable element of visitor satisfaction." Indeed, by the 1970s, statewide curricula in Hawai'i often echoed the themes of tourism marketing materials, with textbooks closely resembling guidebooks and lesson plans focused on preparing students to be tourism workers.[58]

These changes were accompanied by a new rhetoric of systematization. HVB executive Mark Egan, addressing an audience of Honolulu Rotarians in 1966, compared Hawai'i to a corporation, which had "many inter-related sub-systems, each with related components." With that in mind, he argued, there should be "a conceptual approach appl[ied] to the total economy of Hawaii." The visitor industry, he implied, would serve as fulcrum in the Hawai'i corporation. Such a reorientation, according to Egan, meant that any effort to develop Hawai'i tourism would necessarily summon the participation of all Hawai'i's people. Epitomizing the management argot of the day, Egan told his audience: "This involves everybody and the total area of Hawaii and all of the other systems and sub-systems as they are inter-related."[59]

Within a decade of statehood, cracks in the system had begun to emerge. Despite HVB efforts to acclimate Hawai'i residents to tourism's hegemony, the Aloha Spirit was showing signs of wear. This was of great concern to a statewide committee on tourism appointed by the HVB, which in a 1969 report worried that "an increasing population and number of visitors is eroding the spontaneous expressions of Aloha." Unsurprisingly, the solution proposed by the report was not to slow tourism growth, but rather to integrate tourism planning "in relation to the total environment—both human and physical," while at the same time fostering acquiescence to its inevitability. This could be achieved in part by making sure "our people [are] decently housed, properly educated, meaningfully employed, culturally enriched." Echoing the sentiments of the HVB, the committee took an expansive view on the role of tourism in Hawai'i society. The social program outlined in the report was one for which the visitor industry had "a desirably selfish, as well as a selfless, stake" in achieving. Moreover, it had a particular responsibility in ensuring the Aloha Spirit's durability, the report continued, as it had had a hand in creating it. "The widespread use of the word, 'Aloha,'" it claimed, "coincided with the building of Hawaii's first hotel."[60]

For all its high-minded rhetoric about social progress, the report also had a cynical take of the origins of the Aloha Spirit. While it had "evolved in part in our Island society as a way of getting along as painlessly as possible," it was also, the committee admitted, a contrivance—one "'manufactured' to serve commercial ends." Committee member Thomas Hamilton, former president of the University of Hawai'i, questioned whether expressions of the Aloha Spirit had any correlation to the state of Hawai'i society at all, suggesting that what was more important was "the educational force of and the character change which is sometimes induced by role-playing." According to Hamilton, the Aloha Spirit was, at best, a highly effective—yet artificial—social lubricant. "The 'Aloha Spirit' does make the gears of inter-action mesh more smoothly," Hamilton said. "Thus even if the impetus is artificial, it is more than possible that the individual will become habituated to the Aloha way."[61] This view was endorsed by the Hawaiian Travel Industry Congress the following year, when delegates agreed that "even where [the Aloha Spirit] might be ersatz it is still an important lubricant in a gritty society and one worth preserving."[62]

Hawai'i's policymakers thus self-consciously championed the tourism industry's practice of what Dean MacCannell calls "staged authenticity."[63] The people of Hawai'i were being asked to sell a market-tested imitation of Hawai'i society—and of themselves. The Aloha Spirit had served to mask the inequality between locals and tourists, but now that mask was cracking. No longer the signal of Hawai'i's exceptionalism that Reverend Akaka extolled, the Aloha Spirit was increasingly seen as a mechanical display of feigned emotion whose origins were less divine than commercial. For the tourism industry, which relied on Hawai'i's cosmopolitan and welcoming image to market vacations, the task of "habituating'" Hawai'i's people to the Aloha Spirit was thus more necessary, and challenging, than ever. At the same time, however, the demands for a manufactured Aloha Spirit revealed the service relationship at the heart of the multicultural fantasy the tourism industry was selling.

The Hawai'i tourism industry in the 1960s and 1970s clearly believed that multiculturalism was profitable. But not always. Underscoring its often cynical use of multicultural tropes, it was willing to downplay them depending on the consumer. One group of tourists in particular was not lured with the promise of the Aloha Spirit or an exotic adventure: servicemen on leave from Vietnam, who flocked to Hawai'i in droves in the late 1960s and early 1970s. In contrast to many visitors from the mainland who sought a cosmopolitan experience—to "see the Orient"—military personnel traveled to Hawai'i to get away from Asia, where the American encounter with foreign peoples was not going to plan. Hawai'i R&R reached its height during the nadir of the war, when an American victory seemed increasingly impossible and news of the My Lai massacre and other atrocities committed by American troops was undermining any lingering assumptions that the United States was a benevolent force in Vietnam. The program, according to the HVB, "affords the opportunity to turn a favorable spotlight on the Armed Forces" to combat the "anti-Vietnam war image."[64] Rest and relaxation in Hawai'i thus offered not only a diversion from a failing war, but a narrative of redemption for soldiers returning to American soil to see their loved ones. In Hawai'i they could be seen as clean-cut family men rather than marauding grunts.

The Vietnam R&R program in Hawai'i was both separate from the larger practices of the tourism industry and a direct product of it. Rest and relaxation tourists came to the islands for a distinct set of reasons and usually had a different kind of holiday from other tourists as a result. Rest and relaxation stays in Hawai'i were short—six days—and were mostly family affairs, as Hawai'i was the only R&R site that most military dependents could easily reach. There were compelling practical reasons for making Hawai'i an R&R site. For one, it would prevent soldiers from spending U.S. dollars abroad and contributing to the balance-of-payments problem.[65] Just as important, Hawai'i was between Vietnam and the continental United States and, due in part to that geographical convenience, it was the location of the command center for the war in Southeast Asia. This also meant that there was an extensive military presence in the islands—the nearly twenty bases and other installations spread across the state meant that Hawai'i had the highest concentration of military facilities in the United States—that provided an organizational infrastructure for R&R visits.

Such practicalities, of course, were born of U.S. empire in the Pacific. Hawai'i's role as bridge to Asia, a concept seized on by the tourism industry, was originated by the military, and defense buildup largely preceded the explosion of tourism. And as Vernadette Gonzalez shows, tourism and militarism have often gone hand-in-hand in Hawai'i. For instance, the H-3 interstate on O'ahu, one of Hawai'i's "scenic highways" facilitating access to various tourist sites, was first conceived in 1960 as a transport link for the island's military bases.[66] Tourism and American military power have been intertwined in Hawai'i in other ways as well. The Pearl Harbor national monument, which reaffirms the righteousness of the American power in the Pacific, was, and remains, one of the most popular sightseeing activities in Hawai'i for military and civilian visitors alike.[67] Meanwhile, off-duty military personnel stationed in Hawai'i during World War II helped to promote the idea of Hawai'i as a tourist paradise accessible to a wider class of mainland Americans beyond wealthy elites.[68] And since statehood, tourism and the military in Hawai'i have also been connected by the fact that they have become the two largest revenue generators in the state—with both assumed to be necessary to Hawai'i's economic survival.

That Hawai'i should be an R&R site was thus ordained. The program was introduced in 1966, and as one of around a dozen R&R sites, Hawai'i quickly became the most popular (followed by Tokyo, Hong Kong, and Bangkok)—even though its in-demand status meant that servicemen often had to wait longer to take leave.[69] By the spring of 1969, Hawai'i had hosted 1 million servicemen on R&R.[70] At its height a year later, R&R visits accounted for 20 percent of Hawai'i tourists, with sixty-five flights per month coming from Vietnam, bringing with them a total of ten thousand servicemen who were meeting some twelve thousand family members.[71] A major part of the appeal lay in the fact "that it's part of America," offering servicemen the cultural and familial comforts of home.[72] As the *Christian Science Monitor* reported, the men on leave "like the feeling of 'being back in the States.'"[73]

Despite their high numbers, R&R tourists in many ways were not as visible as most other visitors to Hawai'i. They often avoided the kind of interaction with residents that was usually a key selling point of a Hawai'i vacation. Many reports emphasized that R&R men and their wives and families often eschewed going out in public in favor of spending time in their hotel rooms or on private military lands. "The R&Rers have no desire for organized activities, want no more than to be by themselves, to get acquainted with the brides, the infants they hardly know," wrote the *Honolulu Advertiser*. "The hotels have learned to stay discreetly away from the GI families, at least for the first day or two, that most of the young couples put in requests for room service—and little else."[74]

Rest and relaxation visitors were a class apart. They received deep discounts on hotels, restaurants, and other services, and family members were offered reduced airfare to Hawai'i. And many felt they were owed special treatment. One G.I. who was having trouble getting a hotel reservation in advance of a trip to Honolulu wrote to Hawai'i governor John Burns to complain: "I certainly feel that my wife and I are much more deserving of a nice suitable accommodation than the mass of tourist who come to Hawaii."[75] But the soldier, who also sent a copy of his letter Lyndon Johnson, was overlooking the many ways in which R&R tourists were treated as "more deserving" of Hawai'i's pleasures. In addition to discounts at private facilities, they enjoyed access to military-only areas and their accompanying entitlements. Unlike civilians, servicemen were able to take advantage of rock-bottom accommodation rates at the Armed Forces Recreation Area at Fort DeRussy in Waikiki, and visit restricted military beaches, camps, and recreation centers around the state.[76]

This exclusive world within the larger tourism landscape exemplified the ways in which the military in Hawai'i, as Kathy Ferguson and Phyllis Turnbull write, was "hidden in plain sight"—at once dominating and elusive, with little accountability to the local community.[77] Significantly, R&R tourists' privileged access to spaces that were that were off-limits to civilians came at a time when people in Hawai'i were becoming increasingly vocal about an acute shortage of land exacerbated by both military expropriation and tourism development. The armed forces occupied slightly more than 5 percent of Hawaiian land—with the proportion even higher on O'ahu, where military bases were clustered—and hotel development was driving up housing costs and restricting beach access.[78] Against this background, Native Hawaiians and other local groups were beginning to organize around land rights.[79] While residents in Hawai'i clearly chafed at the pressure to perform the Aloha Spirit in interactions with mainland tourists, surely the efforts of servicemen to insulate themselves in private enclaves was similarly vexing.

Any frustration with R&R visitors, however, appears to have been kept under wraps during the war. The soldier, after all, embodied sacrifice and virtue as well as tourist revenue. In press coverage of Hawai'i's R&R program, the holidays enjoyed by enlisted men on leave were held up as overdue reward for months of grueling and traumatic experiences on the front. Such stories perpetuated the stereotype of the combat soldier as representative of military service during the war. Though many of the men who came to Hawai'i on leave had endured horrific ordeals on the ground in Vietnam, many had not. As Meredith Lair shows, the majority of those who served in Vietnam, some 75 percent, had noncombat roles and spent much of the war in "comfortable, well-stocked base camps."[80] Hawai'i, for them, may have been a well-deserved break, but it was not a respite from the battlefield.

Nonetheless, contemporary accounts of R&R in Hawai'i imbued the program with moral purpose and emotional heft. Reporters often focused on the dramatic reunions at Fort DeRussy between servicemen and their wives or girlfriends, and their stories abounded in heart-rending anecdotes: soldiers meeting their babies for the first time, husbands and wives initially passing each other by when they failed to recognize new hairstyles, "deep and immeasurably long kisses."[81] The women, who were said to "go into hysterics," "squeal with delight," or even faint from nervousness, were often at the center of these narratives— perhaps because they helped to domesticate, and humanize, the war-weary soldier.[82] Indeed, the military actively sought to ensure that the women at Fort DeRussy were prepared to help their men readjust to civilian life, if only for a few days. One Army chaplain, known for his energetic and "fun" performances in the waiting area, was put in charge of gearing up the women to perform emotional and sexual labor for the arriving men. He reminded them that the men had been "snatched from the steaming jungles of Vietnam" and urged them to "show some excitement!" and wake up sleeping babies because "You're going to want them to sleep once you and daddy are together."[83] The chaplain, as a man of the cloth and of the U.S. government, suggested that heterosexual romance for soldiers and their wives was not only a form of recreation, but was a religious and national imperative. And for those not yet husband and wife, the military went out of its way to arrange marriage ceremonies, with chaplains reportedly officiating some forty weddings a week.[84]

Such stories conveyed the message that R&R in Hawai'i was about strengthening familial bonds rather than simply entertainment and pleasure. For one Marine wife, Mrs. R. M. Thatcher, this was the "real value" of Hawaii R&R— "that for the first time the Marine Corps sees its fighting man as a family man."

FIGURE 12. Soldiers on R&R greeting their wives in Hawai'i, 1967. *Honolulu Star-Advertiser.*

As she wrote in a letter to *Leatherneck,* "It gives to the military wife the dignity and honor she has long deserved as it recognized the psychological value of six days of family reunion in America's paradise of the Pacific as opposed to yet another solo sojourn on foreign soil."[85]

As suggested by Mrs. Thatcher's disdain for foreign "solo sojourns," R&R generally had a reputation for debauchery. Single men tended to spend R&R

in Asia, "most likely taking advantage of what will be, for most, their one stay on the continent."[86] "Taking advantage" often meant sex with Asian women. Asian R&R destinations, particularly Bangkok and Hong Kong—known to many servicemen as the home of Suzie Wong, the fictional prostitute in Richard Mason's eponymous 1957 novel—were famous for their carnal pleasures. The resulting carousing subverted American efforts to promote the virtue of the U.S. mission in Vietnam. Military leaders, for their part, treated soldiers' sexual exploits during off-hours as a necessary form of recreation and condoned prostitution by dispatching military police to patrol red light districts and Army medics to brothels to conduct regular health checks.[87] Rape committed by servicemen was also disturbingly common—many soldiers referred to R&R as "rape and ruin"—although the military generally favored covering it up and the problem was underreported by the media.[88]

But while the military had grown more lax over the decades when it came to regulating the personal behavior of enlisted men, it remained worried about the potential diplomatic problems caused by local opposition to the presence of rowdy American troops in foreign R&R destinations.[89] Perhaps its greatest concern, however, was the spread of venereal disease among recruits, which had long been a consequence of war and imperial expansion. The military sought to warn servicemen of this hazard through health education films such as "Where the Girls Are—VD in Southeast Asia" (1969), wherein Pete, a naïve young soldier, succumbs to the sexual allure of an Asian woman he meets on R&R. When he returns to the United States to marry Julie, his American girlfriend, Pete learns that he has contracted syphilis in Asia, endangering his engagement to Julie and putting both of their lives at risk.[90]

Had Pete taken R&R in Hawai'i he might have avoided such a fate. In the context of the Vietnam War, Hawai'i offered an antidote to its depravities and a way to disown accountability for them. It was a place where fresh-faced young men could cement relationships with their American sweethearts and avoid the temptations of debased Asian women. Hawai'i R&R was decidedly noninternationalist. As such, it revealed the paradox at the core of American Cold War internationalism, which often resorted to racialized violence in the name of spreading democracy and demonstrating U.S. benevolence. Hawai'i was supposed to be a place that fostered peace between the United States and Asia in part through the friendly interactions of mainland tourists and people in Hawai'i of Asian descent. But as the war in Vietnam exposed the brutality inherent to the American project in Southeast Asia, Hawai'i became for many Americans an escape from the nation's foreign entanglements. For American servicemen, it turned out, the door to the Gateway to the Pacific swung both ways.

The Hawai'i R&R program was scaled back significantly after the withdrawal of American troops from Vietnam in 1973. But the visitor industry had

He's come home to you... in Hawaii.

ROYAL HAWAIIAN $18 single/double

PRINCESS KAIULANI $14 single/double

SURFRIDER $18 single $21 double

You want this special time in your lives to be perfect. So select one of the Sheraton Hotels in Hawaii for your time together . . . while he's on R&R. After Viet Nam and being so far apart, you both deserve the best.

SHERATON-KAUAI on Poipu Beach, Island of Kauai $16.50
SHERATON-MAUI on Kaanapali Beach, Island of Maui $21.25

For Guaranteed reservations at these R&R rates, telephone 800/325-3535 (toll-free) or write

MOANA $16 single $19 double

Sheraton Hotels in Hawaii

SHERATON HOTELS AND MOTOR INNS, A WORLDWIDE SERVICE OF **ITT**

FIGURE 13. Ads directed at R&R tourists did not rely on common tropes of Hawai'i as a multiethnic paradise, instead emphasizing the islands as an escape from Southeast Asia. This one appeared in an R&R guide in 1970. Marriott International.

come to rely on military dollars, and R&R was one of the factors in the over-development of tourism in the islands. In the late 1960s hotel rooms increased by 25 percent, but tourism only rose by 10 percent.[91] By the mid-1970s, with the nation facing an economic crisis that included rising fuel costs and declining disposable income, the downsides to a tourism-driven economy were clear. People in Hawai'i were torn: they were dependent on tourism for jobs and tax revenue, yet it was an industry that was particularly vulnerable to recession. At the same time, even when tourism was booming, many worried about the effects it was having on everyday life, such as its contribution to a rising cost of living, competition for beaches and other public facilities, increased traffic, and environmental degradation.

Surveys of Hawai'i residents from the early 1970s revealed this deep ambivalence. A study conducted by *Sunset* magazine found that while 66 percent of respondents were "friendly" towards tourism, the same percentage believed tourism development was already "big enough" or "too big." An even larger number—74 percent—felt that the opinions of Hawai'i residents had been overlooked in the tourism development process.[92] A survey commissioned by the HVB found similar results. Respondents were largely in favor of tourism, with the vast majority identifying its economic benefit to Hawai'i as its most important feature. But only a minority of 41 percent believed they had personally benefitted from tourism. Despite residents' overall support for tourism, their responses exposed an undercurrent of resentment. Their written answers, meanwhile, offered possible explanations for the decline of the Aloha Spirit. Complaints centered around problems such as the "synthetic selling of Hawaii," "increased congestion," "disparity of income" between hotel owners and workers, "hippies and surf bums," and the ways in which the tourism industry "prostitutes the local people" by providing mostly menial jobs. Notably, younger respondents—those under age twenty-nine—were consistently more negative toward tourism than people in older age groups. They were also least likely to identify "racial harmony" as the "best thing about living in Hawaii."[93] Many of these younger respondents may have been sympathetic to the kind of radical politics represented by the ethnic studies movement at the University of Hawai'i, which, as discussed in chapter 6, challenged the dominant narrative around poststatehood Hawai'i as an exemplar of equality and racial harmony.

Local resistance to the hegemony of tourism—and the continued efforts of the visitor industry to pursue its habituating project—were brought to the fore in Hawai'i's 1978 state tourism development plan. The growth of tourism, Governor George Ariyoshi wrote in the report, "has brought about a parallel growing concern about Hawaii's future, and the effects of such rapid growth on Hawaii's physical, social and economic environments." Ariyoshi's opening note acknowledged that not all of Hawai'i's people were happy with the status quo. In an attempt to assuage opponents of tourism growth and address some of the negative by-products of tourism, the plan went on to recommend that "the adverse effect associated with these conditions may be minimized in part through policy decisions which regard the interests of Hawaii's residents as the more important." Again, however, the report did not recommend that the state seek to slow growth, but to rationalize it through more intensive planning. Its projection that tourism growth would slow to 7 percent per year between 1978 and 1985 (down from an average of 16 percent since 1960) was based not on any notion that the state would intervene to limit tourism's expansion, but on a consideration of external factors such as rising fuel costs and national economic instability. At the same time, pointing to the oversaturation of Waikiki, it advocated that more effort be made to encourage resort development in Hawai'i's outer islands. Such growth-oriented planning was necessary "to maintain Hawaii's competitive advantage over other resort destination areas" and "provide employment opportunities over the coming decade."[94] The tourism juggernaut, it seemed, could not be held back.

While claiming to address local concerns about the "social costs" of tourism and Hawai'i residents' desire for a better quality of life, the report sought to frame tourism itself as the answer to the problems it had created. To reduce the negative impact of the tourism industry, the report argued, tourism needed to become *more* entrenched, not less, in residents' everyday lives. The people of Hawai'i needed more specialized job training and more public education on tourism's benefits so that they would "become aware of the effects and substantial economic contribution of the industry." In addition, in order to maximize tourism's rewards, Hawai'i's people should worry less about themselves and more about the psychic troubles of vacationers. "Residents should be encouraged," the report recommended, "to develop an understanding of the travel experience so they can have empathy with the strains and tensions of the visitor experiences."[95]

Critics of tourism argued that it was undermining racial equality in Hawai'i, which the industry had long promoted as the islands' best feature. "Today, haves and have-nots are as clearly marked and separated in Hawaii as they ever were under the old plantation system," Gavan Daws, a prominent historian of Hawai'i, said in 1977. Tourism, according to Daws, was fueling permanent migration to Hawai'i from the mainland and, as a result, "the new population will resemble to an uncanny but obvious degree the statistical profile as assembled by the HVB. He and she are white, middleaged, and affluent above the national average, and certainly above the Hawaiian average." While Hawai'i became more white, the workforce serving both tourists and the influx of new residents would remain nonwhite, "part of it siphoned off from the labour severed from the declining sugar and pineapple business" and "augmented more and more by recent immigrants—not from the American mainland, but from Asia."[96] The liberatory pretense of the globalizing economy, Daws suggested, masked its effectiveness in achieving conservative ends.

Hawai'i, meanwhile, saw itself as a model for other economies embracing service sector labor. As it had done in Hawai'i, the HVB, through its Pacific Tourism Marketing and Research Institute, formed in 1967, aimed to promote "management concepts [and] technological advancement" in world tourism and encourage the "conversion of attitudes towards employment in the 'hospitality' careers" around the world.[97] Indeed, Hawai'i was representative of a changing global economy, one defined by flexible accumulation, interdependency, and a transition to service sector labor. While the continental U.S. traded factories for finance, Hawai'i traded agriculture for tourism.[98] This transition to tourism was also taking place in former resource-based economies in Asia and the Pacific—with the Hawai'i visitor industry's encouragement and financing from the World Bank and International Monetary Fund.[99] These shifts could be profoundly destabilizing, economically and culturally, as the case of Hawai'i makes clear. With globalization and flexible accumulation, David Harvey writes, "the sense that 'all that is solid melts into air' has never been more pervasive." The postmodern market, in its reorientation toward the consumption of experience over goods, has meant that "tradition is now often preserved by being commodifed."[100]

As Hawai'i became increasingly integrated with global markets, it began attracting affluent tourists from abroad, notably Japan. The 1970s and 1980s saw a huge increase in Japanese tourists to Hawai'i as well as a massive influx of Japanese investment in the islands. By 1987, there were more than 1 million Japanese visitors to Hawai'i annually, and the state remains among the most popular tourist destinations for Japanese traveling overseas. Much of the marketing material geared toward Japanese visitors has used themes similar to those aimed at Americans, wherein Hawai'i occupies a space between the foreign and the familiar. Like continental Americans, Japanese tourists would be comforted by the fact that they could speak their own language in the islands while at the same time experiencing an "exotic" paradise.[101]

The lucrative Japanese market and the loosening of global capital flows helped solidify tourism's hold on Hawai'i's economy. But as the service sector became ever more dominant in Hawai'i and elsewhere, it failed to deliver on its promise to create prosperity for all. Instead, the old categories of racial difference continued to shape social relations and conditions of inequality. The buying power of Japanese tourists in Hawai'i may have represented their economic advancement in relation to the United States, but it also reified Japanese dominance over other Asians, as Filipino and Korean service workers were expected to wait on them while projecting their best rendition of the Aloha Spirit. When people of varying Asian descent came together in Hawai'i with Native Hawaiians and white Americans, it was on dramatically uneven terms. In Hawai'i, as in the rest of the United States, the challenge to the inequalities wrought by the postmodern economy would come in the form of a reassertion of racial identity.

5

Delicious Adventures and Multicolored Pantsuits

GENDER AND COSMOPOLITAN SELFHOOD IN THE SELLING OF HAWAI'I

IN SUMMER MONTHS in the years after Hawai'i statehood in 1959, newspaper society pages chronicled "the luau craze" that had gripped party planners from Boston to Los Angeles.[1] As the *Atlanta Constitution* declared, "Americans have taken the luau to their hearts and made it one of the most popular summer parties."[2] By August 1968, according to the *Los Angeles Times,* luau parties had become so popular in the San Gabriel Valley that "the number and variety of luaus . . . seem to be infinite."[3] Indeed, in Southern California, where Hawai'i's various cultural exports shaped the region's trumpeted "lifestyle," the luau was becoming ubiquitous. Nearly every country club, charity organization, or civic group, it seemed, was riding the wave—among them Armenian churches, synagogue sisterhoods, sorority chapters, local Democrats, local Republicans, opera leagues, the NAACP, the Sons of Norway, even the Chicano Legal Defense Fund, which held a luau fundraiser to aid striking Delano grape pickers.[4] The luau also penetrated American postwar culture on a deeper and more personal level with the proliferation of private parties held in people's homes and backyards.

These luau parties were part of a broader fascination with Hawai'i in American postwar life, which was amplified by statehood. From *Gidget* to the lanai trend to the explosion in pineapple-based desserts, Hawai'i was everywhere—and on a level completely disproportionate to its size or economic importance to the United States. Looking back from the twenty-first century, it is easy to dismiss the backyard luau, the tiki bar, or the muumuu as part of postwar kitsch. But in the 1960s and 1970s the cultural production and consumption of Hawai'i was much more than kitsch, and not merely a backdrop to other social

FIGURE 14. One of numerous fundraising luaus for charity, this one organized by high
school students in the affluent Los Angeles neighborhood of Bel Air, 1958. University
of Southern California Libraries, *Los Angeles Examiner* Photographs Collection.

changes. Rather, they were a means for mainland women, particularly white
middle-class women, to both safely challenge the norms of postwar femininity and assert their racial liberalism by experimenting with racial boundary-
crossing—all without sacrificing the privilege of their whiteness.

Eating and dressing are each intimate, corporeal acts, one involving the
assimilation of food into the body and the other the wearing of a second skin
as part of the material representation of the self. As scholars of gender, food,
and fashion have shown, the performance of self through the seemingly superficial practices of clothing, dining, and personal presentation constitutes a language that signals how people understand their place in society.[5] At the same
time, attention to the ways in which people have talked about eating, dressing,
and other bodily experiences in order to define the parameters of race and
ethnicity—or, in the case here, define what counted as an acceptable breach
of those parameters—can illuminate how social difference is produced.[6] For
American postwar women, to don a muumuu or serve tempura shrimp was, at
once, to get swept up in a popular trend of cosmopolitan consumption and to
make an individual and deliberate choice about what went in or on one's body.
Both require explanation. A muumuu is never just a muumuu.

The muumuu in the postwar era was both a symbol and a practical expression of an emerging multiculturalist ideal, one that celebrated, and commercialized, racial and ethnic difference. The muumuu, along with other Hawai'i-branded products and consumer practices, was also a decidedly gendered commodity. Women were the main targets of marketers of the Hawai'i food, fashion, and design that were exported to the mainland. And by all evidence, they were eager consumers. While we cannot be certain as to why individual women adopted Hawai'i's cultural exports so enthusiastically, the messages conveyed in the selling of Hawai'i provide some insight. Hawai'i fashion and food were promoted as vehicles for personal transformation, one centered on both sexual freedom and the adoption of practices and traditions of nonwhite culture. As many women came to chafe at what Betty Friedan called the "Happy Housewife Heroine" ideal, Hawai'i-themed commodities offered a fantasy of overseas travel—and an encounter with a racially harmonious and sexually open society that could make you more worldly, relaxed, and sophisticated.[7] At the same time, as mainland women donned Hawai'i fashion and hosted Hawai'i-themed events, they were helping to create a commercial multiculturalism that spoke to larger discussions over the value of diversity in American postwar society. Like the famous 1971 commercial in which an ethnically mixed chorus of young people sing, "I'd like to buy the world a Coke," Hawai'i food and fashion promised a multicultural and liberated consumer future.

To some extent, the commodification of Hawai'i in the postwar period drew on older primitivist discourses of Hawai'i as a premodern land of hula girls in grass skirts, ripe for the picking by a colonizing United States. But while other scholars have emphasized these primitivist aspects of Hawai'i imagery in the postwar period, they often overlook the ways in which Hawai'i came to represent novelty and modernity.[8] A primitivist lens also tends to frame Hawai'i as a feminized object of the male gaze, which neglects the role of mainland women as the main consumers of Hawai'i. Women, for instance, made up 55 percent of tourists to Hawai'i in 1965, and it was women who did the most to commodify Hawai'i culture in the continental United States.[9] At the same time, Hawai'i women themselves, as cookbook authors and, less visibly, as garment manufacturers and designers, actively sought to harness Hawai'i's prominence toward their own ends and promote a modern vision of the islands as a center for cultural mixing.[10]

Women's sexuality was central to the postwar consumption of Hawai'i on the mainland. But instead of sexualizing Hawai'i's women for male pleasure, the luau craze of the postwar period served as a conduit for white women to express new sexual freedoms. Wearing Hawai'i fashions or hosting a luau promised mainland women an opportunity to take part in the changing sexual norms of the 1960s and 1970s. The flavorful food, informal and free-spirited parties, colorful clothing, and promiscuous cultural borrowing that Hawai'i represented matched broader cultural trends away from the neo-Victorian social values of the immediate postwar era. Through racial boundary crossing, whether by cooking and eating the Asian cuisine associated with Hawai'i or acting the part of Native Hawaiians at a backyard luau, women could engage in what was portrayed as a newly liberated, modern version of womanhood—one that emphasized both overt sexuality and a cosmopolitan sensibility that could unleash them from older traditions of domesticity. Hawai'i food and fashion tapped into the desires of many postwar middle-class women frustrated by the monotony of homemaking and suburban living by offering excitement and cultural edification. This might have especially appealed to educated women who, after a college experience that "plunged them into a world of ideas," now felt like "shut-ins"—this according to a *New York Times* story from June 1960 that, coincidentally, shared a page with an article on "Sunny Tropical Cottons" from Hawai'i.[11] As Friedan was urging women to reject the "feminine mystique" and explore the world beyond the domestic sphere, many were doing so by embarking on a Hawai'i adventure, if only metaphorically.

Friedan probably would have looked down on housewives seeking fulfillment though food and fashion rather than work or social activism. And indeed, the discourses around Hawai'i in cookbooks and women's magazines were hardly radical. Instead, while they urged readers to use Hawai'i food and fashion to gain and demonstrate knowledge of foreign cultures, such pursuits were often framed as a way for women to heighten their sexual appeal to men.

This gendered performance of cosmopolitanism drew on older Orientalist traditions among bourgeois American women, but unlike earlier movements to "embrace the East," the postwar consumption of Hawai'i achieved widespread, mainstream prominence.[12] It also took on new moral implications against the background of civil rights and the rise of white racial liberalism, as discussed in previous chapters. Whereas white women's Orientalism of earlier periods often explicitly upheld empire and global racial hierarchies, the messages that accompanied Hawai'i food, fashion, and design in the postwar era relied on the rhetoric of cross-cultural understanding that was associated with the fiftieth state. At the same time, however, it could serve to absolve white women of their own responsibility for ongoing racial inequalities, both in Hawai'i and on the mainland, and in the global sphere. During the postwar era, as white women across the United States embraced nonwhite culture in their homes and on their bodies, they did so at a time when many white suburbanites were pushing black people out of their neighborhoods, and when America's engagement with Asian people abroad had become increasingly violent.[13] As in Hawai'i tourism, the performance of racial tolerance via

Hawai'i food and fashion did not need to be accompanied by a commitment to racial equality.

––––––––

Continental Americans had been consuming two of Hawai'i's most important exports—sugar and pineapple—for decades before statehood. If sugar was the backbone of Hawai'i's colonial economy, pineapple was its face, conveying both exoticism and modernity at once. New agricultural science, industrial canning and distribution methods, and advertising brought the Hawaiian-grown fruit to mainland supermarkets in the first decades of the twentieth century. By World War II, Hawai'i was supplying over 80 percent of the world's pineapple.[14]

Along with hula dancers, pineapple—though indigenous to South America—was indelibly linked to Hawai'i. Advertisements for the tropical fruit rarely failed to mention that it came from "glamorous Hawaii" and most drove the point home by using images of Native Hawaiians in outrigger canoes, Diamond Head, or island flowers such as plumeria and orchids. Advertisements also frequently included recipe ideas, from aspic salads with greens and cottage cheese to upside down cake, suggesting to home cooks that they could incorporate some of Hawai'i's glamour into everyday meals.[15] Despite the fact that traditional Native Hawaiian food did not use it, pineapple—a sturdy, sugary and tart fruit with seemingly infinite uses, a standout in produce aisles with its eye-catching, almost opulent exterior—was the food that introduced mainlanders to the idea of Hawai'i cuisine.

If pineapple growers offered the first sweet taste of Hawai'i, savvy restaurateurs promised a more holistic culinary trip to the islands. Ernest Raymond Beaumont Gantt, a former bootlegger better known as Don the Beachcomber, opened the first Polynesian-themed restaurant in Hollywood in 1933. Five years later he was followed, and eclipsed, by Victor Bergeron, who—perhaps to obscure his European ancestry—likewise assumed an alternate identity, as Trader Vic, to front his own Polynesia inspired establishment in San Francisco. The two men, in friendly competition with one another, went on to expand their respective business empires over the next several decades by opening dozens of restaurants across the United States, and later, for Bergeron, around the world.[16] "Tiki" went national after World War II and the trend accelerated with Hawai'i statehood, so much so that by 1962, an executive of the National Restaurant Association estimated that the number of Polynesian-themed restaurants had increased tenfold in the previous five years.[17]

The growth of tiki restaurants was part of a larger expansion of both the size and scope of the restaurant industry, particularly when it came to mid-range and higher-end establishments. French cuisine had long been considered the standard-bearer for gastronomic elegance, but by the mid-1960s, ideas on what constituted modern dining were broadening, creating new debates and divisions. When Jacqueline Kennedy hired René Verdon as the first French chef for the White House since the Jefferson administration, she signaled a new era of chicness in presidential dining. But when in 1965 Verdon resigned his post "in a huff" over a request for cold chickpea soup—the final in a long line of orders from Lyndon Johnson that riled his "Gallic sensibilities"—it appeared to many as an act of ethnic snobbery.[18] Victor Bergeron, for one, was so offended that he took out a full-page protest that ran in San Francisco newspapers. In it, he lambasted Verdon as "old fashioned, archaic and . . . completely out of step with the world." Bergeron, himself of French descent, insisted that French food, which "only a few people" enjoyed, was elitist. "By what stretch of the imagination do you think that French cooking is the only cuisine in the world?" he asked Verdon.[19]

As Americans seemed to be taking more pleasure in cooking and eating, the definition of gourmet was changing. Looking back on the 1960s in 1970, Craig Claiborne, the famed *New York Times* food critic, celebrated the decade as one of "vastly widened horizons." New York City, Claiborne wrote with obvious pride, had witnessed an "awesome debut of restaurants of numerous nationalities" and New Yorkers' palates were becoming more experimental and pluralistic as they devoured sushi and spicy Szechuan food with newfound passion.[20] Among those newcomers were a number of Polynesian-themed restaurants, including the Luau 400, the Hawaiian Room at the Lexington Hotel, the Gauguin Room—which Claiborne rated as highly as the traditionally French Lutèce—and, of course, Trader Vic's.[21] In New York and elsewhere, such restaurants capitalized on the new visibility of the Pacific in U.S. culture. In selling fantasy, they tended to offer a hodgepodge of cultural appropriation, all of it meant to conjure the tropical and the exotic. The décor was aggressively Polynesian, or at least a spectacular imagined version of Polynesia: tropical wood paneling, grass fringe, rattan furniture, carved Polynesian gods. An extensive drinks list of rum-based cocktails traced its lineage to the Atlantic tropics rather than the Pacific.

The food menu, meanwhile, was dominated by Asian fare, most of it Chinese, with a few Japanese and Southeast Asian dishes mixed in. This can be attributed, in part, to Chinese food's long-standing popularity among whites, particularly in cities on the West Coast.[22] But the image of Chinese food was also undergoing a significant shift in the postwar period. The first white clientele at many Chinese restaurants in the nineteenth century were miners and other workers seeking a cheap hot meal. Later, after the Chinese Exclusion Act of 1882, "chop suey houses" proliferated in part because restaurant owners and employees were among the few Chinese migrants exempt from the restriction-ist law.[23] But even as Chinese cooking in the United States expanded to include more refined establishments, it was still often identified with lowly food and a ghettoized community, and plagued by stereotypes that it was unsanitary. One persistent rumor was that Chinese cuisine was full of rat meat, reinforcing the idea that Chinese people themselves were disease ridden and uncivilized.[24]

The decision to serve Chinese fare at tiki restaurants thus drew on an association with the exciting unfamiliarity of "the Orient" as well as the long-standing presence of Chinese eateries. But tiki places—faddish in a way that Chinese restaurants had not been—also helped to normalize Chinese food, and elevate its reputation, among a wider range of white Americans. Mean-while, the link made between China and Polynesia went beyond a shared aura of exoticism. Hawai'i, as a center of Chinese immigration in the nineteenth century, was the connecting thread that brought the two cultures together, both materially and conceptually, as the tiki trend exploded.

Indeed, it was in Hawai'i where Victor Bergeron studied Chinese cooking.[25] Although Hawai'i's Chinese population was relatively small compared to other ethnic groups, by mid-century many Chinese in Hawai'i had left plantation work and found success as owners of restaurants, groceries, and other small businesses—lending Chinese culture outsize influence in the islands. In part because of his time spent in Hawai'i, Bergeron viewed Chinese cooking as the natural accompaniment to the Polynesian atmosphere in his restaurants. In fact, though his menus included various dishes with names that referenced Polynesia, he was generally disdainful of its cuisine. "Real Polynesian food," according to Bergeron, was "the most horrible junk I've ever tasted" and was too "primitive" to be "acceptable to American tastes."[26] Bergeron was hardly alone in this assessment, with many commentators singling out poi—a Hawai-ian staple made from fermented and pounded taro root—as something resem-bling "an immobile goo that tastes like library paste."[27]

The contempt shown for indigenous island culture while appropriating its customs was nothing new—beginning with the arrival of the missionaries in 1820, haoles in Hawai'i had sought pleasure and entertainment by borrow-ing Hawaiian people's practices and simultaneously condemning their way of life. But the lifting up of Chinese culture and Asian culture more broadly in Hawai'i was a departure from pre–World War II portrayals of the islands as an undeveloped Polynesian idyll—it was also part of broader erasure of Native Hawaiians in postwar narratives of Hawai'i as "bridge to Asia."

If Native Hawaiian food represented primitiveness, Asian food was its modern foil. What made Hawai'i modern in such portrayals was its history as a site of immigration and cultural mixing. Though immigration to the United States was at an all-time low for much of the early postwar period (until the overhaul of the quota system in 1965) the celebration of the United States as a "nation of immigrants" was gaining popular currency. The elimination of racial barriers to migration and citizenship, along with texts such as John F. Kennedy's *A Nation of Immigrants* and James Michener's *Hawaii*, endorsed a liberal vision of pluralistic unity. Aiding this newfound reverence for the role of immigrants in American life was a broader glorification of mobility in American society.[28] Whereas pre–World War II mainstream discourse frequently portrayed immigrants, particularly those from Asia, as uncivilized peasants who would infect the United States with their backwardness, increasingly in the postwar era immigrants were held up as models of mobility, as globe-trotting cosmopolitans. Once a scourge, now they were to be admired for their pluck and their cultural flexibility in the face of unfamiliar conditions.

Hawai'i, meanwhile, was frequently discussed in futurist terms—as a place that forged a unique historical path that the world was now catching up to. Hawai'i, insisted August Heckscher in *House & Garden*, heralded "the threshold of a new age." Heckscher, who had served as the first White House cultural advisor, under Kennedy, had clearly imbibed his boss's New Frontier rhetoric. While the islands may have seemed backward to nineteenth-century missionaries, Heckscher wrote, the Hawai'i of the mid-twentieth century embodied "fresh impulses," and its embrace of a "pattern of life freer and less circumscribed than anything in our own tradition" should be emulated.[29]

For many white liberals in this period, emulating Hawai'i and consuming immigrant food—especially Asian cuisine—was a way to demonstrate their own cultural flexibility, their defiance of outdated social boundaries, and thus signal their belonging in the "new age." The food of Hawai'i, frequently referred to as an ethnic "mélange" or "potpourri," gave diners the chance the chance to experiment with several exotic culinary styles at once.[30] The language used to describe this venture into foreign foodways often conveyed exhilaration and novelty. James Michener wrote of encountering "the most exciting food emporium I have ever seen" in a Honolulu grocery store and the "delightful variety and unending pleasantness" of the "delicacies" drawn from the "six great traditions" served on Hawai'i's tables. He also made sure to point out that even "one hundred percent Caucasian" hostesses in Hawai'i never failed to include at least one Asian dish at their dinner parties.[31] Mainland white women, Michener suggested, could likewise be so cosmopolitan.

Just as dining out at Hawai'i-themed restaurants was on the rise, so was dining in on Hawai'i-inspired recipes. One of the ways to measure this growing interest is through the increase in cookbooks and food writing on Hawai'i. Cookbooks, as Susan Leonardi argues, are rarely just lists of rules for preparing various dishes. Recipes—and thereby food writing more generally— are "embedded discourses" that come with "a context, a point, a reason to be."[32] Why certain recipes, and certain cookbooks, were published at particular times, and how their authors justified the appeal of a dish or collection of dishes, can elucidate broader cultural change and the rise of new social norms.[33] By all evidence, the postwar period saw a dramatic increase in the cooking and eating of foods identified as Hawaiian. In an era when the home was sacralized as the moral center of American society, Hawai'i became a physical and emotional feature of the domestic landscape.[34] Cookbook and food writers routinely urged their readers, in an exchange that was usually woman to woman, to bring Hawai'i into the private realm of their kitchens and dining rooms as a way to enhance their family and social lives.

At restaurants like Don the Beachcomber and Trader Vic's, Hawai'i tropes were cast as a form of pure entertainment in a public setting. But in the intimacy of the home, where women generally prepared meals themselves, the escapist promise of Hawaiian food was tempered by the material demands placed on the home chef. Cooking, in short, took work, whether it was "delightful" food or not. And cooking a particular dish engendered a deeper familiarity with it than eating it at a restaurant. Why did so many women take on the labor of Hawai'i food? What meaning was attributed to cooking, serving, and eating dishes associated with the fiftieth state?

Like restaurant dining, home cooking was undergoing profound change in the postwar period. Mass production and distribution of food products meant that home cooks had more choice than ever before. Labor-saving appliances, along with new packaged and processed foods, reduced once-time consuming kitchen tasks to mere seconds. Women continued to spend a significant amount of time in the kitchen, however—some seventeen to eighteen hours a week—and cooking remained central to women's identity in the postwar era. While women were working outside the home in increasing numbers, they were often solely responsible for meal preparation, something that had fallen to live-in maids and paid cooks in middle-class households in the late nineteenth and early twentieth centuries. And they were still doing much of the cooking from scratch: commercially prepared items accounted for a relatively small percentage of the food Americans bought and served in the early postwar period.[35]

At the same time, postwar housewives faced a different set of expectations compared to their mothers and grandmothers when it came to food preparation. Much of the food discourse during the Progressive Era drew on ideas promoted by home economists and food scientists, who argued that the main purpose of eating was nutrition, not pleasure.[36] During the Depression and World War II, women were urged to make the most out of limited resources, which often resulted in simple food that was short on flavor. Indeed, Depression-era food was often deliberately bland, as home economists and those in charge of relief believed that tasty food would cause people to overeat in a time of scarcity.[37] Later, wartime rations called for personal sacrifice on the home front to support the nutritional needs of troops abroad.

After demobilization, however, attitudes toward food and eating underwent a transformation. While a renewed interest in high-end food had begun to emerge during the early 1940s—symbolized by the inauguration of *Gourmet* magazine in 1941—most Americans had to wait until war's end for food culture to change.[38] Against the background of the postwar economic boom, when Americans were again celebrating their nation as a land of abundance, food increasingly came to be viewed as something to be enjoyed. After the austerity of depression and war, home entertaining was on the rise, and many home-cooked meals were more elaborate than their prewar counterparts. House-wives had long been told that nourishing their husbands and children was an act of family, and sometimes national, devotion. They were now encouraged to take new pride not only in food's nutritive value, but in how it tasted as well.[39]

Home cooks were aided in this effort by a slew of new cookbooks. These commercial texts boomed during the 1930s, perhaps due to pressures to economize through homemade food, and had been growing steadily in popularity ever since.[40] Women were increasingly turning to mass-produced cookbooks—such as Irma Rombauer's *The Joy of Cooking,* first published in 1931—along with magazines and newspaper food sections, instead of family recipes or community cookbooks, to learn the art of cooking. American food culture was becoming increasingly national, and local cuisines were spreading across regional boundaries. But it was in the postwar period, and especially after 1960, however, that cookbooks really took off. The 1960s and 1970s, a time when Americans began to cook "with more enthusiasm, in more depth and abandon than ever before," saw a near tripling in cookbook publications compared to the previous two decades.[41]

Some of this can be attributed to the interest sparked in gourmet cooking by the debut in 1961 of Julia Child's *Mastering the Art of French Cooking,* which gently challenged home cooks to try their hand at complicated dishes that had previously been available mainly to those who could afford to eat at fancy restaurants. But a large portion of the cookbooks published around this time spoke to Americans' interest well beyond Western Europe and to their increasingly global sensibilities in an era of jet travel and unprecedented American expansionism. There was some precedence to this. Even during the height of the home economics movement, as Kristin Hoganson shows, food writers often eschewed simple and bland food by including foreign dishes in their recipe recommendations—urging women to transform their kitchens "into sites of geographic knowledge."[42] Although French and Italian cuisine received the most attention, recipes for Latin American and Asian dishes, particularly

Indian curry, introduced adventurous eaters to a broader culinary repertoire.[43] And Americans, native born and nonnative alike, had been crossing ethnic boundaries to sample the foodways of various immigrant groups in restaurants and shops since at least the late nineteenth century.[44]

Before World War II, however, the patronizing of immigrant businesses was generally confined to cities with large foreign populations and the adoption of immigrant food by U.S.-born Americans was hardly widespread. Moreover, cosmopolitan eating in this earlier period took place against a background of high nativism against immigrants from eastern and southern Europe and Asia. Many Progressive Era cookbooks, rather than celebrating foreign culinary traditions, targeted immigrants and sought to assimilate them by ridding their cooking of its "un-American" taste.[45] By contrast, post–World War II cookbooks on the cuisine of second-wave immigrants often played up the foreignness of its flavors. Cookbooks in the postwar period also expanded to include East Asian food as part of what was considered legitimate, accessible ethnic cuisine. Remarking on Americans' expanded palate in the late 1950s, *Los Angeles Times* food writer Clementine Paddleford described a "scramble" to purchase "cookbooks which tumble from the presses, cram-jammed with Far Eastern food and drink ideas."[46]

Cookbooks on and from Hawai'i were a key medium for introducing Americans to Asian cooking. Before World War II, most cookbooks on Hawai'i were community cookbooks or other texts geared toward readers in Hawai'i itself. That all began to change in the mid-1950s, as Hawai'i appeared to be on the path to statehood and the islands gained new cultural prominence in popular media. The first breakout cookbook to come from Hawai'i was *Mary Sia's Chinese Cookbook*, originally published in 1956. Although Sia's text was explicitly a guide to the food of China, not Hawai'i, it was a product of Hawai'i nonetheless. Copyrighted by the University of Hawai'i Press, and manufactured by the Honolulu-based Tongg Publishing, *Mary Sia's Chinese Cookbook* was described on the inside flap as the work of a "thoroughly cosmopolitan" expert with three decades of cooking experience in both China and Hawai'i. In the introduction, Sia, who was born and raised by Chinese parents in Honolulu, wrote of learning to cook first in Hawai'i, before ever setting foot on Chinese soil.

Mary Sia's Chinese Cookbook, which was reissued within a year and has since gone through multiple reprints and four editions, introduced many American readers to the art of Chinese cooking at a time when Chinese cookbooks were still uncommon; it was also one of the first Chinese cookbooks to enjoy mainstream national success. By 1956, Sia was already a pioneer and considered a "famous teacher" of Asian cuisine.[47] Her first book, *Chinese Chopsticks*, which came out in 1935, was one of only a handful of Chinese cookbooks published in the United States at the time. The few English-language texts available on the mainland before World War II were mostly short community cookbooks, with titles such as *What's Cooking in Your Oriental Neighbor's Pot Party*, compiled by proimmigrant groups or religious organizations with missionary ties.[48] By contrast, clocking in at some 150 pages, *Mary Sia's Chinese Cookbook* offered a more comprehensive examination of Chinese cooking and allowed the author space to explain and ruminate on the ways in which food reflected Chinese ways of living and understanding the world.

Although she assumed her audience's general ignorance of Chinese food, Sia "took it for granted that the cuisine commanded respect."[49] She conveyed a straightforward confidence in the complexity and sophistication of Chinese food. Challenging the stereotype, represented by chop suey, that Chinese cuisine was thrown-together peasant food meant to be scarfed down, Sia explained in the book's lengthy introduction that the Chinese took food and its preparation very seriously—because food was something to revere and take pleasure in. "In China," Sia wrote, "cooking has become an art." Even though many Chinese cooking techniques were the result of poverty, Chinese cooks still made sure that their food was tasty, flavorful, and pleasing to the eye.

Sia even made some subtle barbs at Western culture. For one, she claimed, Chinese people exercised more discipline when it came to alcohol. Sia recommended that Americans take up the practice of using chopsticks to signal the end of libations at a feast. "Many an American housewife who frets while her guests continue drinking as the dinner gets cold would enjoy the Chinese system of cutting off the 'cocktail hour,'" by signaling the end of libations by holding up a pair of chopsticks.[50]

At the heart of the narrative presented in the cookbook was Sia herself. Her first-person preface lent the rest of the text a promise of authenticity and her authoritative instructions throughout made the foreign recipes more accessible to American readers. Moreover, her biography in many ways exemplified the emerging image of Hawai'i as "bridge to Asia." She had a sympathetic life story, one that dovetailed with increasingly popular ideas about Asian immigrants' ambition and their devotion to family and tradition. As the child of Chinese-born parents, both of whom were medical doctors, Sia learned classic Chinese cooking at their Honolulu home, where, Sia wrote, her mother's "love of life attracted guests from every part of the world and her warm hospitality included the finest Chinese food."[51] While living briefly in Beijing with her husband, she began teaching Chinese cooking to Western women living in the city, and she reveled in her role as a mediator between East and West— "pleasing the palate," she believed, "could be a bridge between two great cultures."[52] After returning to Honolulu during the war, she continued teaching cooking classes to haole housewives, eventually leading her to write *Mary Sia's Chinese Cookbook*. Though a native U.S. citizen, Sia embodied a vision of immigrant life that was more pluralistic than most prewar iterations. She was, according to a profile in the *Los Angeles Times,* "a cosmopolitan, a product of two worlds."[53] She had not assimilated in the traditional sense—Sia was still deeply enmeshed with China and Chinese culture, which was the very thing that made her book compelling.

Sia also represented a more worldly model of postwar womanhood than the stereotypical suburban mainland housewife. While she expressed dedication to home and family life and frequently directed her advice to housewives, her own claims to expertise were made on the basis of her education—she had a degree in home economics from the University of Hawai'i—her role as a teacher, and significantly, her identification with a trans-Pacific perspective on, and direct experience of, the world. Despite the cultural emphasis on domesticity in the postwar period, women also frequently sought, and were celebrated for, their paid work, volunteering, and other activities outside the home.[54] Perhaps Sia, through her own example and through her cooking advice, appealed to women's desires for a fuller engagement with the world beyond the domestic sphere—a feat that could be accomplished, paradoxically, by bringing the world into the kitchen.

While the Hawai'i-born Sia helped usher in a new fascination with Chinese cooking in American homes, other food writing highlighted Hawai'i's multiple ethnic food traditions. Most cookbooks on Hawai'i opened with an introduction that began by describing the successive waves of migration to the islands and ended with a reflection on the positive impact of migrants on Hawai'i's foodways, or how "the truly cosmopolitan way to life offered in Hawaii permits the savoring of many cultures."[55] Hawai'i food even might go beyond a temporary feeling of pleasure and "become a way of life" that "opens the mind, and, more important, the palate to different tastes, cooking techniques, to cultures and the people [of Hawai'i] themselves," as author Elizabeth Ahn Toupin claimed in *The Hawaii Cookbook and Backyard Luau.* In a book with a foreword by James Michener—and with a rainbow-fonted "Hawaii" on its cover whose design looked suspiciously like the jacket of Michener's *Hawaii*—Toupin invited readers to embark on a "delicious adventure."[56]

Like Sia, Toupin was a daughter of Hawai'i. Born Elizabeth Ahn in Honolulu to Korean parents, her life trajectory in many ways paralleled the increasing prominence of Hawai'i in national politics and culture. In the late 1940s, she collaborated with future senator Daniel Inouye in the local Democratic Party's campaign for statehood, and later served as Inouye's research assistant in Washington, DC.[57] But by the early 1960s, when her husband Richard Toupin's work took the family to Westchester, New York, Elizabeth had become a bored housewife. She turned to cookbook writing and proved to be a savvy author, tapping a rich cultural vein with *The Hawaii Cookbook and Backyard Luau*. The book, which was originally published in 1967 by a small publisher, was quickly picked up by Doubleday's Bantam imprint, becoming the first Hawai'i cookbook authored by a Hawai'i local and published by a major press. It was an immediate success: as part of Doubleday's Cookbook of the Month series, it sold 90,000 copies in its first month, eventually reaching 120,000, with sales reportedly exceeding any other previous title in the series.[58]

Toupin's housewife persona in the accompanying press coverage masked her ambition. With *The Hawaii Cookbook and Backyard Luau*, she used the broader discourses around Hawai'i to her advantage. Seeking to ride the momentum of the 1966 film version of Michener's *Hawaii*, she recruited Michener for the foreword by drawing on their common friendship with Inouye.[59] Toupin also deliberately linked Hawai'i's food to the racial liberalism Michener represented. The dishes in her book, Toupin suggested, were more than the sum of their ingredients. Rather, they could elicit feelings of empathy and tolerance, catalyzing a new worldview. "This memorable encounter [with Hawai'i's food] can only enrich one's life," she wrote, "for preparing and feasting the various cuisines is a way of experiencing life as another lives it." Taste could even offer a lesson in world history. By "drawing the best from each [ethnic] group and combining them expertly," cooking the food of Hawai'i was a sensory manifestation of not only the islands' mixed society, but of larger global processes. The food of Hawai'i, she wrote, represented the legacies of modern migration—by cooking and eating it one was calling up "the history of the culinary arts of the Orient and the Pacific, transported in seed and memory, modified by tropical lands and streamlined by jets, electric kitchens and appliances."[60]

Toupin urged her readers to participate in this ever-accelerating globalization by cooking and eating the food of Hawai'i. In doing so, she infused jet age visions of untrammeled access to the world with higher moral purpose. Toupin presented a vision of female mastery of the world's cultures that seemed increasingly realizable for many American women and a distinct break from the past, when global travel was reserved mainly for privileged men. At the same time, it was couched in decidedly feminine terms; Toupin, herself a woman of Asian descent, invoked empathy and hybridity in her descriptions of Hawai'i's globetrotting food. And yet, such language overlooked the unequal relations of power between white American women and women of color around the world, including many in Hawai'i itself. As in the foreign policy discourses on cultural exchange in Hawai'i, those on Hawai'i food and fashion portrayed America's engagement with Asia and the Pacific as benevolent and mutualistic rather than violent and coercive. To that end, Toupin's idealized representation of Hawai'i's cuisine offered home cooks a more palatable version of the cross-cultural encounter, one in which power was not part of the equation.

As in Toupin's text, the history lessons typically provided in the opening pages of Hawai'i cookbooks made the development of Hawai'i's multiethnic society appear as an inevitable, and wholly successful, product of globalization and modernity. "Time and progress brought many peoples to the island shores," went the *Pacifica House Hawaii Cookbook* (1965). "They liked island life, each new group developed and shared its cultures and customs until now, hundreds of years later, Hawaii has emerged with a way of life which is bound to enrich all those privileged to either visit or to live within its sea-swept boundaries."[61] The gourmet's "paradise unlimited" that resulted from this enviable history was seemingly free of conflict or hardship. It was also a version of history that erased U.S. colonialism in Hawai'i and elsewhere in the Pacific. Instead, cookbook narratives presented Hawai'i's evolution toward cross-cultural understanding and racial equality as complete and coherent.

Hawai'i's food thus represented not only a mixing of cultures, but the tangible, and delicious, fruits of social harmony and global progress. The cookbook of the Hawaii State Society of Washington, DC, argued explicitly that the food itself had produced Hawai'i's famed social relations, claiming, "Out of the acceptance of each other's food came the resultant tolerance for the people and their foreign roots."[62] The benefits of this were said to accrue not only to people of color in Hawai'i, but to its white residents as well, who, according to *House Beautiful,* had become "worldly, urbane, and sophisticated" because they had "thoroughly assimilated the many and diverse cultures of Asia and the Pacific basin" in their entertaining.[63] Here, the usual meaning of assimilation in popular American discourse was turned on its head, with Westerners adapting Asian traditions rather than the other way around. To cook and eat Hawai'i's food was both to endorse this progressive vision and to collect its bounty—to assert one's racial liberalism while enjoying its edible pleasures.

While the promise of furthering positive race relations likely appealed to those readers who chose to join the "delicious adventure" of Hawai'i-style cooking, it could be a potentially vexing trip nonetheless. Unfamiliarity with many dishes and ingredients might be exciting, but it could also be daunting. New cooking techniques could be intimidating and often required the purchase of new equipment, such as woks or hibachi grills. Acquired tastes for foreign flavors took effort. Many cooking tutorials on Hawai'i assumed readers' ignorance of the islands' foodways. Cookbooks typically included a glossary, made up of Hawaiian and Asian food terminology, at the beginning or end of the text. These helped introduce mainlanders to strange ingredients like fresh ginger, sake, and ahi, the Hawaiian word for tuna.[64]

While Hawai'i cooking tutorials were often didactic, they tended to adopt a coaxing tone, straddling the line between entreating readers to experiment and accommodating mainland provincialisms. A Dole luau instructional booklet from 1973, for instance, urged mainland luau participants to try a raw lomi-lomi salmon salad, barbequed spareribs with a sweet and sour marinade, and shrimp tempura, but suggested using rice as an accompaniment instead of poi.[65] The point was to convey authenticity without overdoing it. Similarly, the food section of the *Atlanta Constitution,* in offering a menu that included seafood stuffed pineapples and turkey roast with Chinese sauce, insisted that Hawai'i-style food served on the mainland "should have the authentic feeling of the Hawaiian Islands, yet appeal completely to American appetites."[66]

Others urged mainland cooks to prove their worldliness by suppressing the urge to modify Hawai'i's food. One cookbook recommended that "uninitiated" eaters have several cocktails before trying some of the recipes it contained.[67] Trader Vic, practically goading his cookbook readers to defy his generalization, gave his highest recommendation to sushi and sashimi, saying he was "addicted to it," but that Japanese raw fish dishes were "a seldom acquired taste with Americans."[68] Those who did acquire it, he suggested, would become members of an exclusive club for sophisticated sushi junkies. In labeling raw fish an "acquired taste" but declaring his love for it, Trader Vic at once confirmed and rejected long-held assumptions about non-Western cuisine—exemplified by the Washington lawyer who, at statehood hearings in 1948, chastised Hawai'i residents for serving raw fish to mainlanders because it made the islands appear "not quite civilized."[69] Trader Vic, some two decades later, asserted his own claim to cultural enlightenment by insinuating that most Americans, unlike him, were too provincial to experiment with truly exotic foods.

Trader Vic and other food writers were wrong to underestimate Americans' interest in Japanese raw fish or other "unusual" foods. By the end of the twentieth century one need not go far in most small U.S. cities to satisfy a craving for sushi or many other Asian specialties that would have been wholly unfamiliar in the early postwar period. And indeed it was Trader Vic, Elizabeth Toupin, and others serving and writing about the food of Hawai'i who introduced many Americans to a wide variety of East Asian food beyond chop suey, from teriyaki beef to kimchi to Filipino pancit. For countless home cooks, a Hawai'i cookbook was likely the first place where they encountered non-Chinese East Asian cuisine.

Whether they were modifying their recipes or not, mainland cooks were increasingly able to access the ingredients and equipment needed for the "highly unusual" recipes in Hawai'i food. Many exotic and once-exotic foodstuffs—such as soy sauce, water chestnuts, tropical fruits, and even poi—were available in mainland stores. Cookbooks and newspaper food columns often provided readers with lists of local specialty shops and mail-order companies where they could acquire the necessary supplies. Over time, they began directing their readers to the supermarket, where many of the basic ingredients for Asian cooking were now appearing on store shelves as the corporate food industry awoke to the appeal of "ethnic" cuisine.[70]

Part of that appeal was the notion that the "delectable" food of Hawai'i represented fun, even decadence. Food writers reminded their audience that people in Hawai'i "take time out to enjoy living."[71] When serving food from Hawai'i, readers were frequently told, there should be an abundant quantity on offer to convey festiveness and joy—a marked departure from the scarcity of a few decades earlier. Meanwhile, food writers' emphasis on the novel and intense flavors of many of the "intriguingly spiced" foods associated with Hawai'i, in particular "fiery" Chinese cuisine, underscored its extravagance—standing in stark contrast to the supposed refinement of French food or the blandness of typical American cooking during the first half of the twentieth century.[72]

Spicy and flavorful food had long been linked with sex. Into the twentieth century, many spices were considered to be stimulants like caffeine. Victorian women were exhorted to avoid foods with too much seasoning and to repress their appetites in service of a "delicate" feminine ideal—one that supposedly stood in contrast to the "intemperate" women of Asia.[73] By the postwar period, and particularly after the 1950s, Americans were relishing more flavorful food and all the other sensual implications that came with it. Food writing on Hawai'i in the postwar era played on the identification of foreign foods with sexual appetites, and more specifically, with Hawai'i's reputation as a land of open sexuality, where interracial sex had gone hand in hand with the mixing of cuisines. The fruits of Hawai'i were described as "luscious," the islanders "creative salad making" as "totally uninhibited."[74]

Such language drew on well-established colonialist and Orientalist tropes of the heightened sexuality of nonwhite societies. Hawai'i had long been framed as an object of desire for American men, who sought to possess both the islands and their women, portrayed as sexually available and submissive. Increasingly in the postwar era, mainland women, too, looked to Hawai'i as a site of pleasure. Whereas white women of an earlier period were held up as models of virtue for people of color to emulate, now white women were asked to imitate—perhaps by making an "uninhibited" salad—the supposed sexual liberalism of the people of Hawai'i.

For *Cosmopolitan* editor Helen Gurley Brown, Hawai'i, and its food, were to be viewed as a means of sexual fulfillment. In her *Single Girl's Cookbook*—after exclaiming "Shame on you!" to readers who turned up their noses at "sensuous" foreign food—Brown recommended serving a Hawai'i-inspired menu for women who aimed to win back straying lovers.[75] To stand out above the competition, "cook something *different*." The "chicken luau" dish she recommended included ingredients—such as spinach, mushrooms, and tarragon—that hardly suggested Hawai'i. But Brown played up the exoticism nonetheless. Make him "food he might only have read about in *National Enquirer*," Brown implored.[76] Brown's text was one of a rash cookbooks published in the 1970s that explicitly melded cooking and sexuality by urging single people to view food preparation as "a form of seduction."[77] Published in 1969, *The Single Girl's Cookbook* echoed many of the same themes of Brown's sensational advice manual, *Sex and the Single Girl*, which came out seven years earlier. Both texts celebrated female sexuality outside of marriage as well as a less domesticated version of postwar womanhood, with Brown urging her readers to pursue meaningful careers as well as sexual pleasure. In urging women to live a more exciting life, Brown's was a message that jibed with those embedded in Hawai'i food writing.

But this liberatory premise was undercut by the expectation that women's identities would continue to be determined by their relationships with men, who served as the ultimate arbiters of female desirability and the objects of women's efforts to expand their culinary repertoires. Brown did not call for a transformation of gender norms so much as a modification. Women were now expected to project worldliness and flexibility instead of domesticity and virtue—and to do so to secure their sexual allure to, rather than a marriage proposal from, the opposite sex. Moreover, as much as Brown insisted that women must leave the home, physically and psychologically, her advice did not rescue women from the gendered domain of the kitchen. The key was to feign an attitude of antidomesticity. For Brown, the waning male attention that her Hawaiian menu aimed to reverse constituted "an EMERGENCY," one that made it all the more important "to seem not to have fussed."[78]

Other cultural representations of Hawai'i during this period also centered on white women's heterosexual awakening. Newspapers and magazines reported drolly on the University of Hawai'i's summer school, where the vast majority of mainland students were women—"a most attractive species of migratory fauna," according to *Life*. Though they were ostensibly there to study, usually education, after class they sought out "sun, sea, dancing and summer romances (naval ensigns preferred)."[79] Reinforcing the idea of Hawai'i as a site of female pleasure was a trilogy of Hawai'i films starring Elvis Presley—*Blue Hawaii* (1961), *Girls! Girls! Girls* (1962), and *Paradise, Hawaiian Style* (1966)—that focused on Presley's romantic adventures and featured multiracial casts. These hugely popular films relied on Presley's sexual appeal, as with a *Paradise, Hawaiian Style* poster that promised, perhaps referencing his notoriously energetic pelvis, that "Elvis breaks loose in the swinging, swaying, luau-ing South Seas!" A similarly suggestive scene in *Blue Hawaii* showed him singing and strumming his guitar wearing only a pair of tight swimming trunks and surrounded by Waikiki "beach boys." Meanwhile, the romanticized figure of the Native Hawaiian beach boy featured prominently in the last section of James Michener's *Hawaii,* when Elinor, a young white widow from Boston, falls for Kelly, a pidgin-speaking surf instructor brimming with "amazing manliness" who made women "think of little else" besides sex.[80]

Changing sexual norms linked to cross-cultural experimentation animated the "luau craze" of the 1960s and early 1970s. If Hawai'i's food offered a taste of the fiftieth state and the sexual and racial future it portended, the luau promised that participants could live in that future, if only for the length of the party. It was supposed to be "an escapist's delight" that transported guests "to the Islands by the sense of sight, taste and smell."[81] Indeed, the constellation of sensory stimuli made mainland luaus perhaps the most immersive of Hawai'i consumer experiences outside of a trip to the islands. Many of these luaus were public, or semipublic, events—club parties, neighborhood festivals, fundraisers, apartment complex socials—that helped to popularize the luau as social practice. The vast majority of mainland luaus, however, were private affairs held in people's homes, a nationwide trend spurred by the general fascination with Hawai'i as well as a profusion of advice texts on how, and why, to throw a luau.

The mainland luau demanded a lot of work to produce the casual mood that was supposed to be its hallmark. According to Dole, to create the crucial "relaxed atmosphere," the luau would require "an abundance of food"— multiple meat and fish dishes along with a suckling pig—fruity cocktails, "decorations and costumes in the tropical manner," and an elaborately set table with tropical plants. All these elements together would facilitate "the bountiful feeling a Luau always gives—filled with laughter, light-heartedness, and plenty for all." Neglect any one, Dole implied, and your luau might not capture the aura of Hawai'i it was meant to invoke.[82]

Luau planning required a holistic approach. According to Hilo Hattie, a well-known Hawaiian entertainer, "Food alone does not make a successful luau." Rather, "it is fun and merriment, music, singing and dancing that are the most important fare."[83] Décor was key to setting the merry mood. Like tiki restaurants, the food was mixed Asian and Hawaiian but the setting of a luau was meant to be Polynesian, conjured by fishnets, flaming bamboo torches, flower garlands, papier-mâché volcanoes, and other tropical-looking décor. A number of outlets offered specialized services to aid those looking for the right supplies. Orchids of Hawaii in Manhattan sold the requisite flora, as well as a range of other merchandise, to New York luau enthusiasts. For more high-end party planners, the shop also employed an "entertainment counselor" to help with the arrangements.[84] In Washington, residents had the benefit of a Hawai'i state delegation eager to promote affection for the islands among the national policy elite. As the summer party season ramped up, the *Washington Post* reported in 1965 that "real Hawaiian guests are in much demand" at district luaus.[85] Meanwhile, for those who did not have easy access to Hawai'i politicians or a retail store selling tropical decorations, Dole offered a catalog of "luau kits," complete with die-cut flowers, poly leis, plastic hair flowers, tiki gods, and crepe-paper pineapples.[86] The luau kits represented an attempt to distill Hawai'i—and all the meanings that the Hawai'i signifier evoked—into commodities that allowed anyone to participate in the Hawai'i experience.

The luau, above all, was meant to be relaxed, and relaxing. This was a festive event—the term *luau* was "almost a synonym for a gay, informal party"—not a staid formal affair.[87] Food writers stressed that a luau should be a carefree fete even for the woman throwing it. "This is a dinner planned for the hostess-cook, who doubles in brass—who is maid and dishwasher," the *Los Angeles Times* insisted. "Note there are no last minute preparations and no need to be up and down like a jumping jack during the dinner."[88] However much effort she put into organizing it, the hostess was expected to project a sense of effortlessness to produce an informal mood. Guests, too, should show up to a luau ready to seek out the unfamiliar and shed their inhibitions. The fare was served buffet style, and much of it was in the form of pupu, a Hawaiian word used to refer to finger food ("provide plenty of napkins," *Sunset* warned).[89] Outdoor footwear might be prohibited in the Asian custom, as it was at a luau in the nation's capital where "a front porch covered with shoes (minus owners)" served as a warning to "would-be 'stuffy' guests" that this was "anything but a typical Washington party."[90] In another blow to stuffiness, seating was often on floor pillows or directly on the ground. Liberally served libations, meanwhile, would ease guests into these foreign practices and ensure affability and social mingling.

For housewives, the luau's call for purportedly low-key entertaining promised to lessen the burden of hosting and allow her to indulge in the festivities. Those festivities typically centered around racial imitation, which was often tinged with sex and the loosening of social conventions.[91] According to Trader Vic, luaus appealed to a universal desire "to get out of character now and then, to relax and unleash the shackles of propriety." The Hawai'i theme allowed "the gals . . . to play the siren, dance a little naughty and shake their fannies around. Guys like to get into the act and clown around."[92] To match the multiethnic food on offer, guests might be encouraged to dress in grass skirts or other garments associated with Hawai'i fashion, said to be both more comfortable and more flamboyant than other styles. Some women went

FIGURE 15. Luaus were known for loosening social mores. A Los
Angeles beach club luau, 1951. University of Southern California
Libraries, *Los Angeles Examiner* Photographs Collection.

further in altering their appearance to look less white by using dark wigs to
cover their light hair.[93] Guests could also be expected to engage more freely
in physical contact with other partygoers through a welcoming ceremony
involving the bestowing of leis and kisses.[94] More ambitious hostesses organized hula lessons. This emphasis on racialized playacting, according to one
report, ensured that "even the most staid businessmen and social matrons"
could be found at a luau "happily ensconced on sand or floor attired in typical
costume."[95]

It should be noted that Hawaiʻi cookbooks and food writing often inaccurately represented both older Hawaiian food customs and the everyday
foodways of most people living in the islands in the mid-twentieth century.
In appealing to a mainland audience, food writing at once exotified and
deexotified Hawaiʻi cuisine. Traditional Hawaiian food, for one, was served
cold and was based more on raw fish than meat, which dominated most luau
menus. Precontact Native Hawaiian feasts, meanwhile, were religious events
that were gender and class segregated, "not the convivial, lavish and egalitarian
festivities of popular imagination."[96] The luau, which was a word that did not
exist in precontact Hawaiʻi, was popularized during the late nineteenth and
early twentieth centuries as a form of cultural resistance to Americanization
and annexation.[97] Meanwhile, after statehood, pineapple—used to make any
dish "Hawaiian" despite its South American origins—was increasingly produced in the Philippines and Thailand to reduce labor costs.[98]

PUPUS

tempura shrimp pupus

INGREDIENTS:	PORTION: 25	50	100
Shrimp 16/20 count	2½ lbs.	5 lbs.	10 lbs.
Milk	1 cup	2 cups	4 cups
Egg	1	2	4
Flour	1 cup	2 cups	4 cups
Oil			
Chicken broth	1 cup	2 cups	4 cups
Soy sauce	½ cup	1 cup	2 cups
Pineapple Juice	½ cup	1 cup	2 cups
Brown sugar	2 tsp.	4 tsp.	2½ tbsp.
Horseradish	4 tsp.	2½ tbsp.	5 tbsp.
Cornstarch	4 tsp.	2½ tbsp.	5 tbsp.

DIRECTIONS:

Peel and slit raw shrimp lengthwise, leaving tails on. Remove vein. Beat together milk and egg; add flour and blend until smooth. Do not overbeat. Dip shrimp in batter and fry in 375°F. oil until golden brown. Drain. Mix all remaining ingredients and heat to boiling. Serve as dipping sauce for shrimp.

Size of portion: 2 per person.

Tempura Shrimp Pupus

FIGURE 16. A recipe for tempura shrimp pupus combined multiple food traditions under the Hawaiian label. *A Dole Hawaiian Luau*, 1973. Dole Collection, University of Hawaiʻi Library.

At the same time, many of the foods that were common in twentieth-century Hawaiʻi did not make it into the pages of popular cookbooks. Spam, for instance, became a staple of Hawaiʻi diets after it was introduced during World War II. The cheap canned meat was incorporated into everything from breakfast eggs to tempura, leading Hawaiʻi to become the biggest consumer of Spam in the United States.[99] As the Spam example suggests, the association of Hawai'i cuisine with abundance belied the relative difficulty and expense of eating in Hawai'i itself. In 1970, Honolulu residents spent more on food than Americans in any other major metropolitan area, and some 16–20 percent above the urban U.S. average.[100] This was due in large part to Hawai'i's long-standing dependence on food produced thousands of miles away on the mainland, which was only exacerbated as the land-hungry tourism business became the driver of Hawai'i's economy. Although the Hawaiian islands were self-sufficient for thousands of years before Western contact, the increase in imports since statehood was so dramatic that, by the twenty-first century, Hawai'i was shipping in 85–90 percent of its food.[101] Such realities almost never made it into Hawai'i cookbooks and newspaper recipe pages.

Like Hawai'i food writing, the discourses of the Hawai'i fashion industry were wrapped in a haze of promises of personal transformation. Promoters of Hawai'i fashion attributed its appeal to its emphasis on color, comfort, and multiethnic influences, which in turn reflected Hawai'i's much-lauded diversity and social laxity—qualities that mainlanders were said to be embracing themselves. Hawai'i had become "a well-spring of casual fashion," a 1966 promotion claimed. "Our colors, our styles are now emulated all over the world. The whole world is moving toward a more casual way of life, and since that is what Hawaii has always stood for, it is moving toward us."[102] Part of that "casual way of life" was Hawai'i's supposedly easy mixing of Asian, Polynesian, and Western cultures, which informed Hawai'i designs. Indeed, many of the defining features of Hawai'i fashion did emerge out of the particularities of Hawai'i society, as boosters claimed. But those particularities were not always the ones highlighted in popular images of Hawai'i apparel, which tended to naturalize Hawai'i as a "well-spring" of cosmopolitan fashion rather than a place whose local political economy, social relations, and labor conditions shaped the clothing it produced.

Modern garment production in Hawai'i began with the "Mother Hubbard" dress introduced by American missionaries in the early nineteenth century. This was a floor-length, high-necked, long-sleeve garment that served as the basis for a number of "Hawaiian" styles to come, notably the muumuu (originally worn as an undergarment). Many older sources claimed that missionaries foisted this garment on Hawaiian women in an effort to cover up their naked bodies, though more recent accounts claim that royal Hawaiian women actively sought out the style for themselves, with the Mother Hubbard adapted for tropical temperatures by removing the waist and replacing it with a yoke above the bust. Even this early, Western-inspired garment, however, was Pacific in orientation as many of the original fabrics used were painted silks and brocades from Asia.[103]

During the late nineteenth and early twentieth centuries, the local clothing trade was comprised of small shops, the vast majority of which were owned by Asian immigrants.[104] The industry expanded in size and scope during the interwar period as factories opened and tourism increased. By the mid-1930s, manufacturers were producing "aloha shirts"—Western-style casual men's button-down tops made with colorful tropical-themed printed fabric. During World War II, the shirts became must-have souvenirs for GIs and production of aloha shirts soared after the war, with new pattern themes that increasingly showcased Asian iconography in addition to "traditional" images of leis, pineapples, and tropical flowers.[105]

But it was women consumers who transformed the Hawai'i garment industry into a multimillion dollar global business. In the postwar period, the vast majority of garments produced in Hawai'i were women's wear.[106] The muumuu provided the initial spark. Beginning after World War II, female tourists helped make the muumuu—a short-sleeved, waistless shift—an iconic garment in the growing casual-wear market. According to the Hawai'i garment industry, mainland women's discovery of the muumuu was a revelation: a rejection of conformity and confinement that inaugurated "a fashion shot heard round the world." After realizing they could "zip off their girdles," women "leaped into [muumuus] as soon as they got off the boat, giggled a bit when they made their first self-conscious appearance, and then relaxed as they saw how they melted into the Waikiki scene."[107]

Despite its reputed origins with puritanical missionaries, the muumuu was described by its mid-twentieth-century advocates as a way to rebel against old-fashioned ideas of female sexuality. In fact, the muumuu's predecessor, the Mother Hubbard, had become a favorite of prostitutes in the 1880s, and even a target of vice law in some U.S. cities, because it made sex easier.[108] The muumuu of the later era was similarly associated with a rejection of physical restriction. Fashion writing often traced its popularization on the mainland in the late 1950s to college "co-eds"—specifically a group at the University of Ohio, according to one report—who, in the name of comfort and relaxation, felt free to discard the fashion rules their mothers followed.[109] The muumuu thus had a certain youthful cachet. But older women also cottoned to the muumuu. According to one *Los Angeles Times* fashion writer in 1963, the muumuu appealed to all women, and for a multitude of reasons. Working women liked it because, "after a busy day at the office bound in rigorous foundations" they could "shed these pinching, cinching underpinnings and [retire] to muumuu bliss." Housewives attending to homemaking duties appreciated that they "could execute them in comfort." And women with "figure problems" liked that the muumuu's "sheer vastness" provided cover. The muumuu, the author suggested, even had a transformative effect on women's self-perception, leading them to feel more at ease in their own bodies, if only in private: "What the muumuu taught a woman is that she could and should be unfettered and comfortable at home."[110]

Indeed, whether it changed the way women thought of their bodies, the muumuu represented a form of liberation from the constricting styles popular in the 1950s, which required tight undergarments to achieve a cinched waist and lifted breasts. A muumuu's defining characteristic was its looseness, effected by an abundance of fabric that grazed the body rather than encased it. Muumuus could be worn with no undergarments at all.

While the muumuu would remain a staple of the Hawai'i fashion (despite perennial declarations of its demise), with statehood the Hawai'i garment industry began to produce a much wider range of styles, and by the 1960s apparel constituted the islands' third most profitable commodity, behind sugar and pineapple. This was an expansion aided by support from the state for a Hawai'i fashion guild, as well as large-scale tie-in partnerships with mainland department stores, malls, and magazines.[111] Although garment manufacturing remained a smaller part of the state economy compared to tourism or government spending, its expansion heralded the broader success of the marketing of "Hawaii" as a way of life. As Hawai'i fashion exploded in the late 1950s and early 1960s, the growth in garment manufacturing in the islands outpaced that of any other nongovernment industry in Hawai'i and at a rate double that of the national garment industry as a whole.[112] Over the next decades, the local industry continued to swell, particularly in the increase in "exports" to the mainland, which constituted more than a third (some $23 million) of Hawai'i's manufacturing output by 1976.[113]

Local manufacturers sought to create a distinct aura around garments produced in Hawai'i. Many began affixing a "Made in Hawaii" label to garments, which, like "Made in France" or "Made in Italy" signaled the islands as a place known for a unique aesthetic and sensibility: in this case bright and colorful prints, Asian-inflected silhouettes, informality, and cosmopolitan sophistication. Sales on the mainland continued to be referred to as "exports" well after statehood, underscoring the notion that Hawai'i fashion was somehow foreign, constituting a market separate from the national garment trade. This was reinforced by the proliferation of specialty shops and department store sections devoted to Hawai'i clothing and other items in major urban centers across the United States. According to the *Los Angeles Times,* as early as 1961, there were some twenty Hawai'i-themed retail outlets scattered throughout Southern California, leading the paper to report that "the 'Made-in-Hawaii' tag on merchandise has created for most Hawaii products a tailor-made sales department" in the region, with a $10 million annual market.[114]

FIGURE 17. Muumuus promised liberation from the constricting
styles of the 1950s. Polynesian Patterns, ca. 1960s.

In many respects, Hawai'i's garment industry was distinct, helping to produce the "Made in Hawaii" look. For one, most garment businesses were small,
often husband-and-wife teams.[115] While these smaller firms were unable to
produce the same textile yardage as large factories on the mainland, Hawai'i
plants were nimbler, and small yardages meant a greater variety of prints, with
manufacturers often creating exclusive prints for particular mainland retailers.
Hawai'i firms also set themselves apart by relying mostly on screen printing, a
method best suited for smaller-scale production, and one that allowed for use
of more—and more brilliant—colors.[116]

Hawaiʻi itself informed the look of island fashion, which was "as varied and colorful as Hawaii's racial patterns," in other ways as well.[117] Just as local material conditions influenced the hues and prints that Hawaiʻi clothing was known for, so too did the ethnic traditions of garment manufacturers guide local style. East Asia's presence in Hawaiʻi clothing went back to the early nineteenth century, when members of the monarchy began importing Chinese silks. Later, Asian migrants to Hawaiʻi and their descendants came to dominate the garment trade in the islands; they helped popularize a mix of East Asian styles and print motifs, first within the local market and then in the fashion exported to the continental United States. While white textile designers entered the Hawaiʻi market in significant numbers in the postwar period, it appears that most of the original creators of Hawaiʻi-style prints were of Asian descent, and many of them were women.[118] Hawaiʻi manufacturers also continued to use Asian-made fabrics, particularly from Japan.

The "oriental glamour" of Hawaiʻi fashion was a large part of its appeal.[119] As explained in 1965 by *Paradise of the Pacific*, a Hawaiʻi magazine with a large circulation on the mainland, "The flavor of local design had to be, of necessity, a rich broth brewed from many international ingredients."[120] One local publication went so far as to credit Hawaiʻi-made garments with opening "the window of Asia to the rest of the United States."[121] Some garments, such as the Japanese kimono or mandarin collar blouse, were imported whole cloth. But East Asian design also had a more diffuse impact on Hawaiʻi fashion: "The Japanese contributed their kimono comfort, their shibui concept of beauty; the Chinese their side-slit *cheong-sams*, their classic simplicity and elegance; the Filipinos added *pina*, their gauzy pineapple cloth, their fantasy of butterfly sleeves, their lavish embroideries and beading." This all added up to "FASHION, PACIFICA," embodying "a more carefree and casual way of life."[122]

The ethnic backgrounds of Hawaiʻi's people were said to determine the quality of the garments as well, as most garment workers were of Asian descent and therefore came from "a strong tradition for patient painstaking work."[123] This was supposedly cultivated in Hawaiʻi homes, where Asian immigrant parents taught their children to sew, creating "a large reservoir of Oriental island seamstresses."[124] Commentators also praised the attention to detail of textile exporters from Japan, where "they take personal pride in their work," in contrast to the "mass-production minded" United States.[125] Whether garment workers in Hawaiʻi fulfilled the model minority cliché of the diligent Asian laborer, it was indeed the local industry's mostly Asian workforce that made the explosion of Hawaiʻi fashion possible.

But while Hawaiʻi's seamstresses were often romanticized in the fashion press, they reaped limited benefits from the popularity of the items they made. The extraordinarily tight profit margins of Hawaiʻi's small factories meant their wages were generally lower than in mainland firms, despite Hawai'i's high cost of living. Meanwhile, Hawai'i garment workers, the majority of them female and almost all of them nonunionized, earned well below the average manufacturing wage in the islands.[126] Production of the cosmopolitan fashions produced in Hawai'i thus relied on the toil of low-paid women of color, whose strained eyes and hunched backs were obscured by the message of freedom and comfort that Hawai'i garments projected onto the women who wore them. Increasingly that labor would move to Asia, where mostly female garment workers, not unlike the Asian women of Hawai'i, were extolled for their innate sewing skills while earning a fraction of American workers' wages. This globalization of the apparel trade, though spearheaded by large multinationals like Wal-Mart, was anticipated by the Hawai'i garment industry in both its outsourcing and nonunion labor practices and its celebration of "fashion, Pacifica."[127]

As it grew in popularity, Hawai'i fashion local designers increasingly aimed for a "more universal resort look" consisting of a variety of dress shapes, separates, and swimwear that went beyond muumuus and bright floral prints.[128] If muumuus represented at-home comfort, these newer styles produced in the fiftieth state were the requisite attire for the modern, jet-setting woman: "Lifestyles have changed. Jets take us, within hours, to the sun. Times are relaxed. Emily Post is simply a nice old lady, no longer the czarina of behavior." Whereas Paris, New York, and Rome were the traditional fashion centers, their stodgy garments no longer represented the vanguard. Those fashions asked women to "be happy in basic black." By contrast, "with its multihued prints and relaxed styling, the Hawaiian look suits a new age. It is contemporary. It is now."[129]

Indeed, Hawai'i-made garments were at the forefront of a larger movement toward more informal attire. During the 1960s and 1970s a growing number of American women were dressing in sportswear—originally developed for affluent elites to wear only for recreation—as everyday fashion. Characterized by separates, ease of movement, and low-maintenance fabrics, sportswear's popularity "coincided with the attitude that 'dressing down' in an elegant, comfortable manner was a subtle sign that one did not have to keep up appearances."[130] With its growth after statehood, the Hawai'i garment industry became evermore legitimate in eyes of the arbiters of high fashion.

Vogue, perhaps the most influential fashion magazine, was particularly invested in promoting Hawai'i and Hawai'i fashion. Under the editorial leadership of Diana Vreeland, who pushed the publication toward riskier, more artistic fashion coverage in the 1960s, *Vogue* portrayed Hawai'i clothing as chic expressions of a more relaxed way of life. Signaling its endorsement of Hawai'i as a fashion center, *Vogue* highlighted the fiftieth state in its November 1966 issue, which included dozens of pages of articles, fashion stories, and advertisements on the islands. In one, a photo spread featured German supermodel Veruschka posing yogically on a Hawaiian beach wearing "deft and delectable" muumuus and sarongs said to represent the "crest of a Hawaiian wave."[131]

Vogue's support for Hawai'i's garment industry underlined the idea that Hawai'i, like fashion houses such as Dior or Paco Rabanne, was a brand unto itself. And just as it cultivated relationships with labels and designers, *Vogue* often collaborated with Hawai'i officials and other state boosters to nurture Hawai'i fashion. The offices of Governor Burns and Senator Daniel Inouye, for instance, worked directly with the magazine to devise story ideas and coordinate advertising for *Vogue's* special issue on Hawai'i in November 1966.[132] A few years later, the Hawaii Visitors Bureau, together with the Cotton Producers Institute, arranged for an advertorial in *Vogue,* featuring Hawai'i fashion brands.[133]

The advertorial, which tied into the HVB's 1970 Golden People campaign to increase off-season tourism, dramatized the evolution of the Hawai'i garment industry from clothing aimed at a local and tourist market to fashion geared toward the readers of *Vogue.* In keeping with the typical themes of Hawai'i fashion discourse, the text emphasized "unexpected color combinations" and "*comfort* and coolness." But the *Vogue* reader targeted by the advertorial was more mobile and sophisticated than the housewife doing chores in her muumuu. With looks "designed to assert [their] vivid beauty under the most glaring sun" these were clothes created and marketed with the traveling woman in mind.[134] Or at least the woman who longed to travel. But even as it evoked the personal independence associated with the jet age, the rhetorical emphasis on casualness and comfort could also obscure the more restricting aspects of some newer Hawai'i garments. Whereas muumuus were notable for their lack of tailoring, the advertorial's Kahala pant set was "beautifully tailored to emphasize a trim waist, to discipline a curved hip."[135] Hawai'i fashion was not necessarily as freeing as it claimed to be; like the luau, it celebrated women's sexuality while asking women to conform to disciplining ideas of gender difference.

As the Hawai'i apparel industry moved into "fashion," its garments became less explicitly geared toward comfort even as it was helping to promote more casual styles. In this way, Hawai'i fashion was in line with larger trends in women's personal presentation. Women may no longer have felt pressure to wear confining girdles and bullet bras, but they were nonetheless expected to perform a particular kind of femininity—cool and "carefree," but also slim and attractive to men. The muumuu, meanwhile, continued to be seen as a kind of antifashion garment, precisely because its chief design feature was comfort.

Perhaps no one was more infatuated with the casual (if not always comfortable) Hawai'i aesthetic than residents of suburban Southern California. It wasn't just the region's similar climate and its relative proximity to Hawai'i that

FIGURE 18. A 1970 ad in *Vogue*—part of an HVB tie-in—promoted high-fashion Hawai'i clothing. National Cotton Council of America.

made luaus and muumuus so appealing. It was also the notion that Hawai'i offered a set of attitudes and practices that meshed with the emerging "California lifestyle." Hawai'i was vaunted for its informality, its relaxed mores, and its decidedly Pacific orientation. Hawai'i shaped, and helped legitimize, California's claim that the U.S. West was the main generator of American culture in the postwar period. In stark contrast to the East Coast, with its Puritan roots, its stodgy food and fashion, and its traditional architecture and design borrowed from the Old World, Hawaiʻi, California, and the rest of the U.S. West were promoted by cultural producers as the bellwether of the future. California had once been dismissed as "social Siberia," the *Los Angeles Times* wrote. But "no longer does it kowtow to condescending Eastern cousins. It's fun and it knows it."[136]

With the rise of Hollywood in the early twentieth century, California was already a major source of American popular culture; that influence amplified during and after World War II as California and many other parts of the region became a center of defense and electronics production, drawing millions of new residents and other industries westward. Many of the defining characteristics of American postwar life, from suburban development to the reliance on the automobile to new social movements, were taken to extremes in California and elsewhere in the West, where available land, economic opportunity, and the perception of a physical and cultural clean slate propelled a belief that the region was at the forefront of modernity.[137]

Hawaiʻi, as the newest, and farthest west, of American states, appeared to many to be the most different from the traditional, Eastern arbiters of U.S. culture. Its food, fashion, home design, and social norms signified a departure from the past in favor of a more relaxed and adventurous way of living. These were tropes that tapped into suburban Californians' self-image as pioneers of a new casual lifestyle, one defined by an innovative and eclectic design aesthetic, an embrace of the outdoors, informal dress, and a love of leisure.

Surfing was perhaps the most visible tradition that Californians borrowed from Hawaiʻi, though, ironically, its Hawaiian origins were frequently downplayed as California surfers claimed the pastime as their own. As an article in the *Los Angeles Times* declared, it was Southern California, not Hawaiʻi, that was the "true utopia" for surfers—mainly because of its more consistent waves but also, the author suggested, because it was Californians who had modernized surfboard design.[138] The notion that white Americans could improve on the Hawaiian sport, as Scott Laderman shows, went back to the early twentieth century, when haoles in Waikiki sought to master surfing as proof of their racial superiority over both Hawaiians and Asians.[139] By the time surfing exploded along the Southern California coastline in mid-century—due in large part to *Gidget,* the popular book, film, and television franchise that centered surfing culture in Malibu—it was one among several cultural practices linking California to Hawaiʻi.

Sunset magazine, a publication with a circulation of 800,000 in 1965 and key chronicler, and promoter, of life in the U.S. West, routinely drew the connection between Hawaiʻi and the West Coast.[140] The California-based *Sunset,* which boasted what it called a "second home" office in Honolulu and carried at least one article on Hawai'i in every issue, was one of the state's most vocal advocates.[141] It frequently urged readers to experiment with exports from the islands—not only luaus, but other practices and goods common to the fiftieth state.

Hawai'i was an important contributor to the West's informal living movement, which broke with older design traditions.[142] In the early postwar era, home design in the eastern United States was dominated by houses that relied on a Victorian sensibility, which called for numerous rooms with separate functions and a sharp delineation between private family areas and public spaces reserved for visitors.[143] By contrast, Hawai'i and West Coast homes in the postwar era used open floor plans with multipurpose rooms that allowed easier access to outdoor space, a feature that had become central to the notion of "good living" in the postwar West.[144] According to the *Los Angeles Times*, the ability to dine in one's own outdoor space, in particular, was a "pleasure of living" that Californians had borrowed from others and perfected.[145]

The lanai, "a shoes-off kind of room" that eroded the distinction between indoors and outdoors, was perhaps the most popular Hawai'i design innovation to be exported to the West Coast and beyond during the postwar period.[146] The lanai in Hawai'i homes was a fully incorporated, furnished, wall-less room intended to be used daily, "with no barriers or sense of visual separation" from the rest of the house or the outside.[147] It was, in part, a product of Hawai'i's calm tropical climate. But for many, the lanai also represented a broader philosophy of openness to nature, to the future, and to other people. Hawai'i homes and—by implication, their inhabitants—were celebrated in *Sunset* for being "open to the air, the trees, the sea, and the horizon beyond."[148] Similarly, *House & Garden*, in a special issue devoted to Hawai'i, extolled islanders' "exceptional talent for living." This included not only airy physical spaces, but also a "distinctly unhidebound" approach to decorating that embraced "carefree mixtures" of different ethnic furniture styles.[149]

Hawai'i's particular take on modern design was exemplified by its new state house, which was said to reflect the "unaffected democracy" of Hawai'i society, and whose plan featured a roofless inner court accessible from the street by the building's open sides and overhanging eaves that referenced Asian architecture.[150] The flexible, borderless, unrestricted sensibility of Hawai'i design was of a piece with the islands' image as a land of easy cultural mixing, relaxed social mores, and openness to new experience. Governor John Burns, upon inaugurating the capitol in 1968, made these linkages explicit. The building was a symbol of Hawai'i's "open arms and open hearts," Burns said. He went on to allude to Hawai'i's designated role as bridge between East and West, where America's commitment to inclusion was most fully realized. "It is by means of [the] striking architecture of this new structure," Burns claimed,

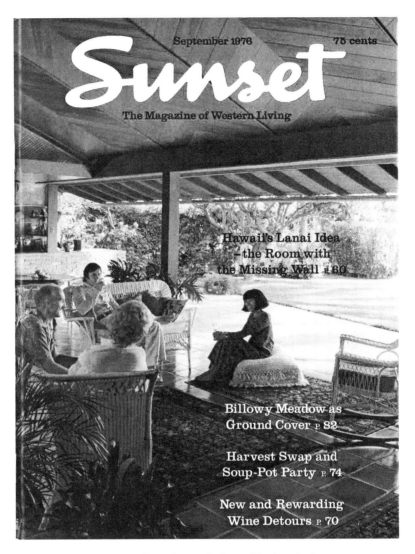

FIGURE 19. *Sunset* frequently featured lanais and other
design ideas from Hawai'i. *Sunset*, September 1976.

"that Hawai'i cries out to the nations of the Pacific and of the world, this
message: We are a free people . . . we are an open society . . . we welcome all
visitors to our Island home."[151]

Against this background, it was not only the aesthetic qualities of Hawai'i's
cultural exports, but the outward-looking worldview they signified, that
appealed to enthusiasts of Hawai'i food, fashion, and design. And yet, for all
the emphasis on worldliness, the consumption of Hawai'i on the mainland

largely took place within the insular space of the home. The Hawaiʻi-inspired products and activities so popular in the 1960s and 1970s were consumed and enacted in suburban houses that may have signaled an openness to the horizon beyond, but that were nonetheless bounded by a property line.

The ubiquity of the backyard luau was made possible by the postwar boom in homeownership and a housing market that promoted detached, single-family dwellings with their own outdoor space. At the heart of postwar housing discourse was a preoccupation with privacy—in terms of both private property and noninterference from the outside world—that shaped the suburban landscape and social practices. Suburban developments were often touted for their community life but also for their exclusivity, for their ability to provide family seclusion as well as protection from people deemed undesirable neighbors, notably poor people and people of color.

African Americans, in particular, were deliberately prevented from purchasing housing in many suburban areas, and from purchasing housing in general, through widespread discrimination among realtors, residents, lenders, local governments passing restrictive zoning laws, and the Federal Housing Administration's mortgage insurance program. All this led to the creation of what David Freund argues was a new racial formation that associated whiteness with property ownership.[152] Owning a home in the suburbs was also for many an emblem of white middle-class identity, a mark of independence from landlords, extended families, and the obligatory neighborly intimacy of urban living. Property rights and privacy in this context took on an exclusionary logic that left its mark on home design itself. While architects and developers extolled open floor plans for home interiors—and an easy transition between indoors and outside—outdoor areas often sharply delineated the boundaries of private space through fences, shrubbery, and other visual barriers that articulated a sense of separateness. Meanwhile, the decorative and recreational, as opposed to agricultural, uses of yards and gardens conveyed the homeowners' respectability and their capacity for conspicuous consumption.[153]

The luau flourished as backyards became places for entertaining in private, an expression of leisured class status and of distance from the messiness of the urban scrum. This was part of a broader shift away from public life in postwar U.S. society. As white Americans migrated to the suburbs, they traded everyday practices that had once been conducted in public—shopping in downtown commercial districts, going to the movies, or enjoying municipal parks—for consumption and recreation that took place in more rarefied quarters.[154] Enclosed spaces such as malls, country clubs, and the home became the primary sites of entertainment in suburban communities, where unpleasant encounters with people of different backgrounds could be avoided. At backyard luaus, the encounter with other cultures usually took the form of imitation, rather than interaction with people of non-European descent. Hosts and guests could enjoy the benefits of a multicultural lifestyle while avoiding the potentially unsettling consequences of engaging with people of different ethnic backgrounds, whose life experience might not correspond to the idealized portrait of social harmony painted by luau proponents.

It is significant that the peak of Hawai'i's influence on the West Coast, and in the United States more broadly, came as Los Angeles and other cities were deeply divided over issues of racial inequality, de facto segregation, and the generally slow progress of ground-level change for African Americans after civil rights reform. The broader national and global context shaping the racial dynamics of postwar cities meant that not all people of color experienced the same effects. As blacks were locked out of many of the economic opportunities fueled by the postwar boom, Asians came to be held up as America's "model minority."

This represented a significant transformation in status, one that was nowhere more astonishing than in California, which only a few decades earlier had been the center of the Asian exclusion movement. As Charlotte Brooks argues, this shift can be traced, in large part, to concerns about America's image abroad. Resistance by white homeowners seeking to keep Asians out of their neighborhoods now faced popular backlash, and increasingly Californians, including many conservatives, came to see Asian integration as a necessary "sacrifice" to win the Cold War.[155] Integration, however, had limits. The idea that suburban residents were relinqushing anti-Asian tradition for the good of the nation suggests a new willingness among many white Californians to live next door to Asians, and perhaps even patronize their businesses and borrow their cultural traditions, but a reluctance to fully embrace Asians as peers or close friends. And while Asians gained significant residential mobility in the postwar years, black exclusion was exacerbated.

If tourism to Hawai'i offered a physical escape to a place that promised anodyne cross-cultural interaction, the consumption of Hawai'i food and fashion in Los Angeles and elsewhere represented a withdrawal from a heterogeneous but divided city into a largely homogenous world where all the key roles could be played by whites. As riots broke out in black neighborhoods like Watts, where decades of simmering frustration with persistent poverty, inequality, and police abuse boiled over into violence, many white Angelenos defended the necessity of black residential separation while bemoaning the state of race relations in their city.[156] Speaking to this unrest, James Jiminez, the Filipino chairman of L.A.'s Polynesian-American Unity Day luau, insisted in 1971 that "Polynesians have never caused anyone any hassle," while "other minorities are getting a lot of attention through militant actions."[157] The peaceful people of Hawai'i and the Pacific, Jiminez suggested in a nod to the emerging "model minority" discourse, offered an antidote to the militancy of other people of color. For the white hostesses who looked across the Pacific for inspiration, the backyard luau could serve as a refuge from the turmoil of the streets, where one could perform racial liberalism without the hassle of racial discord.

6

The Third World in the Fiftieth State

ETHNIC STUDIES IN HAWAIʻI AND THE
CHALLENGE TO LIBERAL MULTICULTURALISM

THE VISION OF Hawaiʻi as a racial and consumer paradise required a process of both creation and erasure. The efforts of Hawaiʻi's boosters in the postwar era—statehood advocates, tourism industry leaders, and those promoting Hawaiʻi as a site for international exchange—all hinged on constructing an idea of the islands as a place where the practices of social difference were untainted by social struggle. The driving purpose behind that liberal multiculturalist narrative was its perceived role in advancing American economic and military interests in Asia, where the U.S. government sought to prove its racial tolerance and benevolent intent.

Such a project not only obscured the violence and coercion that characterized American intervention in Asia; it also ignored the complexity of life in Hawaiʻi. The multiracial, multiethnic nature of Hawaiʻi society was a direct legacy of American colonialism. Statehood may have formally ended Hawaiʻi's unequal territorial status but it could not undo its effects. That colonial history and its consequences would be reawakened as excitement over statehood gave way to widespread discontent among those excluded from statehood's rewards.

Tourists in Waikiki—sold on a vision of the islands as a bastion of social harmony, a showcase of American democracy, and an escape from the racial tensions of the mainland—would probably have been surprised by the events taking place just a couple of miles from their hotel during the spring of 1972. In late March, students at the University of Hawaiʻi occupied Bachman Hall, the administration building, to protest stalled negotiations over the future of the university's nascent Ethnic Studies Program. The administration, students and other ethnic studies supporters argued, was guilty of institutional racism in its appointment of a largely white faculty committee to advise on whether the program should be made permanent. For the protesters, who chanted, "Our

History! Our Way!" this was the latest in a long line of historical injustices. "We have to get clear in our heads that the Administration is not interested in local people," said Larry Kamakawiwoole, a Hawaiian member of the Ethnic Studies staff. "We have no place in the decision making-process. We are the servants, the singers, bus drivers, and waiters."[1]

Kamakawiwoole and the student activists did not match the image of happy Hawai'i residents that the tourism industry and others worked so hard to construct. Kamakawiwoole, by referencing the servile roles that many Hawai'i residents were expected to play in the tourism industry, offered an oblique denunciation of Hawai'i's poststatehood political economy, one in which some people benefited more than others and many of the old racial and class hierarchies continued to shape Hawai'i society.

This was the context in which tourism promoters raised the alarm about the erosion of the Aloha Spirit in Hawai'i, as discussed in chapter 4. Although they espoused only the most superficial understanding of its causes, those lamenting the Aloha Spirit's supposed decline were right to worry. By the late 1960s, Hawai'i's history of colonialism and racial inequality, which since World War II had been effectively contained through a discourse of progress and anti-colonialism, was coming under growing scrutiny within the state itself. And indeed, the Aloha Spirit, however real it ever was, appeared increasingly fragile as challenges to this dominant discourse grew louder. A newly vocal contingent of Hawai'i locals, galvanized by an emerging language of radical critique and frustrated with the gap between the state's rhetoric of inclusion and the reality of persistent inequality in the islands, offered a very different take on the defining characteristics of Hawai'i's history and culture. In this alternative analysis, Hawai'i was not a model of racial harmony; rather, it was a complex society that had not solved the mainland's racial problems, but shared them. Where state boosters saw amity, radicals saw simmering conflict.

The radical challenge to liberalism in the fiftieth state coalesced around the movement for ethnic studies at the University of Hawai'i. The university, one of the key institutions behind the effort to establish Hawai'i as the vanguard of multiculturalism, now found itself at the center of new debates over the nature of that multiculturalism in an era of radical ethnic activism. Students and faculty at UH, galvanized both by revolutionary movements on the mainland and in the Third World, and by local disillusionment with the poststatehood status quo, called for a new curriculum and pedagogy that reflected Hawai'i's complex multiethnic society. An ethnic studies program, they argued, would not only unveil a more accurate, and more troubling, history of Hawai'i, but would engender a new sense of ethnic pride among UH students that would give them the necessary tools to fight for social change beyond campus boundaries. It would also, according to its supporters, bring a much-needed local perspective to analyzing social relations in Hawaiʻi, one that emphasized Hawaiʻi's uniqueness and ran counter to the notion that Hawaiʻi was representative of the broader United States. The structure of the program, and the pedagogy behind the curriculum, meanwhile, were intended to represent a definitive break with past higher education approaches to the study of race, as students were given a role in programmatic decision making and their classes called for active community engagement.

The movement for ethnic studies, however, was not purely a product of grassroots agitation, despite the claims of many activists to the contrary. It also grew out of the mainstream discourses around Hawaiʻi as a multicultural paradise. And while it served as a correction to that idea it did not fundamentally overturn it. Hawaiʻi may not have been a paradise, according to ethnic studies activists, but its multiculturalism was worth celebrating. Earlier efforts to commend and institutionalize Hawaiʻi's diversity—whether through the East-West Center, Peace Corps training, or the tourism industry—helped set the stage for, and make palatable to policymakers and administrators, the radical multiculturalism promoted by ethnic studies. What was different about this version of multiculturalism was its emphasis on conflict and contestation as well as its ultimate aims. Radical ethnic activists saw group identification as a means to promote social justice and empowerment and, often, to fundamentally alter the political and economic system in which they lived, whether on a local or national level. Difference was at once the basic problem and the solution.

By contrast, those seeking to turn Hawaiʻi into a center for global cultural exchange saw the celebration of difference as a way to preserve and expand a status quo that was sound in theory, if not always so in practice. To them, the American way of life and its political institutions should be extended around the world, and this necessarily called for new—but limited—accommodations to difference. A basic rejection of capitalist development, for instance, was a difference too far. At the same time, this new liberal framework for making sense of difference, while largely doing away with a rigidly stratified understanding of race, nonetheless served as a system of measurement, assigning differing values to separate groups depending on their perceived contribution to the national project. Successful Asian Americans in Hawaiʻi, for instance, were seen by the U.S. government as helpmates in extending American influence to the Pacific.

The basic conflict between these two multiculturalisms would come to a head once Ethnic Studies was established as a provisional program at UH. Initial administration support for Ethnic Studies was at once an effort to accommodate and to rein in an increasingly vocal radical movement. The contradiction between these two administration goals, as well as the clash between liberal and radical multiculturalism, would play out over the course of the 1970s as the Ethnic Studies Program fought to become permanent. Neither side would emerge unchanged.

————

One of the earliest advocates in Hawai'i of what would take the form of ethnic studies was Governor John Burns. Ten years after statehood—and less than a year after the assassination of Martin Luther King—Burns delivered a State of the State speech in February 1969 that, in contrast to his usual pronouncements, struck a tone of unease over the status of racial progress in the United States. As students in California were striking to demand the establishment of ethnic studies at state universities, and their counterparts in Hawai'i were looking on with interest, Burns acknowledged that there was reason for such discontent. He began his address by hitting all the familiar notes: Hawai'i was "a source of inspiration which leads to righteous revolutionary improvement in this world," it was "the throbbing Heart of the Pacific," and a model of "deep empathy" for the people of the globe. But then Burns stepped back from the utopian vision of Hawai'i he had done so much to create and devoted most of the rest of his speech to addressing what he identified as "a sense of uncertainty that gnaws at the conscience of many of our citizens." This uncertainty was due, he surmised, to "a subtle 'inferiority of spirit,'" particularly among the descendants of immigrant plantation workers. Despite being "totally unwarranted" this ethnic self-doubt had become "a social and psychological handicap in life." Although Burns suggested that this phenomenon was being fanned by "outbreaks of civil unrest in our sister states on the Mainland," he nonetheless argued that the lack of a strong ethnic identity among many in Hawai'i was a problem that needed to be tackled:

> They should be proud of their ethnic roots, of the riches and treasures of their Pacific and Asian cultures. I submit further that they should be given every opportunity—even in our public school system—to learn more about their own people's rich past, to understand the sources of inspiration which motivated their fathers and their ancestors before them. . . . What our people have done under the conditions of yesteryear—the story of the different waves of immigrants who came to Hawaii—the education of the immigrants' children—their rise into the professions, into government— the development of the cultural heritage we have today—all these stories are vital to the history of our State. Our children should know it, as should their children and all future generations of Hawaii. In short, we must safeguard their identity so that they will be secure in their future. We must do

this so that every child in Hawaii will have an opportunity to grow up with
supreme confidence in the dignity and value of his own person and his own
heritage. It is through an understanding of our backgrounds, our heritage,
that we can best achieve amicable accommodation of the diversity of views
that is the hallmark of a truly democratic society.[2]

Burns ended his speech by for calling for people in Hawai'i to reject division
and seek unity through diversity—likely an implicit criticism of the activists
causing "civil unrest" on the mainland.

And yet Burns, a consummate postwar liberal, was also embracing aspects
of the radical ideology fueling that civil unrest. His reference to the importance of ethnic pride echoed the arguments of ethnic studies advocates, Black
Power activists, and other ethnic solidarity movements—many of whom had
been inspired by anticolonial revolutionary Frantz Fanon, who used his training as a psychiatrist to assert that racism and colonialism caused deep psychological damage among people of color. Certainly, Burns was not supportive
of the revolutionary aims of these activists. But he was ready to concede that
they had legitimate grievances, and that those grievances needed to be dealt
with for the sake of local and national consensus.

Burns, like a number of other members of the political establishment,
appeared to be rethinking the causes of and solutions to racial inequality in
the wake of civil rights reform. While many white liberals were repelled by
the radicalism of black activism in the late 1960s and adopted a "color-blind"
notion of racial politics, others were more receptive to claims of persistent
poverty and discrimination and demands for deeper policy change that took
race into account. The report of the Kerner Commission, appointed by President Johnson in response to the urban "disorders" that broke in Detroit and
Watts, was notable for its sympathetic take on the motivations of the rioters.
Published in 1968, the report baldly asserted that the segregation and poverty
that led to the recent riots were the fault of white action and inaction: "What
white Americans have never fully understood," it declared on its first page, "is
that white society is deeply implicated in the ghetto. White institutions created
it, white institutions maintain it, and white society condones it." Calling for
a broad-scale national response and redistributive measures—including new
taxes, "if necessary"—to overturn the racial status quo, the report insisted
that it was "time to make good the promises of American democracy to all
citizens—urban and rural, white and black, Spanish-surname, American
Indian, and every minority group."[3]

Lyndon Johnson's short-lived War on Poverty initiative represented the
federal response to the challenge of how to address inequality after the end
of legalized racism—a response that paradoxically worked to meet radicals'

demands and to contain them. Its Community Action Program, for instance, melded radical calls for self-determination with capitalist notions of self-sufficiency in an effort to bring impoverished communities into the national fold.[4] Major private funders, in particular the Ford Foundation, enthusiastically funded ethnic studies throughout the United States and also many initiatives of the Black Power movement in a parallel effort to address poverty. Though its ultimate goal, argues Karen Ferguson, was liberal, elitist, and individualist—the foundation aimed to "restore social stability through black leadership development"—it nonetheless served to expand the terms of racial debate in the post–civil rights era as well as control them.[5]

Against this background, higher education became a key site of both contestation and cooperation between establishment liberals and young ethnic radicals. The striking students in California—made up of a multiracial coalition calling itself the Third World Liberation Front—found initial success at San Francisco State, where in the fall of 1969 they succeeded in convincing administrators to inaugurate the nation's first ethnic studies program, with separate departments of Black Studies, American Indian Studies, Asian American Studies, and La Raza Studies. Berkeley followed close behind, with an ethnic studies department housing multiple programs along the lines of the departments at San Francisco State. Those events catalyzed a broader national movement to create academic programs and curricula aimed at empowering students of color to examine their ethnic histories and experiences from the perspective of people of color themselves. Such programs sought to challenge the racism and Eurocentrism they saw in most of the scholarship and teaching in the humanities and social sciences. Emerging as it did from the student protest movement, the goal of ethnic studies was not only to create a new paradigm for scholarship but to serve as a platform for activism and social change.[6]

As elsewhere in the United States, African American students in Hawai'i—despite their relatively small numbers—were the instigators of the campaign for what would become Ethnic Studies at UH. Though it began as a push to create a black studies program, the effort was soon broadened as the university's own Third World Liberation Front, composed of a multiethnic coalition of students, made demands for a more comprehensive ethnic studies program. They criticized the university for its failure "to present a complete and accurate representation of Third World people," and argued that "Hawaii, with such a large, varied population of Third World peoples, should be leading the trend in the nation to establish Ethnic Studies as a vital educational area."[7]

The UH students, much like their mainland counterparts, initially conceptualized ethnic studies in global terms. The intersection of decolonization and the problem of racial difference in the United States framed their understanding of the issues at hand, as it had for statehood advocates and officials of the

East-West Center and the Peace Corps. Like many racial liberals, they too were responding to Third World calls for a toppling of global racial hierarchies. But for these students, Hawai'i was not proof of America's benevolence to the decolonizing world or of the progress of civil rights in the United States. Instead, they flipped the script: the decolonizing world should serve as a model for Hawai'i, and for the United States more broadly. The Black Students Union, for example, made the case that black studies was necessary not only because there was lack of attention to the African American experience in U.S. history, but because recent world events made that experience more relevant: "The sudden transformation of Colonial Africa into imposing, independent sovereign states," the Black Students Union argued, "has created an urgent need for comprehensive information on the black American."[8]

Such rhetoric came on the heels of a series of talks at UH by radical black activists who argued that the struggle for racial justice in the United States was part of a worldwide awakening. Stokely Carmichael, who visited campus in 1968 and spoke to a crowd of seven thousand people at the university's Andrews Amphitheater —reportedly one of the largest turnouts the venue had ever had—gave a fiery speech that embedded the Black Power movement in "a revolution of the third world—the world of color." Carmichael told his audience to embrace "racial violence" and reject liberalism, which he said was ineffective because it sought to avoid confrontation by asking for sacrifice from the racially oppressed rather than their oppressors.[9]

Students at UH may not have heeded Carmichael's call for revolutionary violence, but they responded to the notion of identifying as part of an oppressed racial group that transcended national boundaries. In taking up the mantle of the "Third World," ethnic studies advocates situated themselves as part of the "world of color" that Carmichael evoked. This called for both a nationalist understanding of ethnic self-identity and an assertion of transnational solidarity among people of different races and ethnicities who were nonetheless united by their oppression under systems of racism, slavery, and colonialism.

This notion of the Third World, in contrast to the view of the U.S. government, posited that it was not a distant geographical space—one that represented what America was not—but a conceptual framework that denoted long-standing global hierarchies and inequalities based on both race and region. It was not backwardness or "tradition," but the legacy of Western domination that defined the Third World and its peoples, who brought that legacy with them as they moved about the globe. The Third World could thus exist outside of *and* within the United States. This was a way of thinking that drew on older pan-Africanist and colonial solidarity movements, which thrived in the interwar period by underlining the similarities between Jim Crow and

European colonialism. But activists in the 1960s and 1970s were also a product of the postcolonial, post–civil rights era.[10] With the formal structures of racial discrimination supposedly dismantled, to deliberately align oneself as part of the Third World, with all of negative connotations that term evoked, was to call attention to the limits of top-down change as well as to the ongoing possibility for grassroots action on a global scale. Decolonization may not be complete, but its future was still unfolding.

In Hawai'i, the effort to create an ethnic studies program began much less acrimoniously than it did in California. Indeed, this relative lack of controversy was not surprising, given the state's eagerness to lay claim to being America's most racially progressive community. But the initial support of Hawai'i's political and educational establishment for ethnic studies also belied the tensions and disillusionment that motivated many of the activists. These would soon come to the surface once ethnic studies was established and debates erupted over how it should be implemented, who it was for, and what its ultimate purpose was.

In the spring of 1969, the Black Students Union and the Third World Liberation Front submitted separate proposals for new programs—the former outlining a plan for black studies that would eventually be folded into ethnic studies—and the administration was mostly enthusiastic about the general idea. According to a report from the office of the Dean for Academic Development, the kind of research and teaching that ethnic studies promised was "long overdue" at UH. Ethnic studies, it argued, would "provide a creative arena for educational development relevant to the lives and existence of Hawaii's minority ethnic groups." But while recognizing that UH lagged behind many other institutions when it came to diversifying its curriculum, the report also struck a self-congratulatory tone. Whereas ethnic studies elsewhere came about "almost spontaneously under pressure from minority students (mostly blacks)," the report asserted that administrators at UH "have, fortunately, not felt this pressure." Rather than acknowledging the role played by students in persuading UH to introduce ethnic studies, the administration seemed insistent on taking all of the credit for its embrace of curricular change.[11] Ethnic studies, it suggested, was the natural outgrowth of Hawai'i's tradition of racial enlightenment. The lack of bad blood over ethnic studies was thus further proof that Hawai'i, and UH, were ahead of the curve on issues of race relations—a sentiment that was of a piece with the discourses around statehood and Hawai'i's special role as bridge to Asia.

Despite the appearance of consensus, the early discussions on ethnic studies revealed some of the latent fault lines that would crack open just a few years later. Like the student activists, the Academic Development office report emphasized that the "real experience" of Hawai'i's ethnic groups had gone ignored. But administrators and activists disagreed on the consequences and causes of such ignorance. The administration endorsed the liberal idea that the biggest problem with the lack of knowledge about Hawaiʻi's different ethnic groups was that this kept those groups "isolated from the larger society" and led to "pockets of poverty in the local community." Such language, while highlighting the economic plight of many in Hawaiʻi, implied that their poverty was an anomaly that defied Hawaiʻi's promise. The less privileged among Hawaiʻi's nonwhite ethnic groups, through their poverty and isolation, were thus deviating from mainstream norms. The report left the causes of this deviation rather vague, but indicated that the blame lay with individual racism. "Even in such an area of heavy Asian concentration as we have here in Hawaii," the report stated, "many continue to see these ethnic groups through the veil of stereotypes." This reference to racial attitudes tapped a broader liberal discourse on race, what Leah Gordon calls the theory of "racial individualism," that argued that inequality was the consequence of personal prejudices multiplied many times over—rather than something baked into a wide range of institutional structures.[12]

Although the administration and activists agreed that education was a necessary corrective to racism, the dean's office report appeared to endorse the idea that racism could be solved simply by fostering greater respect among whites towards nonwhite cultures. The activists, meanwhile, had a different take on the role of education, the causes of racism, and the relationship between the two.

Activists, though they too lamented the lack of respect for nonwhite culture and the concentration of poverty among people of color in Hawaiʻi, were less concerned than administrators over whether Hawaiʻi's minority groups were isolated or deviant from an imagined ideal; instead they spoke more forcefully of the need for economic equality, and asserted that *inequality* was the norm, one they sought to break. Moreover, for ethnic studies proponents, racial inequality did not derive so much from individual acts of discrimination. Rather, they saw racism "as an overriding reality, a systematic process structuring the entire society and its institutions."[13] According to the Third World Liberation Front, the educational system's failure "to present a complete and accurate representation of Third World peoples' roles in the past and present conditions of this State and Nation" was a symptom of larger structural forces maintained by people in power, most of them white. In their proposal for Ethnic Studies, they suggested that the state and the university were deliberately ignoring the experiences and needs of people of color. The "institutionalized condition of negligence and ignorance by the State's educational system," they argued, "is an integral part of the racism this country has perpetuated upon nonwhite peoples."[14] By laying blame for racism on the state, rather than individuals, Third World Liberation Front students challenged Hawai'i's official narrative of racial progress.

There were other, subtle dissonances between the administration report and the Third World Liberation Front proposal. In emphasizing the potential for Ethnic Studies to lift "the veil of stereotypes," the administration conceived of the new program as part of the larger state project to encourage "mutual understanding" between different national groups—a project sold to whites during the Cold War on the basis of its benefits to America's global stature. Mutual understanding would supposedly help people in the Third World, meanwhile, by bringing them into the Western fold while allowing them to retain aspects of their cultural heritage—a form of compensation for accommodating Western influence on economics and politics. At the same time, in keeping with domestic racial liberalism, the report suggested that social unity should be the ultimate goals of ethnic studies. The Third World Liberation Front activists, by contrast, were less interested in changing white attitudes or creating mutual understanding for the benefit of the nation as a whole. They saw the relationship between whites and nonwhites, on both the national and global stage, as one marked by a lack of equal power rather than mutual understanding. Cultural respect and self-respect were tools of power to be used by people of color for emancipatory ends, not an end unto themselves.

While these preliminary discussions on ethnic studies at UH portended later debates over the purpose of ethnic studies, in 1969–70 any tensions were dampened in the service of getting the program off the ground. By the fall of 1970, UH—with a mandate from the Hawai'i legislature and a sixty-thousand-dollar appropriation for the first year—had established Ethnic Studies on a provisional basis.[15] The evidence suggests that the design of the program and the curriculum was left largely to its relatively young program staff, initially under the leadership of founding director Dennis Ogawa—a new assistant professor in the UH American Studies Department who had helped found the Asian American Studies Center at the University of California-Los Angeles while pursuing his doctorate in sociology. The official outline of the program, written by Ogawa, sought to strike a balance between satisfying activist demands and catering to administration concerns. It made clear that it intended to complicate the popular image of Hawai'i as a racial paradise. The curriculum, it insisted, "will avoid saccharine myths about minority success stories or fond overtures proclaiming the Aloha given to all men regardless of skin pigmentation, eye contour or speech accent." At the same time, courses would avoid the usual pitfalls of racial theory, wherein people were portrayed "as either all alike or totally different."[16]

But ultimately, the emphasis of ethnic studies, at UH and across the United States, was on difference over similarity. While claiming that the Ethnic Studies

Program courses would "strive to create a recognition of the ways people are similar," program materials stressed that it would also foster "a respect for the ways they are different and distinct."[17] The balance of curriculum themes demonstrated that more weight was placed on the latter. Only a few of the eleven courses offered for the 1970–71 academic year, such as "Ethnic Groups in Hawaii" or "Roots of Racism and Group Prejudice," dealt with broad theoretical approaches to race or social relations. The remaining courses were organized by the particular ethnic group they studied: Japanese Americans, Chinese Americans, Korean Americans, Samoan Americans, Black Americans, and Hawaiian Americans. The administrative structure of the program paralleled that of the curriculum. Corresponding to the seven courses on different ethnic groups was a set of committees at the programmatic level made up of representatives of each group. The goal was to ensure that "persons who are knowledgeable and deeply concerned about individual ethnic groups have a voice in the decision-making process affecting respective groups in the programs."[18] Indeed, this was part of an effort that lay at the heart of the ethnic studies idea: to broaden the range of voices students encountered in both course content and behind the lecture podium, to elevate the role of minority communities in academic literature and in academic employment. At the same time, in the service of representation, the organization of the program and the curriculum worked to delineate ethnic boundaries.

This delineation was also one of the philosophical and methodological underpinnings of the nascent discipline of ethnic studies, which in its early years tended to treat ethnic groups as discrete units. On the one hand, such an approach drew on older sociological understandings of ethnicity, in which ethnic identity was predetermined by the family or community one was born into. In doing so, it tended to downplay more recent work that took intergroup relations as its main object of study. It also largely ignored research that focused on intermarriage and interracialism, much of it led by UH sociologist Romanzo Adams, who had looked to interwar Hawai'i as a "laboratory" of cross-cultural mixing. The research lab Adams founded during the 1920s was, in 1961, folded into the larger Social Science Research Institute, which had a much broader interdisciplinary mandate to deal with what were considered to be the major economic and political problems of the day. Meanwhile, futurist theories, academic and otherwise, on Hawai'i's role in pioneering the formation of a new "golden" race made up of a blend of Pacific and European lineages, were less interesting to the new Ethnic Studies Program than studying ethnic groups as separate entities.

If anything, "golden race" ideas fundamentally contradicted the political aims of the Ethnic Studies Program, which often spoke explicitly of the need to reject the notion of Hawai'i as the "melting pot" of the Pacific. The melting pot was a "widely-held, highly attractive, and very marketable stereotype" that portrayed Hawai'i as "a charming, even romantic confluence of peoples of diverse ethnic backgrounds merging together in happy cultural and biological fusion." But this idea ignored "extremely interesting and important differences in the sociological, political, and economic experiences—past and present—of Hawaii's ethnic groups."[19] To call Hawai'i a melting pot was to suggest that people in Hawai'i had assimilated to Euro-American norms, and that assimilation represented progress. To some extent, critiques of the melting pot idea relied on a straw man—many in Hawai'i and elsewhere in the United States, as we have seen, had long since moved away from the traditional assimilationist model as a national ideal. University of Hawai'i president Harlan Cleveland, for example, argued in 1974 against the simplistic principal that "all men are brothers—or that we are all sisters under the skin." Rather, "multicultural living" required learning "a harder lesson, that all brothers are different, and the differences are to be honored and cherished, not homogenized in an undifferentiated Americanism."[20] This was a view that echoed the East-West Center's earlier call for rejecting "bland assimilation." But the liberal multiculturalism promoted by the state and by the tourism industry nonetheless shared certain assumptions with the melting pot paradigm, particularly in its emphasis on all things "intercultural" and the premise that social harmony was the ultimate goal of democratic society.

The late 1960s and early 1970s, however, was not a time of harmony in American politics or culture. The most visible issue of contention in this period was America's involvement in the Vietnam War. But the national consensus of the early postwar era, forged in the crucible of unprecedented affluence and Cold War anxiety, showed signs of breakdown in other corners of American life. Americans across the political spectrum were beginning to question the traditional authority of the WASP establishment class. This questioning took many forms, from leftist social rights movements such as Black Power to right-wing Christian movements that believed powerful liberals were trying to erode divine will through secularism. Meanwhile, a series of revelations of government lies about U.S. actions in Vietnam and other areas of the Cold War, along with the Watergate scandal of 1972, led to mass disaffection with American politics and politicians.[21]

Within the context of this crisis of authority, Americans were less likely than they were at the beginning of the 1960s to associate strongly with the nation as a whole, and instead to see themselves as members of specific ethnic groups or local communities, or to base their identity on other shared traits or interests. Against this background, many Americans were seeking to uncover their ancestral lineages. The hugely successful television miniseries *Roots*, which ran in 1977 and was based on Alex Haley's Pulitzer Prize winning book of the same name, chronicled the history of a black family in America, beginning with the life of a captured African slave and up through his ancestors' emancipation during the Civil War. The story expressed the widespread belief that people were shaped by their personal ethnic history. *Roots,* wrote James Baldwin "is a study of continuities, of consequences, of how a people perpetuates themselves." It was a story that "suggests, with great power, how each of us, however unconsciously, can't but be a vehicle of the history which has produced us."[22]

The white descendants of first- and second-wave immigrants were likewise beginning to emphasize their ethnic heritage. Where many of their ancestors had laid claim to an undifferentiated white identity to head off prejudice against non-Anglo culture, now Americans with Jewish, Irish, Slavic, or Italian backgrounds were increasingly identifying themselves as "hyphenated Americans" in what Matthew Frye Jacobson calls a shift from "Plymouth Rock whiteness" to "Ellis Island whiteness."[23] The movement to reclaim ethnic identity was even recognized by Congress, which offered funding for educational programs on ethnic culture through the Ethnic Heritage Studies Act of 1972.[24]

The appeal of ethnic identity was a trend already identified in 1963 by Nathan Glazer and Daniel Patrick Moynihan in their book, *Beyond the Melting Pot: The Negroes, Puerto Ricans, Jews, Italians, and Irish in New York City.* "The point about the melting pot," they wrote, "is that it did not happen." It was time to put this fiction to rest: "The notion that the intense and unprecedented mixture of ethnic and religious groups in American life was soon to blend into a homogenous end product has outlived its usefulness, and also its credibility. In the meanwhile, persisting facts of ethnicity demand attention, understanding, and accommodation."[25] Ethnic groups, they insisted, had retained distinct identities even several generations after their ancestors migrated to the United States. Eight years later Michael Novak's *Unmeltable Ethnics* made a similar case, though in more impassioned and political terms, as it called for a "new cultural pluralism" to challenge the "irrepressible condescension" and longstanding nativism of American WASPs.[26]

The emergence of ethnic studies as its own discipline must be understood as part of this larger ideological moment when many Americans were seeking to "discover their roots." The broader discussions around the "persisting facts of ethnicity" and family heritage in this period tended to treat ethnic identity not as a mutable discourse shaped by the present moment, but as an essential key to selfhood, one that was long-buried and waiting to be unearthed from layers of assimilationist sediment. Once exhumed, that identity could be deployed in multiple ways—as a basis for community building in the face of national disunity and distrust of traditional institutions, as an object of commodification, as a psychological bulwark against the alienation of modern life. For many, it was also a political organizing mechanism, or more slippery tool for asserting cultural power. This was the case not only for people of color, but for many whites who declared their own ethnic pride as a way to counter both WASP dominance and the claims of newly emboldened minorities who asserted their entitlement to public services and political representation.[27] Though ethnic identity was embraced by many white leftists—Tom Hayden, for instance, identified with the radical political tradition of his Irish ancestors—it also offered a new language of grievance for whites who insisted that they faced ethnic prejudice akin to that of racial minorities.[28]

However its adherents chose to use it, the notion of ethnic identity that emerged in the late 1960s and 1970s insisted on pluralism over cosmopolitanism or hybridity. This way of thinking anticipated what Daniel Rodgers calls the "Age of Fracture," in which the presumed cohesion of American society, however fictional it may have been, gave way to self-conscious assertions of difference, particularity, and discord.[29] In the United States in the late twentieth century, as discourses of ethnic identity took both the individual—as the person journeying toward self-discovery—and the isolated group as its objects of concern, questions of society, nation, and intergroup relations were pushed to the sidelines. The trend away from analysis of the nation, and of the "Great Men" who made nations, was reflected not only in ethnic studies, but in academia more broadly. American scholars of the new school of social history, inspired by the work of E. P. Thompson and others who sought to rescue ordinary people "from the enormous condescension of posterity," focused much of their attention on the experiences of those who did not conform to the white, male, Protestant norm: slaves, immigrant workers, women.[30]

If America's origin story had once been told, with little opposition, as one that began with heroic English migrants disembarking on New World shores in the seventeenth century, now a host of alternative genealogies sprang up to challenge this homogenous and Anglocentric narrative. The United States, social historians argued, had countless points of origin, each one contributing to, and disrupting, the historical linkages connecting the Mayflower pilgrims to the America of the late twentieth century. Such studies tended to be highly local and specific, borrowing the ethnographic techniques of anthropology to reconstruct tight-knit community worlds. At the same time, while the preceding generation of historians had emphasized consensus in American life—for some, as a lamentable feature of U.S. politics that limited the scope of debate— these younger historians stressed contestation and conflict.[31]

Ethnic studies activists in Hawai'i were part of this broader national turn toward local and community concerns and toward distinct identities. Although UH Ethnic Studies Program materials stated that it did not "cater to ethnic enclaves in which students only pursue studies of their own ethnic group," it was nonetheless expected that students would flock to the courses

that examined their own ancestral roots—an expectation that proved accurate.[32] An administration report from 1974 found that "the title of the ethnic
identity courses is related to student composition," with the majority of students in most courses identifying as a member of the ethnic group covered by
the syllabus. Of the students enrolled in "Japanese Americans in Hawaii," for
example, 80 percent were identified as having Japanese ancestry.[33] Reinforcing this trend, an assignment for the course "The Chinese in Hawaii" in the
spring of 1975 asked students to investigate "your family and the conditions in
China when they left" in order to "help you examine the factors that shaped
your own identity." The task presumed that the enrolled students were all of
Chinese descent.[34]

As indicated by the ancestry assignment, the strengthening of students'
personal ethnic identity was seen as a core program goal. Education on one's
own history would help to spur activism outside the classroom by helping
students to understand the roots of ongoing injustices they had themselves
experienced. Ethnic Studies described its mission as one of "building a sense
of one's history, of finding one's roots, and of developing a positive sense of
identity." This process would allow students to see themselves as part of an
ongoing "history of struggle to better oneself and Hawaii. It follows that struggles to solve contemporary problems is just part of a continuum of struggles
by our ancestors."[35]

Ethnic Studies also sought, more generally, to foster a sense of personal
self-worth among Hawaiʻi's people. Echoing John Burns's state of the state
address of 1969, program materials argued that young people in Hawaiʻi were
"a lost generation" with "no sense of identity, of pride in being themselves." The
results were socially harmful. "In many of them this lack of self-knowledge has
bred shame; in others, a deep-seated sense of frustration and anger."[36] This language drew on popular psychological theories of the time, particularly those of
Erik Erikson, who coined the term *identity crisis*, which he characterized as an
affliction common among adolescents and caused by a struggle to figure out
their place in society.[37] As "identity" increasingly came to be associated with
one's ethnic background, many in Hawaiʻi and elsewhere in the United States
spoke of the need to learn about their ancestry in order overcome such a crisis
and achieve full human development. University of Hawaiʻi Ethnic Studies
students themselves spoke in these terms, saying that the lack of "understanding of their own history or the conditions their parents have struggled under"
had "led to an 'ethnic generation gap' where the youth acquire values and
concepts that are different from their parents."[38] Here Hawaiʻi's young people
turned the "generation gap" cliché on its head. Rather than bemoaning their
parents' traditionalism, they expressed regret for their own lack of tradition.

FIGURE 20. Poster for rally in support of Ethnic Studies, 1971.
By John Kelly, courtesy of Colleen Kelly.

Unlike the state boosters who emphasized Hawai'i's novelty, Ethnic Studies students expressed nostalgia for an ancestral past.

Ethnic Studies challenged the New Hawai'i image in other ways as well. The notion of a "lost generation" of alienated Hawai'i locals suggested that mutual understanding was less important than self-understanding. More broadly, Ethnic Studies questioned the value of the cosmopolitan ethos that had characterized much of Hawai'i public discourse in the 1960s. Instead, it called for a more essentialist approach to diversity, to preserve people's "democratic right to maintain and perpetuate their cultural heritage" against the homogenizing tendencies of cultural mixing.[39] Even if Ethnic Studies overstated the persistence of the melting pot idea in Hawai'i, its seeming lack of interest in the gospel of cross-cultural education flouted liberal norms. The UH administration, for instance, would become deeply critical of what it saw as the program's lack of "ethnic interchange," which encouraged students to be "concerned about [their] own ethnic background, but not so concerned about the background of others."[40]

Ethnic Studies defied other shibboleths of the popular image of poststatehood Hawai'i. Where state boosters had sought to make the case that Hawai'i was the embodiment of America's best self—representative of national ideals of democracy and racial egalitarianism—ethnic studies activists labored to disentangle Hawai'i from its established relationship to the mainland. Hawai'i, they insisted, was both exceptional and not exceptional to mainland norms, but not in the way liberals often portrayed it. Rather than being an example of America's racial future, Hawai'i was at once prone to the racism and inequality found on the mainland and was also a singular place whose racial dynamics were wholly separate from those of the rest of the United States. Hawai'i, according to ethnic studies advocates, was a part of the United States, and as such "it must deal with the race problem that is facing America in its most bold and glaring proportions today." But it also "occupies a unique position in the Nation as a whole with its mixed population," and so deserved to be studied on its own terms rather than as an exemplary American community.[41] Underscoring this, the curriculum of Ethnic Studies focused on how ethnicity worked in Hawai'i specifically, not in the United States more broadly. "Hawaii's people are the focal point," program materials made clear. "Mainland United States and international data are drawn upon only if they contribute to a better understanding of Hawaii's situation."[42]

This growing emphasis on Hawai'i's particularity represented a subtle shift away from the founding ethos of the Ethnic Studies Program when it was launched in 1969. The Third World Liberation Front paradigm had sought to link together the struggles of nonwhite people in Hawai'i, the continental United States, and the rest of the world. By contrast, over the course of the 1970s, Ethnic Studies placed increasing political weight on local histories, problems, and social movements in an effort to underscore the uniqueness and agency of Hawai'i's people. This was reflected in the program's broader activist and research work, which focused on local concerns.

Community activism work was integrated into the general program as well as the content of Ethnic Studies classes. Field trips and various "action projects" frequently took students off campus to enable them "to become involved in understanding and helping to solve ethnic problems." This might include activities such as producing community newspapers and authoring other publications focusing on Hawai'i's ethnic makeup.[43] Most notably, beginning in 1976 the Ethnic Studies Program oversaw the development of a large-scale oral history project that aimed to "better understand the forces that blended together to shape Hawaii's economic, political, social and cultural growth"—this would become one of the program's longest-running initiatives.[44] Ethnic Studies students were also encouraged to participate in more overtly political work, particularly around anti-eviction campaigns in ethnic neighborhoods targeted for redevelopment. The program, according to its own materials, "has naturally enough assumed a stance of protest with regard to many current social problems" because of students' own embeddedness within the ethnic communities they studied.[45]

To some extent, the intense focus on Hawai'i's society—to the exclusion of others—was a reflection of the fact that, in many ways, Hawai'i was distinct. For one, unlike most other parts of the United States, "minority" groups in Hawai'i together made up a large majority of the population. And although the state power structure was disproportionately represented by whites, since World War II people of Japanese and Chinese descent had made significant gains in both politics and the local economy. These gains were consolidated in the 1970s, exemplified by the rise of George Ariyoshi to become Hawai'i's first governor of Japanese descent, following Burns's death in 1974. Hawai'i's demographics helped ensure that the Ethnic Studies at UH had a strong base of local support, as evidenced by the legislative mandate for the program.

But Hawai'i's specific racial dynamics also meant that there were long-simmering resentments over the decades of minority rule that characterized Hawai'i's history as a territory and that continued to shape Hawai'i's politics and economy. While whites maintained disproportionate influence, successful Asians in Hawai'i were held up as members of a "model minority," a term used by an increasing number of journalists, politicians, and social scientists to refer to Asian Americans as a whole. The model minority theory posited that Asian Americans, by dint of hard work and family cohesion, had achieved economic and social mobility even in the face of historic exclusion.[46] The model minority concept was not only celebratory or innocuous. It often ascribed

Asian American success to alien, "oriental" traditions that implied Asian Americans would be perpetual foreigners. At the same time, in highlighting the accomplishments of some Asian Americans, it suggested that less successful nonwhites were simply not taking advantage of opportunities available to them. Such a concept offered a particularly compelling message to white Americans after the passage of civil rights legislation failed to bring about full racial equality or stem the tide of racial protest. In doing so, it affirmed America's democratic promise while shifting the blame for other minority groups' continued struggles to their own individual and community shortcomings. On the mainland, African Americans were the primary foils in discussions of Asian American achievement. In Hawai'i, the relative wealth and influence of some Japanese and Chinese obscured the fact that others in the islands continued to struggle under economic inequality and racism. Many poorer Hawai'i residents of Asian descent, particularly Filipinos, continued to experience the social and economic legacies of a plantation labor system that linked race and class, in which Filipinos were segregated into the hardest and least-skilled work.

Meanwhile, Native Hawaiians had gained the least from statehood, which was the latest step in an ongoing process that stripped Hawai'i's indigenous people of land, political power, and cultural autonomy—in part due to the consequences of mass Asian migration and the subsequent rise of an Asian American elite in Hawai'i.[47] Hawaiians' position had in many ways worsened during the postwar period. Whereas they had reaped limited benefits from the political patronage system under the territorial regime, which relied on Native Hawaiian votes to stay in power, they were now under growing pressure to abandon their traditional way of life to make way for accelerating development of the islands. The liberal multiculturalism promoted by the state and the tourism industry often portrayed Hawaiians as one ethnic group among many while romanticizing Asian success. The particular indigenous rights claims of Hawaiians, as well as Hawai'i's history of colonial conquest, were ignored in favor of a portrait of Hawai'i as a site where this triumphant immigrant story was enacted.

But while there were growing tensions between Hawaiians and Asians, there also existed a shared culture of solidarity across ethnic lines among people of color in Hawai'i. Originating during the interwar period, many in Hawai'i increasingly came to identify themselves as "local," imbuing the term with a specific meaning that signaled a nonwhite, working-class identity that relied on its own language—Hawai'i pidgin—and stood in opposition to haole control of the islands. Expressions of solidarity intensified during the "Massie Affair" of 1931–32, when a white naval officer murdered Joseph Kahahawai, a young Hawaiian man, after he and a multiethnic group of friends

were falsely accused of raping the officer's wife. The alleged rape was sensa-
tionalized by the mainland press, which cast the islands as primitive place
where dark-skinned men preyed on white women, and led to rumblings that
the navy might impose martial law in the islands. The incident, scholars have
argued, helped to awaken the political consciousness of many Hawai'i residents, ultimately helping pave the way for the Democratic coalition that swept
the territorial legislature in 1950s.[48]

The localism that resurfaced in the 1970s was again used as way to claim
political power against the mainland. If mainstream discourse in the statehood
era had been characterized by an effort to further entrench Hawai'i in both
U.S. culture and foreign policy, by the early 1970s, Ethnic Studies activists were
seeking to resist the deepening relationship between Hawai'i and the rest of
the United States. Ethnic studies advocates, in particular, used the rhetoric of
localism to defend against the tide of mainlanders who had long felt entitled to
Hawai'i, whether as tourists, missionaries, or academic researchers. To counter
the overwhelming influence of the mainland, many in the Ethnic Studies Program insisted that those researching and teaching about the people of Hawai'i
must be Hawai'i locals. For too long, Larry Kamakawiwoole decried, UH had
been dominated by "foreigners," referring to academics born and educated on
the mainland. Kamakawiwoole, who at the time was head of the Hawaiian section of Ethnic Studies and was concerned specifically with the lack of Native
Hawaiian representation at UH, believed that mainland scholars had distorted
Hawaiian history and crowded out native voices in the process. Courses on
Hawai'i, he said, were "controlled by haoles and taught from a white man's
perspective—the colonizers telling the native they colonized what his/her
problems are and what his/her history has been."[49]

Kamakawiwoole's denunciation of UH policy reflected the ways in which
localist discourse in the 1970s often intersected with an anticolonialist critique.
This unsettled popular ideas about Hawai'i's current and historic relationship
to the United States. Kamakawiwoole, in his explicit reference to the U.S. colonization of Hawai'i, dissented from the accepted liberal account of Hawaiians
as welcoming hosts who embraced American interference in the islands. In
doing so, he articulated the widely held belief among Native Hawaiians that
their islands had been unjustly annexed and their culture exploited. In this
view, Hawai'i was not an integral part of the United States, but a separate and
unequal community whose autonomy had been stolen but not forgotten. This
was a grievance that would coalesce into the Hawaiian sovereignty movement
later in the decade. For now, however, Kamakawiwoole's demands were less
ambitious: he wanted Hawaiians to be given the platform to produce their
own teaching and research. "No longer should Hawaiians," he said, "stand by
and allow foreigners to use local people as 'informants'—as data sources to

provide material for an article here, a book there—for the academic advancement of 'scholars' who have taken our hospitality for granted and invaded the privacy of our lives and our homes."[50]

Ethnic studies advocates also sought to distance themselves from the broader activism of the New Left, which many felt was dominated by haoles who were out of touch with local issues. An editorial in the UH student newspaper, *Ka Leo,* chastised the Hawai'i chapter of Students for a Democratic Society for its inability to rally support at UH. SDS, it said, "for all practical purposes is dead on this campus." This was due in large part to its lack of recognition of the importance of ethnic identity and its connection to community concerns. "The SDS is made up mostly of whites, mostly Mainland whites. Such a group cannot relate as well to the local problems." Though it suggested that many members of SDS were willfully ignorant when it came to local affairs, the editorial also cautioned that even the more sensitive and open-minded members would face backlash if they tried "to tell locals how to solve their problems." The recent ethnic revival among Hawai'i residents had created "a strong resentment of white paternalistic interference, no matter how well meaning." If SDS wanted any traction in Hawai'i its membership would have to "shak[e] off the stigma of being Mainland, white and obnoxious."[51]

The insistence on local control over leftist activism mirrored the Ethnic Studies Program's assertions of autonomy in its relationship to the UH administration. In both cases, ethnic identity was marshaled as an organizing tool and as a rationale for self-determination. Perhaps unsurprisingly, this led to clashes with the administration—over who Ethnic Studies was for, who should control it, and how it should approach teaching and research. The first round of controversy emerged in the spring of 1972, when the Ethnic Studies Program came up for renewal after two years of temporary status. The administration's stated objections focused on the pedagogical approach of the program, arguing that it was not academically rigorous enough—evidenced by the role that undergraduate students played as part of the program's governing structure and as "lab leaders" for Ethnic Studies courses.[52] But the administration also indicated that it was suspicious of what it called the program's "political and ideological orientation," which it characterized as an affront to academic standards. Ethnic Studies, according to university president Harlan Cleveland, had a "short supply of high-grade scholarship so far," which led to a "tendency to substitute rhetoric for research in trying to fill that gap."[53]

Indeed, the program and its pedagogy were unabashedly political. For many students and faculty, the very purpose of Ethnic Studies was to revolutionize academia by blurring the line between teachers and students, and between classroom learning and community action, and by giving students of color a greater voice in decision making as a means of political awakening.

The discipline of ethnic studies, wrote one supporter, questioned "very basic assumptions about the content of our knowledge and the conclusions drawn from it." In asking, "What if our society's way of looking at and understanding history (or art, science, or sociology, etc.) has been basically wrong?," Ethnic Studies was fundamentally "threatening to established institutions."[54] Activists thus saw administration criticism over the program's breaking of academic norms as an effort to "perpetuate the status quo."[55] Somewhat paradoxically, many were also suspicious of the fact that the idea of an ethnic studies program enjoyed broad support in Hawai'i. The legislature's decision in 1971 to appropriate another $100,000 a year for the next two years of Ethnic Studies led to worries that the program would be "establishment oriented and unimaginative"—a concern that seemed to be confirmed when some legislators argued that the Ethnic Studies was too "radically inclined."[56] So when the administration appointed a committee of mostly haole professors to review the program's status, students launched a revolt, leading to a two-hundred-person sit-in at Bachman Hall to demand the creation of a joint student-faculty group that would help decide the future of Ethnic Studies.[57]

And yet despite the threat to the status quo that Ethnic Studies posed, the activists got most of what they wanted in their 1972 fight with the administration, which agreed, in exchange for an end to the sit-in, to recognize the People's Committee on Ethnic Studies—made up of students, faculty, and community members—as the group empowered to develop and propose changes to the program.[58] Soon after, the UH Board of Regents accepted the People's Committee proposal for extending Ethnic Studies, again on a provisional basis. Administration officials seemed reconciled to the inevitability of Ethnic Studies, with president Cleveland predicting, in a tone of resignation, that Ethnic Studies "seems certain to be, in one form or another, a permanent part of what the University of Hawaii should be offering its students."[59] Affirming Cleveland's suggestion that there was too much demand for the program to dismantle it, by the fall of 1972 some 650 students had registered for Ethnic Studies courses. This number was up from the 450 who enrolled in its first year, 1970, and more than three times the expected enrollment when the program was initially being conceived.[60]

Far from resolving the conflict over the future of Ethnic Studies, however, the battle of 1972 exposed the fundamental rifts between activists and the UH administration, and demonstrated the increasingly fraught disagreement between liberal and radical views on race. The debates over who should control the program, while not unusual in any large institution, took on a distinctly racial cast at UH in the 1970s. President Cleveland criticized the protestors for their "anti-haole" rhetoric—which he said was "much more pronounced than he had ever experienced."[61] Meanwhile, the faculty senate initially rejected the

People's Committee proposal for a new course, ES 203: The Caucasian American, because they believed it was "a play on the 'haole guilt complex'" and would be filled by students "who already accept its ideological assumptions."[62] (The course did run in the fall, presumably after some modifications.[63])

The activists, for their part, protested what they saw as administration attempts to marginalize nonwhite voices, especially those of Hawaiians. Larry Kamakawiwoole led the charge against what he called racial paternalism, which "defeats the very purpose of ethnic studies."[64] Hawaiians, he argued, were at a distinct disadvantage in the context of Hawai'i's particular racial politics. "Hawaiians in Hawaii have been treated as incompetent and unqualified to hold responsible positions in society," he said. At the same time, "These are the people upon whom Hawaii is built, the people born to the aloha spirit now so exploited by the tourist industry."[65] Kamakawiwoole had first emerged as a thorn in the administration's side when he clashed with the Ethnic Studies Program's founding director, Dennis Ogawa, who was Japanese-American, in late 1971. Kamakawiwoole, along with a group of other faculty members, called for Ogawa's resignation amid rumors that Ogawa was working with administration officials on a plan to split off Asian Studies from Ethnic Studies, leaving the Hawaiian section "to fend for itself."[66]

The tensions between Kamakawiwoole and Ogawa were marked by a general sense of racial distrust, one that was stoked, in part, by the relatively elevated status of Japanese Americans in Hawai'i. Ogawa appeared to have a friendly relationship with the administration, while Kamakawiwoole was viewed as being too militant in his advocacy on behalf of Hawaiians and unwilling to compromise in the "real multicultural, multiracial world."[67] While Kamakawiwoole accused Ogawa of "stilling the voice and active participation of those Hawaiians . . . who have for too long been left out of the mainstream of Hawaiian society," Ogawa, echoing administration rhetoric, suggested that the Ethnic Studies Program was at risk of fracturing along racial lines.[68] This was due, in part, to "inherent friction involved in delineating specific races for specific courses." But Ogawa also expressed concern that Japanese Americans, in particular, were becoming the targets of suspicion. "I'm really scared for Japanese Americans," he told *Ka Leo*, rather cryptically. "I think they're hated."[69]

Hawai'i's complex local racial dynamics continued to shape the evolution of the Ethnic Studies Program. By the spring of 1972, the embattled Ogawa had resigned and the People's Committee nominated Kamakawiwoole to replace him as director of Ethnic Studies. But Kamakawiwoole's tenure would be even shorter than Ogawa's as he wrangled with the administration over hiring decisions and what Kamakawiwoole saw as anti-Hawaiian prejudice. When President Cleveland refused to approve his appointment of another Hawaiian staff member as program coordinator, Kamakawiwoole, protesting that the move was an insult to "all Hawaiians," stepped down himself. In a letter to Cleveland, Kamakawiwoole insisted that while "Caucasian and Oriental Directors have picked their own staff without such illegal harassment," Kamakawiwoole, as the first Hawaiian to head a program at UH, was being singled out by Cleveland's veto—which "is tantamount to saying, among other things, that you do not feel that a Hawaiian Director is capable of making a wise personal choice."[70]

Whatever the exact circumstances that led to Kamakawiwoole's resignation, it is clear that his more militant approach to Hawai'i politics posed a threat to the established liberal order. Kamakawiwoole was one among a number of Hawaiians who, after decades of discontent expressed in private quarters, were now coming out more forcefully against U.S. annexation of the islands and the continuing legacies of American colonialism. According to Raymond Ako, one of Kamakawiwoole's supporters on the UH advisory board on Ethnic Studies, "The mood of Hawaiians today is no longer one of complacency or submission."[71] The revisionist Hawaiian history promoted by Ethnic Studies was perhaps the most subversive of all of the program's challenges to the status quo. While the narrative around statehood had suggested, often implicitly, that Hawai'i's people of color had suffered racism and injustice under territorial status, statehood was meant to close that unfortunate chapter by giving Hawai'i equal status to other U.S. states. But Hawaiians, by employing the language of colonialism and neocolonialism, were now publicly insisting that statehood could never correct the original sin of U.S. colonization.

At the same time that Hawaiians at UH were writing an alternative history of Hawai'i, Hawaiians were becoming more vocal in the broader political sphere, often with the help of ethnic studies advocates. In the Kalama Valley, on the windward side of Oahu, a group of tenants in 1970 joined up with UH activists—led by Kamakawiwoole—in an attempt to curtail a massive development plan spearheaded by the industrialist Henry Kaiser. Due to tourism and an influx of permanent residents from the mainland, land development had mushroomed since statehood, and was squeezing an already tight real estate market. Many of Hawai'i's largest landholdings were still controlled by descendants of white settlers who leased small plots to Native Hawaiian subsistence farmers. Seeking to cash in on the poststatehood boom, landlords began rapidly selling off their property to developers, who in turn evicted any tenants and, often, denied public fishing access by closing paths to the sea. Many Native Hawaiians were left homeless, resorting to living in tent cities on the beach. Residents, like those in the Kalama Valley, increasingly resisted these eviction efforts. Kalama Valley activists failed to stop the evictions. But the campaign led to the formation of Kōkua Hawai'i, a group that, according to activist and scholar Haunani-Kay Trask, gave birth to the islands' modern sovereignty movement, which would grow in its radicalism and visibility over the coming decades.[72]

For ethnic studies activists, Hawaiian and otherwise, participation in political movements such as the Kalama Valley campaign represented the full expression of the ethnic studies promise to use new scholarship and pedagogy to foster political change. Supporters of Ethnic Studies praised what was called an "affective" approach to learning, in which students "exist in a state of constant and active interaction" that "engendered a sense of activism and participation in those associated with the program."[73] Local community supporters, such as Henry Chun—a neighborhood activist who had worked with Ethnic Studies students to oppose the erection of a garage that would displace residents in downtown Honolulu—likewise praised the program for defying the university's tendency to focus only on "book knowledge" at the expense of its mission "to serve the community." "Knowledge should be shared," Chun insisted.[74]

And yet it was affective learning and political action that put the Ethnic Studies Program in a precarious position at UH. As Ethnic Studies was pushing for permanent status in the mid-1970s, Chancellor Douglas Yamamura questioned "what is meant by 'affective value' of the Program and how this value is related to its academic value, which we consider to be of prime importance."[75] He criticized the program for what he called its tendency "to present one point of view, for to do otherwise would detract from the emotional appeal being made by the instructor." It was, however, "beyond question" that there should be "a rational rather than emotional presentation of history, sociology, political science and related disciplines." This was the mark of "mature academic departments."[76]

By the end of 1976, Yamamura was pushing for Ethnic Studies Program to be abolished and its curriculum distributed to other departments. The move led to yet another bruising round between the administration and Ethnic Studies advocates, who were becoming more explicit in linking racial inequality to class analysis. At a public hearing for supporters of the program, Hawai'i locals argued that administration claims that Ethnic Studies was too political were really a reaction against its promotion of "dangerous ideas" that ran counter to racial liberalism's rejection of class. "The real cause of poverty, racism, and sexism," one resident stated, "is an economic system that rips off huge profits for the few, the ruling class."[77] The university, another supporter insisted, was hypocritical in its claims that academia should be a space free of ideology or politics because the capitalist system in which the university operated was itself was based on ideology. The same criticisms of Ethnic Studies for its "affective" approach, wrote UH professor of English George Simson, "could also be brought against the business school, the law school, and the medical school, in which students, faculty, and the official institutional myths (as in the myths of the state) demand affection." The University of Hawaiʻi, according to Simson, had succeeded in fostering "the kinds of affections the participants in these programs are supposed to exhibit, including a peculiar affection for the local commercial lifestyle. . . . So it is not a matter of whether a program promotes values but which ones."[78]

Yamamura's attempt to shut down the program backfired when it prompted a review by the faculty senate. The senate recommended the program be made permanent, which the Board of Regents approved in June 1977.[79] By this time, UH Ethnic Studies was among the five largest university programs in the nation to offer an Asian American studies curriculum—it was difficult to argue with its success in attracting student interest and carving out a role for itself in campus life.[80]

In the process of establishing itself as a permanent presence, however, Ethnic Studies' attention to the intersections of class and ethnicity gave way to a stronger emphasis on cultural analysis. This was due, in part, to the faculty senate's endorsement of the idea that Ethnic Studies was too political. The program's focus "on the class struggle approach" was "ideologically narrow," stated the final faculty senate report on the matter, and the program "would be strengthened by placing more emphasis on the cultural and historical approaches."[81] By the mid-1980s, the faculty's Educational and Policy Planning Committee was praising Ethnic Studies for successfully evolving "from a controversial, academically suspect program that was given permanent status—in spite of a number of doubts—into one that appears sound and academically responsible." They applauded what they saw as the program's move away from its politically charged mission of the 1970s. For instance, the committee wrote favorably about assignments that took students out of the classroom, which "are now more flexibly oriented towards the personal and cultural interests of those doing the projects and not so rigidly determined by prepackaged sociopolitical objectives."[82]

Other evidence shows that during this period the program did retreat from using class as a central category of analysis in studying Hawaiʻi's ethnic communities. In the program's flagship oral history project, for instance, there was a notable decline beginning in the mid-1980s in interviews covering subjects related directly to labor and working-class experience, such as labor organizing or working conditions on the islands' sugar and pineapple plantations. At the same time, there was an increase in culture-oriented interview topics with subject tags such as ethnic tradition, family life, and education. The transition was reflected in the relative percentages of labor- and culture-related subject

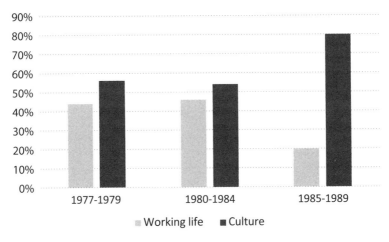

FIGURE 21. UH Oral History Project subject tags.
Center for Oral History Database, University of Hawai'i.

tags attributed to each interview. While the total number of subject tags for working life and culture remained about even in the 1970s and early 1980s, the latter accounted for 80 percent of tags in the late 1980s.[83]

Perhaps it is not surprising that Ethnic Studies, embattled within liberal Hawai'i and entering a conservative decade in American politics, moved toward a less overtly anticapitalist stance. The shift away from class analysis was part of a broader trend in American academia, in which many leftist scholars became increasingly disillusioned with what seemed to be a global failure of the left to enact viable socialism.[84] The fractures within Ethnic Studies itself also surely contributed to the decline of class analysis in the 1980s (although it certainly never disappeared). Against this background, Ethnic Studies would continue to promote an alternative, more pluralistic version of multicultural-ism than that of Hawai'i's liberal establishment. In the process, Ethnic Studies held the university to account for its rhetorical celebration of diversity, which helped lead to an expanded curriculum, a more ethnically mixed student body, and the hiring of more faculty members of color. It ensured that the anodyne multiculturalism promoted by state boosters would continue to be challenged by critical voices. At the same time, however, the program's existence depended on its accommodation to many of the academic norms that it set out to revolutionize in the 1970s and its attempts to overhaul faculty hiring were limited—an administration report from 1989 found that 70 percent of tenured faculty at UH were white.[85]

It would take grassroots social protest, in Hawai'i and in the rest of the United States, to expose the elisions inherent to liberal multiculturalism. But those protests had to confront a powerful story of national progress and the entrenched interests that benefitted from it. At the same time, even the Ethnic Studies paradigm, conceived as a radical rebuke to those interests, struggled to account for the uneven relations of power among Hawaiʻi's nonwhite ethnic groups—or that some might refuse the "ethnic group" label altogether. As the twentieth century drew to a close, a new wave of activism in would challenge just how Hawaiʻi came to be multicultural state.

Epilogue

Legacies of 1959

MULTICULTURALISM AND COLONIALISM
IN THE "DECOLONIZED" STATE

THE PREDICAMENT OF Ethnic Studies at the University of Hawai'i has mirrored the fundamental conflicts at the heart of multiculturalism itself. In whatever form it takes, multiculturalism is a fundamentally unstable concept. Distilled to its most basic elements, it poses a challenge to any kind of universalism that purports to speak for all members of a heterogeneous community. At the same time, however, multiculturalism is often seen as a means of accommodating difference *within* a defined community or political structure, be it a nation, city, or university. It is this tension, between universalism and particularism, that animates multiculturalist discourse, evoking the dilemma between national consensus and respect for minority opinion that Tocqueville identified as a defining feature of American democracy. But the lauding of minority perspectives that multiculturalism entails has been less a solution to the problem of social difference than an indirect acknowledgment of it.

In the decades since the end of civil rights reform and the racial transformations in American academia, multiculturalism has come under fire from opponents across the political spectrum. At the height of the "culture wars," conservative critics such as Allan Bloom and Dinesh D'Souza blamed universities, with their emphasis on multiculturalism, for promoting a radical close-mindedness that prioritized "political correctness," denigrated Western thought and culture, and caved to the demands of activist students at the expense of intellectual rigor.[1] In more alarmist fashion, Samuel Huntington characterized multiculturalism as part of a "clash of civilizations" and a full-frontal attack on "the existence of a common American culture" that would destroy the United States if left unchecked.[2] Ur-liberal Arthur Schlesinger also lambasted multiculturalism, along with right-wing monoculturalism, for leading to the "balkanization" of American society, and pleaded for a return to the melting pot paradigm.[3]

Leftists, meanwhile, critiqued multiculturalism for covering up persistent structural inequality in the United States and for valuing cultural recognition over political power. During the ascendency of conservative politics in the 1980s, as social programs were slashed in the name of reducing the size and mandates of government, the problems of difference and inequality, once a central concern of American politics, were increasingly shunted to the sidelines. As a result, the university became one of the main forums for arguing the merits of various approaches to social difference. But, as many academic critics themselves have argued, talking about difference and its effects has not been a substitute for political action. Academic attention to racism and inequality has done little to curb their persistence in broader American society.

Meanwhile, even as multiculturalism opened new lines of inquiry and allowed for a more diverse range of participation in these debates, the language of multiculturalism could result in conservative ends. Multiculturalism, according to scholars on the left, had been co-opted by white gatekeepers who sought to "manage diversity" toward profitable ends rather than overturn the status quo.[4] Many of these critics were themselves part of the changes to higher education wrought by the ethnic studies movement. While historian Robin Kelley has challenged the idea that universities could ever serve as a site of revolution, African American studies scholar Hazel Carby argued that multiculturalism in the academy too often served as a form of tokenism—a way to alleviate white guilt that favored an integrated curriculum in place of an integrated student body and faculty; whatever its radical promise, it had become "a discourse that seems to act as a substitute for the political activity of desegregation."[5]

Liberal multiculturalist principles could also aid the very conservatives bemoaning multiculturalism, as sociologists Michael Omi and Howard Winant have argued. Multiculturalism, as the name implies, has tended to prioritize ethnicity and culture—rather than race—as organizing social categories. As liberal multiculturalism deemphasized race-based critiques of inequality, conservatives seized the discourse of color-blindness to both disavow racism and criticize "nontraditional" values and cultural practices.[6] According to that logic, if culture was the key to difference, then the relative socioeconomic positions of various groups could be explained solely by reference to group values, social expectations, and "pathologies." Similarly, for Asian American studies scholar Susan Koshy, multiculturalism's celebration of ethnic difference undercut earlier promises of liberation movements based on racial solidarity.[7] Multiculturalism had become an end in itself rather than a means to promote political action.

Even as multiculturalism has acknowledged race as a biological fiction, it cannot undo the continuing salience of race as a shaper of social status. Formal equality did not translate to social leveling. At the same time, this new liberal framework for making sense of difference, while largely doing away with a rigidly stratified understanding of race, could still serve as a system of measurement, assigning differing values to separate groups depending on their perceived contribution to the national project. Here is where looking to Hawai'i for the origins of U.S. multiculturalism is illuminating. Successful Asian Americans in Hawai'i, as we have seen, were seen by the U.S. government as helpmates in extending American influence to the Pacific, and as members of a larger, national "model minority." This in turn had widespread political, social, and cultural effects both in Hawai'i and in the rest of the United States, as this book has demonstrated.

Debates around multiculturalism have played out in particular ways within Hawai'i. Hawaiian sovereignty activists have criticized multiculturalism for the way in which it equated indigenous populations with other nonwhite people under the "minority" label. Native communities, they argued, were not analogous to other ethnic groups that had settled on formerly indigenous land. Hawai'i's people of Asian ancestry were therefore part of the settler colonialist project, and thus had fewer rights claims within Hawai'i than descendants of the Hawaiian Kingdom.[8] Reflecting the idea that Hawai'i's indigenous people constituted their own social and political category, in 1987 the University of Hawai'i established a Hawaiian Studies Center that was separate from Ethnic Studies; it would eventually be housed in its own building on the far east side of the Manoa campus.

The tensions between Hawaiians and Asian Americans in Hawai'i have been amplified by the problem of widening social inequality in the islands. While residents of Japanese and Okinawan descent have the lowest rates of poverty and highest rates of home ownership of any ethnic group, Native Hawaiians, by comparison, have faced disproportionately high rates of poverty, homelessness, unemployment, poor health, and imprisonment.[9] Ongoing inequality both reflects social divisions within Hawai'i and serves as the basis for Hawaiian rights claims.

Hawai'i statehood was intended to solve the dilemma posed by America's possession of an overseas, racially different colony in the context of global anticolonialism and the Cold War. But as the limitations of this transformation were exposed, so too was the incompatibility between "decolonization" and continued U.S. control over a once-sovereign nation. Institutional multiculturalism likewise failed to reconcile this fundamental conflict. Indeed, as Jodi Byrd argues, multiculturalism, whether radical or liberal, often elides America's history of settler colonialism. The national community to which different groups make claims of recognition resides on indigenous land and depends "upon an historical aphasia of the conquest of indigenous peoples."[10]

Yet the debates around multiculturalism and ethnic studies, in Hawai'i and in the rest of the United States, also opened up space for critiques of colonialism. Third World Liberation Front activists, in particular, aimed to expose the interconnectedness of historical colonialism, slavery, and the persistence of domestic racial inequality. Like the liberal multiculturalists behind statehood, they situated Hawai'i in larger global context. But in their global version of Hawai'i history, Hawai'i was not a benign gateway to Asia; rather it was a site of global imperial encounters that continued to shape everyday life.

Hawai'i's history of colonialism had hovered in the background—unacknowledged but always there—of the celebratory narratives about Hawai'i during the statehood debates and in the decade after. This specterlike presence was due in part to the ways in which Hawai'i's racial difference, a direct product of colonialism, was framed as an asset to U.S. foreign policy. While statehood on the American continent served to erase U.S. colonialism by normalizing white settlement of native lands, Hawai'i's particular history of Asian migration, and the global context in which it became a state, made that erasure more difficult.

By the 1970s, the utopian visions of Hawai'i that characterized the statehood era had begun to crumble under the weight of statehood's failure to deliver on its promises. As ethnic studies advocates pointed out, statehood had not overturned racial injustice in the islands, and in many cases it had exacerbated it. As the myths around statehood were being newly challenged, colonialism emerged as a flashpoint in local politics. Activists, many of them drawn from the ethnic studies movement, increasingly came to identify U.S. colonialism as the root cause of inequality in Hawai'i.

In particular, they sought to link the colonial dispossession of native lands to ongoing land struggles. In the wake of the movement to stop evictions in the Kalama Valley, anti-eviction efforts became a primary form of opposition among Hawaiian rights activists. Emerging out of these eviction battles, the nascent sovereignty movement began to coalesce around indigenous land claims and protests against irresponsible land use. The protests also revealed that many in Hawai'i were deeply ambivalent over both tourism and militarism in the islands, which were increasingly linked to each other—and to Hawai'i's history of colonialism. Anti-eviction campaigners repeatedly called for "land for local people, not tourists," and, in one 1971 journal essay, identified urban renewal projects that displaced native communities as "Hawaii's Strategic Hamlets," a pointed reference to America's counterinsurgency efforts in Vietnam.[11] Over the course of the 1970s, such protests shifted in their rhetoric and strategy to deploy cultural pride—reflected in the renewed use of the

Hawaiian language and an emphasis on Hawaiians' special relationship to the land—as part of their organizing strategy.[12]

A twenty-year campaign against the navy's massive bomb testing project on Kahoʻolawe, a small uninhabited island off the coast of Maui, fused environmentalism, antimilitarism, and Hawaiian spirituality to argue for demilitarization of the island.[13] As one Native Hawaiian activist declared in 1977, it was his "moral responsibility to attempt an ending to this desecration of our sacred aina [land] . . . for each bomb dropped adds further injury to an already wounded soul."[14] Although tourism promoters were among the first protesters in the 1970s—a sign of tensions between Hawaiʻi's two major income generators—the Kahoʻolawe campaign came to be dominated by sovereignty activists, who called for the island to be restored to Hawaiians as part of a future Hawaiian nation. (The Navy eventually ended its live-fire exercises on Kahoʻolawe in 1990 and transferred it to state control in 1994.)

Native Hawaiian concerns were also front and center at the state's constitutional convention in 1978. The Hawaiian Affairs Committee, considered a powerless and perfunctory group in past constitutional conventions, dominated much of the meeting and pushed for changes to the state constitution that continue to shape and, often, divide Hawaiian society to this day. Arguing that "a culturally diversified society is a source of strength for a nation," the committee's final report succeeded in securing the passage of several notable amendments, including adding Hawaiian as an official state language; a mandate for the study of Hawaiian history and language in public schools; protections for traditional fishing and religious sites; and the creation of the Office of Hawaiian Affairs (OHA)—a semiautonomous state agency in charge of administering grants and programming for the benefit Native Hawaiians.[15]

The constitutional convention and the creation of the OHA helped to further galvanize the Hawaiian sovereignty movement into an organized force within local politics. Yet the OHA itself, as a state institution, has played a complicated and sometimes contradictory role in this process—exposing the irreconcilable tensions wrought by colonialism and statehood. More radical sovereignty activists rejected the very notion of working within state government structures at all, while others sought to use it to their advantage. In 1993, for instance, sovereignty activists organized a series of OHA-sponsored activities to commemorate the centennial of the 1893 overthrow of the Hawaiian monarchy.[16] Many non–Native Hawaiians, meanwhile, criticized the OHA as an example of "reverse racism" because of a rule that its board be composed of Native Hawaiians who could trace their bloodlines back to the period before annexation. In 2000, after an organized effort led by a white Big Island rancher to challenge the eligibility rules for OHA board membership, the U.S.

Supreme Court ruled in *Rice v. Cayetano* that the Hawaiian ancestry requirement was unconstitutional.[17]

The *Rice v. Cayetano* ruling saw Hawaiians as a race rather than a protected legal class, dealing a blow to sovereignty activists seeking increased federal recognition of their indigenous status. Hawaiians have also faced challenges in attempting to redress grievances through U.S. courts over the corrupt oversight of Hawaiian home lands—property that originally belonged to the Hawaiian monarchy and was eventually transferred to the state government, which in turn is supposed to lease it to people of native ancestry. Despite the fact that few tracts of land have been distributed to Native Hawaiians—while many have gone to the military and to wealthy non-Hawaiians for various commercial enterprises—the terms of the home lands legislation make it difficult to sue the government for mismanagement.[18]

In part because of these legal setbacks, the sovereignty movement has increasingly worked to disentangle Hawai'i from the United States both legally and culturally. A bill proposed in 2000 by Hawai'i senator Daniel Akaka, which would offer federal recognition to Native Hawaiians similar to that of Native American tribes, has divided the sovereignty movement over whether they should continue to work with the U.S. government. Instead of appealing to the U.S. government, some sovereignty activists have attempted to use international law—such as the Law of Nations and United Nations protocol on decolonization—in their arguments for independence.[19] This has been coupled with a powerful discourse of Hawaiian exceptionalism. Some within the movement have explicitly sought to distance Hawaiian rights claims from those of Native Americans, by contrasting Hawai'i's status as a recognized sovereign nation-state at the time of the 1893 overthrow with Native Americans' classification as "domestic dependent nations."[20]

Many continental Americans, too, seem to view Hawai'i as not truly part of the United States—though not necessarily for anticolonialist reasons. The Hawai'i-born Barack Obama was plagued by conspiracy theories about his foreign birth throughout his first presidential campaign and later his presidency. While these claims hinged on his father's Kenyan nationality, the so-called "birther" campaign also drew on Hawai'i's association with foreignness. Rather than denying the validity of Obama's birth certificate wholesale, some conspiracists insisted that Hawai'i had allowed babies born abroad to be registered in the fiftieth state.[21]

Even Obama himself has inadvertently played into the narrative that Hawai'i is not quite fully American. In his political life he has subtly eschewed his Hawai'i roots in favor of his connection to Chicago, with its rich African American history, and with the wider Midwest of his mother's childhood. In the keynote address at the 2004 Democratic Convention that launched

Obama's national career, the future president mentioned Stanley Ann Dunham's native Kansas, but not Hawai'i, where his mother spent most of her life. Later, his choice of Chicago as the site of his presidential library, while perhaps inevitable, broke with the tradition of locating libraries in presidents' home states.

The administration of President Donald Trump, the most prominent "birther" of them all, has not-so-subtly suggested that Hawai'i lies outside the confines of the U.S. nation-state. Trump's former attorney general Jeff Sessions called into question Hawai'i's place in the nation when he attacked a 2017 federal district court decision to block Trump's travel ban on people from Muslim countries. The ruling itself was bad enough, but so too was the fact that it was made in Hawai'i, where the federal court was located. "I really am amazed," Sessions said, "that a judge sitting on an island in the Pacific can issue an order that stops the president of the United States from what appears to be clearly his statutory and constitutional power."[22] Surely Sessions was aware that Hawai'i is a U.S. state and not simply "an island in the Pacific." But he sought to undermine the legitimacy of the ruling by pointing to Hawai'i's geographical remoteness, and thus cultural distance, from the rest of the United States. As a child of the Jim Crow South, Sessions might have heard similar arguments made against Hawai'i statehood.

Indeed, as *Gateway State* has explored, throughout its history as a U.S. territory and later as a state, Hawai'i has occupied an ambiguous position between the domestic and the foreign in U.S. culture. That ambiguity was often purposefully exploited by a range of actors invested in building Hawai'i as "bridge to Asia" during the Cold War. Many in Hawai'i are now seeking to overturn that ambiguity by rejecting at once its relationship to the United States and to Asia in favor of an indigenous, local rendering of the domestic. But while this type of sovereignty claim might serve as a legal and discursive strategy to secure independence, it nonetheless risks distorting Hawai'i's place in both global and American history. It overlooks Hawai'i's fundamental *un*-exceptionalism. Not only must we understand Hawai'i's history as an extension of the European colonial project in North America, we must also locate the colonization of Hawai'i in the global context of modern imperial formation. Hawai'i's own local story of annexation and statehood may have played out in particular ways but it was far from unique. Rather, Hawai'i's modern history exemplified larger interrelated developments of global empire, capitalism, and migration. The settlement of Hawai'i by people of Asian descent was dependent on imperial developments abroad: British intervention in China in the 1840s, America's forced opening of Japan to foreign trade in the 1850s, and the American colonization of the Philippines in 1898 all fueled the mass movement of Asian people around the world. Many of them ended up as contract laborers on Hawai'i's plantations, where they faced grueling conditions and restrictions on their freedom of movement—a fact that argues against identifying them as "settler colonialists" and instead points to the broader colonial history that created Hawai'i's multiethnic society.[23]

Hawai'i may no longer take up the same national political or cultural space that it did in mid-century America. But its history unearths the roots of racial liberalism as we know it today, however embattled it may seem after the election of 2016. Obama himself invoked the multiculturalist ideal so prevalent in discussions around Hawai'i in the 1960s in his 2004 convention speech. Highlighting his "funny name" and the "diversity of my heritage," he insisted that "in no other country on Earth is my story even possible." Hawai'i statehood had appeared to represent a similar promise, of elevating the United States though the embrace of diversity. And yet, in Hawai'i, as in the rest of the United States, the celebration of difference has all too often masked the structures of violence and inequality, both global and domestic, in which difference has been produced and sustained. The liberalism of Hawai'i statehood promised Americans redemption by transforming a history of racism and colonialism into the basis for a multicultural future and a source of American power. This is a narrative that continues to resonate precisely because of what it leaves out.

Subject tags	1977–79	1980–84	1985–89
Cooperatives—Agricultural		2	
Pineapples	18	5	2
Plantation life	22	40	26
Strikes	33	5	3
Sugar cane	3	17	4
Unions	12	3	11
Working conditions	15	17	3
Total	**103**	**86**	**49**
Total # oral history project interviews by date range	171	111	158
Total # of subject tags	233	186	244
Percentage of subject tags	**44%**	**46%**	**20%**
Subject tags	1977–79	1980–84	1985–90
Acculturation	1		
African Americans-Community, Lifestyle, and Family Life			4
Arts			1
Buddhism		1	
Caucasian-Lifestyles		1	
Chinese-Customs and Beliefs, Lifestyles			
Christianity	5	2	
Churches	3	4	5
Community	22	13	3
Customs and Beliefs	6	5	
Dancing	2	1	6
Education	3	5	3
Ethnic Identity			
Ethnic Relations	15	16	33
Family life	24	8	55
Food	4	8	2
Hawaiians-Social life, Customs and Beliefs, Lifestyles,	10	3	31
Japanese-Community, Customs and Beliefs, Lifestyles			21
Language, language schools	4	7	2

Subject tags	1977–79	1980–84	1985–89
Portuguese Community, Customs and Beliefs, Lifestyles		2	6
Recreation	8	10	3
Religion	1	2	2
Social activities	17	2	6
Schools	5	10	12
Total	**130**	**100**	**195**
Total # oral history project interviews by date range	171	111	157
Total # of subject tags	233	186	244
Percentage of subject tags	**56%**	**54%**	**80%**

Source: Center for Oral History Database, University of Hawai'i.

NOTES

Introduction

1. Joseph A. Loftus, "Kennedy Campaign to Open in Hawaii, with Alaska Next," *New York Times*, July 22, 1960, 1.

2. Although Kennedy eventually won 303 electoral votes to Nixon's 219, the 1960 election was the closest in U.S. history since 1916, with Nixon challenging Kennedy's victory in several states; Kennedy's legitimacy was thus bolstered by any additional votes. For more on the Hawaiʻi recount, see Burl Burlingame, "Hawaii Was the 'Florida' of 1960 Election," *Honolulu Star-Bulletin*, November 18, 2000.

3. See Thomas Borstelmann, *The Cold War and the Color Line: American Race Relations in the Global Arena* (Cambridge, MA: Harvard University Press, 2001); Mary Dudziak, *Cold War Civil Rights: Race and the Image of American Democracy* (Princeton, NJ: Princeton University Press, 2002); and Penny Von Eschen, *Satchmo Blows Up the World: Jazz Ambassadors Play the Cold War* (Cambridge, MA: Harvard University Press, 2004.)

4. Thomas Bender, *A Nation among Nations: America's Place in World History* (New York: Hill and Wang, 2006).

5. John D. Kelly and Martha Kaplan, *Represented Communities: Fiji and World Decolonization* (Chicago: University of Chicago Press, 2001), 20.

6. For a discussion on the coming of the Cold War as an "unimagined contingency" in the Global South, see Mark Bradley, "Decolonization, the Global South, and the Cold War, 1919–1962," in Melvyn Leffler and Odd Arne Westad, eds., *Cambridge History of the Cold War*, vol. 1, *Origins* (Cambridge: Cambridge University Press, 2010). For more on American efforts to shape the trajectory of decolonization struggles abroad, see, for example, Odd Arne Westad, *The Global Cold War: Third World Interventions and the Making of Our Times* (Cambridge: Cambridge University Press, 2005); Mark Bradley, *Imagining Vietnam and America: The Making of Postcolonial Vietnam, 1919–1950* (Chapel Hill: University of North Carolina Press, 2000); Douglas Little, *American Orientalism: The United States and the Middle East since 1945*, 3rd ed. (Chapel Hill: University of North Carolina Press, 2008); and Borstelmann, *The Cold War and the Color Line*. For more on the agency of actors in the decolonizing world, see Matthew Connelly, *A Diplomatic Revolution: Algeria's Fight for Independence and the Origins of the Post–Cold War Era* (New York: Oxford University Press, 2002).

7. See, for example, Todd Shepard, *The Invention of Decolonization: The Algerian War and the Remaking of France* (Ithaca, NY: Cornell University Press, 2006); and Jordanna Bailkin, *The Afterlife of Empire* (Berkeley: University of California Press, 2012).

8. As Bonnie Honig argues, foreignness can serve "as an agent of (re)founding," filling the nation's demand for "periodic testimony to the true universality of its principles and the choiceworthiness of its democracy." Bonnie Honig, *Democracy and the Foreigner* (Princeton, NJ: Princeton University Press, 2001), 3, 94.

9. Senate Committee on Interior and Insular Affairs, *Hearings on Statehood for Hawaii*, 80th Cong., 1st sess. (1957), 10. Such notions of Asian American usefulness overseas was gaining popularity among policymakers during the Cold War, as Ellen Wu demonstrates in her discussion of State Department efforts to transform "Overseas Chinese" living in the United States into American cultural ambassadors. See Wu, *The Color of Success: Asian Americans and the Origins of the Model Minority* (Princeton, NJ: Princeton University Press, 2014), 122–138.

10. For an examination of the racialization of European immigrants and their eventual acceptance into the category of "Caucasian," see Matthew Frye Jacobson, *Whiteness of a Different Color: European Immigrants and the Alchemy of Race* (Cambridge, MA: Harvard University Press, 1998). It is important to point out, however, that, unlike Asian immigrants, Europeans were considered "free white persons" under the 1790 Naturalization Act and were thus eligible for naturalized citizenship.

11. "Report on Progress of the Center for Cultural and Technical Interchange between East and West," March 1, 1961, U.S. National Archives and Records Administration, RG 59: Records of the Department of State, Bureau of Educational and Cultural Affairs, Office of the Assistant Secretary, Subject Files, 1961–1962, Box 2.

12. On the conflict between American democracy and settler colonialism, see Jodi Byrd, *Transit of Empire: Indigenous Critiques of Colonialism* (Minneapolis: University of Minnesota Press, 2011).

13. Ian Lind, "Ring of Steel: Notes on the Militarization of Hawaii," *Social Process in Hawai'i* 31(1984–85): 25–48.

14. Michael Hunt, *Ideology and U.S. Foreign Policy* (New Haven, CT: Yale University Press, 1987).

15. Amy Kaplan, *The Anarchy of Empire in the Making of U.S. Culture* (Cambridge, MA: Harvard University Press, 2002).

16. Michael Patrick Cullinane, *Liberty and American Anti-Imperialism* (New York: Palgrave Macmillan, 2012); Ian Tyrrell and Jay Sexton, eds., *Empire's Twin: U.S. Anti-imperialism from the Founding Era to the Age of Terrorism* (Ithaca, NY: Cornell University Press, 2015).

17. The definitive political account of Hawai'i statehood, Roger Bell's *Last Among Equals: Hawaiian Statehood and American Politics* (Honolulu: University of Hawai'i Press, 1984), focuses on the congressional wrangling and sectional debates that delayed Hawaii's admission. For an account of statehood that focuses more on local actors and territorial politics, see John S. Whitehead, *Completing the Union: Alaska, Hawai'i, and the Battle for Statehood* (Albuquerque: University of New Mexico Press, 2004); Tom Coffman, *The Island Edge of America: A Political History of Hawai'i* (Honolulu: University of Hawai'i Press, 2003). For a critique of statehood in relation to the Hawaiian sovereignty movement, see Dean Saranillio, "Seeing Conquest: Colliding Histories and the Cultural Politics of Hawai'i Statehood" (Ph.D. diss., University of Michigan, 2009).

18. See Gretchen Heefner, "'A Symbol for a New Frontier': Hawaiian Statehood, Anti-Colonialism, and Winning the Cold War," *Pacific Historical Review* 74, no. 4 (2005): 545–574;

Giles Scott-Smith, "From Symbol of Division to Cold War Asset: Lyndon Johnson and the Achievement of Hawaiian Statehood in 1959," *History* 89, no. 294 (April 2004): 256–273; and Ann Ziker, "Segregationists Confront American Empire: The Conservative White South and the Question of Hawaiian Statehood, 1947–1959," *Pacific Historical Review* 76, no. 3 (2007): 439–466.

19. For a distillation of many of the themes and debates within the United States and the world literature, see Thomas Bender, ed. *Rethinking American History in a Global Age* (Berkeley: University of California Press, 2002). This transnational approach to American history has often looked beyond the nation-state as the primary subject of study, though it has not discounted the state as a powerful shaper of foreign relations. See, for example, Ian R. Tyrrell, *Woman's World/Woman's Empire: The Woman's Christian Temperance Union in International Perspective, 1880–1930* (Chapel Hill: University of North Carolina Press, 1991); Leila J. Rupp, *Worlds of Women: The Making of an International Women's Movement* (Princeton, NJ: Princeton University Press, 1997); Madeline Hsu, *Dreaming of Gold, Dreaming of Home: Transnationalism and Migration between the United States and South China, 1882–1943* (Stanford, CA: Stanford University Press, 2000); Eiichiro Azuma, *Between Two Empires: Race, History, and Transnationalism in Japanese America* (New York: Oxford University Press, 2005); Jesse Hoffnung-Garskof, *A Tale of Two Cities: Santo Domingo and New York after 1950* (Princeton: Princeton University Press, 2008); and Takashi Fujitani, *Race for Empire: Koreans as Japanese and Japanese as Americans during World War II* (Berkeley: University of California Press, 2011).

20. Bender, "Historians, the Nation, and the Plentitude of Narratives, *Rethinking American History in a Global Age*, 9.

21. One of the first big works to self-consciously embrace this permeability was Daniel Rodgers's *Atlantic Crossings: Social Politics in a Progressive Age* (Cambridge, MA: Belknap Press of Harvard University Press, 1998).

22. Paul A. Kramer, "Power and Connection: Imperial Histories of the United States in the World," *American Historical Review* 116, no. 5 (December 2011): 1348–1391.

23. William Appleman Williams and Walter LaFeber were among the first American historians to frame U.S. foreign policy in terms of empire. See Williams, *The Tragedy of American Diplomacy* (New York: World Publishing, 1959); and LaFeber, *The New Empire: An Interpretation of American Expansion, 1860–1898* (Ithaca, NY: Cornell University Press, 1963). Works emphasizing the links between U.S. expansion in the Americas and later imperial ventures include D. W. Meinig, *The Shaping of America*, vol. 2, *Continental America, 1800–1867* (New Haven, CT: Yale University Press, 1986); Ann Laura Stoler, ed., *Haunted by Empire: Geographies of Intimacy in North American History* (Durham, NC: Duke University Press, 2006); and Greg Grandin, *Empire's Workshop: Latin America, the United States, and the Rise of the New Imperialism* (New York: Metropolitan Books, 2006). For works that demonstrate U.S. cultural and economic enmeshment in global imperial networks, see Walter Johnson, *River of Dark Dreams: Slavery and Empire in the Cotton Kingdom* (Cambridge, MA: Harvard University Press, 2013); Marilyn Lake and Henry Reynolds, *Drawing the Global Colour Line: White Men's Countries and the International Challenge of Racial Equality* (Cambridge: Cambridge University Press, 2008); and Kristin Hoganson, *Consumers' Imperium: The Global Production of American Domesticity, 1865–1920* (Chapel Hill: University of North Carolina Press, 2007). For works on formal U.S. empire after the 1890s, see Paul Kramer, *The Blood of Government: Race, Empire, the United*

States, and the Philippines (Chapel Hill: University of North Carolina Press, 2006); Kristin Hoganson, *Fighting for American Manhood: How Gender Politics Provoked the Spanish-American and Philippine-American War* (New Haven, CT: Yale University Press, 2000); Mary Renda, *Taking Haiti: Military Occupation and the Culture of U.S. Empire, 1915–1940* (Chapel Hill: University of North Carolina Press, 2001); Laura Briggs, *Reproducing Empire: Race, Sex, Science, and U.S. Imperialism in Puerto Rico* (Berkeley: University of California Press, 2002); Amy Kaplan and Donald Pease, *Cultures of United States Imperialism* (Durham, NC: Duke University Press, 1993); Amy Kaplan, *The Anarchy of Empire in the Making of U.S. Culture* (Cambridge, MA: Harvard University Press, 2002); and Alfred W. McCoy and Francisco A. Scarano, eds., *Colonial Crucible: Empire in the Making of the Modern American State* (Madison: University of Wisconsin Press, 2009).

24. For links between colonialism and the development of New World slavery, see Edmund Morgan, *American Slavery, American Freedom: The Ordeal of Colonial Virginia* (New York: W. W. Norton, 1975); Sidney Mintz, *Sweetness and Power: The Place of Sugar in Modern History* (New York: Penguin Books, 1986); Robin Blackburn, *The Making of New World Slavery: From the Baroque to the Modern, 1492–1800* (New York: Verso, 1998); and Sven Beckert, *Empire of Cotton: A New History of Global Capitalism* (New York: Alfred A. Knopf, 2014).

25. For an argument on the centrality of the Pacific in American historical development, see Bruce Cumings, *Dominion from Sea to Sea: Pacific Ascendancy and American Power* (New Haven, CT: Yale University Press, 2009).

26. In the aftermath of the U.S. military's brutal defeat of the Philippine insurrection in 1902, colonial administrators launched a project of "benevolent assimilation" that differentiated between "civilized" and "savage" Filipinos in an attempt to prepare the colony for eventual self-rule. Many on the mainland, however, failed to appreciate the distinction, and attempts by colonial authorities to normalize the Philippines as part of the United States led to a nativist backlash. See Kramer, *Blood of Government.*

27. According to the Supreme Court in a series of decisions collectively known as the Insular Cases, the new colonies were "foreign in a domestic sense" and thus need not be governed by the same legal regime that applied in the continental United States. See Bartholomew Sparrow, *The Insular Cases and the Emergence of American Empire* (Lawrence: University Press of Kansas, 2006); Efren Rivera, "The Legal Construction of American Colonialism: The Insular Cases (1901–1922)," *Revista Juridica Universidad de Puerto Rico* 65 (1996): 225–328; and Christina Duffy Burnett and Burke Marshall, *Foreign in a Domestic Sense: Puerto Rico, American Expansion, and the Constitution* (Durham, NC: Duke University Press, 2001). The new territories' simultaneous inclusion as part of the United States and formal exclusion from its legal protections exemplified what Amy Kaplan calls the "anarchy of empire": the distorting and unsettling impact of empire on American legal, social, and cultural norms. See Kaplan's *The Anarchy of Empire.*

28. Two of the biggest anthologies on U.S. empire, Kaplan's *Cultures of United States Imperialism* and McCoy's *Colonial Crucible,* leave out Hawai'i entirely.

29. For a summary account of Hawai'i's relationship to the United States from the time of the first American settlements, see Gary Okihiro, *Island World: A History of Hawai'i and the United States* (Berkeley: University of California Press, 2008); Gavan Daws, *Shoal of Time: A History of the Hawaiian Islands* (New York: Macmillan, 1974); Lawrence H. Fuchs, *Hawaii*

Pono: A Social History (New York: Harcourt, Brace & World, 1961). Haunani-Kay Trask's *From a Native Daughter: Colonialism and Sovereignty in Hawai'i* (1993; reprint Honolulu: University of Hawai'i Press, 1999), provides a Hawaiian nationalist perspective on the history of American-Hawai'i relations. For a history of early missionary work in Hawai'i, see Patricia Grimshaw, *Paths of Duty: American Missionary Wives in Nineteenth-Century Hawaii* (Honolulu: University of Hawai'i Press, 1989).

30. Christine Skwiot, *The Purposes of Paradise: U.S. Tourism and Empire in Cuba and Hawai'i* (Philadelphia: University of Pennsylvania Press, 2010), 31–48. Fuchs, *Hawaii Pono*, 30–31.

31. See Erez Manela, *The Wilsonian Moment: Self-Determination and the International Origins of Anticolonial Nationalism* (New York: Oxford University Press, 2007); and Elizabeth Borgwardt, *A New Deal for the World: America's Vision for Human Rights* (Cambridge, MA: Harvard University Press, 2007).

32. See Brenda Plummer, *Rising Wind: Black Americans and U.S. Foreign Affairs, 1935–1960* (Chapel Hill: University of North Carolina Press, 1996); Penny von Eschen, *Race against Empire: Black Americans and Anticolonialism, 1937–1957* (Ithaca, NY: Cornell University Press, 1997); and Nico Slate, *Colored Cosmopolitanism: The Shared Struggle for Freedom in the United States and India* (Cambridge, MA: Harvard University Press, 2012).

33. *Current Marketing Report,* Hawaii Visitors Bureau, January 1970, Hawai'i and Pacific Collections, University of Hawai'i.

34. For representative examples, see the essays in the David Theo Goldberg, ed., *Multiculturalism: A Critical Reader* (Malden, MA: Blackwell, 1994); and Charles Taylor et al., *Multiculturalism: The Politics of Recognition* (Princeton, NJ: Princeton University Press, 1994); Barnor Hesse, ed. *Un/Settled Multiculturalisms: Diasporas, Entanglements, "Transruptions"* (London: Zed Books, 2000). David Hollinger, a historian, has written at length about multiculturalism and its problematics, but he too glosses over its historical emergence. See Hollinger, *Postethnic America: Beyond Multiculturalism* (1995; reprint New York: Basic Books, 2000).

35. For a critique of the ways in which multicultural education ignores the lack of diversity on college campuses, see Hazel Carby, "Multicultural Wars," *Radical History Review* 54 (1992): 7–18.

36. See Taylor, "The Politics of Recognition," in Taylor et al., *Multiculturalism.*

37. According to Google Ngram, the word *multiculturalism* began appearing in English-language books in the mid-1970s, rising steadily until 1988, when its usage shot up from less than 0.00005 percent of all printed words in Google's book sample to nearly 0.00025 percent. Globalization also began to take off in the 1970s, at much the same rate as multiculturalism. After the late 1980s it grew more quickly, reaching a usage of just under 0.0007 percent by 2000. The Ngram program allows you to quantify word usage within a 500-billion-word corpus taken from some 15 million books digitized by Google. For more information, see https://books.google.com/ngrams/info; and Jean-Baptiste Michel et al, "Quantitative Analysis of Culture Using Millions of Digitized Books," *Science* 331, no. 6014 (January 2011): 176–182.

38. Lawrence Davies, "Hawaii U. Girds for Future Role; New President Sees School Becoming Major Institution," *New York Times,* May 26, 1963.

39. Horace Kallen, "Democracy Versus the Melting Pot," *The Nation,* February 25, 1915. Diana Selig, *Americans All: The Cultural Gifts Movement* (Cambridge, MA: Harvard University Press, 2008).

40. Matthew Briones, *Jim and Jap Crow: A Cultural History of 1940s Interracial America* (Princeton, NJ: Princeton University Press, 2012), 5.

41. James R. Barrett, "Americanization from the Bottom Up: Immigration and the Remaking of the Working Class in the United States, 1880–1930," *Journal of American History* 79, no. 3 (December 1992): 996–1020.

42. David Hollinger tracks the essential differences between the pluralist and cosmopolitan traditions, and the ways in which they both inform multiculturalism, in *Postethnic America*, 79–104.

43. Christina Klein, *Cold War Orientalism: Asia in the Middlebrow Imagination, 1945–1961* (Berkeley: University of California Press, 2003); and Melani McAlister, *Epic Encounters: Culture, Media, and U.S. Interests in the Middle East since 1945* (Berkeley: University of California Press, 2001). For more on Orientalism and U.S. policy in Asia, see Bradley, *Imagining Vietnam and America*.

44. See Mai Ngai, *Impossible Subjects: Illegal Aliens and the Making of Modern America* (Princeton, NJ: Princeton University Press, 2005).

45. See Klein, *Cold War Orientalism*; and Naoko Shibusawa, *America's Geisha Ally: Reimagining the Japanese Enemy* (Cambridge, MA: Harvard University Press, 2006).

46. Quote from 1973 governor's conference report, *Hawaii 2000: Continuing Experiment in Anticipatory Democracy*, cited in Fuchs, *Hawaii Pono*, xi.

Chapter 1: "The Picture Window of the Pacific"

1. William F. Quinn statehood dedication ceremony speech, November 29, 1959, Records of the Hawaii Statehood Celebration Committee, Hawai'i State Archives, Box 1.

2. Senator Henry Jackson quoted in *Cong. Rec.*, 86th Cong., 1st sess. (1959), 3846.

3. Roger Bell, *Last Among Equals: Hawaiian Statehood and American Politics* (Honolulu: University of Hawai'i Press, 1984), 4.

4. Lawrence H. Fuchs, *Hawaii Pono: A Social History* (1961; reprint New York: Harcourt, Brace, 1983), 45.

5. There is much debate on Native Hawaiian population numbers before Western contact, but nearly all agree that there was a population decline of more than 80 percent after contact. For a helpful summary of these debates, see Gary Okihiro, *The Columbia Guide to Asian American History* (New York: Columbia University Press, 2005), 45–55.

6. Native Hawaiians' adoption of haole religion and law came as the population was being devastated by Western disease, leading to "the destruction of Native self-confidence in their own institutions," writes Jonathan Kamakawiwo'ole Osorio in *Dismembering Lahui: A History of the Hawaiian Nation to 1887* (Honolulu: University of Hawai'i Press, 2002) 13. Sally Engle Merry similarly suggests that Hawai'i's adoption of Anglo-American law was a defensive measure, intended to prove Hawai'i's worthiness as a civilized, independent nation. Throughout the first half of the nineteenth century, the monarchy faced challenges to its authority from foreign governments, notably France and Britain, each of which threatened to overtake the islands at various points in the mid-nineteenth century. See Sally Engle Merry, *Colonizing Hawai'i: The Cultural Power of Law* (Princeton, N.J.: Princeton University Press, 2000).

7. For pre–World War II Hawai'i labor history, see Gary Okihiro, *Cane Fires: The Anti-Japanese Movement in Hawaii, 1865–1945* (Philadelphia: Temple University Press, 1992); Ronald T. Takaki, *Pau Hana: Plantation Life and Labor in Hawaii, 1835–1920* (Honolulu: University of Hawai'i Press, 1984); and Edward D. Beechert, *Working in Hawaii: A Labor History* (Honolulu: University of Hawai'i Press, 1985).

8. For the American annexation of Hawai'i, see Julius Pratt, *Expansionists of 1898: The Acquisition of Hawaii and the Spanish Islands* (Baltimore: Johns Hopkins Press, 1936); Walter LaFeber, *The Cambridge History of American Foreign Relations, Volume II: The American Search for Opportunity, 1865–1913* (New York: Cambridge University Press, 1993); and Noenoe K. Silva, *Aloha Betrayed: Native Hawaiian Resistance to American Colonialism* (Durham, NC: Duke University Press, 2004).

9. Okihiro, *Cane Fires*, 13. See also Evelyn Nakano Glenn's *Unequal Freedom: How Race and Gender Shaped American Citizenship and Labor* (Cambridge: Harvard University Press, 2002), which offers a summary of the legal and social bars to citizenship in postrevolution Hawai'i.

10. Fuchs, *Hawaii Pono*, 80. Native Hawaiians, through the Home Rule Party—founded in 1900 by Robert Wilcox, who had led the resistance to the overthrow of Queen Lili'oukalani—did hold real political power for a few years. Home Rulers were elected to a majority of seats in the territorial legislature, and Wilcox was installed as Hawai'i's nonvoting congressional representative. But haoles managed to convince Prince Jonah Kuhio Kalaniana'ole, a member of the ousted Hawaiian monarchy, to run for congressional delegate in Wilcox's place and join the Republican Party. Kuhio was tremendously popular among Native Hawaiians, and to varying degrees of success, sought to secure them jobs and land in exchange for his cooperation with Republicans. See Fuchs, *Hawaii Pono*, 157–160.

11. Bell, *Last Among Equals* 62–66.

12. Eisenhower objected to Alaska statehood largely for reasons of Cold War policy: Alaska's proximity to the Soviet Union appeared to necessitate the military's control over large swaths of unpopulated land, which might prove unsustainable if Alaska were granted increased self-rule. The final Alaska statehood bill garnered Eisenhower's approval after provisions were inserted that allowed for the federal government to recover sovereignty over certain areas if such action were deemed necessary for national security. See John S. Whitehead, *Completing the Union: Alaska, Hawai'i, and the Battle for Statehood* (Albuquerque: University of New Mexico Press, 2004), 224–225.

13. For more on the Hawai'i territorial elections of 1954, see Tom Coffman, *The Island Edge of America: A Political History of Hawai'i* (Honolulu: University of Hawai'i Press, 2003). For more on Alaska statehood, see Whitehead, *Completing the Union*. Bell's *Last Among Equals* provides a helpful account of the congressional wrangling and sectional debates that delayed Hawaii's admission.

14. For more on how Southern Democrats exercised disproportionate control over Congress and its effects on liberal policy efforts, see Ira Katznelson, et al., "Limiting Liberalism: The Southern Veto in Congress, 1933–1950," *Political Science Quarterly* 108, no. 2 (summer 1993): 283–306.

15. Gretchen Heefner, "'A Symbol for a New Frontier': Hawaiian Statehood, Anti-Colonialism, and Winning the Cold War," *Pacific Historical Review* 74, no. 4 (2005): 559.

16. John Dower, *War Without Mercy: Race and Power in the Pacific War* (New York: Knopf, 1993).

17. "Hawaii on the Threshold of Statehood," 1947, Collection COM-18: Records of the Hawaii Statehood Commission, Hawai'i State Archives (hereafter COM-18), Box 28.

18. House Committee on Public Lands, *Hearings on Statehood for Hawaii*, 80th Cong., 1st sess., (1947), 155.

19. "Hawaii and Statehood," 1950, Hawaiian and Pacific Collections, University of Hawai'i (hereafter HPC).

20. Correspondence between the Hawaii Statehood Commission and the University of Minnesota, May–July 1947, COM-18, Box 4.

21. Letter from George McLane to Henderson Publishing, February 20, 1950, COM-18, Box 7.

22. See Daniel Immerwahr, *How to Hide an Empire: Geography and Power in the Greater United States* (New York: Farrar, Straus, and Giroux, 2019).

23. Letter from David Aitchison to congressional representatives, March 3, 1949, COM-18, Box 17.

24. Correspondence between George McLane and Stewart Fern, November–December 1947, COM-18, Box 8.

25. Letter from George McLane to Norman Meller, November 5, 1947, COM-18, Box 6.

26. Letter from George McLane to the editor of the Worcester Telegram, March 19, 1947, COM-18, Box 4.

27. Census figures printed in Senate Committee on Interior and Insular Affairs, *Hearings on Statehood for Hawaii*, 83rd Cong., 1st and 2nd sess. (1953 and 1954), 205. The same census reported that Hawaiians (including part-Hawaiians) made up 17 percent of the population, Chinese 6.5 percent, and Filipinos 12 percent. Other groups—including Puerto Ricans and Koreans—made up the remaining 4 percent.

28. Letter from George McLane to Thomas J. Lane, April 28, 1947, COM-18, Box 4.

29. Senate Committee on Public Lands, *Hearings on Statehood for Hawaii*, 80th Cong., 2nd sess. (1948), 463.

30. Scholars such as Dean Saranillio have pointed out that the Statehood Commission was involved in coaching local witnesses who testified before visiting members of Congress, but given the divergence between the commission's distortions of Hawai'i's racial makeup and the emphasis on diversity that many residents relayed in their testimony, it seems likely that not all witnesses were coached. See Saranillio, "Seeing Conquest: Colliding Histories and the Cultural Politics of Hawai'i Statehood," (Ph.D. diss., University of Michigan, 2009), 146.

31. Senate Committee on Public Lands, *Hearings on Statehood for Hawaii*, 80th Cong., 2nd sess. (1948), 202.

32. Ibid., 242.

33. Ibid., 67–68.

34. Letter and accompanying materials from Richard McCarthy, president of the Native Sons of the Golden West, to Senator William Knowland, February 14, 1946, Collection M-473: Papers of Joseph Rider Farrington, Hawai'i State Archives (hereafter M-473), Box 13.

35. Associated Press, "Dr. Butler Opposes Hawaii Statehood," March 13, 1947, printed in the *New York Times*.

36. House Committee on the Territories, *Hearings on Statehood for Hawaii*, 79th Cong., 2nd sess. (1946), 244.

37. House Committee on the Territories, *Hearings on Statehood for Hawaii*, 79th Cong., 2nd sess. (1946), 484, 485.

38. Ibid., 482, 491.

39. Saranillio, "Seeing Conquest," 168–172.

40. Minutes of the Hawaii Statehood Commission, December 21, 1951, COM-18, Box13.

41. John S. Whitehead, "The Anti-Statehood Movement and the Legacy of Alice Kamokila Campbell," *Hawaiian Journal of History* 27 (1993): 59, 61.

42. Letter from George Lehleitner to Samuel King, March 19, 1951, COM-18, Box 20.

43. "Race Relations and the FEPC Idea in Hawaii," memo drafted by the Hawaiian Legislative Reference Bureau distributed by the Statehood Commission, January 26, 1953, COM-18, Box 9.

44. Letter from Oren Long to Walter George, February 27, 1953, M-473, Box 18.

45. House Committee on Public Lands, *Hearings on Statehood for Hawaii*, 81st Cong., 1st sess. (1949), 29.

46. *Cong. Rec.* 82nd Cong., 2nd sess. (1952), 1719.

47. Senate Committee on Interior and Insular Affairs, *Report on Statehood for Hawaii*, 81st Cong., 2nd sess. (1950), 56.

48. *Cong. Rec.* 83rd Cong., 2nd sess. (1954), 3485.

49. Moon-Kie Jung, *Reworking Race: The Making of Hawaii's Interracial Labor Movement* (New York: Columbia University Press, 2006).

50. Whitehead, "The Anti-Statehood Movement," 44–45.

51. Amy Kaplan, *The Anarchy of Empire in the Making of U.S. Culture* (Cambridge, MA: Harvard University Press, 2002), 11.

52. Joseph Farrington quoted in a speech to the Women's Patriotic Conference, January 1, 1949, *Appendix to the Cong. Rec.* 81st Cong., 1st sess. (1949), A531.

53. House Committee on Interior and Insular Affairs, *Hearings on Statehood for Hawaii*, 86th Cong., 1st sess. (1959), 22.

54. Farrington at the Women's Patriotic Conference.

55. *Cong. Rec.* 82nd Cong., 2nd sess. (1952), 753.

56. *Cong. Rec.* 83rd Cong., 1st sess. (1953), 1782.

57. Senate Committee on Interior and Insular Affairs, *Hearings on Alaska-Hawaii Statehood, Elective Governor, and Commonwealth Status*, 84th Cong., 1st sess. (1955), 141.

58. *Cong. Rec.* 80th Cong., 1st sess. (1947), 7937.

59. Senate Committee on Interior and Insular Affairs, *Hearings on Alaska-Hawaii Statehood, Elective Governor, and Commonwealth Status*, 84th Cong., 1st sess. (1955), 131.

60. House Committee on Interior and Insular Affairs, *Hearings on Statehood for Hawaii*, 86th Cong., 1st sess. (1959), 151.

61. Paul Kramer, *The Blood of Government: Race, Empire, the United States, and the Philippines* (Chapel Hill: University of North Carolina Press, 2006).

62. Correspondence between William F. Knowland and the State Department, RG 59: General Records of the Department of State, Office Files of Francis O. Wilcox, 1954–57, Box 1.

63. Naoko Shibusawa, *America's Geisha Ally: Reimagining the Japanese Enemy* (Cambridge: Harvard University Press, 2006), 4–5.

64. Charlotte Brooks, *Alien Neighbors, Foreign Friends: Asian Americans, Housing, and the Transformation of Urban California* (University of Chicago Press, 2009), 1.

65. See Bruce Cumings, *Dominion from Sea to Sea: Pacific Ascendancy and American Power* (New Haven: Yale University Press, 2009).

66. Senate Committee on Interior and Insular Affairs, Hearings on Statehood for Hawaii, 81st Cong., 2nd sess. (1950), 68.

67. Senate Committee on Public Lands, *Hearings on Statehood for Hawaii*, 80th Cong., 2nd sess. (1948), 256.

68. Senate Committee on Interior and Insular Affairs, *Hearings on Statehood for Hawaii*, 86th Cong., 1st sess. (1959), 67.

69. Katsuro Miho quoted in Senate Committee on Interior and Insular Affairs, *Hearings on Statehood for Hawaii*, 80th Cong., 1st sess. (1957), 33.

70. Senate Committee on Interior and Insular Affairs, *Hearings on Statehood for Hawaii*, 81st Cong., 2nd sess. (1950), 99.

71. Dwight D. Eisenhower Archives, Papers as President, Ann Whitman Files, Speech Series, Box 14.

72. Dwight D. Eisenhower: "Annual Message to the Congress on the State of the Union," January 5, 1956. Online by Gerhard Peters and John T. Woolley, *The American Presidency Project*, http://www.presidency.ucsb.edu/ws/?pid=10593 [last accessed 5/27/18].

73. On moderate Southern opinion on *Brown*, see Matthew Lassiter and Andrew B. Lewis, "Massive Resistance Revisited: Virginia's White Moderates and the Byrd Organization," in Lassiter and Lewis, eds., *The Moderates' Dilemma: Massive Resistance to School Desegregation in Virginia* (Charlottesville: University Press of Virginia, 1998). For more on the New South, see Lassiter's *The Silent Majority: Suburban Politics in the Sunbelt South* (Princeton University Press, 2006); Kevin M. Kruse, *White Flight: Atlanta and the Making of Modern Conservatism* (Princeton University Press, 2005); and Bruce Schulman, *From Cotton Belt to Sunbelt: Federal Policy, Economic Development, and the Transformation of the South, 1938–1980* (Durham, NC: Duke University Press, 1991).

74. Irwin Unger and Debi Unger, *LBJ: A Life* (New York: Wiley, 1999), 225.

75. "Remarks at the East-West Center in Honolulu," October 18, 1966, *Public Papers of the Presidents: Lyndon B. Johnson, 1966*, vol. 2 (Washington: Office of the Federal Register, 1967), 1221. For more on Johnson's transformation from an opponent to a supporter of Hawai'i statehood, see Giles Scott-Smith, "From Symbol of Division to Cold War Asset: Lyndon Johnson and the Achievement of Hawaiian Statehood in 1959," *History* 89, no. 294 (April 2004): 256–273. For more on Burns and statehood, see Coffman, *The Island Edge of America*, 155–158.

76. Burns claimed in 1959 that "the most effective opposition to statehood has always originated in Hawaii itself." Quoted in Whitehead, "The Anti-Statehood Movement," 44.

77. Senate Committee on Interior and Insular Affairs, *Hearings on Statehood for Hawaii*, 80th Cong., 1st sess. (1957), 10.

78. *Cong. Rec.* 83rd Cong., 1st sess. (1953), 157.

79. *Cong. Rec.* 82nd Cong., 2nd sess. (1952), 1082.

80. House Committee on Interior and Insular Affairs, *Hearings on Statehood for Hawaii,* 86th Cong., 1st sess. (1959), 25.

81. Whitehead, "The Anti-Statehood Movement."

82. For a discussion of the ways in which liberal racial logic during the statehood debate denied claims to Hawaiian sovereignty, see Dean Saranillio, "Colliding Histories: Hawai'i Statehood at the Intersection of Asians 'Ineligible to Citizenship' and Hawaiians 'Unfit for Self-Government,'" *Journal of Asian American Studies* 13, no. 3 (October 2010): 283–309.

83. Senate Committee on Interior and Insular Affairs, *Hearings on Statehood for Hawaii,* 86th Cong., 1st sess. (1959), 3.

84. *Cong. Rec.* 86th Cong., 1st sess. (1959), 3880.

85. Whitehead, "The Anti-Statehood Movement," 43.

86. Saranillio, "Seeing Conquest," 140.

87. According to Resolution 742, adopted by the U.N. General Committee on November 27, 1953, for any status other than independence to be considered a legitimate form of self-government, the population of the territory must have had freedom of choice "between several possibilities, including independence."

88. Daniel Cobb, *Native Activism in Cold War America: The Struggle for Sovereignty* (Lawrence: University Press of Kansas, 2008).

89. These colonial stereotypes of Puerto Rico would continue to shape its unequal relationship to the rest of the United States, exemplified by the use of the island as a testing ground for medical and social engineering projects. See Laura Briggs, *Reproducing Empire: Race, Sex, Science, and U.S. Imperialism in Puerto Rico* (Berkeley: University of California Press, 2002).

90. Mai Ngai, *Impossible Subjects: Illegal Aliens and the Making of Modern America* (Princeton, NJ: Princeton University Press, 2003), 225–264.

91. House Subcommittee No. 1 of the Committee on the Judiciary, *Hearings on H.R. 2580,* 89th
 Cong., 1st sess. (1965), 199.

92. *Cong. Rec.* 89th Cong., 1st sess. (1965), 24444.

Chapter 2: Through the Looking Glass

1. Betty Washington, "Fear Selma March Violence: Excitement Haunts Ala. Rights Workers," *Chicago Defender* (hereafter *CD*), March 20, 1965.

2. Clayborne Carson, ed., *The Papers of Martin Luther King, Jr.,* vol. 5, *Threshold of a New Decade* (Berkeley: University of California Press, 2005), 278.

3. UPI, "Fong Advises Congress Not to Rush Rights Bill," *New York Times* (hereafter *NYT*), August 31, 1959. Fong would eventually vote for the 1964 Civil Rights Act and 1965 Voting Rights Act.

4. Harry S. Truman, "Special Message to the Congress on Civil Rights," February 2, 1948. *Public Papers of the President of the United States* (Washington: Government Printing Office, 1964), n20.

5. Senate Committee on Interior and Insular Affairs, *Hearings on Statehood for Hawaii,* 81st Cong., 2nd sess. (1950), 68. It seems that Chapman's belief that Hawaii might help improve

race relations on the mainland was born of genuine concern. Chapman had long been a supporter of civil rights. As Roosevelt's assistant secretary of the interior he had been instrumental in arranging Marian Anderson's 1939 concert on the steps of the Lincoln Memorial, after the African American contralto had been denied permission by the Daughters of the American Revolution to sing in front of an integrated audience at Constitution Hall. See Allan Keiler, *Marian Anderson: A Journey* (Urbana: University of Illinois Press, 2002), 208.

6. See Thomas Borstelmann, *The Cold War and the Color Line: American Race Relations in the Global Arena* (Cambridge, MA: Harvard University Press, 2001), 85–134; Penny von Eschen, *Satchmo Blows Up the World: Jazz Ambassadors Play the Cold War* (Cambridge, MA: Harvard University Press, 2004), 4–5.

7. News reports from around the world, which Eisenhower and his staff scrutinized, called on the president to take action against Faubus. See Mary Dudziak, *Cold War Civil Rights* (Princeton, NJ: Princeton University Press, 2000), 115–151. Penny von Eschen also suggests that Eisenhower was influenced by Louis Armstrong, who declared his refusal to participate in State Department jazz tours—a project that showcased African American musicians as informal ambassadors to the decolonizing—unless the federal government intervened in Little Rock. See von Eschen, *Satchmo Blows Up the World*, 63–64.

8. Dudziak, *Cold War Civil Rights*, 133.

9. House Committee on Interior and Insular Affairs, *Hearings on H.R. 50 and H.R. 888 to Provide for the Admission of the State of Hawaii into the Union*, 86th Cong., 1st sess. (1959), 39.

10. For more on civic versus racial nationalism, see Gary Gerstle, *American Crucible: Race and Nation in the Twentieth Century* (Princeton, NJ: Princeton University Press, 2001).

11. "No Place for Racism," *NYT*, editorial, July 23, 1950.

12. "Hawaii As an Asset," *Washington Post* (hereafter *WP*), editorial, March 9, 1953.

13. Hodding Carter, "The Case for Hawaii," *Saturday Evening Post*, June 12, 1954.

14. Ann Waldron, *Hodding Carter: The Reconstruction of a Racist* (Chapel Hill, NC: Algonquin Books, 1993), xiii.

15. Gene Roberts and Hank Klibanoff, *The Race Beat: The Press, the Civil Rights Struggle, and the Awakening of a Nation* (New York: Knopf, 2006), 43.

16. Carter, "The Case for Hawaii."

17. Roberts and Klibanoff, *The Race Beat*, 34.

18. ANP, "Southerners Against Hawaiian Statehood," *Atlanta Daily World* (hereafter *ADW*), March 25, 1953.

19. Fleming R. Waller, "Hawaii Strives for Statehood," *Baltimore Afro-American* (hereafter *BAA*) April 27, 1946.

20. Penny von Eschen, *Race Against Empire: Black Americans and Anticolonialism, 1937–1957* (Ithaca, NY: Cornell University Press, 1997), 8.

21. Adam Green, *Selling the Race: Culture, Community, and Black Chicago, 1940–1955* (Chicago: University of Chicago Press, 2007), 8.

22. Ibid., 15.

23. Senate Committee on Public Lands, *Hearings on Statehood for Hawaii*, 80th Cong., 2nd sess. (1948), 156.

24. ANP, "Desirable 49th State: Racial Identities Lost, Hawaii's Fight Vital," *BAA*, August 2, 1947.

25. Fleming R. Waller, "Hawaii—Island of Freedom," *BAA*, October 18, 1947.

26. Enoc P. Waters, "Adventures in Race Relations: A Novel Solution," *CD*, May 15, 1954.

27. Peggy Pascoe, "Miscegenation Law, Court Cases, and Ideologies of 'Race' in Twentieth-Century America," *Journal of American History* 83, no. 1 (June 1996): 49. See also Jane Dailey, "Sex, Segregation, and the Sacred after Brown," *Journal of American History* 91, no. 1 (June 2004): 119–144.

28. For Hawai'i numbers see Thomas P. Monahan, "An Overview of Statistics on Interracial Marriage in the United States, with Data on Its Extent from 1963–1970," *Journal of Marriage and Family* 38, no. 2 (May 1976): 227. For the national figure, see Kristin Bialik, "Key Facts about Race and Marriage, 50 Years after Loving v. Virginia," Pew Research Center report, June 2017, http://www.pewresearch.org/fact-tank/2017/06/12/key-facts-about-race-and-marriage-50-years-after-loving-v-virginia/ [last accessed 5/26/18].

29. Romanzo Adams, "The Unorthodox Race Doctrine of Hawaii," in E. B. Reuter, ed., *Race and Culture Contacts* (New York: McGraw-Hill, 1934).

30. Henry Yu, *Thinking Orientals: Migration, Contact, and Exoticism in Modern America* (New York: Oxford University Press, 2001), 82.

31. See Gessler, *Hawaii: Isles of Enchantment* (New York: D. Appleton-Century, 1937), 307.

32. For more on interwar social science in Hawai'i, see Lori Pierce, "Creating a Racial Paradise: Citizenship and Sociology in Hawai'i," in Paul Spickard, ed., *Race and Nation: Ethnic Systems in the Modern World* (New York: Routledge, 2005); John Rosa, "'The Coming of the Neo-Hawaiian American Race': Nationalism and Metaphors of the Melting Pot in Accounts of Mixed-Race individuals," in Teresa Williams-León and Cynthia L. Nakashima, eds., *The Sum of Our Parts: Mixed Heritage Asian-Americans* (Philadelphia: Temple University Press, 2001); and Christine Leah Manganaro, "Assimilating Hawai'i: Racial Science in a Colonial 'Laboratory,' 1919–1939" (Ph.D. diss., University of Minnesota, 2012).

33. Shelley Sang-Hee Lee and Rick Baldoz, "'A Fascinating Interracial Experiment Station': Remapping the Orient-Occident Divide in Hawai'i," *American Studies* 49, no. 3–4 (fall/winter 2008): 89, 92.

34. Gary Gerstle, "The Protean Character of American Liberalism," *American Historical Review* 99, no. 4 (October 1994): 1066–1067.

35. Albert Barnett, "Jim Crow Infiltration," *CD*, October 30, 1948.

36. Beth Bailey and David Farber, *The First Strange Place: Race and Sex in World War II Hawaii* (Baltimore: Johns Hopkins University Press, 1992).

37. Bailey and Farber, *The First Strange Place*, 150.

38. ANP, "Migrants Take JC to Hawaii," *BAA*, November 23, 1946.

39. "Hawaiian Post Lives Quietly in One World," *CD*, October 12, 1946.

40. Hubert H. White for ANP, "Hawaii Termed Mecca for Sailors: All Personnel Doing Same Work, Says Writer," *BAA*, February 21, 1948.

41. Inaugural issue of *Ebony* from 1945 quoted in Green, *Selling the Race*, 130.

42. Hubert H. White for ANP, "Factions Gird for War in Hawaiian FEPC Fight," *CD*, March 29, 1947.

43. ANP, "American Soil, Isn't It? Housing Restrictions Vicious in Honolulu," *BAA*, January 28, 1950.

44. Davis is referred to several times, as "Frank," in Obama's memoir, *Dreams from My Father: A Story of Race and Inheritance* (New York: Times Books, 1995).

45. John Edgar Davis Tidwell, ed., *Writings of Frank Marshall Davis: A Voice of the Black Press* (Jackson: University Press of Mississippi), xxv–xxvi.

46. Frank Marshall Davis, "Democracy: Hawaiian Style: Land of Ethnic Hash," *BAA*, January 22, 1949.

47. Ibid.

48. Ibid.

49. Obama, *Dreams from My Father*, 24, 82, 115.

50. Moon-Kie Jung, *Reworking Race: The Making of Hawaii's Interracial Labor Movement* (New York: Columbia University Press, 2006), 3. The turnaround was not as "overnight" as it may have seemed. It was rooted, in part, in changes in labor that took place in the prewar period and the prolabor policies of the New Deal, which gave Hawai'i's workers a new measure of state protection and allowed for significantly greater contact with mainland unions and radical organizers from the West Coast, including many communists. Depression-era efforts bore fruit after the end of the war. By 1944, the ranks of the International Longshore and Warehouse Union were estimated at less than a thousand; two years later they had swelled to over thirty thousand and accounted for nearly all union membership in the territory. The 1944 elections also brought fifteen of nineteen ILWU-endorsed House candidates and six of eight Senate candidates to the territorial legislature. See Jung, *Reworking Race*, 147, and Tom Coffman, *Island Edge of America: A Political History of Hawai'i* (Honolulu: University of Hawai'i Press, 2003), 108.

51. Jung, *Reworking Race*, 7. See also chapter 4 of Jung for more on the 1946 strike.

52. "Investigation in Hawaii," *NYT* editorial, April 30, 1950.

53. "The Miracle of Hawaii," *NYT* editorial, March 13, 1959; "Hawaii: Beauty, Wealth, Admirable People," *Life*, March 23, 1959.

54. John Harris, "Hawaiian Statehood Dreams' Fulfillment," *Daily Boston Globe*, March 15, 1959.

55. "The Miracle of Hawaii."

56. "A Melting Pot as Never Before," *WP*, August 23, 1959.

57. "Uncle Sam's New Nephews," *Life*, March 23, 1959.

58. Bosley Crowther, "'Go for Broke!' Tribute to War Record of Nisei Regiment, Opens at the Capitol," *NYT*, May 25, 1951.

59. "Go For Broke!" *WP*, May 15, 1951.

60. J. W. Junker, "Catching the Next Wave," *Billboard*, May 29, 1999, H-8.

61. For more on Kennedy's "A Nation of Immigrants," see Mai Ngai, "The Unlovely Residue of Outworn Prejudices," in Michael Kazin and Joseph McCartin, eds., *Americanism: New Perspectives on the History of an Ideal* (Chapel Hill: University of North Carolina Press, 2006), 116–117.

62. Joseph A. Loftus, "Kennedy Campaign to Open in Hawaii, with Alaska Next," *NYT*, July 22, 1960, 1.

63. Christina Klein, *Cold War Orientalism: Asia in the Middlebrow Imagination, 1945–1961* (Berkeley: University of California Press, 2003), 13.

64. Lyrics from "You've Got to be Carefully Taught" from the musical *South Pacific*, which was written by Oscar Hammerstein and Richard Rogers based on Michener's 1947 book of

short stories, *Tales of the South Pacific*. The theatrical production of *South Pacific* was first staged in 1949 and explored themes of interracial romance and racial prejudice in an American Navy outpost. The 1958 movie version was the highest grossing film of the year.

65. Michael Klarman, *From Jim Crow to Civil Rights: The Supreme Court and the Struggle for Racial Equality* (New York: Oxford University Press, 2004), 365.

66. UNESCO pamphlet from 1950 quoted in Michelle Brattain, "Race, Racism, and Antiracism: UNESCO and the Politics of Presenting Science to the Postwar Public," *American Historical Review* 112, no. 5 (December 2007): 1386.

67. Ibid., 1387–1388. In 1967 UNESCO published a revised "Statement of Race and Racial Prejudice" asserting "that racist doctrines lack any scientific basis whatsoever." For a more indepth look at the UNESCO deliberations on race throughout the postwar period, see also Anthony Q. Hazard, *Postwar Anti-Racism: The United States, UNESCO, and 'Race,' 1945–1968* (New York: Palgrave Macmillan, 2012).

68. Gunnar Myrdal, *An American Dilemma: The Negro Problem and Modern Democracy* (New York: Harper Brothers, 1944), 1023.

69. Ibid., xlviii.

70. Ibid., 1021.

71. James Michener, unpublished book manuscript on racial prejudice, Library of Congress, Papers of James A. Michener, late 1950s (exact date unknown), 1.

72. Ibid., 2.

73. Ibid., 1.

74. Ibid., Hawaiʻi chapter, 5.

75. Ibid., Hawaiʻi chapter, 3.

76. Ibid., Hawaiʻi chapter, 5–6.

77. For more on Michener's attitude toward Native Hawaiian history, see Paul Lyons, *American Pacificism: Oceania in the U.S. Imagination* (London: Routledge, 2006), 161–168.

78. Michener manuscript, Hawaiʻi chapter, 19.

79. Dudziak, *Cold War Civil Rights*, 13.

80. Michener manuscript, Hawaiʻi chapter, 25–26.

81. "It's in Hawaii, Too," *BAA*, April 29, 1961

82. Michener Manuscript, cover note.

83. "UA-Mirisch's $600,000 For Michener's 'Hawaii,'" *Variety*, Aug 26, 1959.

84. Albin Krebs, "James Michener, Author of Novels That Sweep Through the History of Places, Is Dead," *NYT*, October 17, 1997.

85. Joan Shelley Rubin, *The Making of Middlebrow Culture* (Chapel Hill: University of North Carolina Press, 1992), 100. Ads quoted from 100 and 105.

86. Joan Shelley Rubin, "Book of the Month Club," in Paul Boyer and Melvyn Dobofsky, eds., *The Oxford Companion to United States History* (New York: Oxford University Press, 2001).

87. Sutton quoted in Marion Wong Lindley, "Reactions to Michener's *Hawaii*," *Social Process in Hawaii* 24 (1960): 41.

88. Lyons, *American Pacificism*, 164–165.

89. James Michener, *Hawaii* (New York: Random House, 1959), 891.

90. Although I could not find instances where Michener explicitly mentions the work of Adams and other social scientists in Hawaiʻi, it is very likely that he would have known about

these studies, given the amount of time he spent in Hawai'i and the local and national renown of the university's research on race.

91. Michener, *Hawaii,* 981.

92. Ibid., 992.

93. Ibid., 1035–1036.

Chapter 3: The Power of Mutual Understanding

1. Lyndon B. Johnson, "Remarks to the National Review Board for the East-West Center," May 13, 1965, *Lyndon B. Johnson: 1965 (in Two Books): Containing the Public Messages, Speeches, and Statements of the President* [Book 1] (Washington, D.C.: Office of the Federal Register, National Archives and Records Service, 1966), 528.

2. "Public Law 87–293: An Act to provide for a Peace Corps to help the peoples of interested countries and areas in meeting their needs for skilled manpower," (Date: 9/22/1961; enacted H.R. 7500).

3. Hawai'i representative John Burns, Senate Committee on Interior and Insular Affairs, *Hearings on Statehood for Hawaii,* 80th Cong., 1st sess. (1957), 10.

4. "Report on Progress of the Center for Cultural and Technical Interchange between East and West," March 1, 1961, U.S. National Archives and Records Administration, RG 59: Records of the Department of State (hereafter RG 59), Bureau of Educational and Cultural Affairs, Office of the Assistant Secretary, Subject Files, 1961–1962, Box 2.

5. John F. Kennedy, "National Security Action Memorandum No. 52," May 11, 1961, JFK Presidential Library, Presidential Papers, National Security Files, Meetings and Memoranda Series, National Security Action Memoranda.

6. Liping Bu, *Making the World Like Us: Education, Cultural Expansion, and the American Century* (Westport, CT: Praeger, 2004); Zoë Burkholder, *Color in the Classroom: How American Schools Taught Race, 1900–1954* (New York: Oxford University Press, 2011); Nicole Sackley, "Cosmopolitanism and the Uses of Tradition: Robert Redfield and Alternatives Visions of Modernization during the Cold War," *Modern Intellectual History* 9, no. 3 (2012): 565–595; Whitney Walton, "Internationalism and the Junior Year Abroad: American Students in France in the 1920s and 1930s," *Diplomatic History* 29 (April 2005): 255–278.

7. For more on American cultural policy during the Cold War, see Richard T. Arndt, *The First Resort of Kings: American Cultural Diplomacy in the Twentieth Century* (Washington: Potomac Books, 2005); Laura Belmonte, *Selling the American Way: U.S. Propaganda and the Cold War* (Philadelphia: University of Pennsylvania Press, 2008); David Caute, *The Dancer Defects: The Struggle for Cultural Supremacy During the Cold War* (Oxford: Oxford University Press, 2003); Walter L. Hixson, *Parting the Curtain: Propaganda, Culture, and the Cold War, 1945–1961* (New York: St. Martin's Press, 1997); Frank Ninkovich, *The Diplomacy of Ideas: U.S. Foreign Policy and Cultural Relations, 1938–1950* (Cambridge: Cambridge University Press, 1981); Reinhold Wagnleitner, *Coca-Colonization and the Cold War: The Cultural Mission of the United States in Austria after the Second World War* (Chapel Hill: The University of North Carolina Press, 1994). For the U.S. government's uses of covert propaganda tactics, see Kenneth Osgood, *Total Cold War: Eisenhower's Secret Propaganda Battle at Home and Abroad* (Lawrence: University Press of Kansas, 2006); and Frances Stonor Saunders, *The Cultural Cold War: The CIA and the World of Arts and Letters* (New York: The New Press, 1999).

8. See Thomas Borstelmann, *The Cold War and the Color Line: American Race Relations in the Global Arena* (Cambridge, MA: Harvard University Press, 2001); Mary Dudziak, *Cold War Civil Rights: Race and the Image of American Democracy* (Princeton, NJ: Princeton University Press, 2000); Penny von Eschen, *Race Against Empire: Black Americans and Anticolonialism, 1937–1957* (Ithaca, NY: Cornell University Press, 1997); Penny M. von Eschen, *Satchmo Blows Up the World: Jazz Ambassadors Play the Cold War* (Cambridge, MA: Harvard University Press, 2004); Brenda Gayle Plummer, *Rising Wind: Black Americans and U.S. Foreign Affairs, 1935–1960* (Chapel Hill: University of North Carolina Press, 1996).

9. Christina Klein, *Cold War Orientalism: Asia in the Middlebrow Imagination, 1945–1961* (Berkeley: University of California Press, 2003); Naoko Shibusawa, *America's Geisha Ally: Reimagining the Japanese Enemy* (Cambridge, MA: Harvard University Press, 2006).

10. Klein, *Cold War Orientalism*, 43.

11. For the construction of the "Three Worlds" concept, see Carl Pletsch, "The Three Worlds, or the Division of Social Scientific Labor, circa 1950–1975," *Comparative Studies in Society and History* 23, no. 4 (1981): 565–590.

12. For more on competing concepts of modernity between the United States and the Soviet Union, see Odd Arne Westad, *The Global Cold War: Third World Interventions and the Making of Our Times,* (Cambridge: Cambridge University Press, 2005).

13. R. C. Lewontin, "The Cold War and the Transformation of the Academy," in Noam Chomsky et al., *The Cold War and the University: Toward an Intellectual History of the Postwar Years* (New York: The New Press, 1997), 24.

14. For more on area studies, see other essays in Chomsky et al.; Bruce Cumings, "Boundary Displacement: Area Studies and International Studies during and after the Cold War," *Bulletin of Concerned Asian Scholars* 29, no. 1 (January–March 1997), 6–26; and David Szanton, ed., *The Politics of Knowledge: Area Studies and the Disciplines* (Berkeley: University of California Press, 2004).

15. For more on modernization theory, see Daniel Engerman et al., eds., *Staging Growth: Modernization, Development, and the Global Cold War* (Amherst: University of Massachusetts Press, 2003); Nils Gilman, *Mandarins of the Future: Modernization Theory in Cold War America* (Baltimore, MD: Johns Hopkins University Press, 2003); Michael Latham, *Modernization as Ideology: American Social Science and "Nation Building" in the Kennedy Era* (Chapel Hill: University of North Carolina Press, 2000); and Frederick Cooper and Randall Packard, eds., *International Development and the Social Sciences: Essays on the History and Politics of Knowledge* (Berkeley: University of California Press, 1997).

16. See, for instance, Frederick Cooper, *Decolonization and African Society: The Labor Question in French and British Africa* (Cambridge, Cambridge University Press, 1996); Helen Tilley, *Africa as a Living Laboratory: Empire, Development, and the Problem of Scientific Knowledge, 1870–1950* (Chicago: University of Chicago Press, 2011); and Gwendolyn Wright, *The Politics of Design in French Colonial Urbanism* (Chicago: University of Chicago Press, 1991).

17. For a discussion of the differences between modernization theory in the pre- and post–World War II eras—and between European and American understandings of modernization, see Frederick Cooper, "Development, Modernization, and the Social Sciences in the Era of Decolonization: the Examples of British and French Africa," *Revue d'Histoire des Sciences Humaines* 10, no. 1 (2004): 9–38.

18. Ibid., 10.

19. Senate Committee on Interior and Insular Affairs, *Hearings on Statehood for Hawaii,* 80th Cong., 1st sess. (1957), 10.

20. Ellen Wu, *The Color of Success: Asian Americans and the Origins of the Model Minority* (Princeton, NJ: Princeton University Press, 2014), 231–232.

21. David Chang, *The World and All the Things Upon It: Native Hawaiian Geographies of Exploration* (Minneapolis: University of Minnesota Press 2016).

22. Paul F. Hooper, *Elusive Destiny: The Internationalist Movement in Modern Hawaii* (Honolulu: University Press of Hawai'i, 1980), 96.

23. Ibid., 121. The work of the Institute of Pacific Relations would eventually be severely hampered by McCarthyites in Congress, who blamed IPR China experts for the success of the Chinese communist revolution. It officially dissolved in 1961.

24. Bob Dye, *Hawaii Chronicles III*: *World War Two in Hawaii from the Pages of Paradise of the Pacific* (Honolulu: University of Hawai'i Press, 2000), 305.

25. "Resources and Advantages of Hawaii as a Training Center," proposal from the Office of Hawai'i Governor Samuel Wilder King to the U.S. Department of State's Foreign Operations Administration, January 1954, U.S. National Archives and Records Administration, RG 469: Records of U.S. Foreign Assistance Agencies (hereafter RG 469), Geographic Files of the Director, 1948–1955, Box 9.

26. Description of the opening of the International Cooperation Center, May 28, 1954, RG 469, Y. Baron Goto, Mission to Vietnam, Public Administration Division Subject Files, 1954–1956, Box 2.

27. "Resources and Advantages of Hawaii as a Training Center."

28. Ibid.

29. Ibid.

30. "Hawaii's Training Resources—For Use by the Proposed International Center," compiled by the Governor's Advisory Committee, 1959, RG 469, International Cooperation Administration Executive Secretariat, Subject Files of the Director, 1952–1960, Box 45.

31. "Use of Hawaii for Indonesian participants," memo by A. L. Howard, October 3, 1957, RG 469, Office of Far Eastern Operations, Indonesia Subject Files, 1953–1959, Box 66.

32. Letter from Robert Thayer to Robert A. Kevan at the Department of Health, Education, and Welfare, August 24, 1960, RG 59, Bureau of Educational and Cultural Affairs, Office of the Assistant Secretary, Subject Files 1961–1962, Box 2.

33. Letter from Robert Thayer to William Quinn, September 7, 1960, RG 59, Bureau of Educational and Cultural Affairs, Office of the Assistant Secretary, Subject Files 1961–1962, Box 2.

34. Establishment of Center in the State of Hawaii for Cultural and Technical Interchange Between East and West, dispatch from the American embassy in Seoul, October 21, 1959, RG 469, Deputy Director for Operations, Office of Far Eastern Operation, Far East Subject Files, 1950–1959, Box 96.

35. Letter from L. Edward Shuck to Sam H. Linch, September 1, 1960, RG 59, Bureau of Educational and Cultural Affairs, Records of the Chief of the Leaders and Specialist Division, 1950–1962, Box 7.

36. "A Plan for the Establishment of a Center for Cultural and Technical Interchange between East and West in Hawaii: A Draft Report Submitted by the Inter-Agency Group on

International Programs in Hawaii," November 2, 1959, RG 469, International Cooperation Administration, Executive Secretariat, Subject Files of the Director, 1952–1969, Box 43.

37. "Summary of Proceedings of the National Consultative Meeting of the Center for Cultural and Technical Interchange between East and West," 1961, RG 59, Bureau of Educational and Cultural Affairs, Office of the Assistant Secretary, Subject Files, 1961–1962, Box 2.

38. See bibliographic note in the finding aid for the Robert Helyer Thayer Papers at the Library of Congress, http://findingaids.loc.gov/db/search/xq/searchMfer02.xq?_id=loc.mss .eadmss.ms009200&_faSection=overview&_faSubsection=bioghist&_dmdid=d43572e20 [last accessed 5/22/16].

39. William Cullen Bryant, "Some Comments and Recommendations Regarding the Proposal that a Center for Cultural and Technical Interchange between East and West Be Established in Hawaii," Submitted to the Majority Policy Committee of the United States Senate, May 1960, Lyndon Johnson Presidential Library, January–December 1960 Correspondence/ Reports, 1960 Subject Files: Foreign Relations, (many thanks to Giles Scott-Smith for sharing these files with me).

40. East-West Center annual report, 1961, Hawai'i and Pacific Section, Hawai'i Public Library (hereafter HPL).

41. EWC brochure, n.d. (mid-1960s), Brooklyn College Special Collections, John J. Rooney Collection (hereafter Rooney Collection) Sub-Group 1, Series 1, Box 326.

42. EWC annual report, 1961.

43. http://www.un.org/en/sections/member-states/growth-united-nations-membership -1945-present/index.html [last accessed 10/12/16].

44. Frantz Fanon and Richard Philcox, *The Wretched of the Earth* (1961; reprint New York: Grove Press, 2004), 239, 238, 236–237.

45. "Final Communiqué of the Asian-African conference of Bandung," Ministry of Foreign Affairs, Republic of Indonesia, *Asia-Africa Speak from Bandung* (Djakarta, 1955). For more on Bandung see Westad, *Global Cold War,* 97–109; and Christopher Lee, ed., *Making a World after Empire: The Bandung Moment and Its Political Afterlives* (Athens: Ohio University Press, 2010).

46. EWC annual report, 1961.

47. EWC brochure, n.d. (mid-1960s).

48. "Thai Pavilion at EWC," *Ka Leo,* October 9, 1970.

49. Letter from Burns to Mr. Yoshino, November 30, 1963, Records of the Office of Governor John Burns, Hawai'i State Archives (hereafter Burns Collection), Box 70.

50. East-West Theater brochure, 1963, Rooney Collection, Box 326.

51. Jason Parker, *Hearts, Minds, Voices: U.S. Cold War Public Diplomacy and the Formation of the Third World* (New York: Oxford University Press, 2016), 12.

52. Osgood, *Total Cold War,* 34.

53. Everett M. Rogers, *A History of Communication Study: A Biographical Approach* (New York: Free Press, 1997), 2.

54. Daniel Lerner, "International Cooperation and Communication in National Development," in Daniel Lerner and Wilbur Schramm, eds., *Communication and Change in the Developing Countries* (Honolulu: East-West Center Press, 1967), 110–118.

55. Transforming Third World agriculture was central to U.S. geopolitics and modernization efforts during the Cold War. See John H. Perkins, *Geopolitics and the Green Revolution:*

Wheat, Genes, and the Cold War (New York: Oxford University Press, 1998); and Nick Cullather, *The Hungry World: America's Cold War Battle against Poverty in Asia* (Cambridge, MA: Harvard University Press, 2010).

56. EWC annual report, 1961.

57. "Institute of Advanced Projects, Senior Specialists, 1965," included in a briefing book for EWC National Review Board Meeting, January 1966, Burns Collection, Box 71.

58. "Briefing Paper for National Review Board," included in a briefing book for EWC National Review Board Meeting, January 1966, Burns Collection, Box 71.

59. "A Plan for the Establishment of a Center for Cultural and Technical Interchange between East and West in Hawaii."

60. East-West Theater brochure, 1963.

61. Daniel Immerwahr, *Thinking Small: The United States and the Lure of Community Development* (Cambridge, MA: Harvard University Press, 2015).

62. EWC annual report, 1963, HPL.

63. Letter from Representative Tom Gill to University of Hawai'i faculty, July 2, 1963, Rooney Collection, Box 326.

64. Stephen W. Bartlett, "Hawaii's East-West Center: A Dialog Between Cultures," *Saturday Review,* July 18, 1964, reprinted in *Cong. Rec.* 88th Cong., 2nd sess. (1964), 21672.

65. EWC annual report, 1968, HPL.

66. Petition for a University-wide Study of EWC, June 16, 1970, Burns Collection, Box 70.

67. Memo from W.R.N. (staff member in the governor's office) to Burns, February 14, 1964, Burns Collection, Box 70.

68. "East-West Center Annual Evaluation: Counseling and Testing Center Report No. 6," June 1964, Rooney Collection, Box 326.

69. During the course of the 1960s, more than six thousand volunteers—more than 10 percent of all volunteers for the Peace Corps and nearly half of the 13,500 volunteers assigned to East Asia and the Pacific region—passed through the Hawai'i training program. For the six-thousand volunteers statistic, see memo from Joseph Kennedy, "Peace Corps Training at the University of Hawaii," January 20, 1970, U.S. National Archives and Records Administration, RG 490: Records of the Peace Corps (hereafter RG 490), Training Files of the East Asia and Pacific Regional Office, 1961–1970, Box 4. See "Peace Corps: Tenth Anniversary Report," 1971, for statistics on regional and country-by-country distribution of volunteers. Available on the Peace Corps website, http://www.peacecorps.gov/about/policies/docs/cbj/, last accessed 4/12/14.

70. "Peace Corps training in Hilo, Hawaii," RG 490, photo album, still pictures collection.

71. Objectives defined by the Peace Corps Act published in "Peace Corps Facts," brochure, 1960s (exact date unknown), Peace Corps digital library, http://collection.peacecorps.gov/cdm/ref/collection/p9009coll15/id/31, last accessed 7/11/12.

72. "Excerpts from Kennedy's Speech Urging U.S. 'Peace Corps,'" *New York Times* (hereafter *NYT*), November 3, 1960.

73. Shriver quoted in Elizabeth Cobbs-Hoffman, *All You Need Is Love: The Peace Corps and the Spirit of the 1960s* (Cambridge, MA: Harvard University Press, 1998), 28.

74. Memo to Peace Corps Training Officers from L.J. O'Brien, June 28, 1968, RG 490, Training Files of the East Asia and Pacific Regional Office, 1961–1970, Box 2.

75. "Excerpts from Kennedy's Speech Urging U.S. 'Peace Corps.'"

76. See Latham, *Modernization as Ideology*.

77. Molly Geidel, *Peace Corps Fantasies: How Development Shaped the Global Sixties* (Minneapolis: University of Minnesota Press, 2015).

78. Other U.S. aid workers were likewise not as dogmatic in practice. As Daniel Immerwahr points out in *Thinking Small*, much of the current historiography on modernization theory tends to overstate its hegemony within foreign aid circles.

79. Memo to Peace Corps Training Officers from L.J. O'Brien, June 28, 1968, RG 490, Training Files of the East Asia and Pacific Regional Office, 1961–1970, Box 2.

80. Memo from Phillip Olsen to Joseph Kennedy, "Training at Hawai'i—a Briefing," January 19, 1970, RG 490, Training Files of the East Asia and Pacific Regional Office, 1961–1970, Box 4; "The Peace Corps and the University—Materials for Committee," 1968–1969, Training Files of the East Asia and Pacific Regional Offices, 1961–1970, RG 490, Box 4.

81. Memo from Phillip Olsen to Joseph Kennedy; "The Making of a Volunteer: A Review of Peace Corps Training," 1968, RG 490, Planning and Program Review Office, Training Materials, 1964–1970, Box 42.

82. Edward T. Hall, *The Silent Language* (New York: Doubleday, 1959), 49.

83. Ibid., 14.

84. "A Guide to the Selection of Peace Corps Volunteers in Training," 1969, RG 490, Planning and Program Review Office, Training Manuals, 1964–1970, Box 12.

85. "General Criteria of Training Design," draft, 1969, RG 490, Office files of Director Kevin O'Donnell, 1969–1972, Box 3.

86. "A Guide to the Selection of Peace Corps Volunteers in Training."

87. Alyosha Goldstein explores a similar program among Native American communities in New Mexico in *Poverty in Common: The Politics of Community Action During the American Century* (Durham, NC: Duke University Press, 2012), 77–110.

88. "Guidelines for Peace Corps Cross-Cultural Training, Part 1," 1970, RG 490, Office of International Operations, Country Training Case Files, 1961–1087, Box 7.

89. "The Peace Corps and the University—Materials for Committee."

90. "Planning and Evaluation Report on Thailand IV—North Borneo/Sarawak Training at Hilo," February 1963, RG 490, Evaluation Reports of Domestic Training Programs, 1961–1963, Box 4.

91. Memo from Charles Peters to Sargent Shriver, Training Evaluation of Philippines' Elementary Education, August 26, 1963, RG 490, Evaluation Reports of Domestic Training Programs, 1961–1963, Box 4.

92. "Training at Hawai'i—a Briefing."

93. "Peace Corps training in Hilo, Hawaii," photo album.

94. Quote from Peace Corps trainee Barbara Macaulay, who wrote, "Speaking, Eating Thai Style" for the *Christian Science Monitor*, May 29, 1971.

95. Memo from Jack Frankel to Paul Sack, "Report of Hawaii Training Site," August 20, 1968, RG 490, Training Files of the East Asia and Pacific Regional Office, 1961–1970, Box 2.

96. John Griffin, "Philippine Elementary Education Training, University of Hawaii at Hilo," 1963, RG 490, Evaluation Reports of Domestic Training Programs, 1961–1963, Box 4.

97. "Philippine VIII, Hilo, Hawaii: Training Evaluation," 1962, RG 490, Evaluation Reports of Domestic Training Programs, 1961–1963, Box 2.

98. "Training at Hawai'i—a Briefing."

99. "Peace Corps training in Hilo, Hawaii," photo album, RG 490, still pictures collection.

100. "Guidelines for Peace Corps Cross-Cultural Training, Part 1."

101. Bruce Cumings, *Dominion from Sea to Sea: Pacific Ascendancy and American Power* (New Haven: Yale University Press, 2009), 177. For more general histories on the role of the military in Hawai'i, see Ian Lind, "Ring of Steel: Notes on the Militarization of Hawaii," *Social Process in Hawai'i* 31 (1984): 25–48; and Hal M. Friedman, *Governing the American Lake: The U.S. Defense and Administration of the Pacific Basin, 1945–1947* (East Lansing: Michigan State University Press, 2007). Other critical works examine the impact of the military on everyday life in Hawai'i. See Haunani-Kay Trask, *From a Native Daughter* (1993; reprint Honolulu: University of Hawai'i Press, 1999), Kathy Ferguson and Phyllis Turnbull, *Oh, Say, Can You See? The Semiotics of the Military in Hawai'i* (Minneapolis: University of Minnesota Press, 1998); Kyle Kajihiro, "The Militarizing of Hawai'i: Occupation, Accommodation, and Resistance," in Candace Fujikane and Jonathan Y. Okamura, eds., *Asian Settler Colonialism: From Local Governance to the Habits of Everyday Life in Hawai'i* (Honolulu: University of Hawai'i Press: 2008); and Brian Ireland, *The US Military in Hawai'i: Colonialism, Memory and Resistance* (London: Palgrave MacMillan, 2010).

102. Steve Sanger, "Isle Vietnam Death Ratio Leads Nation," *Honolulu Star-Bulletin*, May 19, 1967.

103. Alfred Thayer Mahan, "Needed as Barrier," letter to the editor, *NYT*, February 1, 1893.

104. Fred S. Hoffman, "Troops Overseas Only Nick U.S. Power: Increase Likely," *Washington Post*, May 4, 1965.

105. "Social engineering" and Robert G.K. Thompson on loyalty quoted in Latham, *Modernization as Ideology*, 152, 174. For more on Strategic Hamlets, see Edward Miller, *Misalliance: Ngo Dinh Diem, the United States, and the Fate of South Vietnam* (Cambridge, MA: Harvard University Press, 2013), 214–247.

106. William P. Schoux, "The Vietnam CORDS Experience: A Model of Successful Civil-Military Partnership," paper prepared for USAID's Bureau for Policy and Program Coordination, Office of Development Evaluation and Information, 2006, https://dec.usaid.gov/dec/content/Detail.aspx?ctID=ODVhZjk4NWQtM2YyMi00YjRmLTkxNjktZTcxMjM2NDBmY2Uy&rID=MzQwMDAx [last accessed 8/12/15]. For more on pacification and development during the Vietnam War, see Richard A. Hunt, *Pacification: The American Struggle for Vietnam's Hearts and Minds* (Boulder, CO: Westview Press, 1995); James M. Carter, *Inventing Vietnam: The United States and State Building, 1954–1968* (New York: Cambridge University Press, 2008); Jessica Elkind, *Aid Under Fire: Nation Building and the Vietnam War* (Lexington: University of Kentucky Press, 2016); Jefferson Marquis, "The Other Warriors: American Society Science and Nation Building in Vietnam," *Diplomatic History* 24 (winter 2000): 79–105; and Christopher Fisher, "The Illusion of Progress: CORDS and the Crisis of Modernization in South Vietnam, 1965–1968," *Pacific Historical Review* 75 (February 2006): 25–51.

107. "Second front" quote from Burns letter to Charles Ladenheim, February 21, 1967, Burns Collection, Box 110. "Because" quote from USAID press release, "AID Training Center Will Open in Hawaii," March 11, 1966, Burns Collection, Box 110. "Total environment" quote from memo from Richard Balch to Edward Tennant, "United States Agency for International Development, Asia Training Center," October 25, 1968, Box 16, Hoover Institution Archives, Edward G. Lansdale Papers (many thanks to Simon Toner for sharing this document with me).

108. "Remarks by Governor John A. Burns Videotaped for Hawaii TV Casts, Vietnam-Laos-Thailand Project of AID," December 3, 1965, Burns Collection, Box 110.

109. Ibid.

110. Memo from Richard Balch to Edward Tennant.

111. Ibid.

112. USAID Committee on AID Training, "A Review of AID Training," January 1969, https://dec.usaid.gov/dec/content/Detail.aspx?ctID=ODVhZjk4NWQtM2YyMi00YjRmLTkxNjktZTcxMjM2NDBmY2Uy&rID=MjM2MTU0 [last accessed 8/12/15], 11–12.

113. Simeon Man, "Aloha, Vietnam: Race and Empire in Hawaiʻi's Vietnam War," *American Quarterly* 67, no. 4 (December 2015): 1085.

114. Schoux, "The Vietnam CORDS Experience," 15.

115. Hunt, *Pacification*, 70.

116. Lyndon B. Johnson: "The Declaration of Honolulu," February 8, 1966. Online by Gerhard Peters and John T. Woolley, *The American Presidency Project*. http://www.presidency.ucsb.edu/ws/?pid=27959 [last accessed 5/27/17].

117. Robert Topmiller, *The Lotus Unleashed: The Buddhist Peace Movement in South Vietnam, 1964–1966* (Lexington: University Press of Kentucky, 2006).

118. Letter from Laurence McGinley to Dean Rusk, October 19, 1966, Burns Collection, Box 70.

119. It does not appear that EWC students were particularly active in the antiwar movement, possibly because the majority were there on foreign student visas and thus vulnerable to deportation.

120. John Witeck, "Creating a Place to Be," *Contact,* May 2, 1968, Burns Collection, Box 70.

121. Letter from Howard P. Jones to Governor John Burns, April 12, 1968, Burns Collection, Box 70.

122. Letter from Edward D. Re to Howard P. Jones, May 27, 1968, Burns Collection, Box 70.

123. EWC annual report, 1965, HPL.

124. "Training at Hawaiʻi—a Briefing."

125. See files on the Hilo center in the Burns Collection, Box 68.

126. Michael H. Prosser, "K. S. Sitaram, An Early Interculturalist: Founding the Field May 6, 1970," *International Journal of Intercultural Relations* 36 (2012): 857–868. Sitaram was the author of such works as (co-authored with Roy T. Cogdell) *Foundations of Intercultural Communication* (Columbus, OH: C. E. Merrill, 1976); *Culture and Communication: A World View* (New York: McGraw-Hill, 1995); and (co-authored with Michael Prosser) *Multiculturalism, Cultural Diversity, and Global Communication* (Stamford, CT: Ablex, 1998).

Chapter 4: Selling the "Golden People"

1. Quotes taken from the president's message, *Mainliner* 10, no. 9 (1966), and the United Airlines advertisement in a supplement on Hawaiʻi in *New York Times* (hereafter *NYT*), October 2, 1966.

2. *Latitude 20* 1, no. 4 (fall 1973): 5.

3. See the literature on Jim Crow-era marketing, such as: M. M. Manring, *Slave in a Box: the Strange Career of Aunt Jemima* (Charlottesville: University Press of Virginia, 1998); and

Kenneth W. Goings, *Mammy and Uncle Mose: Black Collectibles and American Stereotyping* (Bloomington: Indiana University Press, 1994). For an examination of American women consuming exotic goods to signal their cosmopolitan sensibilities in the age of high imperialism, see Kristin Hoganson, *Consumers' Imperium: The Global Production of American Domesticity, 1865–1920* (Chapel Hill: University of North Carolina Press, 2007).

4. Francesco Adinolfi, *Mondo Exotica: Sounds, Visions, Obsessions of the Cocktail Generation* (Durham: Duke University Press, 2008).

5. Beth Bailey and David Farber provide a helpful summary of pre–World War II tourism in "The Fighting Man as Tourist: The Politics of Tourist Culture in Hawaii during World War II," *Pacific Historical Review* 65, no. 4 (November 1996): 642.

6. According to Skwiot, American promoters of travel to Hawai'i in the nineteenth century believed increased tourism to the islands would convince whites to move to Hawai'i as a republican settler class. See Skwiot, *The Purposes of Paradise: U.S. Tourism and Empire in Cuba and Hawai'i* (Philadelphia: University of Pennsylvania Press, 2010).

7. Ibid., 11.

8. Ibid., 84–85. See also Gaye Chan and Andrea Feeser, *Waikīkī: A History of Forgetting and Remembering* (Honolulu: University of Hawai'i Press, 2006).

9. Horace Sutton quoted in Hawaii Visitors Bureau (hereafter HVB) report, September 1960, Hawaiian and Pacific Collections, University of Hawai'i (hereafter HPC).

10. Jane C. Desmond, *Staging Tourism: Bodies on Display from Waikiki to Sea World* (Chicago: University of Chicago Press, 1999), 11–12.

11. As Adria Imada demonstrates, up through World War II, hula dancers of Asian descent often hid their ethnic identities onstage. See Imada, *Aloha America: Hula Circuits through the U.S. Empire* (Durham, NC: Duke University Press, 2012), 185–186.

12. Indeed Americans, as James Sparrow argues, often explicitly saw themselves as part of a national project during the period beginning with World War II. See Sparrow, *Warfare State: World War II Americans and the Age of Big Government* (New York: Oxford University Press, 2011).

13. Tourism boosters after the Civil War claimed that vacationing could be a means of "consuming the nation" that led to increased national cohesion. Marguerite S. Shaffer, *See America First: Tourism and National Identity, 1880–1940* (Washington, DC: Smithsonian Institution Press, 2001), 4. For more on the history of tourism in the United States, see John F. Sears, *Sacred Places: American Tourist Attractions in the Nineteenth Century* (New York: Oxford University Press, 1998); David Wrobel and Patrick Long, eds., *Seeing and Being Seen: Tourism in the American West* (Lawrence: University Press of Kansas, 2001); Cindy S. Aron, *Working at Play: A History of Vacations in the United States* (New York: Oxford University Press, 2001); and Hal Rothman, *Devil's Bargains: Tourism in the Twentieth-Century West* (Lawrence: University Press of Kansas, 1998).

14. See Christopher Endy, *Cold War Holidays: American Tourism in France* (Chapel Hill: University of North Carolina Press, 2004). For tourism and modernization, see Dennis Merrill, *Negotiating Paradise: U.S. Tourism and Empire in Twentieth-Century Latin America* (Chapel Hill: University of North Carolina Press, 2009).

15. Christina Klein, *Cold War Orientalism: Asia in the Middlebrow Imagination, 1945–1961* (Berkeley: University of California Press, 2003), 106, 110.

16. Skwiot, *Purposes of Paradise*, 163. Emily Rosenberg first used the term *promotional state* to describe the relationship between business and the federal government in the Progressive Era. See Rosenberg, *Spreading the American Dream: American Economic and Cultural Expansion, 1890–1945* (New York: Hill and Wang, 1982).

17. HVB, "A Report on House Concurrent Resolution No. 78 to the Budget Session of 1966 Third Legislature, State of Hawaii," 1966, HPC.

18. "An Evaluation of Hawaii Visitors Bureau Programs: Report to the Fourth State Legislature of the State of Hawaii," HVB, 1967, HPC.

19. Hawaii State Planning Office, "Visitor Destination Areas in Hawaii: A Program for Development," 1960, HPC.

20. Statistics obtained from the State of Hawai'i's Research and Economic Analysis Division.

21. Statistics from the HVB 1971 annual report, HPC.

22. Stephen James May, *Michener: A Writer's Journey* (Norman: University of Oklahoma Press, 1995), 296. It seems worth noting that Michener's novel about America's other noncontiguous state, *Alaska,* was not published until 1988 and only reached fifth place for the year on the *NYT* bestseller list.

23. HVB Report, September 1960, HPC.

24. "Satisfaction-Motivation Interview Research," HVB, 1961, HPC.

25. HVB Report, October 1960, HPC.

26. "Satisfaction-Motivation Interview Research," HVB, 1961, HPC. Christopher Endy confirms the HVB's interpretation of why Americans chose Europe—and particularly France— over other tourist destinations. Whereas European visitors to France flocked to its beaches and spas, Americans traveled to France to visit museums, chateaux, and other Old World cultural attractions. See Endy, *Cold War Holidays*, 104–105.

27. Use of the term *local color* in conjunction with "Aloha Spirit" can be found in "Essential Areas of Action for the Development of Hawaii's Visitor Industry," Governor's Advisory Committee on the Tourist Industry, 1956, HPC.

28. Rev. Abraham Akaka, "The Meaning of Aloha," *Mainliner* 10, no. 9 (1966), HPC.

29. A number of scholars have critiqued the commodification of the concept of aloha. See, for example, Lisa Kahaleole Hall, "'Hawaiian at Heart' and Other Fictions," *Contemporary Pacific* 17, no. 2 (2005): 404–413; J. Kēhaulani Kauanui, "Diasporic Deracination and 'Off-Island' Hawaiians," *Contemporary Pacific* 19, no. 1 (2007): 138–160.

30. On white ethnic culture in the late twentieth century, see Matthew Frye Jacobson, *Roots Too: White Ethnic Revival in Post-Civil Rights America* (Cambridge, MA: Harvard University Press, 2009), and *Postethnic America: Beyond Multiculturalism* (1995; reprint New York: Basic Books, 2000).

31. Advertising supplement sponsored by the State of Hawai'i, *NYT,* October 2, 1966.

32. "A sense of involvement" quote taken from a January 25, 1971, letter from Thomas Hamilton to John Burns explaining the "More than a pretty place" ad campaign. Found in Box 46 of the Records of the Office of Governor John Burns, Hawai'i State Archives (hereafter Burns Collection).

33. For more on Johnson's efforts to reverse the balance of payments problem by discouraging foreign travel, see Jennifer Van Vleck, *Empire of the Air: Aviation and the American Ascendancy* (Cambridge, MA: Harvard University Press, 2013), 268–271.

34. *Current Marketing Report,* HVB, January 1970, HPC.

35. Letter from the HVB to John Burns, February 12, 1969, Burns Collection, Box 46; *Current Marketing Report,* HVB, January 1970, HPC.

36. Excerpts of testimony presented by James A. Michener, October 28, 1959, part of a special report to the stockholders and employees of Hawaiian Airlines on the trans-Pacific route case, HPC, 14, 17.

37. James Michener, *Hawaii* (New York: Random House, 1959), 891.

38. Ibid.

39. *Current Marketing Report,* HVB, January 1970, HPC.

40. For northern black activism in the late 1960s, see Nikhil Pal Singh, *Black Is a Country: Race and the Unfinished Struggle for Democracy* (Cambridge, MA: Harvard University Press, 2004); Robert Self, *American Babylon: Race and the Struggle for Postwar Oakland* (Princeton, NJ: Princeton University Press, 2003) and Thomas Sugrue, *Sweet Land of Liberty: The Forgotten Struggle for Civil Rights in the North* (New York: Random House, 2008). For white resistance to overturning de facto segregation, see Sugrue, *The Origins of the Urban Crisis: Race and Inequality in Postwar Detroit* (Princeton, NJ: Princeton University Press, 1996); David Freund, *Colored Property: State Policy and White Racial Politics in Suburban Detroit* (Chicago: University of Chicago Press, 2007); and Lily Geismer, *Don't Blame Us: Suburban Liberals and the Transformation of the Democratic Party* (Princeton, NJ: Princeton University Press, 2014).

41. Letter from John Burns to D.L. Hearn, September 8, 1967, Burns Collection, Box 39.

42. Leach locates the emergence of this strategy in the early twentieth century and argues for its hegemonic impact across time and region in *Land of Desire: Merchants, Power, and the Rise of a New American Culture,* (New York: Pantheon Books, 1993).

43. Thomas Frank, *Conquest of Cool: Business Culture, Counterculture, and the Rise of Hip Consumerism* (Chicago: University of Chicago Press, 1997).

44. *Latitude 20,* 1, no. 1 (September 1972): 2, HPC.

45. By the 1920s tanned skin, which had once been stigmatized as a signal of lower class status, was considered, healthy, a sign of sexual modernity, and evidence of the means to take vacation. See Catherine Cocks, *Tropical Whites: The Rise of the Tourist South in the Americas* (Philadelphia: University of Pennsylvania Press, 2013), 110–123. See also Kerry Seagrave, *Suntanning in 20th Century America* (Jefferson, NC: McFarland, 2005).

46. Norman Mailer, "The White Negro: Superficial Reflections on the Hipster," originally published in *Dissent* (fall 1957) and reprinted in *Advertisements for Myself* (New York: G. P. Putnam's Sons, 1959).

47. Jennifer Van Vleck, "The 'Logic of the Air': Aviation and the Globalism of the 'American Century,'" *New Global Studies* 1, no. 1 (2007): 14.

48. Wendell Willkie's text accompanied the Museum of Modern Art's "Airways to Peace" exhibition in 1943.

49. Jennifer Van Vleck, "The 'Logic of the Air'" 3, 14.

50. For the emergence of the airport as the grounded institution of jet-setting society, see Alastair Gordon, *Naked Airport: A Cultural History of the World's Most Revolutionary Structure* (2004; reprint Chicago: University of Chicago Press, 2008).

51. Christine Yano, *Airborne Dreams: 'Nisei' Stewardesses and Pan American World Airways* (Durham, NC: Duke University Press, 2011), 8.

52. Roland Barthes, *Mythologies* (1957; reprint New York: MacMillan, 1972), 71.

53. T. J. Jackson Lears, *No Place of Grace: Antimodernism and the Transformation of Transformation of American Culture, 1880–1920*, (Chicago: University of Chicago Press, 1994) 32.

54. For a discussion of the economic logics behind tourism growth, see Noel Kent, *Hawaii: Islands under the Influence* (New York: Monthly Review Press, 1983).

55. HVB, memo on internal audit report, June 25, 1962, Records of the Office of Governor William F. Quinn, Hawai'i State Archives, Box 6.

56. HVB, "An Evaluation of Hawaii Visitors Bureau Programs: A Report to the Fourth State Legislature of the State of Hawaii," 1967, HPC.

57. Ibid.

58. HVB, "A Report on House Concurrent Resolution No. 78 to the Budget Session of 1966 Third Legislature, State of Hawaii," 1966, HPC. For the parallels between state curricula and tourism literature, see Julie Kaomea, "A Curriculum of Aloha? Colonialism and Tourism in Hawai'i's Elementary Textbooks," *Curriculum Inquiry* 30, no. 3 (autumn, 2000): 319–344.

59. Mark Egan, "Pacific Panoply: New Dimensions for Hawaii," remarks before the Rotary Club of Honolulu, January 4, 1966, HPC.

60. HVB, "A Report of the Committee on Statewide Goals for the Visitors Industry of Hawaii," 1969, HPC.

61. Ibid.

62. HVB, "Recommended Goals for Hawaii's Visitor Industry as Developed by the Travel Industry Congress at Honolulu," 1970, HPC.

63. Dean MacCannell, *The Tourist* (New York: Schocken Books, 1976).

64. Letter from Thomas Hamilton to John Burns, February 10, 1969, Burns Collection, Box 102.

65. Daniel Inouye emphasized the balance-of-payments rationale in a letter dated August 27, 1965 to Assistant Secretary of Defense Norman Paul, Burns Collection, Box 102.

66. Vernadette Gonzalez, *Securing Paradise: Tourism and Militarism in Hawai'i and the Philippines* (Durham, NC: Duke University Press, 2013), 67–70.

67. For more on the messages conveyed by the Pearl Harbor memorial, see Kathy E. Ferguson and Phyllis Turnbull, *Oh, Say, Can You See: The Semiotics of the Military in Hawai'i* (Minneapolis: University of Minnesota Press, 1998), 133–153.

68. Bailey and Farber, "The Fighting Man as Tourist," 641–660.

69. Other R&R destinations were Taiwan, Manila, Singapore, Australia, Malaysia, and locations in Vietnam itself. See "Hawaii: the Pacific's Top R&R Spot," *Hawaii Business,* June 1967.

70. Associated Press, "Hawaii Greets Millionth R-R Guest," *Austin Statesman,* April 9, 1969.

71. "What Lies Ahead for a Troubled Industry," *Hawaii Business,* April 1970; Wallace Turner, "'R&R' in Honolulu a Six-Day Moment of Peace for Soldiers and Their Wives," *NYT,* April 13, 1970. Commercial flights were chartered, and paid for, by the military to fly men to Hawai'i.

72. Jim Elliott, "Hawaii Liberty," *Leatherneck,* September 1971.

73. Barbara J. Fox, "Five Days 'At Home' in Hawaii," *Christian Science Monitor,* April 11, 1967.

74. Marilyn Beck, "Entertainers Add R&R Leave Extras," *Hartford Courant,* October 11, 1968.

75. Letter from H. Michael Coleman to John Burns, December 5, 1968, Burns Collection, Box 102.

76. See the Hawaiian Armed Forces Directory Service, "Aloha R&R in Hawaii," unofficial guide, 1968, HPC; "Soldiering in the Sun," *Army Digest,* June 1970.

77. Ferguson and Turnbull, *Oh, Say, Can You See,* xiii.

78. I haven't been able to find exact figure of the military's landholdings in Hawai'i from the Vietnam War period, but it is likely that they were well over 5 percent. That figure is the lowest estimate in recent accounts; the highest is 23 percent. See Ferguson and Turnbull, *Oh, Say, Can You See,* 1.

79. For land rights protests against the military, see Haunani-Kay Trask, *From a Native Daughter: Colonialism and Sovereignty in Hawai'i* (1993; reprint Honolulu: University of Hawai'i Press, 1999), 68. See also Gonzalez, *Securing Paradise,* 70–75.

80. Meredith Lair, *Armed with Abundance: Consumerism and Soldiering in the Vietnam War* (Chapel Hill: University of North Caroline Press, 2011), 6.

81. Francine du Plessix Gray, *Hawaii: The Sugar-Coated Fortress* (New York: Random House, 1972), 22.

82. Herb Richardson, "Hawaii R&R," *Leatherneck,* April 1969; Charles Turner, "When Johnny Comes Marching to Hawaii on R&R," *NYT,* March 21, 1971.

83. Gray, *Hawaii,* 18–22; Turner, "When Johnny Comes Marching."

84. Gray, *Hawaii,* 20.

85. Letter from Mrs. R. M. Thatcher, *Marine Corps Gazette,* June 1968.

86. "Hawaii: the Pacific's Top R&R Spot," *Hawaii Business,* June 1967.

87. Susan Brownmiller, *Against Our Will: Men, Women, and Rape* (1975; reprint New York: Ballantine, 1993), 94–96. For a broader overview of the role of the American military in the Asian sex industry, see Saundra Pollock Sturvedant and Brenda Stoltzfus, eds., *Let the Good Times Roll: Prostitution and the U.S. Military in Asia* (New York: The New Press, 1992). For a gender analysis of the behavior of military personnel abroad, see Cynthia Enloe, *Bananas, Beaches, and Bases: Making Feminist Sense of International Politics* (1989; reprint Berkeley: University of California Press, 2014), 125–173.

88. Jacqueline Lawson, "'She's a Pretty Woman . . . for a Gook': The Misogyny of the Vietnam War," *Journal of American Culture* 12, no.3 (fall 1989): 59. For more on prevalence of rape during the Vietnam War, see Brownmiller, *Against Our Will,* 86–113; Heather Marie Stur, *Beyond Combat: Women and Gender in the Vietnam Era* (New York: Cambridge University Press, 2011), 168–170; and Nick Turse, *Kill Anything that Moves: The Real American War in Vietnam* (New York: Henry Holt, 2013), 166–174.

89. Chi-Kwan Mark, "Vietnam War Tourists: U.S. Naval Visits to Hong Kong and British-American-Chinese relations, 1965–1968," *Cold War History* 10, no. 1 (February 2010): 1–28.

90. Sue Sun, "Where the Girls Are: The Management of Venereal Disease by United States Military Forces in Vietnam," *Literature and Medicine* 23, no. 1 (spring 2004): 66–87.

91. Barbara Fox, "Is 'Aloha' Wearing Thin in Hawaii?" *The Christian Science Monitor,* March 10, 1970.

92. *Sunset* magazine survey of subscribers, June 22, 1972, Burns Collection, Box 132.

93. HVB, "A Survey of Residents to Determine Attitudes, Awareness, Familiarity and Opinions Regarding the Visitor Industry in Hawaii," August 1972, HBC.

94. Department of Planning and Economic Development, State of Hawaii, "State Tourism Study: Proposal for a Hawaii Tourism Functional Plan," 1978, HPC.

95. Ibid.

96. Gavan Daws, "Hawaii: The Experience of the Jet Age," talk given at the Townsville College of Advanced Education, 1977, HPC.

97. HVB, "Recommended Goals for Hawaii's Visitor Industry."

98. Judith Stein, *Pivotal Decade: How the United States Traded Factories for Finance in the Seventies* (New Haven: Yale University Press, 2010).

99. For more on the transition to tourism-based economies in the decolonizing world, see Stephen Britton, "The Political Economy of Tourism in the Third World," *Annals of Tourism Research* 9 (1982): 331–358.

100. David Harvey, *The Condition of Postmodernity* (New York: Wiley, 1992), 285, 303.

101. Yujin Yaguchi and Mari Yoshihara, "Evolutions of 'Paradise': Japanese Tourist Discourse about Hawai'i," *American Studies* 45, no. 3 (fall 2004): 89.

Chapter 5: Delicious Adventures and Multicolored Pantsuits

1. "Luau Craze Prompts New Anaheim Class," *Los Angeles Times* (hereafter *LAT*), May 17, 1959.

2. "Have Hawaiian Luau in Mainland Garden," *Atlanta Constitution* (hereafter *AC*), July 8, 1976.

3. "Hostesses Seeking Far Out Cuisine," *LAT*, August 25, 1968.

4. "Armenians Plan Luau at Church," *LAT*, July 1, 1965; "Sisterhood Plans Luau," *LAT*, July 26, 1964; "Sorority Plans Luau," *LAT*, August 2, 1967; "Democrats Plan Brentwood Luau," *Los Angeles Times*, August 29, 1963; "GOP Club Prepares for Luau," *LAT*, June 8, 1969; "Opera League Plans Luau," *LAT*, August 18, 1968; "Pasadena Fund Group Gala Luau Saturday," *Los Angeles Sentinel*, July 1, 1965; "Viking Club, Sons of Norway Plan Luau," *LAT*, June 6, 1969; "The Week Ahead: Benefit for Strikers," *LAT*, Sep 22, 1968.

5. On the performance of gender, see Judith Butler, *Gender Trouble: Feminism and the Subversion of Identity* (London: Routledge, 1990); on the cultural significance of fashion, see Anne Hollander, *Seeing through Clothes* (New York: Viking, 1978); on food and society, see Warren Belasco, *Food: The Key Concepts* (London: Bloomsbury, 2008).

6. On the relationships among food, eating, and the production of race in the United States, see Kyla Wazana Tompkins, *Racial Indigestion: Eating Bodies in the 19th Century* (New York: New York University Press, 2012); similarly, Andrew Rotter looks at how the physical senses informed ideas about race and empire in "Empires of the Senses: How Seeing, Hearing, Smelling, Tasting, and Touching Shaped Imperial Encounters," *Diplomatic History* 35, no. 1 (January 2011): 3–19.

7. "Happy Housewife Heroine" was the title of chapter 2 of Betty Freidan's *The Feminine Mystique* (New York: W. W. Norton, 1963).

8. See, for instance, Haunani-Kay Trask, *From a Native Daughter: Colonialism and Sovereignty in Hawai'i* (1993; reprint Honolulu: University of Hawai'i Press, 1999); and Jane Desmond, *Staging Tourism: Bodies on Display from Waikiki to Sea World* (Chicago: University of Chicago Press, 1999).

9. Hawaii Visitors Bureau Annual Report, 1965, Hawaiian and Pacific Collection, University of Hawai'i (hereafter HPC).

10. As Adria Imada notes, even in the colonialist world of the hula circuit, Hawai'i women were not simply sexualized objects, but, rather, they used hula as an expression of cultural pride and a means of self-advancement. See Imada, *Aloha America: Hula Circuits through the U.S. Empire* (Durham, NC: Duke University Press, 2012). Similarly, Christine Yano explores the ways in which Japanese-American stewardesses from Hawai'i embraced the professional opportunities afforded by work for Pan-Am and forged their own cosmopolitan identities in the process. See *Airborne Dreams: "Nisei" Stewardesses and Pan American World Airways* (Durham, NC: Duke University Press, 2011).

11. Phyllis Lee Levin, "Road from Sophocles to Spock is Often a Bumpy One," *New York Times* (hereafter *NYT*), June 28, 1960.

12. For more on American women's Orientalism in the late nineteenth and early twentieth centuries, see Mari Yoshihara, *Embracing the East: White Women and American Orientalism* (New York: Oxford University Press, 2003); and Kristin Hoganson, *Consumers' Imperium: The Global Production of American Domesticity, 1865–1920* (Chapel Hill: University of North Carolina Press, 2007).

13. For more on suburbanization and segregation, see Kenneth Jackson, *Crabgrass Frontier: The Suburbanization of the United States* (New York: Oxford University Press, 1985); Thomas Sugrue, *The Origins of the Urban Crisis: Race and Inequality in Postwar Detroit* (Princeton, NJ: Princeton University Press, 1996); Becky M. Nicolaides, *My Blue Heaven: Life and Politics in the Working-Class Suburbs of Los Angeles, 1920–1965* (Chicago: University of Chicago Press, 2002); and Lizabeth Cohen, *A Consumers' Republic: The Politics of Mass Consumption in Postwar America* (New York: Vintage, 2003).

14. Gary Okihiro, *Pineapple Culture: A History of the Tropical and Temperate Zones* (Berkeley: University of California Press, 2009), 151.

15. Advertisements seen in Dole scrapbook, 1949–1959, Dole Collection, University of Hawai'i (hereafter DC).

16. Lois Dwan, "Trader Vic and the Art of Genuine Imitation," *LAT,* September 6, 1970.

17. Mitchell Gordon, "Jet Travel, Hawaiian Statehood Aid Boom in Polynesian Dining," *Wall Street Journal,* January 12, 1962.

18. Craig Claiborne, "Ex-White House Chef Gets Job Exhibiting Electric Appliances," *NYT,* January 12, 1966; Associated Press, "Johnsons Borrow Blair House Chef," January 27, 1966.

19. United Press, "President's Ex-Chef Called 'Out of Step,'" *LAT,* January 2, 1966.

20. Craig Claiborne, "The 1960's: Haute Cuisine in America," *NYT,* January 1, 1970.

21. Claiborne's ratings were included in *The New York Times Guide to Dining Out in New York,* as described in Sylvia Lovegren's *Fashionable Food: Seven Decades of Food Fads* (Chicago: University of Chicago Press, 1995), 279.

22. For the history of Chinese restaurants in the United States, see Yong Chen, *Chop Suey, USA* (New York: Columbia University Press, 2015); Andrew Coe, *Chop Suey: A Cultural History of Chinese Food in the United States* (New York: Oxford University Press, 2009); and Jennifer 8. Lee, *The Fortune Cookie Chronicles: Adventures in the World of Chinese Food* (New York: Twelve, 2008).

23. Heather Lee, "The Untold Story of Chinese Restaurants in America," *Scholars Strategy Network,* 2015, http://www.scholarsstrategynetwork.org/brief/untold-story-chinese-restaurants -america [last accessed 8/7/17].

24. Chen, *Chop Suey*, 15–20.

25. Dwan, "Trader Vic and the Art of Genuine Imitation."

26. Quoted in "Polynesia at Dinnertime" *Time*, March 31, 1961; and Gordon, "Jet Travel, Hawaiian Statehood Aid Boom in Polynesian Dining."

27. Horace Sutton, "This Side of Paradise," *Saturday Review*, February 21, 1953.

28. For more on Americans' new postwar mobility and its links to notions of modernity, see Jennifer van Vleck, *Empire of the Air: Aviation and the American Ascendancy* (Cambridge, MA: Harvard University Press, 2013); Richard Popp, *Holiday Makers: Magazines, Advertising, and Mass Tourism in Postwar America* (Baton Rouge: Louisiana State University Press, 2012); and Julia Leyda, *American Mobilities: Geographies of Class, Race, and Gender in U.S. Culture* (Bielefeld, Germany: transcript, 2016).

29. August Heckscher, "The Seduction and Challenge of Hawaii," *House & Garden* (hereafter *H&G*) July 1964.

30. Elinor Lee, "A Lazy Luau: Accenting Oriental Dishes," *Washington Post* (hereafter *WP*), August 13, 1970; Roana and Gene Schindler, *Hawaii Kai Cookbook* (New York: Hearthside Press, 1970), 25.

31. James Michener, introduction to Elizabeth Ahn Toupin, *The Hawaii Cookbook and Backyard Luau* (Norwalk, CT: Silvermine Publishers, 1967), 9–10.

32. Susan Leonardi, "Recipes for Reading: Summer Pasta, Lobster à la Riseholme, and Key Lime Pie," *PMLA* 30, no. 3 (May 1989): 340.

33. For more on the history of American cookbooks and food writing, see Sherrie Inness, *Dinner Roles: American Women and Culinary Culture* (Iowa City: University of Iowa Press, 2001); Janet Theophano, *Eat My Words: Reading Women's Lives Through the Cookbooks They Wrote* (New York: Palgrave, 2002); Jessamyn Neuhaus, *Manly Meals and Mom's Home Cooking: Cookbooks and Gender in Modern America* (Baltimore, MD: Johns Hopkins University Press, 2003); and Megan Elias, *Food on the Page: Cookbooks and American Culture* (Philadelphia: University of Pennsylvania Press, 2017).

34. For more on the idealization of domesticity in the postwar period, see Elaine Tyler May, *Homeward Bound: American Families in the Cold War Era* (New York: Basic Books, 1988); Wendy Kozol, *Life's America: Family and Nation in Postwar Photojournalism* (Philadelphia: Temple University Press, 1994); and Lizabeth Cohen, *A Consumers' Republic*.

35. Laura Shapiro, *Something from the Oven: Reinventing Dinner in 1950s America* (New York: Viking, 2004), 46, 20–24.

36. For more on home economics and food science in the early twentieth century, see Laura Shapiro, *Perfection Salad: Women and Cooking at the Turn of the Century* (1986; reprint Berkeley: University of California Press, 2008).

37. Andew Coe and Jane Zigelman, *A Square Meal: A Culinary History of the Great Depression* (New York: HarperCollins, 2016).

38. Neuhaus, *Manly Meals*, 104–105.

39. For more on the rise of gourmet cooking, see Elias, *Food on the Page*, 73–106.

40. Neuhaus, *Manly Meals*, 40–43. See also Harvey A. Levenstein, *Paradox of Plenty: A Social History of Eating in Modern America* (New York: Oxford, 1994), 31.

41. Craig Claiborne, "The 1960's: Haute Cuisine in America," *NYT*, January 1, 1970. Cookbook numbers are based on a Boolean search of "cookbook OR cooking OR cookery" in the

Worldcat database, where I found 9,447 English-language cookbooks published in the 1940s; 13,822 in the 1950s; 20,469 in 1960s; and 41,127 in 1970s. Although Worldcat does not allow you limit searches to country of publication, the vast majority of these cookbooks were published in the United States.

42. Kristin Hoganson, "Food and Entertainment from Every Corner of the Globe: Bourgeois U.S. Households as Points of Encounter, 1870–1920," *Amerikastudien/American Studies* 48, no. 1 (2003): 115.

43. Hoganson, *Consumers' Imperium*, 105–151.

44. See Donna Gabaccia, *We Are What We Eat: Ethnic Food and the Making of Americans* (Cambridge, MA: Harvard University Press, 1998).

45. Neuhaus, *Manly Meals*, 19–20.

46. Clementine Paddleford, "Have a Polynesian Party!" *LAT*, December 7, 1958.

47. Charlotte Turgeson, "According to Taste," *NYT*, December 1, 1957.

48. *What's Cooking in Your Oriental Neighbor's Pot Party* (New York: Common Council for American Unity, 1944).

49. Rachel Laudan, introduction to the fourth edition of *Mary Sia's Chinese Cookbook* (1956, 1957, 1964; reprint Honolulu: University of Hawai'i Press, 2013), xvi.

50. Sia, *Mary Sia's Chinese Cookbook*, 3–4.

51. Ibid., ix.

52. Brown, "Chopstick Ideas Travel Far—Conditions Favor Resolves to Teach All Edibles Needed."

53. Clementine Paddleford, "East Meets West in the Kitchen," *LAT*, June 4, 1961.

54. Joanne Meyrowitz, "Beyond the Feminine Mystique: A Reassessment of Postwar Mass Culture, 1946–1958," in Joanne Meyrowitz, ed., *Not June Cleaver: Women and Gender in Postwar America, 1945–1960* (Philadelphia: Temple, 1994).

55. *Japanese and Chinese Recipes* (Honolulu: Tongg publishing, 1961), 3.

56. Thank you to Lizabeth Cohen for pointing out the similarities in the book jackets!

57. Amy Reddinger, "Eating 'Local': The Politics of Post-Statehood Hawaiian Cookbooks," *Nordic Journal of English Studies* 9, no. 3 (2010): 70; "Biographical Notes on Elizabeth Ahn Toupin," Elizabeth Ahn Toupin Papers, Special Collections at the Schlesinger Library of the Radcliffe Institute for Advanced Study (hereafter Toupin Papers).

58. Figures provided by Toupin herself, as cited in Amy Reddinger, "Pineapple Glaze and Backyard Luaus Cold War Cookbooks and the Fiftieth State," in Gregory Barnhisel and Catherine C. Turner, eds., *Pressing the Fight: Print, Propaganda, and the Cold War* (Amherst: University of Massachusetts Press, 2012), 193.

59. Spring 1966 correspondence between Toupin and Inouye and between Toupin and Michener, Toupin Papers.

60. Elizabeth Ahn Toupin, *The Hawaii Cookbook and Backyard Luau* (Norwalk, CT: Silvermine Publishers, 1967), 13–18.

61. Erma Meeks Boyen, introduction to Don Fitzgerald, ed., *The Pacifica House Hawaii Cookbook* (Los Angeles: Pacifica House, 1965), 4.

62. The Hawaii State Society of Washington, D.C., *Hawaiian Cuisine* (Rutland, VT: Charles E. Tuttle, 1963), 32.

63. "How They Entertain in Hawaii," *House Beautiful*, January 1964.

64. Toupin, *Hawaii Cookbook*, 208.

65. "A Dole Hawaiian Luau," 1973, DC, Cabinet 2, Drawer 4.

66. Grace Hartley, "For a Fancy Feast," *AC*, May 28, 1972.

67. Mary Lou Gebhard and William Butler, *Pineapples, Passion Fruit, and Poi* (Rutland, VT: Charles E. Tuttle, 1967), 9.

68. Victor Bergeron, *Trader Vic's Pacific Island Cookbook* (New York: Doubleday, 1968), 11.

69. Seth Richardson quoted in Senate Committee on Public Lands, *Hearings on Statehood for Hawaii*, 80th Cong., 2nd sess. (1948), 465.

70. For more on the corporate food industry's embrace of ethnic food, see Gabaccia, *We Are What We Eat*, 149–174.

71. Dorothy Crandall, "How the Luau Got that Way," *Boston Globe*, July 6, 1972; Tutu Kay, *Wiki Wiki Kau Kau* (Honolulu: Watkins Printery, 1953).

72. "Hawaiian Dishes Are Intriguingly Spiced," *The Hartford Courant*, September 26, 1971; Claiborne, "The 1960's: Haute Cuisine in America."

73. Billie Melman, *Women's Orients: English Women and the Middle East, 1718–1918* (Ann Arbor: University of Michigan Press, 1985), 126. See also Joan Jacobs Brumberg, *Fasting Girls: The History of Anorexia Nervosa* (New York: Vintage, 2000); Mabel Collins Donnelly, *The American Victorian Woman: The Myth and the Reality* (Westport, CT: Praeger, 1986); and Gail Turley Houston, *Consuming Fictions: Gender, Class, and Hunger in Dickens's Novels* (Carbondale: Southern Illinois University Press, 1994).

74. "Papayas Brighten Brunch," *LAT*, August 1, 1974; Schindlers, *Hawaii Kai Cookbook*, 168.

75. Helen Gurley Brown, *Single Girl's Cookbook* (Greenwich, CT: Fawcett Crest, 1969), 216.

76. Ibid., 304–305.

77. Sherrie Inness, "Impress a New Love with Your Culinary Prowess," in Sherrie Inness, ed., *Disco Divas: Women and Popular Culture in the 1970s* (Philadelphia: University of Pennsylvania Press, 2003).

78. Brown, *Single Girl's Cookbook*, 304–305.

79. "Hawaii's Sunny Summer School," *Life*, August 31, 1959.

80. James Michener, *Hawaii* (1960; reprint New York: Random House, 2002), 958, 961. For more on beach boys, see Andrea Feeser and Gayle Chan, *Waikiki: A History of Forgetting and Remembering* (Honolulu: University of Hawai'i Press, 2006) and Desmond's *Staging Tourism*.

81. Christy Fox, "Welcome-Home Party Puts the 'Wow' Back in Luau," *LAT*, October 2, 1961.

82. "A Dole Hawaiian Luau."

83. Manners, "Hilo Hattie Tells What Makes a Luau."

84. Craig Claiborne, "Hawaiian Dishes: Back-Yard Luaus Are Likely to Become as Popular in U. S. as the Hula Hoop," *NYT*, March 13, 1959.

85. "Islanders Are in Demand When It's Luau Weather," *WP*, July 19, 1965, 7.

86. "Dole Luau Kit," DC, Cabinet 2, Drawer 4.

87. Marian Manners, "Everybody loves a Polynesian party," *LAT*, February 2, 1963.

88. Clementine Paddleford, "Hawaii Is a Cook's Paradise—How to Have a Hawaiian 'Luau,'" *LAT*, May 5, 1959.

89. "When the Luau Idea Crosses the Pacific," *Sunset*, June 1965.

90. "Shoeless Guests Love That Luau," *WP*, August 10, 1959.

91. The notion that white Americans could become freer by play-acting as nonwhites—particularly indigenous people, who were supposedly purer and less inhibited than those of European descent—has a long history in American culture, as Philip Deloria shows in *Playing Indian* (New Haven: Yale University Press, 1998).

92. Bergeron, *Trader Vic's Pacific Island Cookbook*, 89.

93. Christy Fox, "Luau in a Garden Setting," *LAT,* July 29, 1966.

94. "Foreign Fare: Hawaiian Luau Delicious Way to Celebrate," *Baltimore Sun,* June 22, 1972.

95. Louise Meeter, "Luaus Captivate Beach Social Set," *LAT,* August 6, 1959.

96. Kaori O'Connor, "The Hawaiian Luau: Food as Tradition, Transgression, Transformation and Travel," *Food, Culture and Society* 11, no. 2 (2008): 153, 158.

97. Ibid., 162–165.

98. Duane Bartholomew et al., "Hawaii Pineapple: The Rise and Fall of an Industry," *Hort-Science* 47, no. 10 (October 2012): 1390–1398.

99. Rachel Laudan, *The Food of Paradise: Exploring Hawai'i's Culinary Heritage* (Honolulu: University of Hawaii Press, 1996), 66–69; Dan Armstrong and Dustin Black, *The Book of Spam: A Most Glorious and Definitive Compendium of the World's Favorite Canned Meat* (New York: Simon and Schuster, 2008), 135–137.

100. According to the census bureau, the average annual cost of food for a four-person family in Honolulu in 1970 was $2,855, compared to the national urban average of $2,452. Honolulu retired couples, meanwhile, spent $1,367 on food in 1969, compared to the national urban average of $1,131. U.S. Bureau of the Census, Statistical Abstract of the United States: 1971, (Washington: Government Printing Office, 1971), 342.

101. Office of Planning, Department of Business Economic Development and Tourism, State of Hawai'i, "Increased Food Security and Self-Sufficiency Strategy," October 2012, http://files.hawaii.gov/dbedt/op/spb/INCREASED_FOOD_SECURITY_AND_FOOD_SELF_SUFFICIENCY_STRATEGY.pdf [last accessed 8/8/17].

102. Advertising supplement sponsored by the State of Hawai'i, *New York Times,* October 2, 1966.

103. For more on the general history of Hawai'i fashion, see Linda B. Arthur, *Aloha Attire: Hawaiian Dress in the Twentieth Century* (Atglen, PA: Schiffer, 2000); and Emma Fundaburk, *The Garment Manufacturing Industry of Hawaii*, vols. 1–4 (Honolulu: University of Hawai'i Economic Research Center, 1965).

104. Fundaburk estimates that 95 percent of garment shops were owned by people of Asian descent in this period. See Fundaburk, *Garment Manufacturing*, vol. 4, 39.

105. For more on the Aloha shirt, see H. Thomas Steele, *The Hawaiian Shirt: Its Art and History* (New York: Abbeville Press, 1984).

106. *Garment Manufacturing in Hawaii* (Honolulu: Hawai'i Department of Planning and Economic Development, 1979), 125.

107. Advertising supplement sponsored by the State of Hawai'i, *NYT,* October 2, 1966.

108. Sharon E. Wood, *The Freedom of the Streets: Work, Citizenship, and Sexuality in a Gilded Age City* (Chapel Hill: University of North Carolina Press, 2005), 5; Mara L. Keire, *For Business and Pleasure: Red-Light Districts and the Regulation of Vice in the United States, 1890–1933* (Baltimore, MD: Johns Hopkins University Press, 2010), 33.

109. "Local Stylist to Capitalize on Muu Muu Fad on Mainland," *Honolulu Advertiser,* December 26, 1957, reprinted in Fundaburk, *Garment Manufacturing*, vol. 3, 364.

110. Arline Monks, "Style World Applauds News—Muumuu's Back in Town," *LAT*, December 15, 1963.

111. Hawai'i advertising supplement in *NYT*.

112. According to Fundaburk, "In the period 1952 to 1963 apparel and textile industries of Hawaii achieved a rate of growth in employment, wage payments and employer units which exceeded that for total manufacturing industries and for all other types of non-government industries. While employment in textile and apparel industries rose by 201.34 percent from 1951 to 1963, total non-government employment rose by 64.33 percent and total manufacturing employment declined by 0.38 percent." From Fundaburk, *Garment Manufacturing*, vol. 4, 17. She also estimates that, between 1954 and 1962, the Hawai'i garment industry expanded at a rate of 9.24 percent compared to a national rate of 4.22 percent. Fundaburk, *Garment Manufacturing*, vol. 1, 140–142.

113. *Garment Manufacturing in Hawaii*, 10.

114. Dewey Linze, "Made-in-Hawaii Label Popular in Southland," *LAT*, September 10, 1961.

115. Fundaburk, *Garment Manufacturing*, vol. 3; *Garment Manufacturing in Hawaii*, 130.

116. Fundaburk, *Garment Manufacturing*, vol. 2, 168.

117. Hope Dennis, "Comfort Is the Keynote," *Paradise of the Pacific*, November 1965.

118. For more on print designers in Hawai'i, see Fundaburk, *Garment Manufacturing*, vol. 2.

119. "Hawaiian Fashion Group Says, 'Bring Empty Bags,'" *Boston Globe*, November 11, 1962.

120. Dennis, "Comfort Is the Keynote."

121. Sharlene Rohter, "A Wrap Up: The Hawaiian Fashion Business," *Aloha*, July/August/September 1978.

122. Dennis, "Comfort Is the Keynote."

123. Hawai'i advertising supplement in *NYT*.

124. Dennis, "Comfort Is the Keynote."

125. Rohter, "A Wrap Up: The Hawaiian Fashion Business."

126. Fundaburk, *Garment Manufacturing*, vol. 4, 53, and vol. 1, 98.

127. On the rise of the global garment industry, see Jane Collins, *Threads: Gender, Labor, and Power in the Global Apparel Industry* (Chicago: University of Chicago Press, 2003); Nelson Lichtenstein, *The Retail Revolution: How Wal-Mart Created a Brave New World of Business* (New York: Picador, 2009); and Cynthia Enloe, *Bananas, Beaches, and Bases: Making Feminist Sense of International Politics* (1989; reprint Berkeley: University of California Press, 2014), 250–304.

128. "Mildred Briner of Kamehameha: High Fashion Proves Profitable," *Hawaii Business*, September 1972.

129. *Latitude 20*, 4, no. 5 (September/October 1976): 12, HPC.

130. Bonnie English, *A Cultural History of Fashion in the 20th and 21st Centuries: From Catwalk to Sidewalk* (2007; reprint London: Bloomsbury, 2013), 77. For more on the history of sportswear in the United States, see Patricia Campbell Warner, *When the Girls Came Out to Play: The Birth of American Sportswear* (Amherst: University of Massachusetts Press, 2006).

131. "Fashions from Hawaii," *Vogue*, November 1966.

132. See miscellaneous *Vogue* correspondence in Records of the Office of Governor John Burns, Hawai'i State Archives (hereafter Burns Collection), Box 132.

133. *Current Marketing Report*, Hawaii Visitors Bureau, January 1970, HPC; Hawai'i advertorial in *Vogue*, January 1970.

134. Hawai'i advertorial in *Vogue*.

135. Ibid.

136. Kelly Tunney, "Where California's Pacesetters Go to Slow Down," *LAT,* January 25, 1970.

137. For a historical overview of postwar California, see Kevin Starr, *Golden Dreams: California in an Age of Abundance, 1950–1963* (New York: Oxford University Press, 2009).

138. Richard Scott, "Surfer's Utopia . . . That's Southland," *LAT,* June 19,1964.

139. Scott Laderman, *Empire in Waves: A Political History of Surfing* (Berkeley: University of California Press, 2014), 8–40.

140. For more on *Sunset's* influence on the culture of the U.S. West, see Michael Keller et al., *Sunset Magazine: A Century of Western Living, 1898–1998* (Stanford, CA: Stanford University Libraries, 1998). Circulation statistic taken from Kevin Starr's article, "Sunset Magazine and the Phenomenon of the Far West," taken from Keller et al., *Sunset Magazine.*

141. Letter from T. W. Ohliger to Frank Fasi, April 29, 1969, Burns Collection, Box 132.

142. For more on postwar Hawai'i home design, see Dean Sakamoto et al., eds., *Hawaiian Modern: The Architecture of Vladimir Ossipoff* (New Haven: Yale University Press, 2007).

143. For more on Victorian home design, see Clifford Edward Clark, *The American Family Home, 1800–1960* (Chapel Hill: University of North Carolina Press, 1986). See also Richard L. Bushman, *The Refinement of America: Persons, Houses, Cities* (New York: Alfred A. Knopf, 1992).

144. Elizabeth Carney, "Suburbanizing Nature and Naturalizing Suburbanites: Outdoor-Living Culture and Landscapes of Growth," *Western Historical Quarterly* 38, no. 4 (winter 2007): 477–500.

145. Marian Manners, "The Delights of Outdoor Dining," *LAT,* June 12, 1966.

146. "Hawaii's Lanai Idea," *Sunset,* September 1976.

147. "Talent for Living," *H&G,* July 1964.

148. "Indoor-Outdoor Living, *Sunset,* March 1959.

149. "How to Make a Little House Feel Big," and "Ideas to Emulate," both in *H&G,* July 1964.

150. "New Capitol for the Newest State," *Architectural Record,* June 1961.

151. Burns quoted in the *Hawaii Star-Bulletin,* February 23, 1968; original citation in Paul F. Hooper, *Elusive Destiny: The Internationalist Movement in Modern Hawaii* (Honolulu: University of Hawai'i Press, 1980), 29.

152. David Freund, *Colored Property: State Policy and White Racial Politics in Suburban America* (Chicago: University of Chicago Press, 2007). For more on zoning laws, see also Mike Davis, *City of Quartz: Excavating the Future in Los Angeles* (New York: Verso, 1990).

153. For more on how the design of postwar suburban homes communicated notions of privacy and racial and class segregation, see Dianne Harris, *Little White Houses: How the Postwar Home Constructed Race in America* (Minneapolis: University of Minnesota Press, 2013).

154. For more on the privatization of American life, see Cohen, *A Consumers' Republic;* Kevin Kruse, *White Flight: Atlanta and the Making of Modern Conservatism* (Princeton, NJ: Princeton University Press, 2005); Eric Avila, *Popular Culture in the Age of White Flight: Fear and Fantasy in Suburban Los Angeles* (Berkeley: University of California Press, 2004); Lynn Spigel, *Make Room for TV: Television and the Family Ideal in Postwar America* (Chicago: University of Chicago Press, 1992); and Alison J. Clarke, *Tupperware: The Promise of Plastic in 1950s America* (Washington, DC: Smithsonian Institution, 1999). As Elaine Tyler May shows, in

contrast to earlier eras, during the postwar period the biggest increases in consumer spending were on commodities exclusively for use in the home. See May, *Homeward Bound,* 165–166.

155. For more on how the Cold War shaped Asian residential integration in California, see Charlotte Brooks, *Alien Neighbors, Foreign Friends: Asian Americans, Housing, and the Transformation of Urban California* (Chicago: University of Chicago Press, 2009).

156. For more on Watts and the politics of Southern California, see Lisa McGirr, *Suburban Warriors: The Origins of the New American Right* (Princeton, NJ: Princeton University Press, 2001); Gerald Horne, *Fire This Time: The Watts Uprising and the 1960s* (Charlottesville: University of Virginia Press, 1995); Ronald J. Schmidt, Jr., *This Is the City: Making Model Citizens in Los Angeles,* (Minneapolis, 2005); Errol Wayne Stevens, *Radical L.A.: From Coxey's Army to the Watts Riots, 1894–1965* (Norman: University of Oklahoma Press, 2009).

157. Narda Trout, "20-Foot-High, 3 a.m. Fire Just for Dinner," *LAT,* July 9, 1971.

Chapter 6: The Third World in the Fiftieth State

1. Isabel McClendon, "Light Rain Blesses ES Rally," *Ka Leo* (hereafter *KL*), March 24, 1972.

2. Governor John Burns, speech before a joint session of the Hawai'i state legislature, February 20, 1969, Office of the Vice Chancellor for Academic Affairs, University Archives at the University of Hawai'i-Manoa (hereafter VCAA), Box 18.

3. Kerner Commission, *Report of the National Advisory Commission on Civil Disorders* (Washington: Government Printing Office, 1968), 1–2.

4. Alyosha Goldstein, *Poverty in Common: The Politics of Community Action during the American Century* (Durham, NC: Duke University Press, 2012).

5. Karen Ferguson, *Top Down: The Ford Foundation, Black Power, and the Reinvention of Racial Liberalism* (Philadelphia: University of Pennsylvania Press, 2013), 11.

6. While there is no definitive study on the movement for ethnic studies in the United States, the works on black studies help elucidate the goals and ideology behind ethnic studies more broadly. See Martha Biondi, *The Black Revolution on Campus* (Berkeley: University of California Press, 2012); Ibram X. Kendi, *The Black Campus Movement: Black Students and the Racial Reconstitution of Higher Education, 1965–1972* (New York: Palgrave, 2012); Fabio Rojas, *From Black Power to Black Studies: How a Radical Social Movement Became an Academic Discipline* (Baltimore: Johns Hopkins University Press, 2007); Perry Hall, *In The Vineyard: Working in African American Studies* (Knoxville: University of Tennessee Press, 1999) Manning Marable, ed., *Dispatches from the Ebony Tower: Intellectuals Confront the African American Experience* (New York: Columbia University Press, 2013).

7. Proposal for a School of Ethnic Area Studies from the Third World Liberation Front to Richard Takasaki, April 7, 1969, VCAA, Box 2.

8. Proposal for Black Studies Program, from the Black Students Union to the Acting President, April 3, 1969, VCAA, Box 2.

9. Steve Carter, "Carmichael Tells of Racial Violence," *KL,* November 1, 1968.

10. For more on interwar colonial solidarity movements, see Robin D.G. Kelley, *Race Rebels: Culture, Politics, and the Black Working Class* (New York: Free Press, 1994); Brenda Gayle Plummer, *Rising Wind: Black Americans and U.S. Foreign Affairs, 1935–1960* (Chapel Hill: University of North Carolina Press, 1996); Penny Von Eschen, *Race against Empire: Black Americans and*

Anticolonialism, 1937–1957 (Ithaca, NY: Cornell University Press, 1997); and Nico Slate, *Colored Cosmopolitanism: The Shared Struggle for Freedom in the United States and India* (Cambridge, MA: Harvard University Press, 2012).

11. Report by Brett Melendy for President Harlan Cleveland on implementing the Ethnic Studies Program, April 10, 1970, Faculty Senate Executive Committee, University Archives at the University of Hawai'i-Manoa (hereafter FSEC), Box 22.

12. Leah Gordon, *From Power to Prejudice: The Rise of Racial Individualism in Midcentury America* (Cambridge, MA: Harvard University Press, 2015).

13. Quote from 1972 by sociologist Robert Blauner, cited in Miriam Sharma, "Ethnic Studies and Ethnic Identity: Challenges and Issues," in *Social Process in Hawai'i* 39 (special issue): *The Ethnic Studies Story: Politics and Social Movements in Hawai'i* (1999): 21.

14. Proposal for a School of Ethnic Area Studies from the Third World Liberation Front to Richard Takasaki, April 7, 1969, Office of the Vice President for Academic Affairs, Manoa Campus Program, University Archives at the University of Hawai'i-Manoa (hereafter VPAA), Box 2.

15. "Ethnic Studies Program Gets Stamp of Approval from State, *KL*, March 28, 1971.

16. Description of the Ethnic Studies Program by Dennis Ogawa, 1970, VCAA, Box 18.

17. Ibid.

18. Summary of Ethnic Studies, September 18, 1970, FSEC, Box 22.

19. Report of the Arts and Sciences review team on the Ethnic Studies Program, January 1974, FSEC, Box 22.

20. Cleveland speech before the Hawaiian Civic Club quoted in memo from Nancy Young to Stuart Brown et al., February 16, 1973, FSEC, Box 22.

21. For more on the breakdown of consensus in the late 1960s and 1970s, see Thomas Borstelmann, *The 1970s: A New Global History from Civil Rights to Economic Inequality* (Princeton, NJ: Princeton University Press, 2011); Rick Perlstein, *Nixonland: The Rise of a President and the Fracturing of America* (New York: Scribner, 2008); Bruce Schulman, *The Seventies: The Great Shift in American Culture, Society, and Politics* (New York: Free Press, 2001); and Beth Bailey and David Farber, *America in the Seventies* (Lawrence: University Press of Kansas, 2004).

22. James Baldwin, "How One Black Man Came to Be an American: A Review of 'Roots,'" *New York Times*, September 26, 1976.

23. Matthew Frye Jacobson, *Roots, Too: White Ethnic Revival in Post-Civil Rights America* (Cambridge, MA: Harvard University Press, 2006), 8.

24. John D. Skrentny, *The Minority Rights Revolution* (Cambridge, MA: Belknap Press, 2002), 302.

25. Nathan Glazer and Daniel P. Moynihan, *Beyond the Melting Pot: The Negroes, Puerto Ricans, Jews, Italians, and Irish in New York City* (1963: reprint Cambridge: Massachusetts Institute of Technology, 1970), xcvii.

26. Michael Novak, *Unmeltable Ethnics: Politics and Culture in American Life* (New York: Macmillan, 1972), xxvii.

27. For more on white working-class backlash to minority empowerment in the post–civil rights era, see Thomas Edsall and Mary Edsall, *Chain Reaction: The Impact of Race, Rights, and Taxes on American Politics* (New York: W. W. Norton, 1991); George Lipsitz, *The Possessive Investment in Whiteness* (Philadelphia: Temple University Press, 1998); Joseph Lowndes, *From*

the New Deal to the New Right: Race and the Southern Origins of Modern Conservatism (New Haven, CT: Yale University Press, 2008); Ian Haney-López, *Dog Whistle Politics: How Coded Racial Appeals Have Reinvented Racism and Wrecked the Middle Class* (New York: Oxford University Press, 2014).

28. Tom Hayden, *Irish on the Inside: In Search of the Soul of Irish America* (New York: Verso, 2001). For more on conservative white ethnic identity, see Thomas Sugrue and John D. Skrentny, "The White Ethnic Strategy," in Bruce Schulman and Julian Zelizer, eds., *Rightward Bound: Making America Conservative in the 1970s* (Cambridge, MA: Harvard University Press, 2008).

29. Daniel Rodgers, *Age of Fracture* (Cambridge, MA: Harvard University Press, 2011).

30. E. P. Thompson, *The Making of the English Working Class* (1963; reprint New York: Vintage, 1966), 12.

31. For more on the rise of social history, see Peter Novick, *That Noble Dream: The "Objectivity Question" and the American Historical Profession* (Chicago: University of Chicago Press, 1988), 440–445.

32. Description of Ethnic Studies by Dennis Ogawa, 1970, VPAA, Box 18.

33. 1974 report of the Academic Evaluation Office excerpted in memo from Geoffrey Ashton, November 9, 1976, FSEC, Box 22.

34. Syllabus for "The Chinese in Hawaii," FSEC, Box 22.

35. Instructional Program Review of Ethnic Studies, spring 1977, VPAA, Box 18.

36. Memo from Nancy Young to Stuart Brown et al., February 16, 1973, FSEC, Box 22.

37. Erik H. Erikson, *Identity, Youth and Crisis* (New York: W. W. Norton, 1968).

38. Resolution of Associated Students of UH expressing support for Ethnic Studies, March 21, 1972, FSEC, Box 22.

39. Instructional Program Review of Ethnic Studies, spring 1974, FSEC, Box 22.

40. Chancellor's Office recommendation on future of the Ethnic Studies Program, November 9, 1976, FSEC, Box 22.

41. Third World Liberation Front Proposal, 1969.

42. Memo from Nancy Young to Stuart Brown et al.

43. Instructional Program Review of Ethnic Studies, spring 1974.

44. Background information on Oral History Project, Andrew Lind Papers, University Archives at the University of Hawai'i-Manoa, Box 40.

45. Report of the Arts and Sciences review team on the Ethnic Studies Program, January 1974. For more on the role of the Ethnic Studies Program in local activism, see Davianna Pōmaika'i McGregor and Ibrahim Aoudé, "'Our History, Our Way!' Ethnic Studies for Hawai'i's People," in Noelani Goodyear Ka'ōpua et al., eds., *A Nation Rising: Hawaiian Movements for Life, Land, and Sovereignty* (Durham, NC: Duke University Press, 2004).

46. On the rise of "model minority" discourse, see Keith Osajima, "Asian Americans as the Model Minority: An Analysis of the Popular Press Image in the 1960s and 1980s," Gary Okihiro et al., eds, *Reflections on Shattered Windows: Promises and Prospects for Asian American Studies* (Pullman: Washington State University Press, 1988); Robert G. Lee, *Orientals: Asian Americans in Popular Culture* (Philadelphia: Temple University Press, 1999), 145–179; Frank Wu, *Yellow: Race in America Beyond Black and White* (New York: Basic Books, 2002), 39–78; Charlotte Brooks, *Alien Neighbors, Foreign Friends: Asian Americans, Housing, and the Transformation of*

Urban California (Chicago: University of Chicago Press, 2009), 237–239; Henry Yu, *Thinking Orientals: Migration, Contact, and Exoticism in Modern America* (New York: Oxford University Press, 2001), 187–191; and Ellen Wu, *The Color of Success: Asian Americans and the Origins of the Model Minority* (Princeton, NJ: Princeton University Press, 2013).

47. For a critical examination of the role of Asian migrants in displacing Native Hawaiians, see Candace Fujikane, Jonathan Okamura, and Peggy Myo-Young Choy, eds., *Asian Settler Colonialism: From Local Governance to the Habits of Everyday Life in Hawai'i* (Honolulu: University of Hawai'i Press, 2008).

48. John P. Rosa, *Local Story: The Massie-Kahahawai Case and the Culture of History* (Honolulu: University of Hawai'i Press, 2014); David Stannard, *Honor Killing Race, Rape, and Clarence Darrow's Spectacular Last Case* (New York: Penguin, 2005). See also Jonathan Okamura, "Aloha Kanaka Me Ke Aloha 'Aina: Local Culture and Society in Hawaii," *Amerasia Journal* 7, no. 2 (1980): 119–137. For a critique of the multiethnic use of "local" in Hawai'i, see Haunani-Kay Trask, "Settlers of Color and 'Immigrant Hegemony': 'Locals' in Hawai'i," in Candace Fujikane, Jonathan Okamura, and Peggy Myo-Young Choy, eds., *Asian Settler Colonialism: From Local Governance to the Habits of Everyday Life in Hawai'i* (Honolulu: University of Hawai'i Press, 2008).

49. Larry Kamakawiwoole, speech on Ethnic Studies, February 16, 1972, FSEC, Box 22.

50. Ibid.

51. "SDS is Dead," *KL*, February 24, 1971.

52. Report on Proposals for Ethnic Studies, April 20, 1972, VPAA, Box 2.

53. Harlan Cleveland, speech on Ethnic Studies delivered before UH Board of Regents, April 27, 1972, VPAA, Box 2.

54. Frank Stewart, "Questioning Basic Assumptions," *Hawaii Observer*, May 19, 1977.

55. Sam Pooley, "CSES and Supporters Occupy Bachman Hall," *KL*, March 24, 1972; Janos Gereben, "UH Is Firm on Control of Program," *Hawaii Star-Bulletin* (hereafter *HSB*) March 22, 1972.

56. Alan Matusoka, "Ethnic Studies Plans Changes," *KL*, November 5, 1971.

57. "CSES and Supporters Occupy Bachman Hall"; Janos Gereben, "UH Is Firm on Control of Program," *HSB*, March 22, 1972.

58. Janos Gereben, "Conditional OK Given to Ethnic Study, *HSB*, May 16, 1972.

59. Harlan Cleveland, speech on Ethnic Studies, April 27, 1972.

60. Janos Gereben, "650 Register for UH Ethnic Studies Despite Crisis," *HSB*, September 13, 1972.

61. Memo on President Cleveland's meeting with People's Committee on Ethnic Studies, April 25, 1972, VPAA, Box 2.

62. Janos Gereben, "UH Regents Turn Down Ethnic Studies Nominee," *HSB*, May 18, 1972.

63. Gereben, "650 Register for UH Ethnic Studies Despite Crisis."

64. Larry Kamakawiwoole, speech on Ethnic Studies, February 16, 1972.

65. Ibid.

66. "Ethnic Studies Has Serious Problems," transcript of speech by Carol Amioka, faculty member of Ethnic Studies, printed in *KL*, February 22, 1972.

67. Gereben, "UH Regents Turn Down Ethnic Studies Nominee."

68. Larry Kamakawiwoole, speech on Ethnic Studies, February 16, 1972.

69. Alan Matusoka, "Ethnic Studies Plans Changes," *KL*, November 5, 1971.

70. Letter from Larry Kamakawiwoole to Harlan Cleveland, June 29, 1972, FSEC, Box 22.

71. "UH Ethnic Studies Director Resigns," *HSB,* August 26, 1972.

72. Haunani-Kay Trask, "The Birth of the Modern Hawaiian Movement: Kalama Valley, O'ahu," *Hawaiian Journal of History* 21 (1987): 126–153. See also Neal Milner, "Homelessness, and Homeland in the Kalama Valley: Re-Imagining a Hawaiian Nation Through a Property Dispute," *Hawaiian Journal of History* 40 (2006): 149–176.

73. Report of the Arts and Sciences review team on the Ethnic Studies Program, January 1974.

74. Letter from Henry Chun to Douglas Yamamura, October 1976, Chancellor's Office, General Correspondence Files, Ethnic Studies Program—Reactions, University Archives at the University of Hawai'i-Manoa, Box 28.

75. Memo from Douglas Yamamura to Fujio Matsuda, July 11, 1975, FSEC, Box 22.

76. Chancellor's Office recommendation on future of Ethnic Studies Program, November 9, 1976, FSEC, Box 22.

77. Testimonies made on October 20, 1976, included in the Instructional Program Review of Ethnic Studies, Spring 1977, VCAA, Box 18.

78. Letter from George Simson to Douglas Yamamura, March 30, 1977, FSEC, Box 22.

79. Program Review of the Ethnic Studies Program by the Educational Policy and Planning Committee, May 1984, VCAA, Box 18.

80. UH was identified as having one of the nation's largest Asian American programs in Frank Ching's article, "Expansion of Asian-American Studies on U.S. Campuses Reflects Growth of Ethnic Consciousness," *New York Times,* July 23, 1976.

81. Faculty senate report on the Ethnic Studies Program, May 4, 1977, FSEC, Box 22.

82. Program Review of Ethnic Studies Program, May 1984. This is not at all to say that critiques of capitalism disappeared in Ethnic Studies after the early 1980s—much of the work produced by Ethnic Studies scholars in the 1990s was deeply critical of economic inequality and the nature of economic development in Hawai'i. (See, for instance, the special issue of *Social Process in Hawai'i* 35 [1994], consisting of articles written by Ethnic Studies faculty members on Hawai'i's political economy.) But, even in these works, class was not always a central category of analysis.

83. Please note that this chart refers to the total number of subject tags in a given time period, *not* the total number of interviews. Each interview might have multiple subject tags. For a detailed chart of subject tag usage over time, see appendix.

84. Novick, *That Noble Dream,* 444. For more on the disillusionment of the left in the late twentieth century, see also Samuel Moyn, *The Last Utopia: Human Rights in History* (Cambridge, MA: Belknap, 2010).

85. Kekailoa Perry, "Make'e Pono Lāhui Hawai'i," in Ka'ōpua et al., *A Nation Rising,* 270.

Epilogue

1. Allan Bloom, *The Closing of the American Mind: How Higher Education Has Failed Democracy and Impoverished the Souls of Today's Students* (New York: Simon & Schuster, 1987); Dinesh D'souza, *Illiberal Education: The Politics of Race and Sex on Campus* (New York: Free Press, 1991).

2. Samuel Huntington, *The Clash of Civilizations and the Remaking of World Order* (1996; reprint New York: Simon and Schuster, 2002), 305.

3. Arthur M. Schlesinger Jr., *The Disuniting of America: Reflections on a Multicultural Society* (1991; reprint New York: W. W. Norton, 1998).

4. David Thomas and Robin Ely, "Making Differences Matter: A New Paradigm for Managing Diversity," *Harvard Business Review* 74, no. 5 (September–October 1996): 79–90.

5. Robin D.G. Kelley, "Black Study, Black Struggle," *Boston Review,* March 7, 2016; Hazel V. Carby, "The Multicultural Wars," *Radical History Review* 54 (1992): 16.

6. Michael Omi and Howard Winant, *Racial Formation in the United States: From the 1960s to the 1990s* (1986; reprint New York: Routledge, 1994).

7. Susan Koshy, "Morphing Race into Ethnicity: Asian Americans and Critical Transformations of Whiteness," *boundary 2* 28 (spring 2002): 153–194.

8. For more on indigenous exceptionalism, see the essays in the edited collection by Candace Fujikane and Jonathan Okamura, *Asian Settler Colonialism: From Local Governance to the Habits of Everyday Life in Hawai'i* (Honolulu: University of Hawai'i Press, 2008). See also Cynthia Franklin and Laura Lyons, "Remixing Hybridity: Globalization, Native Resistance, and Cultural Production in Hawai'i," *American Studies* 45, no. 3 (fall 2004): 49–80.

9. Lilikalā Kame'Eleihiwa, "The Hawaiian Sovereignty Movement: An Update from Honolulu," *Journal of Pacific History* 28, no. 3 (January–August 1993): 65. More recent studies show that Hawaiians remain among the poorest people living in Hawai'i, but that rates of poverty are higher among Vietnamese and other Pacific Islanders. See Anita Hofschneider, "Racial Inequality in Hawaii Is a Lot Worse Than You Think," *Honolulu Civil Beat,* March 27, 2018, http://www.civilbeat.org/2018/03/racial-inequality-in-hawaii-is-a-lot-worse-than-you-think/ [last accessed 5/20/18].

10. Jodi Byrd, *Transit of Empire: Indigenous Critiques of Colonialism* (Minneapolis: University of Minnesota Press, 2011), xxvi.

11. Simeon Man, "Aloha, Vietnam: Race and Empire in Hawai'i's Vietnam War," *American Quarterly* 67, no. 4 (December 2015): 1102.

12. Haunani-Kay Trask, "The Birth of the Modern Hawaiian Movement: Kalama Valley, O'ahu," *Hawaiian Journal of History* 21 (1987): 126–127.

13. Mansel G. Blackford, "Environmental Justice, Native Rights, Tourism, and Opposition to Military Control: The Case of Kaho'olawe," *Journal of American History* 91, no. 2 (September 2004): 544–571. For more on the Kaho'olawe campaign, see also Jonathan Kamakawiwo'ole Osorio, "Hawaiian Souls: The Movement to Stop the Military Bombing of Kaho'olawe," in Noelani Goodyear Ka'ōpua et al., eds, *A Nation Rising: Hawaiian Movements for Life, Land, and Sovereignty* (Durham, NC: Duke University Press, 2004).

14. George Helm quoted in Blackford, "Environmental Justice, Native Rights," 544.

15. Tom Coffman, *The Island Edge of America: A Political History of Hawai'i* (Honolulu: University of Hawai'i Press, 2003), 311–312.

16. Lilikalā Kame'Eleihiwa, "The Hawaiian Sovereignty Movement: An Update from Honolulu," *Journal of Pacific History* 28, no. 3 (January–August 1993): 64.

17. J. Kēhaulani Kauanui, *Hawaiian Blood: Colonialism and the Politics of Sovereignty and Indigeneity* (Durham, NC: Duke University Press, 2008), 171–183.

18. Susan Faludi, "Broken Promise: How Everyone Got Hawaiians' Homelands Except the Hawaiians," *Wall Street Journal*, September 9, 1991.

19. Kauanui, *Hawaiian Blood*, 188–194.

20. See Byrd, *Transit of Empire*, 147–183, for a critique of the effort to differentiate Hawaiians from Native Americans.

21. Ben Smith and Byron Tau, "Birtherism: Where it All Began," *Politico*, April 22, 2011, https://www.politico.com/story/2011/04/birtherism-where-it-all-began-053563 [last accessed 5/26/18].

22. Charlie Savage, "Jeff Sessions Dismisses Hawaii as 'an Island in the Pacific,'" April 20, 2017, https://www.nytimes.com/2017/04/20/us/politics/jeff-sessions-judge-hawaii-pacific-island.html [last accessed 5/26/18].

23. For plantation labor conditions, see Gary Okihiro, *Cane Fires: The Anti-Japanese Movement in Hawaii, 1865–1945* (Philadelphia: Temple University Press, 1992); for critique of Asians as "settler colonialists" in Hawai'i see Fujikane and Okamura, *Asian Settler Colonialism*.

SOURCES

Archives and Manuscript Collections

Brandeis University
    Papers of Lawrence Fuchs
Brooklyn College Special Collections
    John J. Rooney Collection
Dwight D. Eisenhower Library
    Papers of Fred Seaton
    Records of the Office of the Staff Secretary
    White House Central Files
Hawai'i Public Library
    Hawai'i and Pacific Section
Hawai'i State Archives
    Papers of John Burns
    Papers of Joseph Rider Farrington
    Records of the Office of George Ariyoshi
    Records of the Office of Governor John Burns
    Records of the Office of Governor William Quinn
    Records of the Hawaii Statehood Commission
    Records of the Statehood Celebration Committee
John F. Kennedy Presidential Library
    Peace Corps Records
    Returned Peace Corps Volunteer Collection
Library of Congress
    Papers of James A. Michener
National Archives and Records Administration
    Record Group 59: Records of the U.S. Department of State
    Record Group 469: Records of U.S. Foreign Assistance Agencies
    Record Group 490: Records of the Peace Corps
New York University Fales Library and Special Collections
    Cookbook Collection
Radcliffe Institute for Advanced Study, Special Collections at the Schlesinger Library
    Elizabeth Ahn Toupin Papers
University of Hawai'i Library
    Dole Collection

Hawaiian and Pacific Collections
Oral History Center Database
University of Hawaiʻi, University Archives
Records of the Faculty Senate Executive Committee
Records of the Office of the Vice Chancellor for Academic Affairs
Records of the Office of the Vice President for Academic Affairs
Records of the Romanzo Adams Social Research Laboratory
University of Miami
Records of Pan American World Airways

Newspapers and Periodicals

Aloha
Atlanta Constitution
Atlanta Daily World
Army Digest
Austin Statesman
Baltimore Afro-American
Baltimore Sun
Better Homes and Gardens
Boston Globe
Chicago Defender
Chicago Tribune
Christian Science Monitor
Collier's
Ebony
Harper's Bazaar
Hartford Courant
Hawaii Business
Holiday
Honolulu
Honolulu Advertiser
Honolulu Star-Bulletin
House Beautiful
Home & Garden
Jet
Ka Leo

Latitude 20
Leatherneck
Life
Los Angeles Sentinel
Los Angeles Times
Mademoiselle
Mainliner
Marine Corps Gazette
Newsday
Newsweek
New York Amsterdam News
New York Herald Tribune
New York Times
Paradise of the Pacific
Philadelphia Tribune
Pittsburgh Courier
Saturday Evening Post
Saturday Review
Seventeen
Sunset
Time
Vogue
Wall Street Journal
Washington Post
Women's Wear Daily

Published Government Sources

Congressional Record
House Committee on the Territories, Congress of the United States, 79th Congress, 1st
Session, Hearings on H. Res. 236, A Study and Investigation of the Various Questions
and Problems Relating to the Territories of Alaska and Hawaii, January 7–15, 7–18, 1946.
Washington: U.S. Government Printing Office, 1946.

House Committee on the Territories, Congress of the United States, 79th Congress, 1st Session, Hearing on H.R. 3646, A Bill to Enable the People of Hawaii to Form a Constitution and State Government to Be Admitted into the Union on Equal Footing with the Original States, June 4, 1946. Washington: U.S. Government Printing Office, 1946.

House Committee on Public Lands, Congress of the United States, 80th Congress, 1st Session, Hearings on H.R. 49, Statehood for Hawaii, March 7, 10–14, and 19, 1947. Washington: U.S. Government Printing Office, 1947.

House Committee on Rules, Congress of the United States, 80th Congress, 1st Session, Hearings on H.R. 49, Statehood for Hawaii, April 17 and 23, 1947. Washington: U.S. Government Printing Office, 1947.

House Committee on Public Lands, Congress of the United States, 81st Congress, 1st Session, Hearings on H.R. 49, Statehood for Hawaii, and Related Bills, March 3 and 8, 1949. Washington: U.S. Government Printing Office, 1949.

House Committee on Interior and Insular Affairs, Congress of the United States, 83rd Congress, 1st Session, Hearings on H.R. 49, 205, 1745, and 2981, Statehood for Hawaii, February 23–24, 26–27, 1953. Washington: U.S. Government Printing Office, 1953.

House Committee on Interior and Insular Affairs, Congress of the United States, 83rd Congress, 2nd Session, Hearings on Statehood for Hawaii, December 16–17, 1954. Washington: U.S. Government Printing Office, 1954.

House Committee on Interior and Insular Affairs, Congress of the United States, 84th Congress, 1st Session, Hearings on H.R. 2535 and 2536, Statehood for Hawaii and Alaska, January 25, 28, and 31, February 2, 4, 7–8, 14–16, 1955. Washington: U.S. Government Printing Office, 1955.

House Committee on Rules, Congress of the United States, 84th Congress, 1st Session, Hearings on H.R. 2535 and 2536, Statehood for Hawaii and Alaska, April 19–20, 1955. Washington: U.S. Government Printing Office, 1955.

House Committee on Interior and Insular Affairs, Congress of the United States, 85th Congress, 1st Session, Hearings on H.R. 49, 339, and 1246, Statehood for Hawaii, April 8–9, and 16, 1957. Washington: U.S. Government Printing Office, 1957.

House Committee on Interior and Insular Affairs, Congress of the United States, 85th Congress, Executive Session on H.R. 49, Statehood for Hawaii, June 4 and 18, 1958. Washington: U.S. Government Printing Office, 1958.

House Committee on Interior and Insular Affairs, Congress of the United States, 85th Congress, 2nd Session, Hearings on Various Bills, July 29, 1958. Washington: U.S. Government Printing Office, 1958.

House Committee on Interior and Insular Affairs, Congress of the United States, 85th Congress, 2nd Session, Executive Session on H.R. 49, Statehood for Hawaii, July 30–31, August 6, 1958. Washington: U.S. Government Printing Office, 1958.

House Committee on Interior and Insular Affairs, Congress of the United States, 86th Congress, 1st Session, Hearings on H.R. 50 and H.R. 888 to Provide for the Admission of the State of Hawaii into the Union, January 26–28, 1959. Washington: U.S. Government Printing Office, 1959.

House Committee on Interior and Insular Affairs, Congress of the United States, 86th Congress, 1st Session, Executive Session on H.R. 50 and Bills Related to Hawaii Statehood, January 29–30 and February 2–4, 1959. Washington: U.S. Government Printing Office, 1959.

Senate Committee on Interior and Insular Affairs, Congress of the United States, 80th Congress, 2nd Session, Hearings on Statehood for Hawaii, November 1, 7–12, 1948. Washington: U.S. Government Printing Office, 1948.

Senate Committee on Public Lands, Congress of the United States, 80th Congress, 2nd Session, Hearings on H.R. 49 and S. 114, Statehood for Hawaii, January 5–9, 14–20, and April 15, 1948. Washington: U.S. Government Printing Office, 1948.

Senate Committee on Interior and Insular Affairs, Congress of the United States, 81st Congress, 2nd Session, Report No. 1928, on H.R. 49 to Enable the People of Hawaii to Form a Constitution and State Government and to Be Admitted into the Union on an Equal Footing with the Original States. Washington: U.S. Government Printing Office, 1950.

Senate Committee on Interior and Insular Affairs, Congress of the United States, 81st Congress, 2nd Session, Hearings on H.R. 49, S. 156, and S. 1782, Statehood for Hawaii, May 1–5, 1950. Washington: U.S. Government Printing Office, 1950.

Senate Committee on Interior and Insular Affairs, Congress of the United States, 83rd Congress, 1st Session, Hearings on S. 49 and S. 51, Statehood for Hawaii, March 6, 12–13, 17, 1953. Washington: U.S. Government Printing Office, 1953.

Senate Committee on Interior and Insular Affairs, Congress of the United States, 83rd Congress, 1st Session, Hearings on Statehood for Alaska and Hawaii, May 14, 1953. Washington: U.S. Government Printing Office, 1953.

Senate Committee on Interior and Insular Affairs, Congress of the United States, 83rd Congress, 1st and 2nd Session, Hearings on S. 49, S. 51, and H.R. 3575, Statehood for Hawaii, June 29–30, July 1–3, 6–7, 9, and 11, 1953, and January 7–8, 1954, Washington: U.S. Government Printing Office, 1954.

Senate Committee on Interior and Insular Affairs, Congress of the United States, 83rd Congress, 2nd Session, Hearings on S. 49, S. 51, and H.R. 3575, Statehood for Hawaii, January 13–15, and 19, 1954, Washington: U.S. Government Printing Office, 1954.

Senate Committee on Interior and Insular Affairs, Congress of the United States, 84th Congress, 1st Session, Hearings Alaskan-Hawaii Statehood, January 31, 1955. Washington: U.S. Government Printing Office, 1955.

Senate Committee on Interior and Insular Affairs, Congress of the United States, 84th Congress, 1st Session, Hearings on S. 49, S. 399, and S. 402 on Alaska-Hawaii Statehood, Elective Governor, and Commonwealth Status, February 21–22, and 28, 1955. Washington: U.S. Government Printing Office, 1955.

Senate Committee on Interior and Insular Affairs, Congress of the United States, 85th Congress, 1st Session, Hearings on S. 50 and S. 36, Bills to Provide for the Admission of the State of Hawaii into the Union, April 1–2, 1957. Washington: U.S. Government Printing Office, 1957.

A NOTE ON THE TYPE

This book has been composed in Arno, an Old-style serif typeface in the
classic Venetian tradition, designed by Robert Slimbach at Adobe.